D1552607

WANG GUNGWU

ZHENG YONGNIAN

DAMAGE CONTROL

The Chinese Communist Party in the Jiang Zemin Era

EAI
EAST ASIAN INSTITUTE
NATIONAL UNIVERSITY OF SINGAPORE

EASTERN UNIVERSITIES PRESS

© 2003 Times Media Private Limited

First published 2003
by Times Media Private Limited
(Academic Publishing) under the imprint
Eastern Universities Press
by Marshall Cavendish

Times Centre, 1 New Industrial Road,
Singapore 536196
Fax: (65) 6284 9772
E-mail: tap@tpl.com.sg
Online Book Store:
http://www.timesacademic.com

All rights reserved. No part of this publication may be reproduced, stored in a retrieval system, or transmitted, in any form or by any means, electronic, mechanical, photocopying, recording or otherwise, without the prior permission of the publishers.

Printed by Vine Graphic Pte Ltd, Singapore
on non-acidic paper

National Library Board (Singapore)
Cataloguing in Publication Data
Damage Control: The Chinese Communist Party in the Jiang Zemin Era /
[edited by] Wang Gungwu, Zheng Yongnian. –
Singapore: Eastern Universities Press, 2003.

p. cm.
ISBN: 981-210-259-0
ISBN: 981-210-251-5 (pbk)

1. Jiang, Zemin, 1926-
2. Zhongguo gong chan dang.
3. China – Politics and government – 1976-
I. Wang, Gungwu.
II. Zheng, Yongnian.

DS779.26
320.951 — dc21
SLS2003021981

London • New York • Beijing • Shanghai
• Bangkok • Kuala Lumpur • Singapore

Contents

Editors & Contributors

EDITORS

WANG Gungwu, Director, East Asian Institute, National University of Singapore

ZHENG Yongnian, Senior Research Fellow, East Asian Institute, National University of Singapore

CONTRIBUTORS

Kjeld Erik BRODSGAARD, Professor, Department of International Economics and Management, Copenhagen Business School

CHEN Weixing, Associate Professor, Department of Political Science, The East Tennessee State University, U. S. A.

Lance L.P. GORE, Assistant Professor, Government and Asian Studies, Bowdoin College, U.S.A.

HE Baogang, Senior Research Fellow, East Asian Institute, National University of Singapore

LAI Hongyi, Research Fellow, East Asian Institute, National University of Singapore

Ignatius WIBOWO, Head of the Center of Chinese Studies, Jakarta and Lecturer at the University of Indonesia

John WONG, Research Director, East Asian Institute, National University of Singapore

XIAO Gongqin, Professor, Department of History, Shanghai Normal University, China

YOW Cheun Hoe, Research Officer, East Asian Institute, National University of Singapore

ZHAO Shikai, Research Fellow, Development Research Center, the State Council, China

ZHENG Shiping, Associate Professor, Department of Political Science, University of Vermont, U.S.A.

ZHONG Yang, Associate Professor, Department of Political Science, The University of Tennessee, Knoxville, U.S.A.

ZOU Keyuan, Senior Research Fellow, East Asian Institute, National University of Singapore

Introduction: Jiang Zemin and His Reign Over the Party

WANG GUNGWU AND
ZHENG YONGNIAN

The Chinese Communist Party (CCP), with its 66 million members, is the largest ruling political party in the world. Scholars and policymakers are watching whether the party will wither away as a result of drastic socio-economic changes. With the decline of Marxism and Maoism, will the party be able to renew its ideology to justify its existence? Will it be able to stay relevant? Will it be able to govern 1.3 billion people effectively? Will it be able to introduce democracy as China's new organisational base? In fact, the significance of the Party goes far beyond its national boundary. The CCP is not just a Party, as understood commonly in the West. The latest version of the Party Constitution states that the party is the vanguard of not only the working class, but also the Chinese people and the Chinese nation. The party will to a large extent decide what role China will play in world politics. Western powers as well as China's neighbours have good reason to have their eyes intently fixed on the party, fully aware that its ambitions will have an important impact on regional peace and security.

At the party's 16th Congress in November 2002, Jiang Zemin stepped down as Secretary General. This was the first time in the history of the People's Republic of China (PRC) that a physically healthy party boss stepped down without intensive political struggles among top leaders. This is clearly a good time to review the CCP under Jiang Zemin. The development of the CCP has been one of the major areas that the East Asian Institute has monitored over the years. This collection represents a joint effort by scholars in the institute to understand the CCP under Jiang Zemin. All the papers were previously circulated as working papers and background briefs produced by the East Asian Institute, and were refined and updated for this publication.

This introduction attempts to provide a general overview of the changes that have occurred within the CCP under Jiang Zemin's leadership and to summarise the major points in these papers. The book comprises four sections. The first section, the Introduction, outlines the situation in which party-building was carried out under Jiang. The second section shows how the party experienced ideological and organisational decline with the deepening of reforms and the open-door policy in the 1990s. The third section discusses how the party responded to the decay in these important areas and struggled for control and relevance. And, finally, the fourth section explores how the party made efforts to engage itself in the transition of the party from a traditional Marxist-Leninist party to something else.

JIANG ZEMIN: PARTY DE-CONSTRUCTOR AND PARTY BUILDER

Jiang was born on 17 August 1926 in Yangzhou, a city in east China's Jiangsu Province. He received his higher education at Jiaotong University in Shanghai, majoring in electrical engineering. During his college years, Jiang participated in the CCP-led student movements and joined the CCP in 1946.

After the founding of the People's Republic, Jiang served as an associate engineer, deputy director of a factory, and section head of an enterprise. In 1955, he went to the then Soviet Union and worked in the Stalin Automobile Company as a trainee for one year. After he returned home, he served as a deputy division head, deputy chief power engineer, director of a branch factory, and deputy director, and then director of factories and research institutes in different parts of China including Changchun, Shanghai and Wuhan. In the ensuing years,

Jiang served as deputy, then director of the foreign affairs department of the No. 1 Ministry of Machine-Building Industry.

The reform and open door policy was a turning point in Jiang's political career. In 1979 when the late Chinese leader Deng Xiaoping proposed to build Special Economic Zones (SEZs), Jiang was sent to Shenzhen. He served as deputy director and concurrently as secretary general of the State Import and Export Administration and the State Foreign Investment Administration. In 1982, Jiang became a member of the 12th CCP Central Committee. At the same time, Jiang was appointed Vice Minister of Electronics Industry, and became Minister in a few months. In 1985, Jiang was appointed Shanghai Mayor. In November 1987, Jiang was elected a member of the Political Bureau, the most powerful decision-making body of the party.

Even though Jiang was able to climb up China's political ladder, he probably never thought that he would become the party's General Secretary one day. Without the pro-democracy movement in 1989, Jiang would not have been in a position to take over the post of party General Secretary. During that event, Zhao Ziyang was ousted for his "wrongdoings" in dealing with the student movement. Jiang was suddenly appointed party General Secretary in June 1989 when the pro-democracy movement was still going on. Five months later, he was appointed chairman of the CCP Central Military Commission (CMC). In 1992, Jiang was reappointed General Secretary. One year later, he became State President and continued to be chairman of the CMC. From then until 2002, Jiang was the most powerful political leader since Mao Zedong. He concurrently held the three most important party positions, i.e., General Secretary, State President and Chairman of the CMC.

Indeed, Jiang Zemin was the core of the third generation leadership. The great power that these institutions granted to Jiang Zemin largely ensured that all changes that occurred to the party were associated with Jiang himself, his vision and his capability. During his *Zhongnanhai* (refers to the CCP leadership compound west of Beijing, the centre of party power) career from 1989 to 2002, Jiang's endeavour to rebuild the party can be divided into three stages.

1989-1992: Politics of Survival

Before Jiang was appointed party General Secretary in 1992, he had no experience in *Zhongnanhai* politics at all. He had spent most of his life in the government sector rather than party affairs. He had no knowledge of the operation of the party machine. During this period, all Jiang's political actions were dominated by the politics of survival. To survive, Jiang had to devote himself to making his own political network. He had to deal with the party elders. Most party elders such as Deng Xiaoping, Chen Yun and Li Xiannan were still alive at that time. While Jiang was nominally number one, real power was in the hand of party elders. He had to follow all sorts of instructions from party elders. Furthermore, Jiang also had to deal with his colleagues. Many of his colleagues, such as Li Peng and Yao Yilin, had more experience in *Zhongnanhai* and were probably more ambitious politically. While Jiang did not expect to be promoted to Beijing when he dealt with the pro-democratic protestors in Shanghai, Li Peng had political ambitions when doing so in Beijing. The fact that the party elders chose Jiang as party General Secretary instead of Li Peng and other political leaders who showed their loyalty to the party elders during the student movement made Li Peng and other politically ambitious leaders quite uncomfortable. Although Deng Xiaoping appointed Jiang to serve as the leadership core, other leaders were not so convinced. Without their cooperation, Jiang could hardly have survived *Zhongnanhai* politics.

To survive politically, Jiang decided he could not and should not take any initiatives that would depart from previously established policies. As a matter of fact, during this period, many policy initiatives that Jiang accepted were initiated by the conservatives. This is especially true over the issue of how the CCP could strengthen itself in the aftermath of the crackdown on the pro-democracy movement in 1989. During the student movements, many private entrepreneurs showed their support for the movement. Some helped organise the movement while others contributed financial support. After the crackdown, party conservatives initiated a policy regulation to prohibit private entrepreneurs from joining the party. Jiang immediately showed his strong support for this new regulation.

To be fair to Jiang, no one would have undertaken any initiatives to reform the party during this period. Both the internal and external environments pressurised party leaders to accord the highest priority to party survival. Many factors such as the 1989 pro-democracy movement and the collapse of the communist regimes in the Soviet Union and Eastern Europe threatened the very existence of the communist regime in China. Party conservatives regarded all of these as the consequences of radical political liberalisation. What the CCP leadership did during this period was simply to strengthen the monopoly of power by the party, and no political reforms were carried out.

1992 to 1997: Politics of Power Consolidation

In 1992, Jiang was reappointed General Party Secretary at the party's 14th National Congress. In early 1992, Deng Xiaoping initiated a landmark southern tour since he was extremely unhappy with the conservative policy orientation that the Jiang Zemin leadership had adopted since 1989. During the tour, Deng made several important speeches and called for more radical reforms to be implemented. Jiang's political "enemies" made use of this opportunity to pressurise Jiang. Jiang was politically sensitive enough to change his previously conservative stand and show his full support for Deng's reform policies. At the 14th Party Congress, Jiang gained Deng's full support, without which Jiang would not have been able to battle with his enemies, especially the Yang brothers, i.e., Yang Shangkun (State President) and Yang Baibing (military man). Furthermore, Deng's ideas were integrated into the party Constitution and laid down the guidelines for the party leadership.

Although Deng's support enabled him to keep his position, Jiang had to spend most of his energy consolidating his power before he could take any initiatives of his own. Another important factor was that Deng and other party elders were still present, though their political influence gradually faded away. During this period, no substantial reform measures were carried out. Jiang skillfully initiated a campaign against party corruption and ousted

Chen Xitong, then Mayor of Beijing, who challenged Jiang's power. Jiang also gained support from the military. Apparently, during this period, party building was not Jiang's highest priority, nor even on his priority list.

1997 to 2002: Politics of Party Transition

During this period, Jiang shifted his focus to the task of party building. Several factors enabled him to do so. First, through enormous efforts, Jiang had consolidated his power. Second, at the 15th Party Congress in 1997, Jiang succeeded in forcing Qiao Shi, his only potential political threat, to gracefully "exit" politics. Third, Deng and other party elders passed away. These new developments enabled Jiang to become his own man.

Nevertheless, the question of how to push forward the work of party building was another matter. It took Jiang many years to figure out his own approach. Overall, he approached the issue on the two fronts, i.e., party ideology and organisation. Even before the 15th Party Congress, Jiang began to pursue a new ideology suitable for the party in a time of drastic socio-economic changes. In 1996, he raised the concept of "*jiang zhengzhi*" (literally "talking about politics") and asked party cadres and government officials to pay attention to political correctness. Two years later, Jiang initiated a more aggressive campaign, i.e., "*jiang zhengzhi, jiang zhengqi, jiang xuexi*" (literally, "talking about politics, virtue and political learning"). Both campaigns received a cool reception.

It was not until 2000 that Jiang realised that the Maoist political campaign had become ineffective, even counter-productive in an age of capitalistic economic development and globalisation. That year, Jiang raised a new concept aimed at rebuilding the party, the "three represents", meaning that the party represents the most advanced mode of production, the most advanced culture and the interests of the majority of the people. The concept opened the party to different social classes, especially newly rising ones. One year later, Jiang formally declared that the party would admit private entrepreneurs and other advanced elements in the Chinese society as members. At the 16th Party Congress, the "three represents" became an integral part of theory, following Marxism, Maoism and Deng's theory. It marked a new beginning for the party.

On the organisational front, he was not able to carry out any major restructuring. Instead, Jiang focused on elite recruitment and the issue of meritocracy. As of June 2002 before the latest Party Congress, the CCP membership nationwide had reached 66.4 million, up from 59.4 million in 1997. From 1997 to the end of 2001, the party accepted 5.3 million new members nationwide. Meanwhile, 124,000 party members were asked to leave the party due to their various wrongdoings, mainly acts of corruption.

Among all new recruits, young members under the age of 35 numbered 14.8 million, or 22.3 percent of the total. According to the categories defined by the Organisation Department of the CCP, 29.9 million party members are from among urban and rural workers, farmers, herdsmen and fishermen, representing 45 percent of the total; 14 million are from among civil servants, enterprise managers, soldiers and armed police, 21 percent of the total; and 7.7 million are from specialised professions, 11.6 percent of the total. In terms of educational background, almost 35 million party members have received above senior middle school education, about 53 percent of the total. Of them, 15 million have received university or college education, about 23 percent of the total.[1]

Jiang Zemin has left his own legacy for the party. With all these changes, the party is in ferment, uncertain of its direction and what enormous difficulties lie ahead. In the following sections, we shall summarise the main points made in the chapters that follow. We first identify the areas where the party has shown decline, and then discuss how the party has responded, and finally highlight major efforts by the Jiang leadership to transform the party.

IDEOLOGICAL AND ORGANISATIONAL DECAY

What the party leadership did under Jiang Zemin was largely a reaction to party decay in the past decade, which can be understood from both ideological and organisational perspectives. In Chapter 1, Lance Gore highlights the political significance of organisation and ideology in the communist system by comparing China and the Soviet Union. Gore attempts to answer the question that has troubled social scientists for many years, that is: Why was no one able to predict the collapse of communism in the Soviet Union and Eastern Europe? Implicitly, Gore also wants to answer another equally important question: Why have different predictions of the fall of the Chinese Communist Party been wrong so far? During the Cold War, scholars paid enormous attention to the communist system and developed various theories to explain its birth and development. Nevertheless, even the most critical scholars failed to predict its fall. After the fall of communism in Europe in the early 1990s, many scholars began to predict a fall of the communist system in China, but this has not happened.

To explain the fall of communism, Gore focuses on the organisational and ideological aspects of communism and places the legitimacy problem at the center of his analysis. It seems to him the communist system by its nature suffered organisational defects or "structural contradictions," such as fixity, corruption, division and stagnation. All these organisational defects were the consequences of total bureaucratisation after the initial communist revolution. Total bureaucratisation froze the revolutionary spirit, generated corruption and power abuses, led to societal divisiveness, and finally caused economic stagnation.

Central to the political stability of the communist system was the regime's ability to justify its legitimacy by delivering economic welfare to its people. Nevertheless, all these organisational defects rapidly undermined the basis of the legitimacy of the communist regime. In the Soviet Union and Eastern Europe, according to Gore, a legitimacy crisis was created by the simultaneous emergence of three conditions: glaring failure of the dominant ideology to rationalise the existing order; the emergence of competing ideologies capable of mobilising and legitimising opposition from both within and outside the establishment; and a change in the opportunity cost structure in society so that the cost of defiance was no longer prohibitive.

While Gore's explanation can be regarded as a kind of after-the-event wisdom, his emphasis on organisation and ideology is certainly helpful to our understanding of regime survival in China. We will see in later chapters that both decay and revival of the CCP can be perceived from the organisational and ideological perspectives. As Gore indicates, it was changes in organisation and ideology that have differentiated the CCP from other communist regimes.

In Chapter 2, Xiao Gongqin discusses the ideological decay of the CCP, using the Falun Gong movement as a case. On April 25, 1999, over 10,000 Falun Gong followers in Beijing grabbed the headlines of the international news media by "laying siege" to the communist leadership compound, *Zhongnanhai*, and staging a "sit-in" to complain about the persecution of Falun Gong followers in Tianjin and demand official recognition of its status as a respectable body. The top leadership was unnerved by such a development which its public security services had failed to prevent. More seriously, the five government representatives in the Falun Gong negotiation team were cadres from core organisations of the CCP itself, including the Supervisory Department, Railway Department, Second Headquarters of the General Staff, Public Security Department, and Beijing University. It was no exaggeration to say that Falun Gong had pierced the stomach of the party. For the party leadership, this was a very threatening sign of party decay.

According to Xiao, many factors contributed to the rise of Falun Gong during a period of rapid economic growth. First of all, Falun Gong served the people's need for faith and belief. People seem to be more eager to search for faith moorings when the society experienced a collapse of the old belief system. Second, the movement satisfied the need for social interaction among lonely aged people, laid-off workers, and others of the disadvantaged strata that are marginalised in a market economy. Third, it attracted the lower classes who sought a sense of security. The disadvantaged groups are easily affected by all kinds of risk and experienced great difficulties in getting family and social protection, and Falun Gong created an opportunity for its members to help each other. Fourth, Falun Gong also satisfied those who were discontented with the system over questions of justice.

Rapid socio-economic transformation has led to the collapse of socialist beliefs and values as well as the collective protection systems. The resultant social injustice, as well as moral decline, have caused the people to have a stronger desire for justice. Falun Gong came into being to fulfill these social needs. It became popular not only among ordinary people, but also among the party cadres and government officials. Although the CCP regime has cracked down on the Falun Gong movement, the battle is not yet over. The communist regime since 1949 had never witnessed such a massive and sustained nationwide opposition movement as Falun Gong. As long as there is a spiritual vacuum, religious movements are likely to grow, be it Falun Gong or some others.

Corruption is another major source of party decay. In the pre-reform era, coercive organisational and ideological measures imposed from above contained corruption quite effectively. However, this is no longer the case in the reform era, especially since the early 1990s. In Chapter 3, Zou Keyuan discusses the implications of corruption for the CCP. Zou believes that corruption could not only cause social instability, but also arouse the people's defiance of the CCP and cast doubts about its legitimacy to rule the country. In other words, corruption has made it difficult, if not impossible, for the CCP to justify its political legitimacy.

It is hard to say that the party leadership did not realise the negative consequences of corruption for the party. Under Jiang Zemin, the party leadership initiated waves of campaigns to crack down on corruption. The leadership also imposed laws in trying to cope with corruption. Nevertheless, the party faced insurmountable difficulties in its efforts to contain corruption. Although Jiang consistently called for the rule of law, the CCP continued to monopolise power. The monopoly of power by the CCP is significant for the sustained corruption among party cadres. As Zou correctly points out, as long as the power of the CCP is not effectively checked and supervised, such power can still give rise to corruption. Highly centralised power is vulnerable to corruption since there is no reasonable division of power and no effective check in the use of power. Law is useful in deterring and controlling corruption, but it is not a panacea. The real victory against corruption lies in effecting further political reform. For instance, one characteristic of China's anti-corruption campaigns is the superiority of party's policy over state laws as guidelines to launch such campaigns. The party wants to control the campaign so that such a campaign will not become a threat to the party. So long as the party stands above the law, how could anti-corruption campaigns become effective?

In Chapter 4, Zhong Yang looks at party decay in terms of central-local relations. While the power of the CCP is highly centralised, Chinese local officials do not always comply with central government policies. Why is this so? According to Zhong, the institutional setting of the party dominance presents a paradoxical situation for center-local relations in China. In the old days, the central government controlled local government mainly via three measures, i.e., party discipline, ideology and the centrally planned economic system. However, the latter two have been significantly weakened as a result of reforms. The only viable control mechanism that the center is counting on is party organisation and discipline. This explains why the local party organisation and party secretary have been given so much power by higher party authorities. Unfortunately, Zhong points out, this power can easily be abused by local party chiefs, and they can use this power to effectively build "independent kingdoms" that give them the latitude to disobey higher administrative authorities or to drag their feet in carrying out the center's policies, particularly in the absence of an effective monitoring system.

Ideological decay has also had an important impact on local officials. Zhong observes that in the reform era, official status and power have become more important due to decentralisation, the weakening of ideology and the deterioration of morality, with official positions carrying possibilities for material gain. For Chinese local officials, official positions equal power equal material gains. When power and material gains became the career objective, it is understandable that local officials behave independently from central party authorities.

Nevertheless, Zhong also stresses, while the increasing resistance to and distortion of central policies at local levels becomes a major issue, localism is easily exaggerated. It is too simplistic to say that central policies are always ignored or distorted. Compliance varies according to the issue. The balance of central mandate and local needs is necessary for local party cadres. In any case, the fundamental principle is that local government officials want to put in the least amount of effort to achieve maximum results.

Organisational decay is more serious at the village level, as Zhao Shikai discusses in Chapter 5. Zhao observes that despite rapid socio-economic transformation at the village level, the grassroots organisations have not made any significant improvement in the methods of handling rural affairs, and they still operate under the old regime. There is grave disaccord between the organisations and peasants, as well as within the internal system of the organisations themselves.

In China's villages, the main institutions include village-level branches of the CCP, self-elected government committees and economic organisations. All these organisations have been in decline over the past two decades. Few village-level economic organisations have performed well, and in most villages, the organisations are either only nominal or simply absent. However, the peasants need the kinds of organisations that can provide services for their economic activities. While officials are there, they only come to villages to collect taxes and fees. In the late 1980s, a system of self-government was established. Since then, village elections have been developed and peasants are allowed to elect their leaders. Nevertheless, according to Zhao, the party cadres do not really like the idea of peasant autonomy, and they want elected village leaders to control the villagers and implement policies initiated at higher levels. In all village-level organisations, the core is still the party branches, with branch secretaries in charge of everything important in the villages. Conflicts between the party and village committees become inevitable. Since the legitimacy of the village committees is based on the will of the people, village heads often try to end party-branch dominance and thus pose a direct challenge to the existing power structure.

Efforts have also been made to resolve the conflicts between the party branches and village committees. For instance, there is the "two vote system" in which the party members receive votes of confidence from villagers. The system was meant to ensure that villagers support the branches and thus strengthen the branches' position in village affairs. Another measure is the system called "one shoulder with all burdens" which integrated the party and self-government by appointing one particular person to represent two organisations. Nevertheless, such a "two-in-one" system often led to the creation of a local autocracy in the village.

When facing exploitation within the grassroots organisations, the peasants often cannot help but accept them. But Zhao also observes that the discontent among peasants could lead to individual and even collective resistance. The Chinese peasants do not have any mechanisms to air their voices and protect their rights. So long as there are no institutions to organise and represent peasant interests, rural stability will continue to be problematic.

In Chapter 6, He Baogang discusses the impact of kinship on rural governance. In traditional China, kinship was an important political force in rural areas. It was the CCP that completely changed the rural social structure. After 1949, particularly after the agrarian collectivisation, the clan system was almost eliminated. However, the introduction of village elections has provided an opportunity for the family clan to revive. Today, clan power attempts to re-emerge through the governance of the rural community. Manifestations of the effect of kinship on the elections are many and clan culture may have a subtle influence on the villagers' value system. It has also generated a disparity in the chance of winning between candidates from a major clan and those from a minor clan. Its influence could be more powerful when it is backed by wealth.

While recognising the influence of kinship, He also points out its limitations. He observes that candidates from small clans were frequently elected, whereas those from the major clans were not. Among other factors, according to He, village party organisations have contributed to local variations. If the village party organisation is strong, it is likely to contain the influence of kinship and not to do so if the organisation is weak. The presence of lineage influence takes place when the village party secretary is incompetent. Needless to say, though clan forces do not constitute a serious problem for village elections, and kinship does not undermine the CCP significantly, the party leadership still needs to address the issue of how to build effective rural party organisations to balance clan forces.

DAMAGE CONTROL AND RESPONSE: STRUGGLE FOR RELEVANCE

The CCP is undoubtedly China's most important institution with vast vested interests. While the party has experienced serious decay, the Jiang leadership also made great efforts to control the damage caused by the decay. Five papers in this section address this issue.

In Chapter 7, Zheng Shiping addresses one of the most important issues in Chinese politics, i.e., the age factor in leadership transition and power succession. As mentioned earlier, the party is highly centralised and leadership stability is the key to regime stability. Strong leadership is needed to curb the negative impact of rapid socio-economic changes on the party. Power struggles among major leaders under both Mao Zedong and Deng Xiaoping caused great political chaos and weakened the party leadership. How power struggles could be avoided was an important issue for the Jiang leadership. Moreover, when younger leaders come to power, they have to find a new base for their legitimacy. While such older generation leaders as Mao Zedong and Deng Xiaoping gained their credentials from revolutionary experience, younger leaders have to turn to other factors.

Jiang was not without any success in this regard. The establishment of "age" as an institutional factor regulating power succession was an example. Under Jiang, the credentials of guerrilla warfare and mass mobilisation were rapidly replaced by the credentials of education and work performance, especially in project management and economic development. More importantly, the new factor of age emerged to shape China's political process. Zheng points out that the "age limit" was chosen since it was an objective criterion, non-political and non-ideological, which the Chinese leaders could use openly and effectively to speed up leadership renewal at various levels of the party and government. While the party leaders under Deng began to use the "age limit" to regulate leadership succession and personnel reshuffling, Jiang had consolidated the system and made it more institutionalised. Today, the "age limit" applies to recruitment and retirement of party cadres and government officials at all levels. The emergence of the "age limit" is important for Chinese politics. To a degree, informal power politics is still relevant in deciding who gets what official position. Jiang himself used the age limit as a convenient political instrument to force his political rivals to step down. However, formal rules and regulations have become increasingly important. As Zheng observes, never before has the age of top leaders become such a relevant and key factor in politics.

In Chapter 8, Ignatius Wibowo discusses changes over the recruitment policy of the CCP. The most significant development under Jiang was that the party legitimised the admission of private entrepreneurs. Wibowo argues that this policy change was largely determined by three factors, i.e., the crisis of recruitment, the pressure by private entrepreneurs and Jiang's desire for personal glory.

Wibowo noted, in the late 1980s, students of prestigious universities were more eager to follow the black path (studying abroad) than the red path (joining the party). To the students, joining the party was considered to be a game of snakes and ladders where people could rise and fall all of sudden, and consequently it did not offer certainty. Such a situation did not change for many years. For example, as Wibowo points out, there are areas where fewer young peasants want to join the party. Certainly, the recruitment problem was a major factor pushing the party to admit private entrepreneurs. But it is also worth noting that to admit fewer peasants might be a part of the party leadership's effort to transform the party.

Furthermore, the admission of private entrepreneurs occurred due to pressure from this newly rising social class. Chinese private entrepreneurs, or capitalists, are not particularly different from their counterparts in other countries. When they become rich, they begin to ask for political power. In fact, private entrepreneurs have entered the Chinese political scene at different levels long before the party's decision to legitimise their political power. The party had silently "implemented" experiments on the impact of private entrepreneurs on the party. Only after leaders found that capitalists did more good than harm did they legitimise the admission of capitalists.

And finally, according to Wibowo, Jiang Zemin's personal motivation also played a role in legitimising capitalists' party membership. This goes back to the point Zheng Shiping raised in the previous chapter that informal politics is still relevant in China today. In the Chinese political context, it is understandable that political leaders want to leave their own legacies for later generations and thus in Chinese history. This was also true for Jiang who vigorously fought for his historical legacy before the 16th Party Congress. Actually, the legitimisation of the admission of capitalists has become Jiang's legacy for both the country and the party.

In Chapter 9, Kjeld Erik Brodsgaard discusses the CCP's cadre management system. Central to all Leninist party-states is the nomenklatura system, which consists of a list of positions over which the party committees have the authority to make appointments. Since the reform policy, China's nomenklatura system has undergone several major changes. In 1984 when the party was under Hu Yaobang's leadership, the direct management power of the Central Organisation Department (COD) was limited to one level down. It conformed to the leadership's attempt to limit the reach of party power and to empower the State Council's Ministry of Personnel. To do so, the leadership expected that the merit-based civil service system could be improved. But in 1989, in the aftermath of the crackdown on the pro-democracy movement, the nomenklatura system was recentralised. Under Jiang, the centralisation of party power was greatly strengthened. In 1998, under the directorship of Zeng Qinghong, Jiang's close aide and confidant, the COD took back its appointment authority of the *ju*-level leaders at the central level, meaning that in certain areas the nomenklatura system went back to the pre-1984 period.

While the COD reinforced its centralisation efforts, it has also limited its scope of cadre management. As Brodsgaard notes, the COD has increasingly focused on the management of leading cadres, which constitute only about 8 percent of the cadre corps in government organs. About 92 percent of them are cadres working at the provincial level and below such as local city and county party secretaries. The most important of leading cadres are those at the ministerial or provincial level and above. This downsising of management scope tends to increase effectiveness of the cadre management system. Leading cadres are now managed according to detailed regulations relating to recruitment, appointment, performance evaluation, training, etc. The objective of cadre management is to make sure that professionally competent people are recruited and promoted and that these remain loyal to the party's ideological and political line.

While the leadership had aggressively used party power to govern the government sector, it also strengthened the efforts to implement legal reform. In Chapter 10, Zou Keyuan highlights the progress and limitations of legal reform under Jiang with regards to reform of the judiciary. The rule of law was given the highest priority at the 15th Party Congress in 1997. In 1998, a major wave of judicial reform was implemented, aiming at realising judicial independence. The party wants to use the legal system to govern the country more effectively. Progress has been made. Nevertheless, Zou notes that the judicial reform was greatly constrained by the party's monopoly on power. The goal of the rule of law requires the development of a judicial system that is relatively autonomous of the executive and legislative powers of the government. But under the one-party system, an independent judiciary is virtually impossible.

According to Zou, since law is made by the legislature, those who control it can make law to reflect their will and to attain their goals. In China, as the National People's Congress (NPC) is under the control of the CCP, then in principle there should be no law which could be in conflict with the party's interest and/or inconsistent with the party's policy. Once the ruling status of the party is threatened by the use of law, the party may not tolerate it. Although the party wants to use the judicial system to enforce law, it also wants to control the judicial system. Thus, loyalty became a principal requirement of recruitment for the judiciary.

Besides the difficulties resulting from the party's monopoly on power, China's judicial system has other significant problems, with judicial corruption the most serious phenomenon. Judicial corruption has taken place in different ways, including: judicial local protectionism and department protectionism; adjudication in violation of statutory procedures or overdue adjudication; abuse of power to detain interested parties or lawyers or limit their personal freedom; abuse of judicial power to extort property, services, or collect fees at random; and breach of the law to protect private interests or the interest of relatives or friends at the expense of the interest of others.

Though supervision of judicial function is regarded as one of the measures to curb judicial corruption and to improve judicial practice, supervision has not proved to be effective. While the main supervision is provided by the People's Congress, the party organisations are still beyond the control of any institutional organs. Zou points out that there are two main obstacles for China to realise judicial independence: first, the CCP's interference, which is illustrated by the presence of the political and legal committees within the party which have power to decide the judgment of some cases; and second, the financial and human resources in support of the judiciary which come from the relevant governmental departments and party units. Indeed, both problems are related to the party's monopoly on power.

Another important area Jiang emphasised to consolidate the party's power was party-military relations. The military has always been the most important pillar of the communist rule, as Mao Zedong had argued earlier that political powers came out of the barrel of a gun. The one single important principle for the communist regime is that the party commands the gun, and the gun must never be allowed to command the party. For the party, nothing else can replace the military in protecting the country. How the Jiang leadership institutionalised party-military relations is the theme of Chapter 11 by Zheng Shiping.

Zheng observes that under Jiang's reign from 1990 to 2002, the PLA overall became more professionalised, modernised, and regularised. Jiang also succeeded in establishing himself as the actual commander-in-chief of the military. When Jiang came to power, he did not have any revolutionary credentials which were often regarded by the military as the most important source of individual leaders' legitimacy to rule the military. So, Jiang had to turn to other institutional factors. According to Zheng, Jiang's first move was to expand the membership of the Central Military Commission (CMC) so that he would be able to put a few faces in that institute. Jiang frequently used his position as the chairman of the CMC to promote military leaders to the rank of general, the highest rank in the PLA. While promoting younger military leaders, Jiang also pushed for more military leadership changes by enforcing the retirement system effectively to his advantage. During Jiang's tenure, a new precedent was established in the military in which one's seniority and biological age had to be compatible. Besides these institutional means, Jiang also resorted to political and legal means. He frequently emphasised that the military had to accept the absolute leadership of the party. After 1996, Jiang made special efforts to promote the concept of ruling the army by law. The 1997 the National Defense Law served an example.

Zheng contends that with all these developments, China's party-army relations under Jiang looked more like a negotiated partnership. While the military takes orders from the party, the party has to provide military benefits of various kinds. For example, after 1989, the world witnessed spending on defense increasing at a double-digit rate every year. Also, during Jiang's tenure, the PLA continued to play a significant role in China's policymaking process. In the NPC, the PLA delegates constituted the largest group. From 1997-2002, the PLA managed to set the percentage of military representation to be at about one-fifth of the full membership in the Central Committee though there was no military man in the Standing Committee of the Political Bureau.

A PARTY IN TRANSITION

A careful examination of what was done to the party under Jiang leads us to see that many measures taken by the party leadership were actually beyond that of damage control. From the above discussions, we can sense that the Jiang leadership had begun to engage the party in transition. The four papers in this section identify main areas where party transition has taken place. These chapters also try to locate the sources that the leadership has used to engage such a transition and their limitations.

In Chapter 12, Chen Weixing explores a general trend of the party transition, i.e., from Deng Xiaoping's party of economics to Jiang Zemin's party of the people. Chen contends that Chinese domestic politics had undergone two distinctive periods before the 16th CCP National Congress in 2002: the politics of transformation under Deng from 1978 to 1992 and the politics of adaptation under Jiang from 1992 to 2002. Deng's politics of transformation concerned transforming the CCP for economic growth, while Jiang's politics of adaptation concerned attuning the CCP to the conditions of the CCP decay and the erosion of China's social solidarity.

Under Deng, the leadership gave the highest priority to promoting economic growth by introducing market-oriented reforms. To do so, the leadership had to de-politicise the Chinese polity, economy, and culture. Rapid socio-economic transformation led to party decay, as we discussed earlier. For the Jiang leadership, the party had to not only continuously promote economic growth, but also carry out party transition in order to accommodate rapid socio-economic transformation. Many measures were taken to make such a transformation. After the mid-1990s, Jiang began to make efforts to revive party ideology. From the "*jiang zhengzhi*" ("talking about politics") to the "three represents" theory, the Jiang leadership initiated a series of ideological campaigns to revive the party ideology. More importantly, the establishment of the "three represents" as the pillar of party ideology means that the party leadership had begun to consider its relevance to the majority of the people. In this sense, Chen believes that the party is in a transition to a party of the people.

If the "three represents" theory represents the party's transition to the party of the people, as Chen argues, how the interests of the majority of the people can be represented by the party is still unclear. No institutions exist for social forces to articulate and aggregate their diverse interests. Needless to say, the party is not ready to grant social forces the freedom to organise themselves. In Chapter 13, Xiao Gongqin explores the possibility and the limits of the emergence of opposition parties in the post-Deng era, using the case of the China Democratic Party (CDP). Xiao argues that the rise of the CDP towards the end of the 1990s was due to various factors. By that time, Jiang had been in power for more than a decade and his political base had been greatly consolidated after Deng passed away. Moreover, the Chinese leaders had also realised how widespread and serious corruption had become. For leaders with liberal minds, popular freedom could serve as an effective monitoring mechanism initiated from below to check corruption practices.

Then, why did the party leadership initiate a campaign to crack down on the CDP? According to Xiao, this was also due to various factors. The leadership went through the political crisis of the 1989 pro-democracy movement and political insecurity still was on their minds when the problems relating to the CDP came to surface. Top leaders believed that the unsolved problem of the 1989 pro-democracy movement, bureaucratic corruption, laid-off workers, and domestic financial crisis could trigger discontent from the lower classes and might even lead to political turbulence. Therefore, while the party leaders wished to implement relatively liberal politics, they also worried about the risk of losing political control. This dilemma confronts the post-Deng technocratic leadership in a unique way. When the top leaders sensed that the CDP had become a "threat" to the party, they became intolerant. So the crackdown followed. However, it is worth noting, as Xiao emphasised, that the radicalisation of the CDP movement was also a major factor leading to the crackdown. The radicalisation often meant that it became difficult for the party leadership to make any concession to the CDP.

Xiao observes that, despite the crackdown, the leadership's response was quite limited compared to many other political campaigns during the Mao and Deng eras. When the leadership explained the crackdown, it regarded the CDP as undermining political stability and domestic security. It did not carry out massive arrests of the democracy activists. By treating them on an individual basis, the leadership tried to minimise the social implications of the CDP event.

Xiao calls the current regime the post-totalitarian regime. Such a regime has two basic features. On the one hand, it inherits the legacy of the totalitarian regime concerning social control, which is manifested in the strong public security system, the bureaucracy system and mechanisms assuring the implementation of political order from top to bottom, the control of media and propaganda, and so forth. On the other hand, different from the totalitarian era, the post-totalitarian era witnesses the retreat of the leftist ideological force and revolutionary senior statesmen and the rise of the technocratic leadership. Overall, the regime continues to be fragile and not stable enough to bear all kinds of political challenges. It is unlikely that the party leadership will tolerate the rise of opposition parties to challenge the CCP. Political liberalisation, participation and democracy are still remote to such a party regime.

Apparently, the party leadership is not willing to accept political freedom and democracy as the formula to revive the party. Then, what sources can the party use to revive the party and engage the transition from the traditional Marxist-Leninist party to something else? In Chapter 14, Zheng Yongnian and Lai Hongyi examine how the Jiang leadership appealed to Chinese traditional factors to revive the party. While the Jiang leadership made great efforts to revive the party, there were enormous difficulties. A new ideology cannot be easily established and party ethics continue to decay. The party's organisational coercion cannot effectively regulate the behaviour of millions of party members. Rampant corruption continues. Rule of law is virtually impossible due to the party's unwillingness to give up its monopoly of power. Jiang, as a technocrat, is a pragmatist. He does not believe that there is one single formula which can revive and transform the party. He tried to borrow many "good" factors from

China's rich traditions. The campaign of the so-called "rule by virtue" serves an example.

The "rule by virtue" doctrine is inherent in the Confucian tradition. In the pre-reform period, the party regarded all kinds of Chinese traditions as barriers to China's modernity, and frequently initiated cultural and political movements to destroy them. This was no longer the case under Jiang and the new leadership. Jiang called for the party to represent the most advanced culture. But this does not prevent him from borrowing traditional factors for contemporary use. In fact, Jiang tried to combine different factors such as Confucianism, socialism, and the rule of law. Somehow, he believed that such a combination would enable the leadership to establish an effective ideology for the party.

In Chapter 15, John Wong and Zheng Yongnian discuss another source for the party transition, i.e., newly rising private entrepreneurs or capitalists. As discussed above, several our authors have discussed why and how the party leadership decided to admit capitalists. According to Wong and Zheng, the admission of private entrepreneurs is not only a matter of party recruitment. More importantly, it is a matter of party transformation. In the long run, nothing else will be more important for the party than the admission of capitalists.

Needless to say, the admission of capitalists is a formal declaration by the party leadership that the CCP is no longer a traditional communist party whose aim was to eliminate all capitalists. The admission of capitalists in the context of the "three represents" theory also implies that the party leadership has begun to consider the party's relationship with the people, as Chen Weixin suggested in his chapter. Nevertheless, how the party can represent diverse social interests remains a big question mark. Without developing various institutions for social forces to articulate and aggregate their interests, "three represents" will not materialise. Furthermore, no one in the party leadership is sure that different social interests can co-exist peacefully under one party's umbrella. Indeed, the "three represents" theory has been very controversial since its birth. Although Jiang was able to establish it as a new pillar of party ideology, this does not mean that the party as a whole has accepted it and is prepared to absorb its consequences. Party leftists believe that capitalists may eventually take over the party's leadership.

Certainly, by admitting capitalists into the party, Jiang Zemin also introduced enormous contradictions into the party. Suffice it to say that with capitalists inside the party, they will certainly act as potential catalysts to quicken the transformation of the party. Jiang might genuinely believe that he had done what it took to strengthen the party-state by broadening its social base. In the future, as the party steps up its process of metamorphosis and evolves into a kind of social democratic party, he will still be favourably judged by history for leading the way for such a transformation. In a positive sense, by doing so, Jiang might have left a legacy of both strengthening the party and facilitating its transformation. But in a negative sense, as Wong and Zheng stress, the loser might be the Chinese Communist Party itself. In admitting capitalists, the party also let in the Trojan horse. How can the party cope with the consequences resulting from the admission of capitalists? What direction will the party take for its transition? How can it succeed in making that transition? All such questions await the new leaderships in the coming decades.

ENDNOTE

1 All figures are from the *People's Daily*, 2 September 2002.

The editors are grateful to Dr. Yow Cheun Hoe for his assistance in the process of editing.

PART 1

Ideological and Organisational Decay

CHAPTER 1

Rethinking the Collapse of Communism: The Role of Ideology Then and Now

LANCE L.P. GORE

More than a decade has elapsed since the dramatic demise of communism in the former Soviet Union and its satellite states in Eastern Europe and Mongolia. The utter unpreparedness of even the most prominent scholars of communism for a historical event of such epical proportions is not only humiliating but also humbling: it exposes the inadequacy of our understanding of the inner dynamics of communist politics as well as deficiency of the conventional tools of political analysis. How could it be possible that these powerful and well-entrenched[1] states, which in most cases (with the possible exception of Poland) faced no significant organised opposition during their entire existence, should have collapsed almost overnight? How could a strong and all-encompassing system, into which generations of people were born and socialised as the only way of life they knew, suddenly lose all its legitimacy and staying power and become the target of mass hatred? What is it in this system that could produce both the mass compliance that had sustained its reproduction for decades and the potential for eruption of widespread defiance and revolt that immediately threatened its very existence? Most importantly, why did the reform leadership, represented by Gorbachev of the former Soviet Union, launch such sustained assault on its own party-state establishment, and was so weak and indecisive responding to the ensuing crisis even with its extensive apparatus of repression still in place? To dramatise a bit: why did these regimes commit suicide?[2] The 1989 Revolution seems to defy all conventional political wisdom.

The collapse of communist regimes in a reverse domino, courtesy of Dean Acheson, is not just another irony of historical accidents; it reveals powerful forces at work that we are yet to understand. Not all, however, communist regimes are swept away by the storm of 1989. A telling contrast to what happened to the former Soviet Bloc is China, where the domino was set in motion from the Tiananmen Square in Beijing. In the decade after 1989, China (also its anxiously watching neighbour and imitator communist Vietnam[3]) has evolved along a completely different path. Its rapid transformation into a market economy and seemingly irreversible integration into the capitalist world economy have not, as many had hoped, "withered away" the communist regime. To the contrary, the country's phenomenal economic growth has boosted the confidence of the Chinese Communist Party (CCP), which, after a prolonged soul search in the wilderness of ideological pauperism and political orphanage, has in recent years begun to reassert the fundamentals of the communist ideology. Under the stewardship of General Secretary Jiang Zemin,[4] the CCP has made sustained effort to rejuvenate the spirit of the party through renewing and revising the party ideology. To strengthen its grip on power the CCP is also revamping the sprawling party organisations and expanding them into areas of society that the party-state has since 1978 ceded to the market.[5] In countering the broad trend towards secularisation,[6] the CCP is eyeing the role as the champion of what it calls "socialist spiritual civilisation" or "advanced culture". It attempts to regain the moral high ground lost in the 1989 bloodshed by capitalising on the ever-growing disillusionment and discontent in society with, on the one hand, the soul-depriving materialism and, on the other, the dislocations and injustices rendered by the new capitalistic economy.

However, reminiscent of its totalitarian past, the CCP approaches this by a return to the past—to its Maoist traditions. Unlike in the immediate aftermath of the Tiananmen massacre when people generally laughed at the regime's attempt to resurrect Mao-style spiritual campaigns such as "learn from Comrade Lei Feng", this time around the Maoist reincarnation seems to have found a more receptive audience. The spontaneous mass nostalgia of 1995 at Mao's 100th anniversary, the wildfire-like spreading of religions across the land, the resilience of the Falun Gong "evil sect" under the party-state's all-out crackdown etc., all point to a craving in society for things spiritual. Here the CCP sees an opportunity to redeem its moral authority.

What then are the political implications of the CCP's resumption of a vanguard role in promoting a "spiritual civilisation"? If people responded to the preaching, brainwashing, and manipulation by the Leninist vanguard party with mass revolt in 1989, what is likely to happen when the CCP attempts the same but in a completely different environment created by the open-door policy and market-oriented reforms? Ultimately, what is likely to be the future of the communist regime?

In addressing these questions, this study first delineates the dynamic processes that led to the crisis of communism, using the two communist giants–the USSR and the PRC, where the communist revolution was endogenous–as primary cases. The focus of the analysis is to specify the role of the ruling ideology in the perpetuation as well as destruction of communism. In an integrated analysis of ideology and structure, the study will demonstrate how the unique role of ideology in communism creates an inherent contradiction between ideology and structure that inevitably leads to a crisis situation. With the sudden collapse of communism thus accounted for, the paper proceeds to examine the situation in reform China and work out the political implications of the CCP's recent move.

CONTENTIONS ABOUT COMMUNISM

As political scientists, we are trained to look for power and interests as the basis of analysis. As a result, the conventional wisdom of communism tended to highlight the stability and staying power of the system.[7] Despite the various well-documented and well-analysed malaise of the system, a structural analysis of power distribution in it has always pointed to the overwhelming superiority of the party-state over any of its real or potential opposition, and the incentive structure in the system is such that openly opposing the system is against almost anyone's self-interests.[8]

Modernisation theory regards communism as a response of "backward" societies to the onslaught of Western industrial civilisation; communism represented an alternative route to the common destiny of our era–industrialisation and modernisation. From this perspective, the reforms and eventual demise of communism simply represent the maturation of the forces of modernisation inherent in an industrial society: forces driving toward social, political, as well as economic pluralism. Modernisation theorists have long predicted a "convergence" of all industrial societies regardless of their political genre.[9] Although useful in broad outlines in bringing communism to a macro-historical perspective, modernisation theory ignored the specific features of communist politics. As a result, it expected an evolution instead of a revolution in the course of the transformation of communism. The legitimacy[10] aspect so characteristic of the collapse of communism is almost totally out of its scope of analysis. It is therefore ill-equipped to account for the dramatic way in which the events in the communist world following the Tiananmen Incident of 1989 unfolded.[11]

Retrospective reflections of the collapse have emphasised the sub-par performance of the economy as the main factor that brought down the whole system.[12] In contrast to the postulates of modernisation theory, this economic performance-centred perspective identifies the failure to modernise as the key to understanding the demise of communism. However, failure to modernise is prevalent in Third World countries and the former communist regimes were not too shabby on that record in comparison. Furthermore, poor economic performance has long been recognised as an integral feature of the Stalinist system after its initial success in rapid industrialisation. Long before the collapse of communism, the economic weaknesses of the system had been well documented, but no communist watchers had derived from these any clue of an imminent total collapse of the system. Like modernisation theory, poor economic performance alone could not explain the suddenness of the collapse either.

The totalitarian model, on the other hand, similarly discounts the importance of the legitimacy aspect of the system by overemphasising the total power of the party-state, its atomisation of society that eliminates the social foundation of any significant opposition. In this image, communism is self-perpetuating, with the all-encompassing party-state organisations grown over time into a vast structure of overlapping privileges, controls, rewards, and vested interests upon which almost everyone in society becomes dependent.[13] Despite the various malaises well documented and analysed by the best scholars of communism, the totalitarian model allows no possibility for a sudden collapse of the system. These malaises at best contributed to an "aging" process, at the end of which the most likely result is for communism to join the rank of the authoritarian states typical of the Third World.[14]

The neo-traditional image of communism,[15] in contrast, captures the dynamic interactions between state and society. It relaxes the rigidity of the totalitarian model by positing "a rich subculture of instrumental-personal ties"[16] around the formal communist institutional hierarchy. Through these informal networks of personal ties, individuals pursue private interests and personal advancement within the limits set by the system. Because of its focus on the state-society relationship, this model is in a good position to analyse the moral and legitimacy aspects in the actual operation of the system. However, it opts for concentrating on the self-interest aspect of this relationship. Consequently, it in fact reaffirms with added reasons the strength of the system: upon the total power and control emphasised by the totalitarian model, it adds a network of entrenched self-interests, for these informal relations and subcultures of self-seeking behaviours should actually strengthen the bond of interdependence of the various actors in the system and hence reduce the incentives as well as the chances for individuals and groups to turn against "the establishment". Hence it too fails to foresee the possibility of a total collapse.

The failure of the above mainstream approaches to discern the possibility of a catastrophic outcome points to the inadequate attention paid to the role of ideology in the structural design of the system in which the danger is embedded. We failed to see that, besides power and self-interests, moral indignation and problems of legitimacy cumulated in the daily interface between state and society (which the communist total system has so intermeshed together) could also serve as a basis of social actions, especially revolutionary actions that often defy the logic of narrow self-interests. The post-1989 retrospective analysis of communism has belatedly awakened to the importance of morality and legitimacy; but, as Daniel Chirot points out, we social scientists do not yet know how to study these intangible concepts.[17] Moreover, a conflict between ideals and reality is perhaps common to all political systems, as is the cant used to reconcile the discrepancy. What made a sudden collapse in the absence of significant shift in power distribution or class alignment uniquely "communist" are the structural features of the system and its mode of operation.

In what follows I will present a structural model that puts the legitimacy problem at the centre of our analysis of communism. I will first provide a narrative account that sorts out the key factors underlying the legitimacy problems of the communist system and identify the concrete roles the official ideology played in the dynamic change and crisis of communism. Then I will recast the narrative into a simple path model for further clarity.

THE STRUCTURAL CONTRADICTION

The under-appreciation of the structural importance of the legitimacy aspect of communism by previous studies is rooted in a deficient understanding of the role of the official ideology, with its vision of the common destiny of humanity and programs for speeding up its actualisation. In the face of grim realities of communist societies, scholars tend to downplay the official ideology or take a cynical view of it.[18] In the former case, the existing structure of power distribution and power relations are considered the only significant factors shaping the historical evolution of communism, and hence the ideological principles that designed the system in the first place are either marginalised in analysis or regarded as insincere, superficial and thus unimportant. In the latter case, the ideology is considered but a deceptive device to cover up the harsh reality of repression and domination, and a means of manipulation to mobilise mass compliance. A central argument of this study, in contrast, is that *it is to a great extent the "unexpected sincerity" of the communist elites in their ideological faith, together with its related visions, and the moral convictions that drove the changes in communism and eventually led to its demise.*

Structurally, the relationship between ideology and society in communism is an inverse to the norm: in the basic design of the system, ideology is not supposed to justify social reality but social reality must be altered to validate the ideology. As a result, communism contains an inherent contradiction between the ideology (with the comprehensive set of values and moral standards it upholds) and the corruptive tendencies in the total system it has created to serve the ideology. The reason that this contradiction is inherent (or structural) is because both power abuse and the high moral expectations are products of the same ideology put to practice. More specifically, a main source of corruption or power abuse is centralisation of decision-making, which in turn is directly related to the ideological prescription for a "planned economy" as both a defining feature of and a pre-requisite for the transition to communism.[19] The high expectation of virtuous behaviours of communist cadres is a result of the party-state's efforts to create a "communist new man" appropriate and in preparation for the coming new society and the associated propaganda of "new communist values and moral standards". Again, according to the ideology, these are indispensable to a successful transition to communism, and the elite–members of the vanguard party–must serve as role models to the masses in this unprecedented societal transformation. This contradiction produces, in reality, a perennial cognitive dissonance between the perceived corruption and power abuses among cadres and the widespread expectation (both justified and encouraged by the regime's ideological effort) that cadres be role models or the embodiment of the moral standards and code of behaviour called for by the ideology. This discrepancy was at the root of the legitimacy problem of communism.

From Lenin's invention of "Saturday Volunteer Labour" to Mao's "Learn from Lei Feng" campaigns,[20] communist regimes spared no effort to mold people's way of thinking and heighten their moral aspirations in conformity to the ideal communist society. However, the voluntary contributions and sacrifices demanded from the masses crucially depend on the party-state's ability to inspire and maintain people's faith in the communist cause. Such faith in turn depends critically on the moral performance of the members of the ruling party who daily preach communist morality and therefore are naturally expected to exhibit loftier behaviours, and to sacrifice and contribute more and before the masses. Indeed, the constitutions of both CPSU and CCP thus specify the codes of conduct for their members. The widespread use of role models in the communist method of rule also reflects this ideological necessity and imperative of operating a system based on faith.

The common tragedy for all communist regimes, given their monopoly of power, is that they could never prevent corruption and power abuse from spreading among the cadre class. The dual task of the communist state to comprehensively plan the economy and to create a whole generation of the "communist new man" led to inflated party-state apparatuses in both functions.[21] It is in this bureaucratic establishment that all the fundamental problems of communism and the sources of its crisis are located.[22] There have been many excellent analyses of the problems of total bureaucratisation under communism.[23] I will highlight here four fundamental ones that contributed to change and crisis of communism, namely, bureaucratic *fixity*, *corruption*, *division* and *stagnation*. Each in its own way contributed to the crisis of legitimacy in communism, but all four represent continued tension between reality and the officially espoused ideology, inciting repeated effort from both above and below for change, and finally leading to the fundamental transformation of communism through either revolution or reform. Let's briefly examine them one by one.

Fixity. Total bureaucratisation froze the revolution. In the context of bureaucratic proceduralism,[24] the grand ideological vision of a more humane society envisaged by Karl Marx decomposed into sets of impersonal rules and prescribed answers that governed a mundane life deprived of individual choices. In the absence of an invigorating vision and hence ideological motivation, the vast number of middle level bureaucrats became a possessing elite who ruled in the name of vested power of office alone. A bureaucratic mentality prevailed. This situation inevitably caused great concern for the master revolutionaries at the top, for bureaucratic immobility and fixity ran directly contradictory to the nature and spirit of the revolution with which top leaders tend to identify more than the rest of the cadre class. They took as their responsibility to periodically shake up the bureaucracy in an effort to keep the revolution alive. Typical examples were Stalin's purge in the 1930s and Mao's Great Leap Forward (1958) and Cultural Revolution (1966–76).

Corruption. Total bureaucratisation generated corruption or power abuses in several ways. The monopoly of power by cadres in the communist hierarchy created numerous "petty tyrannies"[25] out of the officialdoms at all levels. The regime's heroic effort to re-educate and re-socialise the cadres as well as the masses into the communist ideal inadvertently magnified the issue of corruption and thereby made cadres and the system they personified vulnerable to legitimacy challenges. In the all-inclusive communist hierarchy where every individual's life chances were structured and hence controlled by the cluster of cadres around him/her, "ideological and political education"[26] was a very personal matter in the sense that the interaction between state (cadres) and society (the masses) was daily and face-to-face, and in which people fought for their life chances with few possibilities for "exit". While cadres frequently turned "ideological education" into a political ritual to reiterate their domination over their subordinates, the masses could also conveniently use the moral principles of the official ideology as a convenient "weapon of the weak" to contradict cadres' claims for moral authority. Understandably such counterattacks were ineffective in general, but they were nevertheless structurally encouraged by the ideology underpinning the basic system, and frequently by the elite core of the party-state. The encouragement by the top leadership of the people's fight against corrupt officials can be interpreted as an attempt to pin attention to individual cadres so that the fight would not evolve into open questioning of the legitimacy of the whole system. However, it was always possible to draw that linkage by the people and more importantly, as we shall see later, by elements of the elite.

This possibility was enhanced by the following fact of life under communism: because of the party-state's monopoly of distribution of rewards, individuals would seek to gain privileged access to these rewards by cultivating personal ties to individual cadres–the gatekeepers of state resources. The Chinese *guanxi* (connections) were highly exclusive networks that bred corruption, friction, and popular discontent. Distribution by *guanxi* networks produced a distinctive pattern of stratification and an insulated privileged class not dissimilar to the one the revolution set out to destroy in the first place. It flew in the face of the party-state's claim of legitimacy on grounds of social justice and mocked its effort to create an unselfish "communist new man". With an ideology hostile to market exchange, communism ironically represented a step backwards from a class society to a status society. The neo-traditional model of communism correctly identified this aspect of life under communism, but failed to explore its implications for a general legitimacy crisis and hence the possibility of a genuine social revolution.

Division. Total bureaucratisation is socially divisive. In a closed system in which neither democratic nor market mechanisms were available to flush people in and out, individuals constantly found themselves locked in a zero-sum competition with their "comrades" for opportunities and rewards. In the absence of an "exit", political infighting in communism was exceptionally cruel and destructive. At the grassroots level, this is captured in Susan Shirk's concept of "virtuocracy" which she argued is divisive because "virtuous" behaviour necessarily involves actions that are costly to one's colleagues.[27] She found that the interests of political activists (those trusted by cadres) and the ordinary people were inherently in conflict: activists wanted to demonstrate their "virtuous behaviour" in order to monopolise the rewards of political status, but doing this entailed blocking and harming non-activists. For the non-activists, the resultant distribution of rewards could hardly be accepted as "selection by virtue". Bitterness, resentment and cynicism grew abundant as a result of political favouritism. It was in these discontented, disillusioned, and excluded masses that the raw energy was stored that fueled any political movements that were anti-status quo, ranging from the fierce purge in the USSR, the mass campaigns in China, and finally the 1989 Revolution that demolished the communist camp.

Stagnation. Total bureaucratisation also caused economic stagnation that was of particular concern for the top leadership. Due to the inflexibility of bureaucratic planning and economic management and to the lack of exposure to the dynamism of the world market, the communist economy was, as one observer remarked, stuck with "the world's most advanced late nineteenth-century economy, the world's biggest and best, most inflexible rust belt".[28] A main claim of legitimacy by communists was superiority of the system in economic performance; but after the initial stages of rapid industrialisation under Stalin and even Mao, economic growth became increasingly unsustainable, and the regime had to lie to maintain the myth of economic superiority.

Despite these malaises, the communist system was structured in such a way as to allow the party-state and its cadre class to enjoy extraordinary staying power. As long as the party-state apparatuses remained coherently organised under a unifying ideology, as long as society was atomised in the tight organisational grip of the party-state, as long as the gradually swelling middle class (resulting from the increasing complexity of the economy) did not constitute an autonomous political force[29] but was constantly incorporated into the status quo interests and became part of the establishment as was generally the case in Eastern Europe and former Soviet Union, there was no social foundation for significant opposition to emerge and grow, and the hegemony of the party-state would remain uncontested. Any opposition and contestation for power would have to come from within the party-state itself, and cleavages within the party-state would be the prerequisite for such developments.

REFORMS WITHIN THE COMMUNIST GRAND TRADITION

Fighting bureaucratic fixity, corruption, division and stagnation was the main driving force in the historical evolution of communism. The problems of bureaucratisation caused tension and discontent not only among the masses below, but more importantly in the leadership core above. Whereas mass discontent and resistance had only limited overall impact on the system, the strategies deployed by the leadership to cope with them shaped the history of communism. Initially top leaders dealt with the problems strictly within the parameters of Marxism-Leninism. In both the USSR and China, the leadership attempted to maintain the vitality of the revolution against the fixity of bureaucracy, with Stalin resorting to purges and the reign of terror by the secret police and Mao tapping into the grassroots for direct support for his revolutionary ideal. Both failed because the problems of communism were structural. It is in the context of this failure that both Deng's and Gorbachev's reform and the eventual collapse of communism could be better comprehended.

For decades the communist socialisation system[30] had been painstakingly turning out generations of communist idealists. Instead of merely becoming disillusioned in the face of the harsh reality created by the system, some of them managed to keep their faith alive. And because the communist promotion system was inherently politically and ideologically geared, many true believers came to occupy leadership positions at various levels, Gorbachev being a prominent example.[31] In fact, the top echelon was more likely to be filled with committed communists even though at lower levels the usual bureaucratic mentality prevailed. The logic flows like this: in the party-state hierarchy characterised by a top-down organisational centralism, the prestige of the first generation master revolutionaries (Lenin, Stalin, Mao and Deng, etc.) ensured their life tenures as paramount leaders, which allowed them to accumulate enormous personal power and to have a decisive voice in the choice of their own successors. Inevitably they chose people who shared their visions and were committed to their ideals. The centralisation of the system meant that the higher one's position was in the party-state hierarchy, the more freedom he enjoyed to exercise his political idealism, while lower level cadres in general carefully toed the lines set from above and strove to conform. The combined result was that most innovations came from above and true believers tended to cream up at the top.

It is the nature of the future-oriented communist ideology that its true believers will never be satisfied with the status quo. In their pursuit of the ideal society, the true communists are doomed to forever criticising and trying to alter the existing order so as to move the revolution one step forward, even if this order is of their own creation. Stalin's purge was an expression of this systemic imperative. According to Brzezinski, the purge performed several vital functions in the system: to facilitate destruction of the old system and the transformation to the new one immediately after the revolution; to sustain revolutionary momentum; to keep the system pure of dangerous contamination and fight hostile penetration; to resolve inner power struggles and provide for the inflow of new members. The purge was therefore a permanent feature of Stalinism.[32]

As industrialisation deepened, however, the purge with its enormous destructiveness was no longer viable as a method of rule. The Khrushchevian de-Stalinisation and the ensuing Brezhnevian bureaucratic conservatism were responses to both the excesses of the Stalin era and to the demands of an increasingly industrialised and complex economy. By now the central leadership turned supportive to the bureaucratic establishment of the party-state, which had become increasingly indispensable for managing a complex industrialised economy on socialist principles. The state bureaucracy itself began to shed its characteristics as a revolutionary organisation modeled after the vanguard party and became increasingly technocratic in nature and status quo-oriented. The "normal" channels of social mobility of a modern industrial society, e.g., via education, skills and merits, began to supplement the predominantly political channels, much in the way modernisation theory anticipated.

However, over-bureaucratisation eventually led to economic stagnation and institutional decay. The receding revolutionary purges and campaigns were not being replaced by either invigorating market mechanisms or competitive political pluralism. In the meanwhile, the routinised communism in the USSR still retained the basic structural design for a revolution, but with the revolutionary momentum gone, the whole system became an anomie, infected with corruption, lies and cynicism. By the time Gorbachev rose to power, the industrialised communism of the former USSR had exhausted both its revolutionary and developmental potentials.

The problems of bureaucratisation were acutely felt by Mao and his leftist colleagues. Like Lenin and Stalin before him, Mao proceeded to deal with the issue strictly within the Marxist grand tradition, in particular, blaming all the evils of the system on the "class enemies" of the revolution. For him, the Soviet experience under Brezhnev depicted a grim picture of "a revolution degenerated", which prompted his search for a more radical solution. The one he found was guided mass movements which he envisaged would periodically shake up and rejuvenate the massive party-state bureaucracy, and his theoretical formulation behind this was the "Continued Revolution under the Dictatorship of the Proletariat" based on his new class analysis of socialism.[33]

Underlying Mao's new class theory was a more dynamic orientation toward a continued revolution. China under Mao was still a country submerged in a sea of peasants and there was not an urban-industrial base comparable to that of the former USSR for Mao and his leftist colleagues to appreciate the inevitability of the Brezhnevian bureaucratic conservatism. Therefore, in line with his nature as a peasant rebel, he turned to a revolutionary radicalism and eventually launched his most spectacular offensive to save the revolution, the Cultural Revolution, in which he directly reached out to the masses to mount a massive assault on the party and state apparatuses which he believed to have been infiltrated by "capitalist roaders"[34] and become the hotbed for a "new bourgeoisie". Mao's action indeed effectively saved the legitimacy of his leftist core of the party leadership by differentiating himself from the prevalent corruption and abuses in the establishment, by championing the fight against the evils in the system, by providing the masses hitherto excluded from privileges with an open avenue to vent their pent-up anger and frustration, to attack corrupt officials in the name of the revolution, and to strip them off their power as indeed happened on a massive scale during the Cultural Revolution.

However, the Cultural Revolution was immensely destructive; it not only pushed China to the brink of economic disaster but also created a jungle-like world of incessant political in-fights, in which life became almost truly "nasty, brutish and short". By the time of Mao's death and after ten years of "all-out civil war",[35] the economically underdeveloped Chinese communism also exhausted both its revolutionary and developmental potentials.[36]

THE CRISIS

In sum, major movements in communism were inherently self-destructive: in a similar vein as Mao's Cultural Revolution was a destructive change to the left, the reforms of Deng Xiaoping and Gorbachev were to the right, both demonstrating an unusual willingness to dismantle the establishment. All communist reformers, by virtue of their reaching the apex, were at least initially true believers who came to power through a long, battle-hardened career that was full of trials, scrutiny and patronage by their mentors from the older generation of revolutionaries. As far as the commitment to the core values and goals of communism is concerned, Deng and Gorbachev differed little from Lenin, Stalin, Khrushchev and Mao, and it was their commitment to these values that drove their tireless search for alternatives. The reform in China and the Soviet Union started from very different initial conditions, with China still reeling in the stormy Cultural Revolution and the Soviet Union crawling in Brezhnevian stagnation (so-called "mature socialism"), but the impetus for structural reform originated from the same ideological ground that had exhausted its options within the communist grand tradition. The search for a solution had to extend beyond the existing paradigm, a move proven fateful to communism.

The sudden demise of communism in Europe after so many decades of fairly stable and disciplined rule[37] was triggered by the unraveling of the ruling ideology as a result of the new initiatives from the top leadership. This revelation is in no way to deny the fact that the official ideology had long lost its appeal or even relevance among the populace and that cynicism rather than revolutionary zeal defined the public attitude toward the official ideology. Rather, it highlights the Achilles heel of the communist system–its dependence on the official ideology to maintain cohesion within and justify repression without. When reforms extended beyond the communist grand tradition and the new top leaders began to renounce or reformulate some of the sacred tenets of the official ideology[38] in an attempt to accommodate structural reforms aimed at revitalising the ailing economy and rejuvenating the morale of society, the whole system was thrown off balance. In particular, ideological reformulation weakened the communist apparatus of repression from within by depriving cadres their usual justification for repression. Such ideological reformulation inevitably created disorientation as well as divisions within the party-state establishment. While the overall distribution of power remained unchanged, the political will and the effectiveness of using force and repression were weakened considerably.

And the people were quick to sense this. Ideological reformulation by the top leadership provided the window of opportunity for rapid political mobilisation, unleashing the enormous frustration and discontent long simmering in the masses as well as among underprivileged segments of the cadre class. The crisis of 1989 was characterised by a mass indignation, one arising not only from long pent-up frustration but also out of a sense of being cheated or betrayed, for the *glasnost* in the USSR and the *kaifang* ("open-door") policy in China unmistakably demonstrated to the people that they had lived in a lie for all those years: they saw now that their system's chief contenders in the West (as well as the newly industrialised economies of East Asia) had scored infinitely better even measured by the yardstick of the core values of the communist ideology.

The communist ideology is by its very nature vulnerable to challenges from the liberal ideology. Being the off-spring of the progressive age of the Renaisscance, the Enlightenment and the Industrial Revolution, the two share many core values such as popular sovereignty, freedom, equality, faith in human reason and so forth, differing mainly in their respective means of goal attainment. This sharing of core values inevitably pitched the two in an intense competition and made the losing side especially susceptible to a massive defection to the other side.[39] And it was this massive "defection"[40] that caused the collapse of communism. Therefore the crisis of communism in 1989 was fundamentally a crisis of legitimacy that swept the party-state from without and incapacitated the regime from within.

The legitimacy crisis is the simultaneous emergence of three conditions: glaring failure of the dominant ideology to rationalise the current order, the emergence of competing ideologies capable of mobilising and legitimising opposition from both within and outside the establishment, and a change in the opportunity cost structure in society so that the cost of defiance is no longer prohibitive.[41] The key mechanism in the communist system that built up the pressure was the self-defeating ideology: the future-goal orientation of the communist ideology necessitated on the one hand the system's operation to be ideologically inspired and rationalised and, on the other, an organisational centralism (necessitated by central planning) that structurally facilitated (by concentrating too many decision powers into the hands of cadres) self-seeking behaviours among its cadre-bureaucrats. Cadres as revolutionary vanguards preached on a daily basis the communist virtues and therefore were expected by both the party and the masses to become exemplars of such virtues. Self-seeking behaviours were unmistakably perceived as "corrupt" and "immoral" by the masses, and constantly highlighted by the ever-promulgated official ideology. The discrepancy between words and deeds, between ideal and reality, spawned mass discontent and prompted frequent campaigns launched by the top leadership to battle against corruption and decay. This fight was of an ideal turning against the reality it was responsible (albeit inadvertently) for creating; it provided the main impetus for reforms and change in communism. Because the problems were structural and could not be eliminated within the existing parameters of communism, the process soon had to repeat itself. Repetition led to erosion of faith in the current system, a general low morale, and widespread cynicism, as represented by the innumerous political jokes and black humours during the latter days of communism in Eastern Europe.

This condition, however, was not life threatening. It led at most to the "aging of communism"[42] but would not automatically lead to the volcanic events as we saw in 1989. The masses were too atomised and structurally too dependent on the existing system for their livelihood, and the party-state's machinery for repression was too powerful. The repeated failure of communism to live up to its ideological expectations on both moral grounds and on grounds of economic performance eventually forced the leadership to seek solutions outside the established orthodoxy–a structural overhaul so drastic that it necessitated a radical reformulation of the ruling ideology as a prerequisite.[43]

To improve economic performance was often the initial motive of reforms in communism, and it was only natural given the intense and very conscious economic rivalry with liberal capitalism. In the case of the former Soviet Union, the Gorbachevian reform started as an attempt to halt the slow but steady economic downslide that had started in the 1970s under the aging Brezhnev. Gorbachev identified serious problems in the economy as low efficiency, inferior technological development, lack of work incentives, and exhaustion of the potentials of extensive growth (i.e., growth by more input of labour and natural resources), and their combined result of the USSR "lagging further and further behind the advanced nations."[44] He realised that tinkering with the existing system as his predecessors had done would not work, and that an overhaul or "restructuring" of the system was required to steer the economy out of dire straits–

hence the famous *perestroika* of his. However, measures taken to cure economic malaises necessitated new and bold political-ideological initiatives, not only to clear the way for economic restructuring but also to rejuvenate the national spirit needed for drastic reforms. This was the genesis of his refreshing but politically naïve ideas of *glasnost*. A similar process occurred earlier in China in the late 1970s when Deng and his fellow reformers promoted "ideological emancipation" (*sixiang jiefang*) as a way to break the straitjacket of the Maoist neo-orthodoxy and facilitate the national re-orientation toward economic development. The Dengist reform, however, took great care not to undermine the foundation of the CCP power. From the outset Deng clearly set the political limits to reform with his infamous "four cardinal principles"[45] and remained unabashed to the end about his "dictatorship of the proletariat". In comparison "Gorby" was much more endearing to the West. His approach to reform led to rapid political mobilisation and democratisation, sweeping away the foundation of communist power like a tidal wave.

In both cases, repudiation by the top leadership of some basic ideological tenets in an environment of low faith, low morale, mass discontent, and widespread cynicism quickly and effectively discredited communism in its totality. The reforms of the 1980s turned into variables the two constants that had undergirded the stability of system in the pre-reform era: first, the command economy, upon which every individual of society was made dependent; and second, the ideological orthodoxy, which justified repression by whatever means. Accordingly the 1989 crisis was set off through two interactive chains of causal relations that undermined fundamentally the architecture of the whole system and led to its crumbling. The first is ideological. Ideological reformulation from the top betrayed a rare humility on the part of the regime in admitting the problems of the system, and demonstrated an unprecedented openness to liberal capitalism and other ideas. This attitudinal change greatly reduced the certainty with which the cadres of various levels traditionally enforced their domination on the ground of ideological orthodoxy. It effectively loosened the party's ideological control, allowing wider freedom of thinking and expression, freer flow of information, and spates of new ideas, theories and proposals. These in turn led quickly to the rise of powerful competing ideologies, and hence the second condition of a legitimacy crisis.

The prolonged low faith in the pre-reform era also increased the eagerness in people's search for "alternatives". Such a psychological urge could have allowed any counter ideologies to gain wide currency. Quickly, ideological reform degenerated into wholesale abandonment of the communist ideal by the masses as well as by large sections of the ruling elite. Faced with mass non-compliance or even revolts, the regime suddenly found out that it no longer possessed the reliable and effective organisational means of repression it had taken for granted–even the army and police became untrustworthy, harbouring dangerous tendencies as well as elements.[46]

The second causal chain is structural: decentralisation (or as Gorbachev preferred, democratisation) of economic management and the lifting of the ban on market and private enterprises designed to revitalise the economy expanded people's economic freedom and reduced their structural dependency on the command economy.[47] Reduced dependency also reduced the costs of disobedience. The system could no longer effectively generate compliance through structural coercion because people were less in danger of being punished for dissent, and many now had the alternative of "exit". By now, all three factors in a legitimacy crisis were present. It took only a spark to turn the prairie into an inferno.[48]

The radically different results of the crisis in the former USSR and PRC[49] had more to do with the different stages of communist development they were in than, as suggested by many, with their respective cultural and historical traditions. More decisively, however, it had to do with the drastically different reactions by the top leaderships of the two countries to the spreading of social and political unrest. With a limited level of industrialisation, an economy badly battered by the prolonged and violent Cultural Revolution and the resulting popular distaste for continued political turmoil, China's reform was from the beginning concentrated on the economy. In the more industrialised Soviet Union, in contrast, a generally well-educated population and a large, politically conscious middle class meant that from the start the reform was blown into full-scale ideological movements and rapid political mobilisation. The resulting democratisation sounded the death knell of the communist dictatorship in Russia.

To be sure, both states possessed sufficient power and resources to suppress almost any mass rebellion.[50] It all boiled down to mustering the necessary political will to effectively put to use the extensive apparatuses of repression. Faced with the prospect of having to use naked force on the rebels on the Tiananmen Square, the divided leadership problem was resolved in China simply by the influence of the battle-hardened first-generation revolutionaries like Deng, who did not shrink from the prospect of bloodshed.[51] In contrast, no one in the Soviet Union's third generation leadership had the preponderance of power and prestige to do so.

CHINA NOW

If we are to name only one lesson the CCP has learned from the 1989 fiasco or to identify only one political teaching the post-Deng leadership has followed religiously from the late patriarch, it will have to be the determination to maintain stability at any cost and by any means. The post-Tiananmen "Beijing consensus" is to crash with iron fists any real or potential political opposition and "nip it in the bud".[52] The CCP regards it a matter of life and death after watching in jaw-dropping amazement the unfolding drama of the fall of the world's first ruling communist party and the disintegration of the mighty Soviet Union, the world's number-two superpower. The CCP conducted extensive studies of the causes of the catastrophic events in the former communist camp,[53] from which two main conclusions have emerged. First, it must continue with the market-oriented reforms in order to deliver material benefits to the people; the CCP regime regards it as the key to regain legitimacy and moral authority, now that the ruling ideology has exhausted all its appeal and credibility.[54] Second, it must stay vigilant and decisive in dealing with potential political "turmoil".[55] The political line crystallised from this soul search is summed up by the CCP as to "be strong with both hands": strong with reform and opening on one hand and strong with political control on the other (euphemised in the CCP terminology as "upholding the four cardinal principles"). So far this strategy seems to be working: the CCP has not only maintained adequate internal cohesion but also succeeded, for the time being, in selling its "no-nonsense" crackdown policy as imperative for national survival and prosperity, appealing to the patriotism of the Chinese people, especially the traditional social elite and the "conscience of society"–urban intellectuals and college students.[56]

Because of its "failure to collapse" the CCP has preserved its Leninist organisational structure and mode of operation. It has hence inherited the systemic imperatives explored in the preceding discussions. After an interim under Deng's reign, in which we seem to witness the "end of ideology" and the rise of a down-to-earth pragmatism,[57] from the middle of the 1990s on we began to see the return of ideology under Jiang Zemin's stewardship,[58] and with it many old communist tactics of rule and mind control developed under Mao. These include ideological campaigns, party rectification, and the extensive use of role models–not only has Comrade Lei Feng been resurrected but he has found numerous reincarnations in the reform era such as Kong Fansheng. The CCP has greatly intensified its efforts to build a "socialist spiritual civilisation" (*shehuizhuyi jingshen wenming*). In 1991 the Central Committee passed "The Resolution on the Guideline of Socialist Spiritual Civilisation" and in 1996 "The Resolution on Several Important Problems in Strengthening the Construction of Socialist Spiritual Civilisation".[59] In 1999 the CCP officially launched its hitherto largest ideological campaign to promote the "three emphases", which Jiang had tested on various occasions since 1995. The three emphases are on "politics, study, and moral integrity" (*jiang zhengzhi, jiang xuexi, jiang zhengqi*). With all the ambiguities typical of the political language of the CCP, the "emphasis on politics" roughly means to renew Marxist faith, to stay vigilant against any attempts to undermine the communist party rule and socialism, and to maintain the unity of the CCP and the authority of the party center. The emphasis on study roughly means to keep abreast with the developments of the world, learning new knowledge and technologies, and changing leadership style and methods accordingly. The emphasis on moral integrity means roughly to stay morally upright and be resilient against the corrupting influences of the capitalist world economy.[60]

The campaign was a classic feat of communism. It consisted of an elaborate scheme typical of the Maoist tradition dated back to the Yenan era:[61] engaging cadres full-time in protracted political study sessions, "criticism and self-criticism", *xiangdang jiaoxin* (pouring one's heart to the party) or "confessions to the party" of one's own wrongdoings and reporting of others' misdeeds, group rating and assessments of the progress made by individual cadres, and topical discussions that supposedly lead to new political and ideological consensus and renewed revolutionary spirit.[62] The campaign was an ideological house-cleaning operation aimed at shoring up the authority of the top leadership, maintaining the internal cohesion of the party, boosting the morale of party members, increasing the effectiveness of implementing the policies and development programs of the party center, and fighting the pervasive corruption among cadres that was causing widespread resentment and and undermining the legitimacy of the communist rule. Clearly the same political dynamic depicted above is at work in the reform era, and the CCP, unlike authoritarian regimes such as that of Suharto of Indonesia where corruption was taken for granted by the both rulers and the people, is compelled to fight corruption in its own ranks as a political imperative.

At the same time, however, the CCP also has to adapt to the new socio-economic reality created by market-oriented economic reforms. In particular it needs to incorporate the new social elite—mainly the professionals and private business owners—into the status quo. In February 2000 Jiang first proposed his now infamous "three represents"[63] in a speech delivered in Gaozhou municipality of Guangdong Province: "Our Party will forever stand on unfailing ground as long as it remains the loyal representative of the requirements of the development of China's advanced social forces of production, of the direction of development of China's advanced culture, and of the fundamental interests of the broadest majority of the Chinese people".[64] This is a major step away from the class struggle-centered ideology of Mao, which is considered too destructive of China's modernisation, and a step closer to Khrushchevian idea of a "party of the whole people" and "a state for the whole society",[65] which was fiercely assaulted by Mao and his leftist clique as "Soviet revisionism".

The way in which the CCP regime under Jiang deals with the perennial problem of corruption and decay is not to democratise as many China watchers believed to be in the regime's own interests to do,[66] but a combination of strengthening party discipline, building up the rule of law, intensifying the campaign against corruption, and resorting to the Maoist tradition of party rectification and moral purification. It is a partial fallback on the Maoist ideal of "winning people's hearts but not their votes" through "whole-heartedly serving the people" (*quanxing quanyi wei renmin fuwu*).[67] This is by no means accidental: it reflects the nature and imperative of communism as a type of regime and is also rooted in China's imperial traditions and political philosophy.[68] Because of its inherent inability to live up to the ideal it propagates or reach the tall bar it perhaps inadvertently sets for itself, the whole exercise amounts to self-ridicule. Predictably the "three represents" quickly became a laughingstock, fueling the political jokes on the eve of the party's 16th Congress.[69]

Cynicism aside, should we not expect the drop of the mighty China as the second shoe following the one 13 years ago? Can China marketise but not privatise and democratise? Most would probably respond with an emphatic "no". However there is a distinctive possibility that this communist political holdover will last much longer than expected, and in the meanwhile transform into a butterfly of a different color.

In the above model of two causally interactive chains, the ideological chain continues to create political dilemmas and generate cognitive dissonance as well as accumulate psychological stresses both in and outside the party-state, albeit in a much more relaxed environment with freer flows of information and ideas. The structural chain, however, is fundamentally altered after two decades of reform and rapid economic growth. The cost of rebellion remains high but the opportunity cost drastically reduced. It is now possible and even easy for people to retreat into the marketplace and pursue other opportunities; the interface between the party-state and ordinary citizens has shrunk considerably, and the necessity to confront the state also diminished. Marketisation in a communist political context leads not to rapid political mobilisation but to depoliticisation of more and more spheres of social life and hence, to depressurisation of the political sphere. The reason is simple: once allowed other opportunities and alternative outlets of their energy, people will be less inclined to stick out their necks to challenge a still very powerful apparatus of repression unless absolutely necessary.

Marketisation therefore is also a process of "irrelevancing of politics" for many in the Chinese context, creating an elastic and mixed[70] buffer zone between state and society that has reduced the urgency of fundamental political reforms. There are good reasons to account for Oksenberg's observation that there has been "little overt indication that the population demands political reform".[71] With timely and suitable adaptations such as: maintaining a popular reform programme; expanding grassroots elections; incorporating capitalists into the ruling status quo; embracing the market in the ruling ideology; intensifying anti-corruption campaigns; making policy and behavioural modifications in response to the increased international scrutiny of the regime's political conduct; and the greatly strengthened apparatuses of repression, and so on. The regime is much better positioned now to cope with crisis situations than a decade ago.

Make no mistake it is still a repressive regime, but its policies are broadly supported. The reformed political economy has enormously expanded the living space for the coexistence of the increasingly diverse and complex social classes and foreign influences compared to either Mao's China or the former Soviet Union. The CCP by nature will attempt to capitalise upon society's need for a conscience and for moral anchors amidst rampant money worshiping and base materialism that are depriving life of its meaning.[72] In its Leninist incarnation, as we have seen, the CCP is doomed in that role. However, it is not entirely inconceivable that a positive dynamic may develop in the interaction between the party and the people, provided the CCP undergoes an identity change or transformation. The key to a successful transformation is to modify its ideological claims (to lower the bar) and drastically reduce its political liability by cutting down the size of its sprawling organisations and membership that are generating this liability every minute. In other word the CCP ceases to be a Leninist party with Stalinist scope of social exposure.

So far the CCP's effort in this regard has been ultra-conservative and utterly wrong-headed. Not only the party itself is, as Oksenberg points out,[73] the least reformed institution in China amidst the vast socioeconomic changes, but also it attempts to cast its already vast organisational net even wider, to cover the newly emerging market sectors such as the mushrooming new firms in the non-state sector–private firms, foreign businesses, joint-stock companies, cooperative enterprises, *getihu* businesses and so on, and market intermediaries (the so-called *liangxin zhuzhi*–"the two new types of organisations") and other social/communal organisations.[74] Furthermore it also seeks to resurrect the Confucian-Maoist virtuocracy. The CCP leadership seems to be still under the delusion of "power from organisations" and "virtue breeds legitimacy", forgetting that it was ultimately the opposition from within the party-state that brought down the Soviet Union, and that the vast majority of the flags, banners and signposts flooding the Tiananmen Square in the 1989 protests bore the titles of various prominent party-state organisations.[75] The CCP has yet to recognise that its colossal organisational outlay and its still deep (by world standard) involvement in micro-managing a vast array of affairs of economy and society is not strength but a liability. The paradox of a Leninist party is that its insatiable search for power and control inadvertently puts it in a vulnerable position. This remains the Achilles heel of communism now as well as then. Fundamental structural changes in the economy may have increased the margin of error, but legitimacy remains a latent problem that may haunt the CCP forever.

CONCLUSION

This study has demonstrated the dynamics of change inside communism and the critical role played by the vanguard ideology in both the existence and demise of communism. The collapse of communism was at the most fundamental level caused by its self-defeating ideology. In the pursuit of an ideal society, communism created a monstrous bureaucratic establishment whose daily operation produced socio-political and economic consequences that in every way contradicted its own ideological claims of moral as well as economic superiority. Poor economic performance was long recognised as an integral feature of the Stalinist system; important as it is as an contributing factor, its role in the collapse of communism will have to be appreciated in the context of rivalry between communism and liberal capitalism of the West. This brings us back to the issues of ideology and legitimacy, and to a new appreciation of the leadership's perennial efforts at reforming the system. It is in the leadership's ceaseless fight against the inherent systemic malaises that communism invalidated itself. Therefore, the crisis of communism came not as a result of class struggles or factional political in-fighting but as a revolt of a system against itself.

With its "organised dependency"[76] of the people and its extensive apparatuses of repression, communism was not vulnerable to rebellion from below. It was however extremely vulnerable to assaults from above. With its future-orientation towards an ideal society, the communist ideology was doomed to forever criticising the reality it had created, even as the ordinary people accepted the permeating malaise and decay as a fact of life. Contrary to the prevailing interpretation of the crisis of 1989, the collapse of communism was not caused by mass revolts (which were a consequence); instead, it resulted from the repeated assaults on the system by forever unsatisfied leadership (which was the cause) that eventually deprived the system of any ideological justification in the eyes of the people as well as many in the elite, without whose support all previous rebellions had ended up in crushing failure. The seemingly bottom-up revolution of 1989 was in fact top-down initiated and led by segments of the ruling elite. For compelled by the cognitive discrepancy between the ideal and reality, even those elites who fared well within the system could be motivated to rebel.[77] The primary basis of such motivation was neither rational self-interests nor power calculation (although these played an important role), but moral indignation stemming from ideological conviction that communist regimes were so thorough in indoctrinating the population. The rapid deterioration of the state's coercive competence shown during the crisis was a consequence–not a cause–of a more general regime decline centered on a moral decay from within.

The suddenness of the collapse was also due in significant measure to the fact that the totalitarian design of the system had eliminated the many other forms of passive resistance that might have conceivably dissipated some of the pressure built up in the system–such as to "exit" or retreat to private business concerns–to make the revolution in the communist world less explosive. In contrast, the existence of these "exits" has traditionally provided a "safety valve" in authoritarian countries. Here is where communism differed from other corrupt and repressive regimes: by structuring the system around a vanguard ideology, it had built-in mechanisms to turn into action the moral indignation against corruption, decay and stagnation, supplying the system with a "historical necessity" for change. This is why, as a historical irony to Jean Kirkpartrick's once-famous thesis,[78] many of the weaker authoritarian states persisted[79] while the much stronger communist regimes perished.

This political dynamic is still at work in China now. The CCP's heroic effort to stay a vanguard party on top of a capitalist revolution in the economy is yet another historical irony, but it is also inevitability driven by the internal logic of communism. Its headlong drive to champion moral values and traditional virtues in the middle of pervasive corruption, while manifesting an organisational imperative of communist rule, is also a sure way to fritter away its credibility and undermine its legitimacy. No doubt there is a real socio-psychological need to counter-balance the ubiquitous materialism that in other societies is fulfilled by institutions such as the church, community service and political activism, however these are systematically suppressed or adulterated under communism. Its political domination and the extensive organisational outlay makes the party-state ill-suited as the champion of society's moral conscience.[80]

To speculate on the future of communism in China is beyond the scope of this paper. Market communism[81] is infinitely more complex and very different from classical communism. Nevertheless it seems reasonable to suggest that it is likely to end with a whimper rather than a bang, and in a transformation than a revolution. For the society is so much diversified as well as "distracted"—its destructive energy is no longer focused solely on the party-state as in the era of command economy. While the party's ideological innocence may never be redeemed, the state repression apparatus has been beefed up considerably since Tiananmem, and the current battle-hardened regime is unlikely to cringe from using it. The looming danger for the regime that has attracted the most attention is the spectre of social unrest similar to those that haunted previous rulers of China for centuries. The fact that it arises from the successes of economic reforms and in a time of unprecedented prosperity bodes ill for the regime's hope to ride on popular support generated by economic success. The massive unemployment and social dislocations follow naturally from structural reforms of the political economy and increased efficiency of enterprises, and there is no sign indicating these will abate any time soon. The party-state will have to be prepared to wrestle with these tough problems for the long haul. It may be able to keep them from blowing off the lid as long as the disfranchised and disillusioned are kept atomised and their protesting remains sporadic. The regime is keenly aware of this and has been very vigilant on signs of organised activities and stirrings of unsanctioned political mobilisation, evaluating every spontaneous social grouping for its long-term political implications regardless of its current political orientation. As China enters a potentially very long period of social instability, the regime will necessarily become politically more repressive.

However, the real challenge to the party is from within. Its survival is hinged on its ability to maintain internal cohesion in an environment where marketisation has fundamentally transformed the incentive structure facing individual cadres, party members and the various organisations in the sprawling party-state establishment. The sheer size of the CCP alone–65 million members and three million party cells and other organisations nationwide–makes it a "mission impossible" in the long run. However, we will probably never see the passionate and idealistic revolutionary movements of 1989 again because both state and society are deeply imbued in the "economic foundation" or materialist interests. The next "revolution" is likely to be quiet usurping and consolidation of the status quo interests emerging from the "historical stage" of market communism, along the lines of "privatisation" and driven by greed rather than ideals. By then the elite members of the cadre class will merge effortlessly into "successful" capitalists as they did after the fall of the Soviet Union. Some will undoubtedly return to politics with cash to perpetuate their "success".

ENDNOTES

1 Or well institutionalised. The strong institutions and the resulting political stability of the communist political system were highlighted and even admired by prominent political scientists such as Samuel Huntington, see Huntington, *Political Order in Changing Societies* (New Haven: Yale University Press), 1968.

2 Of course the regimes did not intend it; nevertheless the effects of the top-down structural reforms were the same—the collapse of the system in its totality.

3 Recently North Korea also seems to be teetering on the edge to follow suit.

4 Jiang retired at the 16th Congress of the CCP of November, 2002, and passed the baton to Hu Jintao, the man hand-picked by the late paramount leader Deng as the core of the fourth-generation leadership in 1993. However, Hu has been under Jiang's tutelage ever since.

5 For discussion of this issue, see for examples Edward X. Gu, "State corporatism and civil society", in Wang Gungwu and Zheng Yongnian (eds.), *Reform, Legitimacy and Dilemmas: China's Politics and Society* (Singapore: World Scientific, 2000); Pei Minxin, "Chinese civil association: an empirical analysis", *Modern China*, Vol. 24, No. 3 (July 1998); Gordon White, Jude Howell and Shang Xiaoyuan, *In Search of Civil Society: Market Reform and Social Change in Contemporary China* (Oxford, UK: Oxford University Press, 1996); Jonathan Unger, "'Bridges': private business, the Chinese government and the rise of new associations", *The China Quarterly*, No. 147 (September), pp. 795-819.

6 Or a brassy materialism and money worshipping. Communism, especially its Maoist variant, can be appropriately considered a secular religion.

7 For examples of such, see Robert Wesson, *The Aging of Communism* (New York: Praeger Publishers, 1980); Samuel Huntington, *Political Order in Changing Societies* (Yale University Press, 1968).

8 In Robert Wesson's analysis, the persistence of communism despite its serious problems is in part due to a unique incentive structure created by the system in which everybody had a stake in the system. A pathological dependence by almost everyone upon the system helped to perpetuate it. See Robert Wesson, *The Aging of Communism* (New York: Praeger Publishers, 1980), Chapter 3.

9 A representative work of the convergence theory is Chalmers Johnson (ed.), *Change in Communist Systems* (Stanford, California: Stanford University Press, 1970).

10 The concept of legitimacy is notoriously slippery. For the present purpose, however, "legitimacy" is understood as the grounds on which the validity of political authority is voluntarily accepted.

11 I will later deal with the apparently very different results between the Chinese case and the cases of Eastern Europe and the former Soviet Union, but the spontaneity, the explosiveness, and the unexpectedness of mass revolts in all these countries are quite similar. They differ primarily in the reactions from the authorities.

12 For example, Samuel Huntington, *The Third Wave: Democratisation in the Late Twentieth Century* (Norman: University of Oklahoma Press, 1991). Huntington calls 1989 "a crisis of performance".

13 Wesson, *The Aging of Communism*, Chapter 3.

14 Ibid., p. 109. This is the prediction made in the concluding section of Robert Wesson's otherwise very remarkable book of 1980. As to the prospect of a reform to renew the system, Wesson bluntly states, "The capacity for substantial reform of the communist system is slight and probably decreasing. Its special difficulties arise from monopolistic power, and reform violates the first axiom of the system. Hence, there may be no remedy available within the parameters of the system."

15 See Kenneth Jowitt, "Soviet Neo-Traditionalism: The Political Corruption of a Leninist Regime" in *Soviet Studies*, 35:3 (1983), pp.275-297; Andrew Walder, *Communist Neo-Traditionalism: Work and Authority in Chinese Industry* (University of California Press, 1986).

16 Walder, *Communist Neo-Traditionalism.*

17 See Daniel Chirot, "Preface", in Daniel Chirot (ed.), *The Crisis of Leninism and the Decline of the Left: The Revolutions of 1989* (Seattle: University of Washington Press, 1991).

18 Indeed, the official ideology did appear irrelevant to the daily life of the masses both before and since the reforms of Deng and Gorbachev. This observation seems to justify a cynical view of the communist ideology. However, as the ensuing analysis should make clear, this should not lead us to discount the structural importance of the communist ideology as demonstrated by the quick crumpling of the

whole system when its ideological premise was challenged from within the power elite.

19 In the latter case, concentration of resources in the hand of the state was meant to serve both the needs for rapid (and forced) industrialisation and the "dictatorship of the proletariat" which was to eliminate the economic foundation of capitalism and suppress the former bourgeoisie.

20 Lei Feng is a legendary hero in communist China whose altruistic deeds were used widely for communist education and socialisation by the government.

21 In the former there is the planning apparatus and in the latter a massive army of "political and ideological workers".

22 Here "bureaucracy" is not used in the Weberian sense. Bureaucracy is highly politicised under communism; it is organised more on political principles than on principles of rational efficiency. Therefore, the word here is used to refer to the peculiar mixture of functionaries and political organisations found in the party, the state, the economy as well as social, cultural and educational sectors, all performing political and ideological tasks in addition to their normal functions.

23 For example, Wesson, *The Aging of Communism*, esp. pp.20-30.

24 Refers to the routinisation of the system's operation, although nowhere in the communist world has proceduralism reached a level of technicality as that found in some Western bureaucracies.

25 Daniel Chirot, "Preface", p. 11.

26 A catch phrase used by Mao's cadres in their routine evaluation of an individual within their jurisdiction and metering out reward and punishment accordingly is "political and ideological consciousness and performance" (*zhengzhi sixiang juewu* and *zhengzhi biaoxian*).

27 Susan L. Shirk, *Competitive Comrades: Career Incentives and Student Strategies in China* (Berkeley: University of California Press, 1982).

28 Daniel Chirot, "Preface", pp.5-6.

29 The totalitarian system structurally ensured this politically and economically, but not ideologically.

30 While far from being effective, it was a much more comprehensive and penetrating one than those found in any other social systems. It included not only the educational system but also a massive army of professional "ideological workers", the whole cadre class, the whole ideologically geared promotion system designed to award the ideologically "advanced", as well as the frequent ideological mass campaigns (the famous one being the institutionalised "criticism and self-criticism" sessions in Maoist China).

31 The fact that upward mobility in the communist system often required political skills that involved "corruption" alone does not erase the total effect of ideological socialisation. In fact, "political and ideological consciousness and performance" (*zhengzhi sixiang juiwu he biaoxian* in China and the Soviet term) are an important factor in the communist *nomenclature* that facilitated the rise of many communist idealists to key positions.

32 Zbigniew K. Brzezinski, *The Permanent Purge: Politics in Soviet Totalitarianism* (Cambridge, Mass.: Harvard University Press, 1956), Chapter 10.

33 A vivid account of the evolution of Mao's class theory is provided by Richard Kraus. He divides the development of Mao's class theory into three phases: the first phase followed strictly the Marxist property-related concept of class. In the second phase, Mao believed that the old socio-economic basis of class analysis no longer existed under socialism; a new criteria of class had to be found on the consciousness plane. An important aspect of this second theory of class, then, became the notion of "cultural revolution": transformation of the economic base alone was insufficient to root out class enemies of the revolution; only when China possessed truly proletarian culture and institutions could its socialism be secure. In the third phase, Mao attempted to overcome the ambiguity in the "cultural concept" of class that could be used by almost anyone to his or her own advantage. In this last effort, Mao tried to isolate more accurately the social basis of the "new bourgeoisie": the new exploiting groups found their strength precisely in the institutional structures the revolution had established in order to remake society. A structural inequality was built into the socialist institutions of the People's Republic of China and was perpetuated in socialist society. The "bourgeois right" to inequality found its ultimate expression in the state apparatus through which that right was enforced.

34 A term used by Mao during the Cultural Revolution to refer to people whom he regarded not as real communists, but "co-roaders" who had joined the revolution for different purposes.

35 *dadaoyiqie, quanmianneizhan*, Mao's characterisation of the stormy Cultural Revolution.

36 Of course, one may point out that China still had the Soviet road to go before it reached the level of industrialisation achieved under Brezhnev. However, China's two decades' of fight against the Soviet "revisionism" (in which Deng himself played an important part) and the ailing example of the Soviet economy in the late 1970s had conceptually precluded this possibility in the mind-set of the Chinese leadership at the initiation of the reform.

37 After all the stability was what so impressed Huntington.

38 Such as the downgrading of planning as a central feature of socialism and the endorsement for a role of the market in a socialist economy, the *glasnost* and *perestroika*. Reform always starts from reformulating the official ideology. In China, the movement of "ideological emancipation" and in the Soviet Union, the "new thinking" preceded structural reforms in both economic and political spheres.

39 As Bzrezinski observed, the human rights and democracy offensive from the West had quickly put all communist regimes on the defensive, because there is no easy justification within the communist ideological formulations to fence off demands for human rights and democracy. See Zbigniew K. Brzezinski, *The Grand Failure-The Birth and Death of Communism in the Twentieth Century* (New York: Charles Scribner's Sons, 1989), p. 256.

40 This refers not so much to open-armed embracement of the liberalism as to wholesale abandonment of communism. Liberalism served initially as an idealised frame of reference just as communism used to in the revolutionary era; however disillusionment eventually sank in as in both cases.

41 Note that the third condition pertains only to the break down of consent or compliance and may tell nothing about the state of regime legitimacy. But it usually does co-occur with the other two conditions and is a necessary manifestation of a crisis.

42 Wesson, *The Aging Communism*.

43 Drastic changes and new departures were most likely to be introduced by a new top leader, who needed to step out of the shadow of his predecessor, consolidate his power and establish his own identity. For example, as the new general secretary Gorbachev described the CPSU's program he had just inherited as "laughably outdated". See Mikhail Gorbachev, *Memoirs* (New York: Doubleday, 1996), p. 172.

44 *Ibid*., p. 173.

45 These are: 1) the leadership of the CCP; 2) the socialist road; 3) the dictatorship of the proletariat [later changed into a more smoothening but awfully awkward term "the people's democratic dictatorship"]; 4) Marxism-Leninism and Mao Zedong Thought. See Deng Xiaoping, *Selected Works of Deng Xiaoping*, Vol. III (Beijing: Renmin Chubanshe, 1993), p. 324.

46 For example, the commander of the 27th army stationed near Beijing initially refused to obey crackdown orders and Ceausescu's army turned against him. For an analysis of "institutional dualism" of communism (that is, opposition growing from within and parasitic on the party-state establishment), see X.L. Ding, *The Decline of Communism in China: Legitimacy Crisis 1978-1989* (New York: Cambridge University Press, 1994).

47 Such reduction was in fact two-fold. In addition to opening up new opportunities in the non-state sector, in an attempt to reduce fiscal burdens, the regime also reduced the people's structural dependency on the state in another way: by withdrawing many benefits and guarantees that were formerly boasted as the "superiority of socialism" over capitalism but now regarded as sources of inefficiency in the economy, such as job security, free medical care, housing and food subsidies, and even free college education, etc. People are thus forced to improvise on their own, often by, as the Chinese call it, "plunging into the sea" of the market.

48 Perhaps we can say that this is how historical accident embedded in historical necessity in general.

49 This is a topic of heated discussion among social scientists of all persuasions. See, for examples, Barry Naughton, *Growing out of the Plan: Chinese Economic Reform 1978-1993* (New York: Cambridge University Press, 1995); Peter Nolen, *China's Rise, Russia's Fall: Politics, Economics, and Planning in the Transition from Stalinism* (Basingstoke, Hants.: MacMillan; New York: St. Martin's Press, 1995).

50 Wesson once observed that both these regimes had "enormous reserves of authority" and "the Communist state stands out for serenity, certainty,

and security in a world of philosophical chaos" (Wesson, *The Aging of Communism*, p. 152). If one looks at the power aspect of the system alone, one has to agree with him.

51 Even though it meant temporarily resurrecting the dated Marxist theory of "class struggle" (see Deng, *Selected Works of Deng Xiaoping*, Vol. III, pp. 364-5).

52 *Xiaomie yu mengya zuangtai*, a Chinese phrase used by Jiang Zemin when he launched the crackdown on the newly organised China Democratic Party immediately after his return from the historical visit to the United States in 1998.

53 Published studies include: Anonymous, *Fengyun bianhuan de sulian dong'o junshi* (Treacherous Storms of the situation in the Soviet Union and Eastern Europe) (documents for internal circulation, 1990); Huang Hong and Gu Shong (compiled), *Dong'o jubian yu zhizhengdang jianshe* (Catastrophic Changes in Eastern Europe and the Building of the Ruling Party) (Beijing: Hongqi chubanshe, 1991)(for internal distribution); Lu Nanquan and Jiang Changbin (eds.), *Sulian jubian shenchenciyuanyin yanjiu* (A Study of the Deeper Causes of the Catastrophic Changes in the Soviet Union)(Beijing: Zhongguo Shehui Kexue Chubanshe, 1999); Tang Zhuchang (ed.), *Eluosi jingji zhuangui toushi* (In-depth Analysis of Russia's Economic Transition) (Shanghai: Shanghai Shehuikexueyuan Chubanshe, 2001); Huang,Weiting, *Sulian wangdang shinianji* (Commemorating the Tenth Anniversity of the Demise of the CPSU) (Nanchang: Jiangxi Gaoxiao Chubanshe, 2001).

54 In fact Deng himself attributed the CCP's survival and the CPSU's fall to the successful economic reforms in China. See Deng, *Selected Works of Deng Xiaoping*, Vol. III, p. 354.

55 Part of the CCP's diagnosis is that the CPSU was too divided and indecisive, and Gorbachev was a captive of "bourgeois liberalisation".

56 Anecdotal evidence suggests that, despite their pioneer role in the 1989 democracy movement that nearly toppled the regime, intellectuals and college students have turned anti-West after the collapse of communism in Eastern Europe. This unexpected about-face can be attributed at least in part to the sharp contrast between Russia and China after 1989, one that the CCP has taken full advantage of.

57 Ironically it was Deng who complained about the laxity of the party's ideological "education" during the booming 1980s, which he believed to have contributed to the 1989 "turmoil". See Deng, *Selected Works of Deng Xiaoping*, Vol. III.

58 For a discussion of this phenomenon and the forces driving it, see Wu Guoguang, "The return of ideology? Struggling to organise politics during socio-economic transitions", in John Wong and Zheng Yongnian (eds.), *The Nanxun Legacy and China's Development in the Post-Deng Era* (Singapore: Singapore University Press and World Scientific Press, 2001).

59 *Documents of the Sixth Plenary Session of the 14th Central Committee* (Beijing: Renmin Chubanshe, 1996).

60 For an authoritative explanation of the "three emphases", see Jiang Zemin's speech commemorating the 78th anniversary of the founding of the CCP

on July 1, 1999 (LINK "http://www.peopledaily.com.cn/zdxw/4/2000323/200032341.html" http://www.peopledaily.com.cn/zdxw/4/2000323/200032341.html).

61 See Mark Seldan, *China in Revolution: The Yenan Way Revisited* (Armonk, NY: M.E. Sharpe, 1995) for a recent account of the "Yenan Way".

62 The web edition of the official *People's Daily* maintained a special *sanjiang* site posting on-going discussions of the campaign (http://www.peopledaily.com.cn/).

63 Jiang Zemin, *Lun "sangedaibiao"* (On "Three Represents") (Beijing, Zhongyang wenxian chubanshe, 2001)

64 Xinhua News Agency: March 2, 2000.

65 Nikita Khrushchev, *Socialism and Communism, selected passages, 1956-63* (Moscow: Foreign Languages Publishing House, 1963), pp. 129-130 & 167.

66 For example, Michel Oksenberg, "Will China democratize?", *Journal of Democracy*, Vol. 9, No.1 (1998).

67 And also somewhat away from the Dengist developmental legitimacy. This may be associated with the inevitable slowdown of the economy in recent years.

68 Indicative of this reunion of Chinese tradition and communist necessity is Jiang's resurrection of the Confucian notion of "rule by virtue" in recent years. For a discussion of this new development see Zheng Yongnian and Lai Hongyi "Rule by Virtue: Jiang Zemin's New Moral Order for the Party", *EAI Background Brief* (Singapore: 12 March 2001).

69 One such joke in Beijing goes: Bush, Putin and Jiang finally agreed to do away with Sadam Hussein. Bush suggests killing Sadam by sending three B2 bombers to flatten his house. Putin offers three Russian blonds to "exhaust him to death", but Jiang declares that his plan guarantees 100% success: to discuss the "three represents" with Sadam and he is sure to be bored to death. (Reported by Asian Times on-line, Nov. 6, 2002)

70 Because there isn't a recognised boundary between the two in the Chinese political philosophy and both state and society can cross it or erode it.

71 Oksenberg, 'China's Long March Ahead', *South China Morning Post*, Oct. 1, 1999.

72 Or what sociologists call "anomie". The sudden burst of Mao nostalgia in the middle of 1990s is in part a reflection of this social psychology.

73 Oksenberg, "China's Long March Ahead".

74 See for examples, Jiang Zemin, *Lun "sangedaibiao"*, esp. pp. 11-15; Luo Ye, et al., (ed.), *"Liangxin zhuzhi" de dangjian chuangxin* (Innovations in Party Building in the Two New Organizations) (Nanjing: Jiangsu Renmin Chubanshe, 2001); Ye Wuxi and Shao Yunduan, *Xiandanqiye dang de jianshe* (Party Building in Modern Enterprises), Beijing: Zhongguo Fangzhen Chubanshe, 1996); Wu Jixiang (ed.)*Shehuizhuyi shichang jingji yu zhizhengdang jianshe* (Socialist Market Economy and the Construction of the Ruling Party) (Nanchang: Jiangxi Renmin Chubanshe, 1994); Organizational Department of CCP Ganzhou Municipal Committee,

Jiangxi Province (compiled), *Xiagangzhigong dangyuan peixun jianminjiaochai* (A Short Training Course for Laid-off Party Members) (Beijing: Dangjianduwu Chubanshe, 1998).

75 Such "parasitic opposition" is the thesis of X.L. Ding's 1995 book.

76 Walder, *Communist Neo-Traditionalism*.

77 Mao was a classic example. The difference is that he rebelled towards the radical left, but he shared the same discontent with the rebels of 1989.

78 Jean Kirkpatrick was the United States' ambassador to the UN under the Reagan Administration. Her foreign policy recommendation, which later became part of the foundation of the Reagan Doctrine, was based on the view that communist regimes had more staying power and hence were inflexible, non-responsive to external pressure; in contrast, authoritarian regimes were less stable, more flexible, more responsive to outside criticisms, and therefore possible to move towards democracy. Consequently, she believed that while the U.S. could work with the authoritarian regimes, it must fight communism.

79 And their recent transition toward democracy is infinitely more peaceful in comparison. The simple fact is that authoritarian regimes have much less to do with the daily life of ordinary citizens.

80 It is however not entirely impossible, but the pre-requisite is a fundamental transformation of the party-state.

81 See Lance L.P. Gore, *Market Communism: The Institutional Foundations of China's Post-Mao Hyper-growth* (Hong Kong and New York: Oxford University Press, 1998).

CHAPTER 2

The Falun Gong and Its Conflicts with the Chinese Government: A Perspective of Social Transformation[1]

XIAO GONGQIN
Translator: YOW CHEUN HOE

INTRODUCTION

On 25 April 1999, without the knowledge of the Chinese government, as many as 11,000 followers of Falun Gong secretly arrived from the provinces in North and Northeast China and gathered in Zhongnanhai, where the central government is based. The Falun Gong representatives made a number of requests to the government. These, among others, included a recognition of the organisation, a clarification that it was not an "opposition organisation," a release of its 45 followers arrested a week earlier by the Tianjin Public Security Department, and a request that the government would not take action against those involved in the gathering. Surprisingly, the five representatives negotiating with the government were cadres from some core organisations of the Chinese Communist Party (CCP) itself. Respectively, they were from the Supervisory Department, Railway Department, the Second Headquarter of the General Staff, the Public Security Department, and Beijing University. This has caused an official of the Political-Legal Committee to shriek, "Falun Gong has pierced into the stomach of our party!" In response, the government clarified that it was merely an individual act of He Zuoxiu, an academician of the Institute of Chinese Sciences, to get an article published in newspapers and that the government never said Falun Gong was an opposition organisation. Thinking they had basically achieved "the goal of explaining to the government and making it understand them," the Falun Gong members eventually went away.

Since then, a series of conflicts has been unfolding between millions of Falun Gong followers and the Chinese government. The government determined that Falun Gong had great potential to challenge the ruling regime and political stability. On 22 July 2002, three months after the April 25 Event, the government made a national announcement that Falun Gong was an "illegal organisation that disseminated heretical beliefs." It outlawed the Study Society of Falun Beliefs and arrested some of the core members of Falun Gong for long-term imprisonment. Later on, the followers staged demonstrations in Beijing, through street sit-ins, distributing leaflets, disseminating messages across the Internet, and even using some radical methods to challenge the authority of the government. All these caused the government to further declare Falun Gong an "evil cult" and it mobilised all its resources to suppress it. Since the CCP came to power, China had never witnessed such a massive and sustained nationwide opposition movement. Without doubt, the conflicts will go on in the foreseeable future.

This chapter attempts to adopt a sociological perspective and analyse the rise of Falun Gong. It also examines the dual identities of the organisation, the political motives for the government to carry out the suppression, and the factors determining the seesaw conflicts between them. Finally, it investigates the future development of this social opposition movement.

THE RISE OF FALUN GONG: A FUNCTIONALISM EXPLANATION

Why did Falun Gong emerge after two decades of reform in China and reach a scale of as many as several million people? From the perspective of functionalism in sociology, the wide acceptance of a social organisation results from its ability to satisfy certain social needs through various means, some of which might be abnormal and radical. As pointed out by such sociologists as Kang Xiaoguang at the Domestic Studies Centre in the Chinese Academy of Sciences, in the period in which drastic social changes took place, Falun Gong met at least four important social needs of a considerably large number of the people. The four social needs are as follows.

First, Falun Gong served the people's need for faith and belief. The staunch vitality of Falun Gong lies in the fact that it, through its religion-like manner, satisfies the faith hunger of large numbers of people. Faith not merely establishes life goals and meanings, but also sets up moral and behaviour standards. People will appear more eager to search for faith moorings when the society experiences a gradual collapse of old belief systems and witnesses a prevalence of lost morals.[2] It is worth noting that mainland China in fact lacks traditional religious resources, and Buddhism, the most influential among the Chinese people, has been declining for the past few decades. Secularisation and corruption among monks have led to lessened appeal to followers.[3] This has created a breeding ground for some other beliefs to expand their follower base and become new religions.

Second, Falun Gong satisfied the need for social interaction. Humans are social animals. People need to mingle with each other to get affirmation, recognition, sympathy, understanding, and help from others. They need to live in groups that reflect their own values of existence in the collective life. This need for interaction is more important than the need for faith, particularly for lonely and aged people, laid-off workers, and others from disadvantaged strata that are marginalised in a market economy. Through collective practice and training, Falun Gong has offered a sound space for social interaction, satisfying the need of the lower class to communicate with one another.

Third, Falun Gong fulfilled the need of the lower class to have a sense of security. Being in the marginal zone, the disadvantaged group is more likely to be hit by all kinds of risks and have more difficulty in getting family and social protection. Falun Gong has created an opportunity for its members to help each other. Healthcare reform in China has brought about serious social problems for the disadvantaged groups. In this regard, physical exercise, such as the ones practiced in Falun Gong, offer hope to those lacking healthcare protection.

Fourth, Falun Gong satisfied those who are discontented with the questions of justice. Benevolence and pursuing justice is part of human nature. In the midst of the many social problems arising from the economic reforms, the concept of "Truth, Benevolence, and Forbearance" delivered by Falun Gong enabled its followers to feel spiritually uplifted and make themselves comfortable by using "forbearance" to make sense of the social injustices. Being in the organisation and doing its practices, the followers felt superior to others in terms of justice and morality; Falun Gong thus satisfied their need to pursue justice.

In fact, in any society and any period of time, people do have the aforementioned needs, that is, pursuing faith, security, justice, and interaction with other people. The question prompted here is why the movement of Falun Gong did not appear in the first half-century since the founding of the People's Republic of China?

Basically, in the socialist totalitarianism period, the ideology and work units under the collective system should, to a large extent, have served the aforementioned needs. The ideology of a socialist nation provides standard answers as to what justice, truth, benevolence, and beauty should be. Under a closed system, the morals and beliefs of "communism" are repeatedly inculcated among the people who in turn will be satisfied through pursuing equality in a lopsided way. We can even say that the participation of massive numbers of youths during the Cultural Revolution was that it was an outlet satisfying their spiritual hunger and need. Besides, in a planned economy, the people would have their sense of economic security assured by collective system including purchasing and selling processes as well as career assignment.

The repercussions of social transformation in China, however, have included the collapse of socialist beliefs and values as well as that of collective social protection systems in the two decades of economic reforms. Meanwhile, the resultant anomie and social injustice, as well as moral decline, have caused people to have a stronger need for justice. With this situation, if the Chinese government permits religious activities, the religious systems, to a large extent, will take over to fulfill the social needs, thus lessening the tension between the needs and the social allocation system. However, worried about losing its social grip, the leaders have a strong distrust of those religions not controlled by the government. With the announcement that all religious organisations without government recognition were illegal, the autonomous religions have lost their chance to effectively resolve the spiritual and moral problems in the society.

Although the self-initiated communities and social organisations can also, amidst the social transformation, substitute to satisfy the social needs, the government's control over the organisations has been increasingly tightened since the June Fourth Incident. The government has been worried that the social organisations, which are not government-controlled and which are self-initiated, are likely to be exploited by the dissenters to challenge government authority and harm political stability. More specifically, the collapse of socialist regimes in Soviet and East Europe has provoked the Chinese leadership to sense the possibility that the social organisations will ally among themselves and constitute a thorough political challenge to the ruling regime. Based on the principle of "stability is the utmost priority," the government has taken all kinds of measures to diminish all "destabilising factors" right from the "embryonic stage." This was manifested in the strict policy concerning the registration of social organisations. The requirements have been purposely raised and those that cannot meet the requirements are outlawed. With these measures, the government does not allow the existence of autonomous organisations, particularly those with political elements or colours.

Thus, the social organisations have been blocked to fully carry out their functions and the people have remained hungry for faith, justice, interactions, and security. It is from this situation that Falun Gong emerged and has been expanding rapidly across the country. It filled the gap with its easy-to-learn physical exercises and training, its highly moralistic slogan of "truth, benevolence, and forbearance" as well as its function of satisfying the aforementioned four needs.

However, the complexity of the question lies in the fact that Falun Gong is not similar to other voluntary organisations. In some way it resembles a religion with its perverseness, exclusiveness, and closeness. It can satisfy the aforementioned needs through its religion-like spiritual control and close spiritual environment in which its followers repeatedly chant the "scriptures". Because of the high level of concentration required and the spiritual tension, coupled with such mysticism as "open the sky eye" and "turn the dharma wheel," it can easily induce morbid psychology and hallucinations.[4] In addition, the irrational worship of the leader, Li Hongzhi, can induce its followers to being obsessed, perverse, and illogical. There even appeared some extreme cases in which the followers had burned themselves, committed suicide, and murdered others. Thus, when the government officially announced that Falun Gong had caused 1,700-odd casualties, it was considerably based on objective facts.

We can thus observe that the emergence of Falun Gong as a unique cultural phenomenon amidst the social transformation has two main features. First, at a time when mainstream ideology cannot satisfy people's spiritual needs, it has served them through means that can be easily comprehended and that accord well with the Chinese traditional mentality and customs. Second, it has religion-like irrationality.

These two features have engendered the following repercussions. Falun Gong organisations and their sympathisers have emphasised the first feature. They explain that the membership expansion has no political intention; all they want to do is to exercise and get their bodies healthy and they are just ordinary and good people. They have, however, often avoided talking about or even covering up the second feature associated with Falun Gong. In the 2001 Spring Festival, some of its followers, originating from Kaifeng in Henan province, burned themselves in Tiananmen Square. In December of the same year, a devotee in Beijing, Fu Yibin, killed his parents and wife. In response to these two cases, the overseas Falun Gong pamphlets and websites either claimed that they were fabrications or arrangements made by the Chinese Communist Party, or simply said that the people involved were not their followers. On the other hand, the Chinese government, in order to diminish the influence of Falun Gong, has repeatedly highlighted its nature as an "evil cult." The antagonism between the followers and the government regarding the nature of the organisation is crucial to understanding the ongoing political conflicts triggered by Falun Gong.

WHY DOES THE CHINESE GOVERNMENT WANT TO SUPPRESS FALUN GONG?

Approximately one month after the April 25 Event, Jiang Zemin gave a serious warning in an important document released to the whole country. He viewed the event "the most serious one since the political storm in 1989." Why did the Chinese government exercise such great caution and have such a strong reaction towards the event, in which the followers surrounded Zhongnanhai and requested that Falun Gong could exist legally? Where the issue of suppression is concerned, the response of the international human rights institutes and Western mainstream societies have mainly revolved around the autocracy of the Chinese government. As a political scientist concerned about contemporary Chinese politics, I think there is a need to examine the political logic revealed in the Chinese government suppressing Falun Gong. Only with this can we understand the political decisions made by the government in dealing with the issue. This section will analyse the political logic of the suppression. From the government's viewpoint, Falun Gong has four essential features, the combination of which will possibly lead to a crisis that the government will find hard to control and that could eventually stir up a political chain reaction worse than that of the June Fourth Incident.

First, the Falun Gong leader has strong anti-government motives. According to the government, Falun Gong is not similar to other quasi-religious and sport organisations. Though the majority of the participants might not have political intentions, there is no doubt that the leader has a strong motive for opposing the government. This is evident in a secretive letter given by Li Hongzhi to his subordinates on the eve of the April 25 Event, in which he said, "it is good to shed blood and the more chaotic it is, the better it is." The Chinese Central Television even broadcasted the original copy of the letter. According to the investigation by the government, in order to carefully prepare to surround Zhongnanhai, Li personally flew back to China and made the necessary deployment. It was not until the day before the event that Li left China through Hong Kong, so that it would not draw the attention of the government. From the viewpoint of the government, Falun Gong has political intentions and great energy to ignite political activities, making it politically more dangerous than such *qigong* (breathing exercise) organisations as "*Zhonggong*" and "*Xianggong*." More importantly, the Falun Gong leader has absolute religion-like autocracy and power to appeal to his followers. Thus, when the leader thinks the conditions are mature enough, he can mobilise his followers, who though not interested in politics, can quickly move up to the political stage and form a massive nationwide movement opposing the government. The April 25 Event itself is a telling example.

Second, Falun Gong has high ability to mobilise its followers. What makes the government worried is that Falun Gong has unexpectedly demonstrated great ability concerning the mobilisation of its followers. Its strength lies in its pyramid power structure that enables Li Hongzhi to fully control the organisation from top down to the bottom. More specifically, the autocracy of Li as the leader has not merely been derived from his own extraordinary charisma, but also has been consolidated with the pyramid organisation system. Within this system, an internal group of the organisation can follow the leader's will and take united action by making use of the information dissemination procedure and mobilising, whether or not politically, the followers. According to the analysis by a Chinese sociologist, Kang Xiaoguang, Falun Gong has a unique way of expanding its organisation, as follows.

> It can send its high-ranked members to set up new basic units. It can also, without the effort made by the high level, let the basic units to have self-spilt and grow into new ones. When the numbers reach a certain level, some followers will automatically spilt away to establish a new base for doing the physical exercises. Even after the smash by the government, this expanding process will recover itself and the organisation will keep on expanding.[5]

The high organisational capability of Falun Gong, as shown in the following event, certainly shocked the Chinese Communist Party leaders who originally started as revolutionaries. Within a span as short as a few hours, more than 10,000 Falun Gong followers came from various parts of the country, gathered themselves and surrounded Zhongnanhai, without the awareness of the Public Security Department. We can imagine how insecure Jiang Zemin felt when at midnight more than 10,000 persons were making noise outside the walls of Zhongnanhai, his residence. More surprisingly, during the process of making requests that lasted 16 hours, the followers complied with their own internal discipline, shouted not a single slogan, and did not block traffic. They also did not answer questions and left behind not a single piece of paper or cigarette when they had all gone. Even the public security officers could not identify who the commander was after having watched the spot for such a long time. Was this not frightening? This has shown that the organisation has great mobilisation power and appeal among its members. Reinforcing the strength of Falun Gong are the use of modern communication methods, such as mobile phones, the Internet, and long distant telephone service, and the support the leader has in the United States of America.

Third, Falun Gong's base is founded in the disadvantaged social stratum. An unspoken worry that the government has is that the majority of the Falun Gong members are from the disadvantaged groups in the lower class. Amidst the process of social stratification since the introduction of economic reform in 1978, the lower class has increasing felt frustrated and discontent about the current economic development and political regime. Interactions within the organisation itself has made it easier to reinforce discontent among its members. According to the government, this makes the organisation easier to be manipulated and exploited by those "having an axe to grind."

Fourth, the greatest danger of Falun Gong is that it can "act irrationally." If legalised, the organisation, with its feature of religion-like irrationality, will go into the society and adopt nonsensical measures for its political struggle. They can totally ignore the rules of the game, thus making its activities unpredictable. When the conflicts with the government accelerate, both parties cannot communicate with each other at a rational level. This is most evident in the case of He Zuoxiu, an academician in the Chinese Academy of Sciences. He published an article criticising Falun Gong in a not well-known journal by the Tianjin Education College. In response to this, Falun Gong mobilised more than 10,000 followers from various provinces to surround Zhongnanhai and impose pressure on the government. Thus, the government is now worried that, if there is a bigger conflict, the organisation will possibly mobilise more than 10,000 or even one million of its followers to go on a hunger strike in the Tiananmen Square. If it is the case, the repercussions will likely be tenfold more serious than that of the June Fourth Incident.

To sum up, the Falun Gong leader has political intentions and the organisation has a tightly-structured system of mobilisation. Its membership is largely composed of those disadvantaged in the social stratification. It does not act rationally and has religion-like secretive features. From the viewpoint of the government, all these will likely lead to the following situations.

First, the Falun Gong leader will make use of his many followers to expand the organisation's activities. Would there be any acceleration of antagonism, this may lead to more serious conflicts as well as other more provocative events.

Second, with his anti-government intentions, the Falun Gong leader will certainly utilise his religion-like appeal (or what in sociology is called charisma) to mobilise his followers to challenge the government. Hundreds of thousand followers will go to street, challenge the authority of the government, and make requests the government will find hard to accept.

Third, with its base in the disadvantaged groups, the organisation will rapidly mobilise those people who are discontented with the government, and further spread the antagonism to other groups in the society, bringing about the "domino effect." Entering the tough stage of economic reform and social stratification, China has witnessed a lot of problems, such as the laid-off workers, corruption, and the economic bottleneck. From the viewpoint of the government, the combination of these social discontents with the antagonism of Falun Gong will likely, within a short span, lead to a nationwide massive political conflict, which will in turn gain support from the international "anti-China forces." This will accelerate political and social crisis.

Fourth, if the government rejects all of its requests, it is likely that Falun Gong, based on its irrational nature as discussed earlier, will adopt radical strategies. For instance, it will mobilise all the followers in the country to go on a hunger strike in Beijing and commit suicide to pursue its aims to the "fullest." Without doubt, once this happens, the degree and scope of the repercussions will be much greater than that of the June Fourth Incident.

The discussion above is based on the features of Falun Gong and the possible outcomes of the interactions between the organisation and the government. The government might not have said this openly, but it is politically logical to have all these possibilities.

THE FORMATION OF THE SEESAW BATTLE

In fact, the suppression of Falun Gong has been based on political considerations. In the public announcement, however, the most effective strategy is not to highlight the harm Falun Gong brings to the security and unity. The best is to point out its nature as an "evil cult" and deny its legal rights to conduct any political activity. The government has been adopting this strategy of revealing the "evil cult" nature of Falun Gong. Indeed the organisation has the foundation to develop into being an "evil cult." This is clearly reflected in the cases in which its devotees committed suicide, murdered others, and harmed the public security. The government has evidence to prove that the organisation is similar to other evil cults and thus it has reasons to suppress it.

However, as discussed previously, Falun Gong has another important feature. This has to do with the fact that the organisation has served the spiritual needs of his many members for faith, interaction, justice, and security. The majority of the followers actually do not have political intentions and joining the organisation is for the purpose of pursuing truth, benevolence, and beauty. They no longer feel spiritually empty after they become members. Thus, they cannot accept at all the government's announcement that Falun Gong is an "evil cult." In their view, it is a serious case of injustice. When the government banned the organisation, they shouted,

> Don't we want to be good persons? You do your bad persons, and we do our good persons. Can't we just be like 'the well water never invades the river water?' Why do you want to ban and deprive us of our rights to be good persons?

For sure, the members who consider themselves as having no political intentions will defend themselves when the government declares Falun Gong an evil cult and Li Hongzhi the leader of the cult.

What has complicated the situation is that the organisation has an irrational "adverse mentality." When confronted with challenges to existence, this mentality makes the members highly cohesive and strengthens their resolve and obligation to "defend the truth". From their viewpoint, the suppression of Falun Gong is but "an attempt by the evil to destroy the dharma". Countering the suppression, they will think, is a great opportunity the master Li gives them to "diminish their own sin". For them, in order to pursue the "fullness", they have to fight against the suppression until death.

This "adverse mentality" is clearly reflected in an article in the website "Minghuiwang" run by the overseas Falun Gong organisation. The article points out, "The present suppression conducted by the government is a precious opportunity hard to find once in a thousand years". "Only by participating in the process of *zhengfa* (execution), we can be united with the dharma. Otherwise we cannot reach the fullness through the *zhengfa* process". In another article, a follower writes,

> Every report that the followers were tormented until death is a challenge to every follower. One day, I came out with an idea that if I were dead of torment I will awake more followers and other people. If needed, I am willing to sacrifice my life and contribute my body to the *zhengfa* team.

Thus, the suppression made by the government is now conceived as the devil wanting to destroy the dharma and as a good opportunity for the followers to achieve "fullness". Under the irrational mentality and values, the suppression actually reinforced the strength of the organisation.

The suppression will likely cause Falun Gong to have his antigovernment sentiment increased, to take initiative to fight against the government, and to demonstrates the insistence and endurance of its struggle, as a Chinese saying goes, "resolutely going into the tiger mountain, even though knowing there is a tiger".

We can thus see the vicious circle formed because of the conflict between the organisation and the government. Out of the consideration of political stability, the government is harshly suppressing the organisation. On the other hand, the suppressed organisation has it members, influenced by the religion-like sentiment, brave enough to die for it. Based on the four reasons discussed above, the government has to smash the organisation. Meanwhile, the Falun Gong members, based on their personal experience, view they are misjudged as they think they really do not have "political ambitions". On the other hand, Li Hongzhi is now staying abroad. The international fight between Li Hongzhi and the government has translated into the continuous domestic conflicts between the followers and the government. This has determined the conflicts to become a seesaw battle.

It was not until the 2001 Spring Festival that the development turned to be in favour of the Chinese government. This has to do with the incident that happened at the Tiananmen Square, where the followers from Kaifeng in Henan province gathered and burned themselves. The government has fully utilised the incident as a case to portray and prove Falun Gong as an evil cult. The report has been repeatedly broadcasted on television, delivering the most scarring visual effect. At the end of the same year another incident occurred in which a Beijing follower, Fu Yibin, killed his whole family. Shown in the television is how Fu vehemently declared that the murder was to pursue "fullness". This has further worsened the image of Falun Gong.

These two incidents have a very important implication. Amidst the suppression process prior to the two incidents, there was a considerable number of ordinary people and intellectuals who, for the reasons of human rights and freedom, sympathised with the suppressed members. After the incident happened, the intellectuals and ordinary people shifted to be inclined to the government. Since then the pressure that the government faces in carrying out the suppression has been lessening. Within the country, Falun Gong is gradually losing its power to challenge the government. However, as discussed earlier, due to its religion-like mentality and spirit, the organisation is able to generate power strong enough to continue its struggle. This has caused the conflicts to continue, without a sign of coming to an end.

CONCLUDING REMARKS

In the current situation, there is unlikely to be any change in the factors, as discussed earlier, that determine to the seesaw battle between the Chinese government and Falun Gong. Without doubt, the conflicts will happen from time to time for a long time to come. However, in the wake of the June Fourth Incident and Deng Xiaoping's Southern Tour, the main development has been that China is gradually moving into an era of post-totalitarian authoritarianism. From the totalitarian era, China has inherited the mechanism of full control over the country. This includes the basic unit of the Chinese Communist Party, the Public Security Bureau and Intelligence Bureau, and means of propaganda, which are all thoroughly penetrating the society. As a result, the government is able to fully utilise these organs, which are substantially financed, as well as the local administrative powers, to suppress the quasi-religious activities such as Falun Gong. Since 2001 the influence of Falun Gong in Chinese society has been declining and it is likely to be further weakened in future. As the government has badly damaged its foundation in China, the recovery of Falun Gong will encounter many impediments. Moreover, since the leader is staying abroad and thus is unable to directly exercise his influence, it is unlikely that the organisation will court any bigger challenge.

Since the Chinese government at present thinks that it has been successful in the suppression policy, it is unlikely to make any fundamental changes in the foreseeable future. In his speech in the recent Working Conference of the Religions in China, Jiang Zemin revealed some subtle changes concerning the religious followers, which shifted from strict control and harsh suppression to uniting and guiding. According to some analysts, it shows that the Chinese government will increasingly loosen its control over religion. As the main trends go on, it is expected that the Chinese government will be more and more tolerant where religious matters are concerned. However, in the short term, a loose policy on religions is unlikely to come out and there will not be much change in regard to the decision to harshly suppress Falun Gong.

Will the new leadership adopt a looser policy towards Falun Gong? In my opinion, as long as the organisation is weakening, there will be much room to allow policy changes. The first change is likely to be an attempt to differentiate more clearly the members from the leader so as to incorporate them into the nation.

On the other hand, the opposition movement of the overseas Falun Gong organisations will continue. According to some sources, the overseas members have expanded to 47 countries. The majority of these countries have a higher level of economic development and living standards. Many of the overseas members are from the middle class and are well-educated, thus less influenced by superstitious folk beliefs and seldom taking irrational actions.[6] Furthermore, with the protection of the laws of the host countries, they will not be affected by the suppression by the Chinese government. As a result, they will go on to exist for a long time, constituting resources supporting the Falun Gong organisation in China. As the main trend shows, the overseas Falun Gong organisations will take over their counterparts that are suppressed in China and form an opposition power to the Chinese government. Indeed, it has a symbolic implication when the Western followers of Falun Gong did exercises in the Tiananmen Square in November 2001.

The conflicts between Falun Gong and the Chinese government lie in the combination of two factors. First is the high sensitivity of the government, as a result of the June Fourth Incident, that has obstructed the healthy and full development of the Chinese society amidst the economic reforms. Second are the social problems that have lead to the people's spiritual emptiness and hunger. From the long-term perspective, only with healthy socioeconomic development, will the social problems and conflicts be reduced and the freedom of religion be larger. Under the condition that the society develops autonomously, Falun Gong will lose its attractiveness to fill social needs and such religious movements will be unable to attract large numbers of followers. However, as a new quasi-religious organisation, the vitality of Falun Gong is still indomitable.

ENDNOTES

1 Translated from a revised version of a paper written by the author when he was a visiting research fellow at the East Asian Institute, National University of Singapore, from September 2001 to February 2002. The original version was published as "*Falun Gong* yu Zhongguo zhengfu de chongtu yu qi qianjing zhanwang" *EAI Working Paper* (Chinese Series), No. 36, 11 January 2002.

2 The author visited a temple in Wutai Mountain in Shanxi province in 1999 and encountered an old woman who stayed in the temple. Originally an accountant in a village in Shandong province, she practised in the temple because she could not stand the corruption and harassment of the village cadres. Unable to complain and uneasy with such behaviour, she was trying to keep peace of mind by practising to be a good person herself. The attitude of the followers of Falun Gong was very similar to this woman. From this, we can see the social foundation of Falun Gong concerning the belief of "truth, benevolence, and forbearance".

3 In explaining why he abandoned Buddhism and followed Falun Gong, one recollected, "We once stayed in a famous temple for a few days. What confused me was that in that temple the monks lived together with nuns, having meals and reciting scriptures together". "In a banquet, there was a Taoist priest who was eating meat as well as seafood. I asked him if that was appropriate. He answered that religions also need to follow the trend. I came to religion because of not being comfortable with the secular world, whereas he wanted the religion to follow the secular world. As time passed by, I found that this was not a pure land and I thus felt increasingly depressed" (from an article written by a Falun Gong follower – "My heart goes to the belief and I will resolutely do the practice"). The phenomenon is now prevailing among the temples across the country. The author encountered the same case in Jiuhua Mountain where the monks cared for nothing else except collecting money.

4 A follower expressed his experience in a pamphlet disseminated by the Singapore Falun Gong. After being a Buddhist for 18 years, he converted to Falun Gong and had the following experience: "After I sent away the Buddhist idols, I could not sleep at night. I was troubled by misgiving and the devil that arose in my heart. I either recited the Buddha name or said something bad about Falun Gong. During the daytime, I also did not feel easy with all evil thoughts, such as trying to see what it would feel by jumping from the fourth floor or what it would turn out to be if my house was on fire. In order to get rid of these wicked ideas, I chanted the "turning dharma wheel (*zhuan falun*)" loudly and was awakened immediately. No doubt, what tormented me were devils. I shouted loudly that I would never burn incense and kowtow wrongly. I shouted to the devils, "Don't ever think of stealing away and eating my joss sticks. Get away!"

This writing demonstrates in detail the illusions and psychological change a follower would have before being further spellbound with Falun Gong. It is through this process that many went into the tragedies in which they committed suicide or murdered others. The most recent instance was that in December 2001 when a Beijing resident, Fu Yibin, who was troubled by illusions and lost his control over spirit, killed his whole family in order to achieve what was perceived "fullness" in Falun Gong.

5 Kang Xiaoguang, "Guanyu Falun Gong wenti de sikao," on the website of "Shiji Zhongguo".

6 In the interviews I conducted in Singapore with the local Falun Gong members, they said in their daily life they never heard of any case in which other members committed suicide or hurt themselves. They said, "If we did hear of these kinds of things, who still want to take part in Falun Gong?" To some extent, this shows that, because of different socioeconomic conditions, the overseas development of Falun Gong is not the same as in China.

CHAPTER 3

Why China's Rampant Corruption Cannot Be Checked by Laws Alone

ZOU KEYUAN

CURRENT CORRUPTION SITUATION IN CHINA

Corruption is simply defined as the abuse of public office for private gain. The 2000 Corruption Perceptions Index of Transparency International ranked China as 63rd among 90 countries. Corruption in China is still on the rise despite some of the most draconian crackdown efforts ever made. Premier Zhu Rongji had to admit, in his Work Report to the National People's Congress (NPC) in March 2000 that "the emergence and spread of corruption and undesirable practices have not been brought under control".[1] A number of surveys conducted locally have also identified corruption as the most serious social problem facing China today.[2]

Since 1993 the number of cases investigated and handled by discipline inspection and procuratorial organs throughout the country has increased 9 percent on an annual basis, and the number of officials given party and administrative disciplinary punishments has gone up 12 percent annually. Between 1990 and 1998, procuratorial organs nationwide accepted and handled more than 1.1 million corruption cases, of which over 500,000 cases were placed on file for investigation and prosecution. More than 600,000 offenders were involved (see Table 3.1).[3] From January to August 2000 alone, the procuratorates throughout the country prosecuted 23,464 criminal cases involving graft and embezzlement.[4] Above all, in recent years, high-ranking officials have also been brought to court on criminal charges (see Table 3.2).

There are three main features of corruption in China: (1) Increasing involvement of high-ranking officials, especially in recent years. The recent cases of Hu Changqing[5] and Cheng Kejie[6] are just two typical examples. (2) Increased group corruption involving many officials in a particular department or local government since the 1990s. Clearly, corruption in China has gradually become an organised crime, particularly when it is related to smuggling, such as the widely publicised *Zhanjiang* and *Yuanhua* smuggling cases.[7] (3) The monetary amount of bribes and embezzled funds has become larger and larger. For instance, in the past two years, 77 of the 589 cases of corruption investigated by the Beijing procuratorate involved RMB1 million (US$120,000).[8] The executed Cheng Kejie solicited and accepted RMB41 million (US$4.9 million) in bribes in collaboration with his mistress, Li Ping.

TABLE 3.1: RISING TREND OF CORRUPTION IN CHINA

Year	Cases Reported	Cases under Investigation	Persons Implicated
1991	81,110	45,155	51,705
1992	66,477	36,533	47,873
1993	92,136	44,540	391,173 (93-95)
1994	102,112	50,074	Ibid.
1995	102,038	51,089	Ibid.
1996	100,383	46,314	495,503 (96-98)
1997	116,961	53,533	Ibid.
1998	89,544	64,439	Ibid.
1999	130,414	n/a	132,447

Source: *Law Yearbook of China*, various years and other sources.

TABLE 3.2: CORRUPT HIGH-RANKING OFFICIALS CONVICTED IN RECENT YEARS

Name	Position When Caught	Sentence/Year of Conviction
Cao Xiukang	Head, Zhangjiang Customs	Death/99
Chen Xitong	Party Secretary, Beijing	16-year jail term/98
Cheng Kejie	Vice-Chairman, NPC	Death/00
Hu Changqing	Vice-Governor, Jiangxi	Death/00
Huang Jicheng	Vice-Chairman, PPCC Beijing	10-year jail term/97
Jiang Diewu	Vice-Chairman, PC Hebei	10-year jail term/98
Li Chenglong	Vice-Major, Guigang, Guangxi	Death/00
Li Jizhou	Vice-Minister, Public Security	In legal process
Li Xiaoshi	Vice-Minister, SCST	20-year jail term/96
Tie Ying	Vice-Chairman, PC Beijing	15-year jail term/97
Wei Zefang	Vice-Chairman, PC Hainan	5-year jail term/97
Xin Yejiang	Vice-Chairman, PC Hainan	5-year jail term/98
Xu Bingsong	Vice-Chairman, Guangxi	Life imprisonment/99
Xu Yunhong	Party Secretary, Ningbo	10-year jail term/00

Source: compiled from various sources.

Corruption can cause social instability. More importantly, it can arouse the people's defiance of the capability of the Chinese Communist Party (CCP) to ensure fairness and cast doubts about its legitimacy to rule the country. In order to maintain its rule in China, it is imperative for the CCP to launch campaigns against corruption. Since the founding of the People's Republic of China (PRC) in 1949, many such campaigns have been carried out. It should be noted that before the economic reform, corruption was not a big problem in China. However, the emphasis on economic development in the last two decades has stimulated the spread of corruption in China in various forms, giving rise to what has been called "systemic corruption".[9] Facing such a serious problem, China must use the law to crack down on corruption, particularly after it introduced the rule of law. The other reason to use the law against corruption is that the CCP came to realise that the use of ideology to crack down on corruption is ineffective, as revealed in the recent "three stresses" (*san jiang*) campaign.[10]

The death penalty for Hu Changqing and Cheng Kejie was hailed as a good and effective means to punish corrupt officials. Many have advocated that heavy punishment be used on corrupt officials since corruption in some areas and departments is so serious, and the criminal activities so rampant. As argued, without heavy punishment, it is almost impossible to deter the perpetrators, ease the resentment of the people, establish the authority of the law, and educate more people.[11] Even the top CCP leader Jiang Zemin recently stressed the necessity of using heavy punishment for corrupt officials, no matter how high their rank is; however, heavy punishment may have the effect of "killing the chicken to frighten the monkeys", that is, only temporarily. Once the anti-corruption campaign ends, new corrupt activities will resurface, as shown in every previous anti-corruption campaign. Therefore, what is most important is to establish the authority of the law and implement it effectively. As has been rightly stated, "The key pragmatic method to combat corruption is to increase the certainty of punishment rather than to rely upon severity, especially on the death penalty, for deterrence".[12]

Realistically, it is impossible for China to completely eliminate corruption; what it can do is only to curb its increase.[13] One reason lies in the fact that China is a one-party-ruled country. As long as the power of the CCP is not effectively checked and supervised, such power can still give rise to corruption. Anti-corruption campaigns have been carried out in China from time to time since the founding of the PRC, particularly after the economic reforms. However, after 20 years of reform, corruption has become even more severe. The reason is simple. Corruption is closely linked to power. When power is unrestricted, corruption breeds quickly.[14] It thus seems a sound system of checks and balances needs to be established urgently. As has been rightly pointed out, "the more checks and balances exist within a society, and the stronger institutions are in place to protect such checks and balances, the fewer opportunities there may be for corrupt practices which remain unchecked or unpunished".[15]

Some may argue that an authoritarian regime can also curb corruption effectively and that there is no inherent correlation between democracy and corruption. A Chinese scholar has noted that in Chinese history there were good emperors and clean officials. Also, the early period of the PRC had shown little corruption. No doubt, highly centralised power is vulnerable to corruption, but this is because there is a lack of reasonable division of power and effective check in the use of power. Thus centralised power or shared power does not matter greatly in the fight against corruption, and they are just two separate management forms.[16] While we acknowledge that the above argument contains a point, it is recommended that a democratic mechanism, not in the sheer Western form, can help to establish a sound system of checks and balances. Before we talk about introducing this mechanism, what is more important currently is the reform of the CCP itself. To rely more on law may be the only feasible solution currently existing in China for the establishment of an effective anti-corruption mechanism.

Law is useful in deterring and controlling corruption, but it is not a panacea. The real victory against corruption lies in effecting further political reform. Secondly, one characteristic of China's anti-corruption campaigns is the superiority of the party's policy over state laws as guidelines to launch such campaigns. Political documents, including speeches of top leaders, play a major role in the current anti-corruption campaign. The active involvement and leadership of the party's Central Commission for Discipline Inspection (CCDI) in corruption cases reinforces the impression that the party wants to control the campaign so that such a campaign will not be a threat to the party. The "double restraint" (*shuanggui*) is an illustrative example: a suspected corrupt official is required by the party's CCDI or by a local party discipline committee to report to the committee according to the time and location set forth by the committee during the preliminary investigation before going to the judiciary. Such a practice clearly undermines judicial independence. In addition, considering the fact that poorly paid and trained judges who have a limited understanding of the law and might misuse the power and be unlikely to enforce laws, it is obvious that the role of law is limited.

It is unfortunate that in the anti-corruption campaigns, the so-called "rule of law" as embodied in the Chinese Constitution is not fully nor wholeheartedly enforced, though the current use of law to crack down on corruption is much better than in the past. In a nutshell, the rule of men, rather than the rule of law, still prevails over the anti-corruption campaigns. The role of law in anti-corruption campaigns is further compromised by the selfish motivation of the CCP leadership. As often reported in the press, the anti-corruption campaign has been used to bring down the opposing forces. One typical example is the Chen Xitong case. On the other hand, loyal followers, even if they were involved in corruption, are exempted from criminal prosecution. The selective punishment in the anti-corruption campaign gives ordinary people the impression that the administration of justice is not fair, which obviously damages the authority of law.[17] Nevertheless, it should be noted that the change of method in fighting graft from using mass movements to the current reliance on law is remarkable progress for the CCP. Thus, despite the limitation, the law is still needed to combat corruption. In terms of legislation, some laws are necessary in the future, such as the Law of Supervision, Law on Corruption, and Law on Property Reporting of Officials. The NPC has included a supervision law in a list of laws it plans to make by 2003. The law will spell out how China should monitor corruption.[18] In terms of law enforcement, the success of the on-going judicial reform will be critical.

ANTI-CORRUPTION LAWS

There are a number of legal measures against corruption in China. According to statistics, the NPC and its Standing Committee have adopted about 200 laws, resolutions and decisions regarding anti-corruption, and the State Council has also promulgated more than 30 administrative regulations, in addition to specific provisions prepared by the party itself.[19] The most important one is the Criminal Law which was first promulgated in 1979 and later amended in 1997.

The Criminal Law categorises corruption as a crime of property violation and that "State personnel who take advantage of their office to engage in corruption involving articles of public property are to be sentenced".[20] However, the 1979 Criminal Law does not deal with corruption in one clause, but rather contains separate provisions dealing with bribery, smuggling, speculation, misappropriation of State funds and materials allocated for disaster relief, stealing public property or obtaining it by fraud, and extortion involving public property.[21] Before the Criminal Law was amended, some separate laws were promulgated as supplements to the Criminal Law for anti-corruption purposes. The 1982 Decision of the Standing Committee of the NPC Regarding the Severe Punishment of Criminals Who Seriously Undermine the Economy and the 1988 Supplementary Provisions on Punishment for the Crimes of Corruption and Bribery were two major ones. They have been replaced by the relevant provisions enshrined in the amended Criminal Law.

The Criminal Law was substantially amended in 1997 and suppression of the crime of corruption is governed by two specific chapters, though still not in one clause: graft and bribery, and dereliction of duty. Crimes of graft and bribery include embezzlement, accepting and offering bribes.[22] Dereliction of duty is another offence relating to official corruption. It refers to the acts committed by state personnel who abuse their power or neglect their duties, causing great losses to public property and the state's and people's interests. The provisions of the Criminal Law which were applied to the Cheng Kejie case are Articles 385 (1) (on crime of bribery), 386 (on aggravated crime of bribery), 383 (1)(a)(b) (on punishment for graft), and 57 (1) (on deprivation of political rights).[23]

In practice, some problems have arisen from the implementation of the amended Criminal Law. For example, can Article 93(2) be applied to the prosecution of corrupt village heads since the status and responsibilities of village leaders have been unclear? If they are not legally defined as civil servants, so the argument goes, they cannot be prosecuted for corruption. To remedy this, the Standing Committee of the 9th NPC adopted an interpretation of Article 93 (2) of the Criminal Law. The Interpretation does not treat the personnel of village committees as civil servants; but when they, in assisting the government in some administrative work, use their official capacity to illegally occupy public property, embezzle, extort, or illegally accept property from others, they shall be punished under the provisions of the Criminal Law applicable to civil servants.[24] The other amendment to the newly-revised Criminal Law was the 1999 Amendment involving eight articles of the Criminal Law regarding economic crimes. One of them is amended to apply the provisions for the dereliction of duty to the corrupt personnel of state-owned companies, enterprises, and institutions.[25] In addition to the Criminal Law, there are other legal documents designed for the fight against corruption (see Appendix 1).

CRIMINAL PROCEDURE FOR CORRUPTION

There is a statutory procedure for the judiciary to deal with specific corruption cases. The amended Criminal Procedure Law is the main legal basis.[26] Due to some newly-emerged problems resulting from its implementation, the Provisions Concerning the Implementation of the Criminal Procedure Law were jointly issued by the Supreme People's Court, the Supreme People's Procuratorate, Ministry of Public Security, Ministry of Justice, and the Working Committee on Legislation of the Standing Committee of the NPC.[27] The Provisions clarify the scopes of jurisdiction among the court, the procuratorate, and the public security department. The procuratorate has jurisdiction over corruption crimes involving officials (civil servants) while the public security department has jurisdiction over crimes of corruption involving those in companies and enterprises.

When criminal cases investigated by a public security department involve crimes of corruption over which the procuratorate has the jurisdiction, such cases should be transferred to the procuratorate. When both the public security department and the procuratorate have jurisdiction over a case, if the principal crime is one over which the procuratorate has the jurisdiction, the procuratorate should conduct the main investigation with the cooperation of the public security department, and *vice versa*. Detention and arrest should be carried out by the public security department. In cases where the procuratorate approves the arrest, the public security department should immediately execute the decision and promptly inform the procuratorate of the execution.

In practice, when the procuratorate has obtained allegations of corruption, it begins the preliminary investigation, which is not open. When the procuratorate thinks that there are criminal facts which should be subjected to criminal liability, it then puts the case on file. Some compulsory measures, such as house arrest, detention, and custody, will then be taken, usually in co-operation with the public security department.[28] However, for some cases, particularly those involving high-ranking officials, the committee of the discipline inspection intervenes first for the preliminary investigation. Cheng Kejie's is a case in point. In August 1999, the CCP Central Committee decided to launch an investigation. It was only on 25 April 2000 that Cheng was placed on the Supreme Procuratorate's file and formally arrested, after being stripped of all his official positions.[29] The ongoing "*Yuanhua* smuggling case" was also first handled by the CCDI.

To coordinate the anti-corruption work among various departments, the Supreme People's Procuratorate, Ministry of Public Security, and eight other ministerial departments jointly issued the Opinion on Strengthening the Co-ordination and Co-operation in Establishing the Handover Mechanism in Dealing with Malfeasance Cases in 1999.[30] For the co-operation between the courts and procuratorates, there is the Opinion on the Establishment of a Co-ordination System between the Supreme People's Court and the Supreme People's Procuratorate adopted in 2000.

OTHER ANTI-CORRUPTION MEASURES

In 1987, the Ministry of Supervision was re-established as a functional department of the State Council with special administrative powers to deter corruption in the government. Its main responsibilities include monitoring the performance of government departments and supervising state administrative organs and their personnel, as well as leading cadres of state enterprises and institutions appointed by state administrative organs.[31] The Interim Provisions on Administrative Sanctions for Corruption and Bribery of Personnel of State Administrative Organs in 1988 granted the Ministry of Supervision the power to impose administrative sanctions. The supervisory organs also have the power to turn law-breakers over to the judiciary for prosecution if they believe the law-breakers have committed crimes. According to the Proposals of the Ministry of Supervision on Arrangement of Supervision Work for the 1999 Law Enforcement Year, the supervision departments at all levels should carry out the law enforcement supervision, which is one of the basic functions of the supervision departments and also an important measure to prevent and control corruption.[32] The Ministry of Supervision also prepared in 1999 the Interim Provisions on Handling of Infractions of Administrative Regulations by Supervisory Organs.

Some of the anti-corruption measures are not strictly laws, but political and disciplinary norms formulated directly by the CCP or jointly by the CCP and governmental agencies. The Central Commission for Discipline Inspection was re-established in December 1978. Since then, it has prepared numerous disciplinary documents aimed at curbing corruption (see Appendix 2). The latest one is the Regulations on the System of Responsibility to Build up party's Atmosphere and Clean Government jointly issued by the CCP Central Committee and the State Council in late 1998, providing for the party committee, government and the leading team in functional departments to take charge of the building up the party and clean governance. Thus, unlike other fields, the anti-corruption measures are drawn from two sides; one from the law and the other from party documents. Such double regulation, on the one hand, reinforces the effectiveness of the anti-corruption struggle, but on the other hand, it decreases the role of law in the anti-corruption campaigns since on many occasions, party documents are regarded as more important than statutory rules.

Nevertheless, in view that corruption involves criminal and non-criminal elements and some corrupt acts are not subject to punishment by law, party documents are very helpful to curb non-criminal corruption.

After the severe punishment of Cheng Kejie and Hu Changqing, the Chinese leadership seems to have strengthened the anti-corruption campaign nationwide. An ensuing document, jointly issued by the CCP Central Committee for Discipline Inspection, the CCP Central Propaganda Department and the CCP Central Organisation Department, was the Opinion on the Alerting Education for the Party Members and Cadres by Using the Paramount Typical Cases of Hu Changqing and Cheng Kejie in 2000. The document was used to educate leading cadres above the county level in the third quarter of 2000 in a further step to crack down on corruption.[33]

RECENT MEASURES WITH ECONOMIC LEVERAGE

Meanwhile, economic sanctions are also necessary for the crackdown on corruption since economic benefits provided the original momentum for the spread of corruption. The National Audit Office has prepared a plan to audit all government and Party officials, including those at ministerial level, when they leave their posts. According to the plan, the auditing system focuses on two things: (1) an investigation to determine whether or not the official has ever violated the country's financial regulations and rules; and (2) an attempt to establish whether or not the official has fulfilled his/her duties. One of the aims is to help uncover clues of corruption and to act as a warning to officials who are still in their posts. While the problem of corruption cannot be solved by this post-departure audit, given that there are a number of difficulties in implementation, the audit system can still play an important part in the anti-corruption campaign.[34]

The other economic measure is the "two separate lines in revenue and expenditure" (*shouzhi liangtiao xian*). The main points of this system are as follows: (1) all items and standards for fees must be approved by the State Council or the government above the provincial level; no unauthorised items for fees shall be made, and the scope of fee-collecting should not be expanded; (2) when charging fees or fines, the unified receipts printed by the central or provincial financial departments should be used, and certificates of identify should be shown; (3) collecting of fees and fines should be made strictly in accordance with the law, and fine-collecting and fee-collecting should be separate; (4) the opening of bank accounts should be approved by finance departments and the people's bank; no bank account should be made without authorisation and no "small treasuries" (*xiaojinku*) should be established in private; (5) all administrative fees and revenue based on fines should be handed over to the national treasury; no amount should be taken in secret; (6) when arranging the budgets for the law enforcement departments, the finance departments should separate the hand-over administrative fees and revenue from fines from their expenditure, and the administrative fees can be used in priority for the necessary expenditure of any relevant work.[35] It is another important measure to prevent and control corruption from the source.

ADMINISTRATIVE MEASURES

The latest measures to combat corruption in China include the reform of personnel and the introduction of a rotation (*lungan*) mechanism in the civil service. In 1996 the Ministry of Personnel prepared the Provisional Measures of Position Change among Civil Servants in accordance with the Regulations of State Civil Servants. Based on these measures, from 1996 to the end of 1998, 400,000 civil servants in 27 provinces undertook the rotation. The mechanism has proven to be effective in reinforcing the supervision of civil servants, and in enhancing the vitality, efficiency and cleanness of the governmental organs. It is an important measure in preventing the breeding of corruption.

For the reform of personnel, the Reform Programme to Deepen the Cadre System of Personnel in 2000 is an important document. The following actions will be taken in the Programme: (1) reinforcing the work of open selection of leading cadres and of allowing official positions to be taken by competition; (2) introducing the open show system (*gongshi zhi*) for leading cadres before taking the position; (3) taking various measures to resolve the problem of cadres stepping down; (4) developing cadre work exchanges; and (5) reinforcing the supervision of the work of selecting and appointing leading cadres and other cadres.[36] The last measure is aimed at reducing corruption in the personnel system. However, it should be pointed out that though the above reform of the personnel system is necessary, other measures should also be implemented, such as adequate pay for civil servants and improving the civil servant recruitment system. Transparency International's Corruption Perceptions Index and Bribe Payers Index show that bribe-taking in many developing countries is extensive, primarily because of low public salaries, and senior public officials' and politicians' *de facto* immunity from prosecution.[37] The professionalisation of the civil service is thus a key element in curbing official corruption. In that case, high-ranking governmental officials should be appointed through the open recruitment system rather than by the CCP Department of Organisation whose operation is often shrouded in secrecy.

APPENDIX 1: ANTI-CORRUPTION REGULATIONS

- Interim Provisions Governing Disciplinary Sanctions against Corrupt Functionaries of State and Administrative Organs, 1988;
- Explanation of the Supreme People's Court and Supreme People's Procuratorate Regarding Matters Relevant to the Implementation of "the Supplementary Provisions for the Suppression and Punishment of Corruption and Bribery", 1989;
- Notice of the Supreme People's Court and Supreme People's Procuratorate Calling for the Offenders of Corruption, Bribery and Speculative Activities to Voluntarily Surrender and Make Self-Confession to the Judicial Organs within the Specified Time Limit, 1989;
- Detailed Opinions on the Supreme People's Court and Supreme People's Procuratorate on the Implementation of the Stipulations in Article 2 of the "Notice", 1989;
- Official Reply of the Supreme People's Court and Supreme People's Procuratorate on Matters Relevant to the Implementation of the "Notice", 1989;
- Circular of the Supreme People's Procuratorate on Relevant Matters Concerning Application of Law Handling Criminal Cases of Personnel of Companies and Enterprises who Take Bribes, Seize or Misappropriate the Funds of Companies and Enterprises, 1995;
- Circular of the Supreme People's Procuratorate on Further Strengthening the Handling of Cases of Malpractice for Personal Gains, 1995;
- Circular of the Supreme People's Court on Printing and Distributing Several Provisions Regarding the Correct Application According to Law of Probation to Criminals of Embezzlement, Bribery Acceptance and the Appropriation of Public Funds, 1996;
- Explanation of the Supreme People's Procuratorate on Several Matters Concerning the Application of Law in Handling Cases of Favouritism, 1996;
- Interpretation of the Supreme People's Court on Issues Related to Specific Application of Laws to Trying Cases of Illegal Appropriation of Public Funds, 1998;
- Decision of the Supreme People's Procuratorate on Several Issues of Anti-Corruption Work by the Procuratorates, 1999.

Source: compiled by the author.

APPENDIX 2: ANTI-CORRUPTION POLITICAL DOCUMENTS

- Opinion on Severely Punishing Economic Criminals, 1983;
- Interim Measures on Severely Punishing Communist Party Members Who Have Violated Laws or Party Disciplines in the Economic Field, 1983;
- Notice Requiring Communist Party to Comply with Professional Ethics in an Exemplary Way, 1987;
- Decision on Firmly Dealing with Communist Party Members Who Extort Bribes, 1988;
- Interim Regulations on Disciplinary Punishment for the Party Members and Leading Cadres Who Have Committed Severe Bureaucracy and Dereliction of Duty, 1988;
- Interim Regulations on Disciplinary Punishment for the Communist Party Members Who Have Violated Party Disciplines in Foreign Activities, 1988;
- Certain Provisions on Punishing Party Members Who Have Breached the Socialist Ethics (Trial), 1989;
- Certain Provisions on Disciplinary Punishment for Communist Party Members Who Have Violated Laws or Party Disciplines in the Economic Field, 1990;
- Provisions on Disciplinary Punishment for Party Organisations and Party Members Who Have Hampered the Investigation of Cases, 1990;
- Regulations on the Work Case of Inspection of the Chinese Communist Party Discipline Inspection Organ, 1994.

Source: compiled by the author.

ENDNOTES

1 See "Nation moves boldly forward", *China Daily*, 6 March 2000.

2 See Chen Wuming, "The Characteristics of the Rampant Corruption and Its Grave Harm", *Seeking the Truth* (in Chinese), 2000, No.8, p. 27.

3 "Major Corruption Cases", *Beijing Review*, 22 May 2000, p. 14.

4 See *People's Daily* (in Chinese), 15 September 2000, p 1.

5 Hu Changqing, former vice-governor of the provincial government of Jiangxi Province, was sentenced to death on 15 February 2000 and was executed on 18 March 2000 for his request and acceptance of large bribes.

6 Cheng Kejie, Vice-Chairman of the Standing Committee of the National People's Congress, was sentenced to death on 31 July 2000 for accepting bribes and executed on 14 September of the same year. He was the first and highest-ranking official to be punished for corruption in PRC history.

7 See Chen Wuming, "Curbing Corruption: A Juncture Which Must be Leaped Over", *Outlook Weekly* (in Chinese), 7 August 2000, 27-28; and Liu Chun, "An Analysis of the Characteristics of China's Corruption in the 1990s", *Orient* (in Chinese), 2000, No.3, 8-9.

8 See Li Ming, "City beefs up anti-graft drive", *China Daily*, 22 April 2000. It is noted that RMB1 million in a corruption case is a huge amount in China when we compare it with the normally low salaries of around RMB2,000 a month for high-ranking civil servants. On the other hand, this amount is only the tip of the corruption iceberg in China and in some cases, the amount of funds would run up to thousand of millions of RMB.

9 For details, see R. Klitgaard, "Subverting Corruption", *Finance & Development*, June 2000, 2-5.

10 The "three stresses" campaign was initiated in 1999 and continued in 2000. It was an effort to revitalise party identity, but could not achieve its goal. See Zheng Yongnian, "The Politics of Power Succession in Post-Deng China", *Asian Journal of Political Science*, Vol.8 (1), 2000, p. 27.

11 Zhong Jixuan, "Reflections on 'Governing the Country by Heavy Punishment'", *People's Daily* (in Chinese), 29 March 2000, p. 4.

12 Michael Levi, "Stealing from the People", *China Review*, Issue 8, 1997, p. 9.

13 Klitgaard asserts that it is impossible to eliminate corruption entirely, that the best any government can do is balance various considerations and determine its own "optimal level of corruption". See R. Klitgaard, *Controlling Corruption* (Berkeley: University of California Press, 1988), p. 24.

14 Li Rongxia, "Inflicting Severe Punishment on Corruption", *Beijing Review*, 22 May 2000, p. 13.

15 Ibrahim Shihata, "Corruption - A General Review with an Emphasis on the Role of the World Bank", *Dickinson Journal of International Law*, Vol.15, 1997, p. 467.

16 See Huang Bailian, *Curbing Corruption: Study on the Procedure and System of Democratic Supervision* (Beijing: People's Publisher, 1997)(in Chinese), p. 92.

17 It is reported that the Chinese leadership has prepared a list of more than 170 corrupt high-ranking officials who are protected from criminal punishment. See Lu Zijing, "Document on the Selective Protection of Corrupt High Ranking Officials", *Cheng Ming* (in Chinese), 2000, No.9, 17-18.

18 Shao Zongwei, "Public asked to help stop corruption", *China Daily*, 15 March 2000.

19 See Liu Jinguo, "Legal Constraints to Power Corruption", *Chinese Legal Science* (in Chinese), 2000, No.1, p. 47.

20 Article 155 of the 1979 Criminal Law. English text is available in Ralph H. Folsom & John H. Minan (eds.), *Law in the People's Republic of China: Commentary, Readings and Materials* (Dordrecht: Martinus Nijhoff Publishers, 1989), 995-1022.

21 Articles 118-119, 126, 152, and 185 of the 1979 Criminal Law.

22 Text of the amended Criminal Law is reprinted in Peng Liming (ed.), *Compendium of the Current Laws of the People's Republic of China* (Beijing:

China Building Materials Publishing House, 1998) (in Chinese), 389-460. The crime of graft is contained in Chapter 8 which has 15 clauses.

23 See Liu Shiyang, "Legal Basis for the Sentencing of Cheng Kejie", *People's Daily* (in Chinese), 15 September 2000, p. 2.

24 The text of the interpretation is reprinted in *Gazette of the Standing Committee of the National People's Congress of the People's Republic of China* (in Chinese), 2000, No.3, p. 223.

25 Text is available in *Gazette of the Standing Committee of the National People's Congress of the People's Republic of China* (in Chinese), 1999, No.7, 694-696.

26 It was first adopted in 1979 and amended in 1996. The amended Law came into effect on 1 January 1997. Text in Peng, *supra* note 22, 355-388.

27 Text (both in Chinese and English) in *China Law*, issue of 30 June 1998, 110-112; and issue of 15 September 1998, 111-113.

28 See "Decision on Several Issues of Anti-Corruption Work of the Supreme People's Procuratorate", in *Communique of Supreme People's Procuratorate of the People's Republic of China* (in Chinese), 2000, No.1, p. 17.

29 See "Destruction of a High Rank Leading Cadre", *People's Daily* (in Chinese), 15 September 2000, p. 2.

30 Text in *Communique of Supreme People's Procuratorate of the People's Republic of China* (in Chinese), 2000, No.2, 20-21.

31 See Helena Kolenda, "One Party, Two Systems: Corruption in the People's Republic of China and Attempts to Control It", *Journal of Chinese Law*, Vol.4 (2), 1990, p. 215.

32 See *Gazette of the State Council of the People's Republic of China* (in Chinese), 1999, No.14, p. 563.

33 Xinhua News Agency, 31 July 2000, available at http://www.peopledaily.com.cn/GB/channel1/10/20000731/166731.htm (accessed: 25 August 2000).

34 See Liu Weiling, "New Move to Fight Graft", *China Daily*, 21 August 2000. It is reported that since April 2000, the National Audit Office has audited the leaders of six major financial institutions when they left their posts. See Wang Ying, "Graft war targets the top", *China Daily*, 27 October 2000.

35 See Circular of the National Audit Office Concerning Further Implementation of the Regulations on "Separation Between Revenue and Expenditure", *Gazette of the State Council of the People's Republic of China* (in Chinese), 1999, No.28, 1999, 1216-1218.

36 See "The Programme on Deepening the Reform of Cadre Personnel System", *People's Daily* (in Chinese), 21 August 2000; and also see "To Provide the Systematic Guarantee for the Building of Cadre Team with High Quality", *Legal Daily* (in Chinese), 23 August 2000.

37 Jeremy Pope and Frank Vogl, "Making Anticorruption Agencies More Effective", *Finance & Development*, Vol.37 (2), June 2000, at page 6.

CHAPTER 4

To Act or Not to Act: Policy Implementation at the County and Township/Town Levels in China*

ZHONG YANG

Entering the 21st century, the Chinese government once again faces serious challenges from its rural areas. A deteriorating rural economy and declining incomes amongst peasants have caused serious concerns for rural stability. Worsening economic conditions in the rural areas have been exacerbated by a static governmental structure and lack of political reforms at the local government level. A limited degree of democratisation, such as village committee elections introduced since the late 1980s, has not proven effective in solving rural political problems. Peasant riots and disturbances are now common in rural areas, even though occurrences are usually spontaneous and poorly-organised.[1] In fact, rural problems have become so acute that the Chinese central government's top policy priority in 2001 was to improve rural living standards.[2] To understand the rural situation in China attention has to be given to institutional arrangements and policy implementation processes at the local level.

Chinese county and township governments have rarely been studied systematically as an independent subject by China scholars in the West. Local politics in the People's Republic of China (PRC) is mostly studied in association with the study of central-local relations, the object of which is still the central government. In fact, in China studies the term "local government" often refers to provincial government. "Localism" and "regionalism" are often used interchangeably. The lack of attention given to government at the county and township levels is due primarily to three factors. First, there is a long-standing tradition in China studies of focusing on the centre, including its institutions and elite, to address topics such as the transformation of party and governmental institutions, elite power struggles and questions of official ideology, etc. A second factor is the focus on politics at the macro level. Studies of political change in the PRC have tended to deal with big issues: civil society, democratisation and the path of economic reforms. A third factor lies in the difficulty in conducting empirical studies at the local level, due to the lack of access to the localities, funding shortages and the need for spoken language skills in carrying out field research.

This chapter is a study of local government and politics in the PRC during the reform era. "Local government" in this paper refers to government at both the county and township levels. I believe that local government at these two levels deserves more attention than it currently receives in the bulk of scholarship on China, for three reasons. First, economic reform and decentralisation in the last decade have brought about profound changes in local government and politics, and they may provide crucial clues as to where China's future development is heading. Second, politics at the county and sub-county levels has its own dynamics that may be different from politics at the central or provincial levels. Third, local government officials at the county and township levels are the foot soldiers and functionaries of the central government in actually governing over 70 percent of the PRC's population. Any study of political, social and economic changes in China that does not touch upon the rural areas cannot provide an accurate and complete picture of these issues and changes.

LITERATURE ON CHINESE LOCAL GOVERNMENT

The Totalitarian Model and the Authoritarian Model

One of the most powerful models for studying communist systems, including the Chinese system, is the totalitarian model that became very popular in the early days of the Cold War. The best-known version of this model was put forward by Carl Friedrich and Zbigniew Brzezinski in the mid-1950s. They stipulated six essential features of the totalitarian system: an official ideology, a single mass party, a system of terrorist police control, a technologically conditioned near-complete monopoly control of all means of mass communication, a near-complete monopoly control of arms and central control and direction of the entire economy.[3] This model quickly came under fire in the late 1950s and early 1960s after Stalin died. A major criticism was of the static nature of the model. In other words, the model did not allow for any changes in the communist system, and failed to explain the dynamic changes that occurred in the Soviet Union from Khrushchev's era.[4]

The totalitarian model was often cited in describing Maoist China, even though many people questioned whether China had a terrorist system of police control under Mao. The implication of this model for local government studies in China was obviously that, if China had a totalitarian system, then local government was merely responsible for handing down the central government's decisions.[5] In that case, there was little need to study local government itself. However, it is highly debatable whether the central government in Beijing has ever achieved complete control over the lower levels of government. Such control certainly did not exist during the Cultural Revolution. Moreover, there were several major efforts towards decentralising the system between the 1950s and 1970s due to economic inefficiencies stemming from the centralised system such as the waste of resources, rigidity and the lack of local initiative. These decentralisation moves reduced the authority of the central government.[6]

In post-Mao China, the totalitarian model has proven even more inadequate for studying central-local relations. Even though debate still exists about whether China remains a totalitarian state or has been transformed into an authoritarian state, most observers believe that there have been significant changes from Maoist to post-Maoist China, particularly in ideology, economy and social and political control of the population.[7] Terms such as "fragmented authoritarianism" and "sporadic authoritarianism" have been used to describe the political system in post-Mao China.[8] Indeed, after over a decade of administrative and economic reforms, the once mighty centre (*zhongyang*) has become increasingly remote and less relevant for many localities (not just the coastal regions) in the PRC. More than ever in the history of the PRC, the old Chinese saying–"the sky is high and the emperor is far away"–accurately depicts the attitudes of Chinese local officials. Studies of central-local relations in China show that central government policies are often ignored. Provincial governments set up barricades to stop goods coming in from other provinces, and local government officials are more interested in building "dukedom economies" (*zhuhou jingji*) than carrying out centrally-directed economic plans.[9] The traditional control instruments such as ideological requisites and central planning mechanisms have been significantly weakened. As a result, the mobilisation capability of the centre has been reduced.

Yet the various forms of the authoritarian model, either fragmented or sporadic, still fail to delineate between areas in which the central government is ineffective and areas in which it controls local governments and mobilises them for policy support and implementation. Moreover, they do not identify the types of mechanisms that the centre uses to ensure that its policies are implemented, especially at the county and sub-county levels. After all, the PRC is still a unitary state, and the central government in Beijing still wields significant power over local governments. Simply put, the authoritarian model has been successful in portraying what is not working in central-local relations in the PRC during the reform era, but has failed to point out what is still working.

Literature on Central-Local Relations

The most useful literature to study in terms of Chinese local government and politics is probably that on decentralisation. In fact, central-local (mostly central-provincial) relations have become a fashionable topic in China studies in recent years.[10] The focus of these studies in the 1980s was overwhelmingly decentralisation (i.e., the delegation of power from the central government to the provinces). These studies tended to look favourably on decentralisation policies; after all, excessive centralisation prior to Deng's reforms was identified as a major cause of the country's economic stagnation. The centre was encouraged to provide more incentives for the provinces to come up with local initiatives and innovations.

Since the 1990s, however, the tone in the studies of China's central-local relations has changed. The predominant view is that, after a decade of decentralisation, the centre is losing control. In particular, the central government is depicted as losing fiscal control, thus causing the overall decline of state capacity. Wang Shaoguang and Hu Angang found that between 1978 and 1992 the central government tax base shrank from 31.2 percent of total GNP to 14.2 percent, even though China's GNP was actually growing at 9.5 percent annually.[11] This runaway regionalism and level of decentralisation implies the possibility of chaos and disintegration.[12] The assessment of the decline of effectiveness in China's political system has achieved what has been described as a state of "consensus" among China scholars.[13]

There are several problems in applying central-local relations literature to the study of local governments in the PRC. First, there has been a tendency to focus on the provincial authorities as "local" government when studying central-local relations. However, below the provinces and the four provincial-status municipalities (Beijing, Shanghai, Tianjin and Chongqing), there are cities, counties, townships, work units and villages that perform governmental duties. When the literature argues that the provincial government is gaining power, does this mean that the sub-provincial level governments have also gained more power? What is the relationship between the provincial government and subordinate units? What is the relationship between county-level government and township-level government? The exclusive focus on provincial government obviously does not tell the whole story.

Second, these studies tend to assume that central-local relations are a zero-sum game. By this logic, gains by provinces and localities are necessarily a loss for the central government. If the local government has gained power, then the central government must have lost power. The relationship between the centre and the provinces is often described in confrontational terms. A crucial point often neglected is that decentralisation has been a strategic move on the part of the central government. Decentralisation in post-Mao China was granted and directed by the centre to spur economic development. In other words, decentralisation in China is a process controlled from above, rather than a spontaneous or a free flow process. The centre decides what to centralise and what to decentralise. By and large, the PRC is still very much a centralised unitary state. As Dorothy J. Solinger has pointed out, "though the game may have changed slightly, it is still the centre that defines its rules and could, presumably, change them once again".[14]

Third, studies of central-local relations tend to focus on the centre or are at least centre-oriented. The centre, its policies, its institutions and its status in the reform era have been given predominant attention. As a matter of fact, when people talk about the decline of state capacity or state power or the effectiveness of China's political system, they are referring to the centre as if the sub-national-level governments are not part of the governmental machine or state apparatus. County and township governments are clearly important governmental bodies in the PRC. They, instead of the central government, actually govern China on behalf of the central government. Farmers and township and town residents interact with the local government, and the local government in their mind represents the central government in Beijing. Therefore, more locally-oriented studies of local governments in the PRC are necessary.

Fourth, too much attention has been paid to the negative aspects of the decentralisation process in China's reform era. The central government's power loss is treated as being by definition undesirable for China's economic development and having the potential to lead to chaos.[15] There definitely have been negative consequences resulting from the decentralisation process in the last decade. However, we should not overlook the benefits that have come from the process. Much of the tremendous economic growth in the PRC in the reform era comes from two sectors: the non-state owned township and village enterprises (TVEs) and foreign investment, both of which have gained substantially from decentralisation and are heavily involved with Chinese local governments. The rapid development of TVEs has particularly benefited from property rights protection, funding support and preferential policies that have been provided by local governments. In many cases, the local government has become a bargainer on behalf of local non-state sectors (primarily TVEs).[16] By contrast, the centre-controlled state sector has slowed the country's overall economy due to its low efficiency and negative profit margins in at least one third of the state-owned enterprises.

Finally, studies of central-local relations tend to be preoccupied with the fiscal relationship between the central and local governments, particularly in revenue-sharing areas. Since the principle that "money talks" seems to be the bottom line in analysing central-local relations, these studies unduly neglect other aspects of central-local relations. Central-local relations possess far more than just the fiscal aspect. The role of the party, the cadre promotion system and the organisational structure of local government are important issues, all of which are indispensable variables affecting central-local relationships.

SUGGESTED FOCI IN STUDYING LOCAL GOVERNMENT AND POLITICS IN THE PRC

My main research question in this chapter is as to when and why local government officials comply with policy directives from above. Put differently, what motivates local party/governmental officials to carry out the policies handed down to them? Some related questions include what mechanisms do the higher authorities use to control local authorities? Under what circumstances are local authorities more or less likely to carry out policies that are mandated from above? The answers to these questions are not simple, and I do not pretend to have found all of the answers. To begin to answer these questions, however, special and sufficient attention should be given to three areas: local communist party organisation, the rational behaviour of local government officials and policy issue areas.

Local Party Organisation

One of the measures in political reforms since the early 1980s (some people would rather call them "administrative reforms") has been the attempt to separate the communist party from the formal structure and function of the government of the state. In Deng Xiaoping's words, "it is time for us to distinguish between the responsibilities of the Party and those of government from top to bottom, and promote a better exercise of government functions and powers."[17] The expectation was that through this separation, party officials could concentrate more on party affairs and interfere less in day-to-day governmental business to raise the organisational efficiency of both the party and the government. The rationale behind this reform measure is compatible with a Weberian model of bureaucracy that emphasises functional specialisation and differentiation.

Yet the actual result has been far from satisfactory, as the party remains an intrusive force in every aspect of local government. This is particularly true at the county and township levels, and in public enterprises and village organisations. The lower the level of government, the less is the functional separation between party and the government. The interlocking nature of the party and government has not changed at the county and township levels. In fact, the commanding role of the party at these levels has been strengthened since the 1989 Tiananmen Square democracy movement, an event whose occurrence was partially blamed on the weakened and paralysed city party structure in Beijing and elsewhere.

More often than not, the party committee and government offices are in the same building at the county and township levels. The party is deeply entrenched in government organisations and work units. There is little doubt that the party committee secretary at various local government levels and organisations is the "first hand" or the most powerful person, overshadowing administrative officials such as the county magistrate, township mayor, villagers' committee chair or factory manager. County magistrates and township mayors typically occupy the position of first deputy party secretary, which is subordinate to the county and township party secretary, even though only the county magistrate or the township mayor can represent the government in signing legal documents (such as contracts) and is the plaintiff in any lawsuit. However, any major decision has to be made first by the party committee (the party standing committee, in the county case) chaired by the party first secretary; the government administrative body merely formally adopts the decision and carries it out. Obviously, if anything goes wrong, then the party secretary bears the main responsibility. The promotion of party and governmental officials is firmly controlled by the party. The party secretary's opinion carries great weight in questions of promotion for the county magistrate and the township mayor. The deference of the county magistrate and township mayor to the party committee secretary is also due to the fact that the party committee secretary may be promoted to a higher position and may still be a direct or an indirect superior boss of the county magistrate or the township mayor.

Party secretaries at various levels are heavily involved in economic matters, which is an unsurprising fact given that economic development has been defined and treated as a central political task for the whole party. All major economic decisions are decided by the first party secretary and then the chief formal governmental administrative official. For example, it is common to see county and township party secretaries participating in business negotiations and business trips that promote local products. The division of labour between the party secretary and the chief governmental functionary (county magistrate, township mayor and head of the village council) is often along the line of different sectors (e.g., industrial sector vs. agricultural sector) and different projects. The main reason for the involvement of party secretaries in economic matters is that the party secretary is specifically charged with checking whether economic decisions that are made by the local government and local organisations are in accordance with policies of the higher state authorities. Put differently, the party apparatus at various levels still functions as the watchdog in all aspects of governmental affairs, including economic matters.

Another area in which the local party organisation has firm control at the county and township levels is the local People's Congress. According to the Chinese constitution, the county and township people's congresses are charged with crucial powers such as electing county and township government officials, discussing and making decisions on the most important matters concerning economics, culture, education and public health, etc., and supervising local government operations.[18] Deputies to both county and township people's congresses are directly elected by eligible voters, and serve terms of four years and three years respectively. Deputies to the people's congresses at both levels are supposed to reflect the composition of the local population in the county or township in terms of gender, occupation and ethnicity. Both congresses have to convene at least one annual meeting, which usually lasts two to four days. During the meeting, the deputies approve a working report by the county or township government, rectify the government budget, appoint key county and township government officials, and approve local policy recommendations that are put forward by the local government.

In reality, however, the people's congresses at both the county and township levels have little substantive power in governmental decision-making processes, and are under the firm control of party organs.[19] Many party members still serve concurrently as the chairman of the county and the township people's congress. The key officials in the local people's congresses are local party committee members. The party sets the agenda for each meeting of the people's congress and nominates candidates for the county or township's key governmental posts (including county magistrate, deputy magistrates, bureau chiefs, township mayors and deputy mayors, etc.). In most cases, the people's congress merely rubber-stamps the party-nominated officials. For a while during the 1980s, there were always two candidates for the position of county magistrate and township mayor: the Party set up a straw candidate to make the election appear more competitive and democratic. However, sometimes, when the real candidate was from outside the county or township while the straw candidate was local, the straw candidate won. Therefore, ever since the late 1980s the party has limited its nominations for these posts to one. However, the number of candidates who are nominated for the positions of deputy county magistrate and deputy township mayor sometimes outnumbers the positions available, thereby making the competition a bit more meaningful.

Due to the limited power of the local people's congresses, most people do not take them or their elections seriously. The general meeting of the people's congress each year is often perceived and handled as a burden. Eligible voters usually show little enthusiasm in participating in the election of deputies to the people's congress at either county or township levels, particularly when candidates are chosen by the party. According to the election laws, each election can only be valid when more than half of the eligible voters participate, and each deputy receives at least half of the eligible votes cast. However, due to the low interest levels, government election offices often have to set up mobile ballot-casting stations (*liudong toupiao zhan*) to solicit votes door to door after the first round of voting fails to produce the magic numbers.

In fact, local people's congresses are not the only local organisations over which the party has firm control. All five sets of local authorities (the local communist party organisation, the local people's government, the local people's congress, the local Chinese People's Political Consultative Conference and the local Party Discipline Inspection Committee—the so-called *wutaobanzi*) are under direct control of the local Party secretary. In many cases, a deputy party secretary concurrently serves as chairman of the local Chinese

People's Political Consultative Conference. Most importantly, the local party secretary is in firm control of personnel decisions in all five sets of governmental organisations.

The institutional setting of party dominance presents a paradoxical situation for centre-local relations in the PRC. There used to be three main mechanisms by which the centre controlled local government: party discipline, ideology and the central economic planning system.[20] The latter two have been significantly weakened as a result of reforms over the last decade. The only viable control mechanism that the centre is counting on is party organisation and discipline. This is the main reason that the centre has always stressed the importance of party leadership at various levels of government and organisations, and why the local party organisation and party secretary have been given so much power. Yet this power can easily be abused by local party chiefs, who can effectively build "independent kingdoms" that give them the latitude to disobey higher administrative authorities (even though open defiance of higher authorities is rare) or to drag their feet in carrying out the centre's policies, particularly in the absence of an effective monitoring system. The system is such that few people dare challenge the party secretary's authority. In fact, there are substantial incentives for them to follow their local party boss' orders. County and township officialdom is often a close-knit social group based in part on blood connections. Numerous reports on corruption reveal that officials tend to protect each other, and that subordinates do not dare not speak out against the illegal activities of superior officials for fear of retaliation. In this institutional setting, the party control system becomes a double-edged sword: it can strengthen the centre's control of the localities, but it can also undermine the centre's efforts or ability to bring localities in line. The ways in which this paradox is played out is our next subject.

Rational-Choice Behaviour by Local Government Officials

A rational-choice approach to political interest calculation assumes that Chinese local government officials, like politicians everywhere, are self-interested and that their main interest is to keep their positions and further their political career. *Guanbenwei* or "official-centredness" is a long-held tradition in China. With official positions and titles come privileges, special treatment and respect. In ancient China, even the number of rooms an official could have, the size of the entrance gate to his courtyard and the decorative colour on the doors of his house were officially regulated by rank.[21] The differential treatment given to the officials was not completely eradicated after 1949, even during the Cultural Revolution. In the reform era, official status and power have become even more important due to decentralisation, the weakening of ideology and the deterioration of morality, with official positions carrying possibilities for material gain. Even though China has been developing a market-oriented economy, the economy is still closely tied to power and governmental intervention. *Guanxi* (network of informal connections and relationships) is still the most important asset in getting things done in China, and is intricately linked with governmental offices and positions.

The material benefits or privileges of being a major county or township government or Party official range from free transportation to free housing. It is legal to receive gifts of less than 200 *yuan* in value;[22] this opens the door for much so-called "grey income" (such as food, cloth, cigarettes and liquor, etc). The salaries of county and township government officials are not high, ranging from 400 to 800 *yuan* a month depending on rank. Yet between subsidies and grey income, their disposable income is much higher than their official salary suggests. More serious is the pursuit of illegal income through corruption, which is reportedly running rampant at local levels. According to Wang Renzhong, a former Vice Chairman of the Chinese People's Political Consultative Conference, in 1991 70 percent of local officials at the municipal and county levels were corrupt.[23]

An inescapable impression that one has after visiting Chinese counties and townships is that official positions equal power equal material gains. The associated material benefits alone are sufficient motives for Party and government officials to retain their positions and to seek promotion. In current Chinese local politics an interesting phenomenon is *paoguan*, or chasing after official positions. The most valuable information amongst government officials is who is going to become the next "first hand" (i.e., the party secretary) of the organisation that they work in, or the next higher level organisation. If they know this, they can get a head start in establishing *guanxi* with that official through whatever means possible, often by bribery or by doing favours. *Guanxi* is the most important factor in promotion in the Chinese nomenclature system; job performance comes in second at best.[24] Even an extraordinarily able individual still needs someone at a higher level to introduce them or sponsor them so that they can be noticed. Obviously, such rent-seeking behaviour and abuse of power are major causes of the undermining, compromising and even outright violation of official rules, laws and regulations, many of which have come down from higher authorities or the central government in Beijing. Local *guanxi* networks thus often torpedo central government policies. Moreover, rampant corruption at local levels poses a serious threat to political and social stability in the PRC.

The career development pattern of local officials can be another important factor in predicting their behaviour in office. I classify Chinese local officials into two categories: terminal officials and promotable officials. Terminal officials are those whose careers have reached dead ends and who do not expect to be promoted to higher positions, primarily due to official regulations such as age limits and educational requirements. Promotable officials are those who have the possibility or expectation of further promotion. Township government officials tend to be promotion-oriented officials. A typical key township official (party secretary, deputy secretary, mayor or deputy mayor) is from a rural area and has a high school diploma or a degree from a vocational school. A typical career pattern might involve progression through the following posts: deputy township mayor, deputy township Party secretary, township mayor and township party first secretary. By the time that an official becomes township party secretary, he or she is about 40 years old. After serving as township party secretary, the most likely next stop is a chief or deputy chief position in a county government bureau or a chief or a deputy chief position in a county people's government general affairs office (*xianzhengfu bangongshi*) or county party committee office. Due to their age at this point and their lack of higher education, very few are promoted to deputy county magistrate or deputy county party secretary. Most reach their terminal position on the nomenclature ladder after acquiring a county government position.

Most county government officials are thus terminal officials, with little prospect of being promoted to the municipal or district levels. Amongst the seven to ten county magistrates/deputy magistrates and county party secretary/deputy party secretaries, two or three are looking forward to further promotion, such as county party secretary or county magistrate. Yet most do not expect to be promoted due to the fact that officialdom is pyramid-shaped: the further you go, the fewer are the positions that are available. The most likely candidates for further promotion are those who are younger, have college degrees, and, most importantly, have *guanxi*. It often happens that the party secretary of the county party committee is flown in from the municipal government or even the provincial government as a *zhongdian peiyangduixiang* (promising future leader) to gain experience at the local level so that they can be promoted later to municipal or provincial positions. Those party/deputy party secretaries and county/deputy county magistrates who are not promoted will become chairman/vice chairmen of the county people's congress or county's Chinese People's Political Consultative Conference, which are semi-retired positions, and will hold those positions until they reach the retirement age of 60.

Most, if not all, county government bureau chiefs and deputy chiefs are terminal officials with no prospect of being promoted to the next level. As mentioned earlier, many bureau chiefs and deputy chiefs are former township/town party secretaries, deputy secretaries or mayors and deputy mayors who are tired of working at township/town government levels; they treat their county government bureau position as the last stop of their official career before retirement. Some of the bureau chiefs and deputy chiefs are former military officers. County bureau chief and deputy chief positions are usually viewed as semi-retired positions.

The existence of two types of officials may offer an explanation for the different forms of behaviour of different local government officials. Promotion-oriented officials tend to be more willing to comply and to carry out policies from above, and are less abusive of their official positions. A good example is township government officials, most of whom, as indicated earlier, are promotion-oriented officials. They are in their late 20s and early 30s, and are energetic and forward-looking. Township government is the most basic government level in China. It can be said that township government officials are the frontline foot soldiers of the CCP, dealing with the peasant masses that make up 70–80 percent of China's population. They are often referred to as *fumuguan* or father-mother officials, as they are supposed to take care of all the needs of the people that they govern on a daily basis. They spend much of their time in the villages, supervising the implementation of government policies. There tends to be a higher degree of compliance by township government officials with implementing policies that are passed on to them by the county government, as their promotion depends heavily on whether county officials think they are co-operative.

Indeed, the reason that township government officials work hard and more faithfully to carry out government policies is concern for further promotion. Their only career goal is to be promoted to a county government position and move to the urban centre where the county government is located. A county government position is much less stressful and more stable–a typical government bureaucratic office job. If one is promoted to a position in a more lucrative bureau such as the Bureau of Power Supplies, the Finance Bureau, the Personnel Bureau or the Tax Bureau, then one can certainly expect "grey income". In addition, the urban centres where county governments are located offer more convenient services and better schools. In fact, many key township government officials keep homes in urban towns where the county government is located while they commute to work in the rural areas where the township government is located. The situation that township party secretaries and mayors try to avoid is being rotated around the townships, serving continuously as township officials. The worst jobs for them are serving in positions in poor and remote townships. This treatment implies demotion, even though their official rank remains unchanged.

Terminal officials tend to behave differently than promotional officials by exhibiting more rent-seeking behaviour and being oriented towards local interests. Often of advancing age and reduced energy, terminal officials are more satisfied with the status quo and more focused on enriching self-interest. A popular phenomenon in Chinese officialdom is called the "60 phenomenon", meaning that officials tend to "grab as much as they can" before retiring at age 60, the official retirement age for middle-level and low-level cadres. In fact, such officials tend to act much earlier these days. As soon as they settle in their terminal official position, they use their power for self-gain. A popular saying in China is that "power expires if you do not use it while you have it". This kind of behaviour is understandable, as these individuals are not concerned with further promotion and career advancement.

Issues and Policy Areas

The increasing resistance to and distortion of central government policies at local levels is a major issue in studying central-local relations. However, localism is often exaggerated. It is too simplistic to say that central government policies are always ignored or distorted; central-local relations are much more complicated than that. In particular, compliance varies according to issue areas, and issue areas are intertwined with the rational career behaviour of local government officials. It is safe to assume that in implementing policies from above, local government officials always want to put in the least amount of effort and to achieve maximum results. However, local officials are legally and politically obligated to implement the policies that are passed on to them. Administrative punishment and removal from office are the most effective mechanisms that the higher authorities possess to force local government officials to carry out and comply with central or provincial government policies. This is why open defiance of higher authorities is rare in China. Nevertheless, there are numerous factors, often conflicting in nature, forcing local officials to take into consideration in implementing policies from above. How to skilfully balance the two sets of concerns is an art that local government officials have to master if they hope for career advancement. The issue area then becomes a crucial factor in predicting the behaviour of local officials. We can tentatively divide policy issues into the following categories: crucial, spotlight, guideline, and routine legal and regulative issues.

Crucial issues are the most important policies passed down from the centre; they are often issues that the central government has declared to be top priorities. These policies are usually stipulated in a joint circular of the CCP Central Committee and the State Council. For crucial issues, the higher governmental authorities usually require the direct involvement and accountability of county/township party secretaries. County/township party officials tend to devote their best efforts to carrying out policies concerning these issues. If they make any mistakes in these policy areas, then they may suffer career-ending consequences.

A recent example of a critical issue is the crackdown on Falun Gong. As Falun Gong has been considered by the Chinese government to be the number one threat to social and political stability in China since 1999, cracking down on it has become a top priority issue for all levels of government, from the central government down to all levels of local government. Party secretaries and chief government officials are held personally responsible and accountable for any open Falun Gong activities in their area of responsibility. For instance, if a protesting Falun Gong practitioner shows up in Beijing, then the chief party and government officials in the locale that the Falun Gong practitioner comes from risk losing their job.

Another related critical issue is maintaining local social and political stability. This has been a paramount concern for the central government since the Tiananmen incident of 1989. Due to declining incomes, excessive fee collection, official corruption and the mismanagement of peasants' complaints, public demonstrations, sit-ins and even riots are not uncommon in rural

China. Such events pose serious threats to China's social and political stability. The central government has repeatedly emphasised the importance of this issue. County and township party officials are held responsible if any large-scale social unrest or disturbance occurs in their area of responsibility.

A long-standing critical issue confronting key county/township Party officials is that of population control. In fact, population control is so crucial that it has been treated as a so-called "veto issue", meaning that failure by key county/township party officials to keep their local birth rate under the targeted rate will end their political careers, even if they perform exceptionally well in all other areas. This type of punishment forces county/township officials to pay especially close attention to population control and sometimes to take extreme measures (such as forced abortion and tearing down peasants' houses) to enforce birth control policies. Usually, a deputy county/township party secretary is in charge of population control on a full-time basis. Due to the importance of this issue, county/township party secretaries are heavily involved in monitoring the strict implementation of birth control policies at the county and township levels.

Many crucial issues, such as local economic development and population control (or family planning), are often quantified with specific numerical targets for policy fulfilment because quantification makes it easier to evaluate policy implementation. The evaluation of key county/township officials is becoming more quantitative; targets that are expressed in numerical terms are commonly perceived to be objective and easier to compare. One specific example is the policy issued by the central government that township government cannot collect fees exceeding 5 percent of peasants' income. The purpose of this policy is to reduce the financial burden on peasants.

However, number or quota-based policy evaluation is not without its problems. One problem is that, due to lack of adequate auditing or monitoring systems, county/township party officials are tempted to play the "numbers game" by inflating or even fabricating results, especially when the output quota is exceedingly high or the issue at hand is unusually intractable. False reporting of achievement, especially in economic areas, by Chinese local officials is endemic.

Spotlight issues are those which have been exposed to the public by the media and which have caught the attention of higher authorities. Whenever this happens, local officials act very quickly to stamp out the fire by taking swift action to get the problems solved. An example of this issue is the fake liquor incident in 1998 in Shanxi Province, where several dozen people were poisoned and died. Party Secretary Jiang Zemin read the news in the newspaper and was reportedly outraged. He personally called the provincial leaders and demanded that the matter be dealt with swiftly, and that the people involved be punished severely. Not surprisingly, the matter was indeed solved very swiftly by local officials.

Guideline and slogan issues refer to policies that are passed down from higher authorities in the form of vague general slogans or guidelines without any specific details or figures for fulfilment, using language such as "all levels of government must pay more attention to the welfare of school teachers", "all levels of governmental officials must remain clean and incorrupt" or "all levels of government should foster the growth of private enterprise". In fact, local officials are given leeway to apply the policies according to local circumstances. In many cases the size of the country and variation in local conditions make it difficult for the centre to set uniform standards. Therefore, local officials are encouraged to carry out policies creatively, meaning that they have to come up with detailed policies by and for themselves. At the local level, the general understanding and practice is that anything that is not specifically forbidden is allowed.

County/township government officials often put less effort into carrying out policy directives or even distorting them. As these policy directives are vaguely worded and lack indicators of success, it is difficult to monitor how well county/township officials carry them out. A usual way that key county/township officials handle these types of policy directives is to hold one or more meetings to pass on their "spirit" to all county/township and village officials.

The last issue category is that of laws and regulations. With the legalisation efforts that have been taking place since the early 1980s, hundreds of thousands of laws and regulations have been passed by the National People's Congress, provincial people's congresses and local congresses. These laws and regulations are routinely violated by local authorities due to a lack of a sense of the rule of law, ignorance of the existence of laws and regulations on the part of local officials, and weak monitoring systems on the part of higher authorities. Stories abound of how county/township officials provide favours to people who have connections and money for bribes; how influential local officials are given preferential treatment by local law enforcement agencies; how local government officials fake birth certificates so that under-aged teenager boys and girls can get married; and how their family members and relatives get special treatment in obtaining scarce resources or material benefits. This category of issues is the most problematic area in the policy implementation process at the county/township levels in the PRC.

CONCLUSION

China's stability and economic development depend heavily on the situation in the country's vast rural areas. County/township governments are the most basic levels of governmental authority, and county/township officials are the foot soldiers governing the vast rural areas on behalf of the central government in Beijing. Over the past decade, due to a combination of misbehaviour and corruption by local government officials and misguided government policies, there has been a general and steady deterioration of stability in rural areas. Peasant riots and disturbances are common these days. Fortunately for the Chinese government, these riots and disturbances are seldom well-organised and tend to be spontaneous and incident-driven.

As the challenges from counties and townships mount, it has become increasingly clear that current institutional arrangements at the county/township levels are no longer adequate for solving problems in China's rural areas. The Chinese government is caught in a dilemma when reforming the county/township governmental system: it must establish an alternative system that increases the accountability of county/township officials without undercutting the communist party's ultimate control. The question is primarily one of accountability; under the current system, county/township officials are made responsible to the higher authorities through the apparatus of the communist party. Yet this system is failing miserably in checking the misbehaviour of local county/township officials.

An alternative is to establish mechanisms that can supervise and monitor county/township officials from below. One concrete measure might be democratic reforms of the county/township governments, such as making the county and township people's congresses a genuine representative body that has real power and authority to supervise the county/township governments and government officials. Obviously, any democratic reforms will inevitably reduce the power of the communist party, which is a prospect that the Chinese government is not ready to entertain.

In a recent meeting, the central government put forward a proposal requiring township governments to publicise their affairs, particularly financial affairs, so that the public can supervise and monitor township government.[25] There are serious doubts about whether such reforms will or could effectively improve the supervision of township government and reduce corruption at local levels, as local officials can always manipulate or even cook up numbers for public consumption, as they are doing now for their superiors. Yet it does not look like the Chinese government will conduct any meaningful institutional democratic reforms anytime soon at the county and township levels, even though this may mean the continuing deterioration of local conditions in China's vast rural areas.

ENDNOTES

1 *The New York Times on the Web*, September 17, 2000.

2 *People's Daily*, 13 February 2001, p. 1.

3 See Carl J. Friedrich and Zbigniew K. Brzezinski. *Totalitarian Dictatorship and Autocracy* (New York: Frederick A. Praeger, 1956), pp. 3-13

4 See Stephen White, John Gardner and George Schopflin, *Communist Political System: An Introduction* (New York: St. Martin Press, 1987), pp.15-16.

5 IV Samuel Humes, IV, *Local Governance and National Power* (New York: Harvester & Wheatsheaf, 1991), p. 97.

6 For more on the decentralisation movements in Mao's era, see Zhao Suisheng, "China's Central-Local Relationship: A Historical Perspective" in *Changing Central-Local Relations in China*, edited by Jia Hao and Lin Zhimin (Boulder, CO.: Westview Press, 1994), pp. 19-34.

7 See Sujian Guo, "Totalitarianism: An Outdated Paradigm for Post-Mao China?" *Journal of Northeast Asian Studies* (Summer 1995), pp. 62-90.

8 See Kenneth Lieberthal and David Lampton, (eds), *Bureaucracy, Politics, and Decision Making in Post-Mao China* (Berkeley, CA: University of California Press, 1992), pp. 1-12. Also see Kenneth Lieberthal and Michel Oksenberg, *Policy Making in China: Leaders, Structures, and Processes* (Princeton, NJ: Princeton University Press, 1988), pp. 131-168.

9 See Christine Wong, "Central-Local Relations in an Era of Fiscal Decline: The Paradox of Fiscal Decentralisation in Post-Mao China," *China Quarterly*, No. 128 (1991), pp. 691-715 and "Fiscal Reform and Local Industrialization," *Modern China*, Vol. 18 (1992), pp. 197-237; Susan Shirk, "Playing to the Provinces: Deng Xiaoping's Political Strategy of Economic Reform," *Studies in Comparative Communism*, Vol. 23 (1990), pp. 22-258; and Shen Liren and Dai Yuanchen, "Formation of 'Dukedom Economics' and Their Causes and Defects," *Chinese Economic Studies*, Vol. 25 (1992), pp. 6-24.

10 A comprehensive review and evaluation of studies of central-provincial relations is offered by Chung Jae Ho, "Studies of Central-Provincial Relations in the People's Republic of China: A Mid-Term Appraisal," *China Quarterly*, No. 142 (1995), pp. 487-506.

11 Wang Shaoguang and Hu Angang, *Report on China's State Capacity* (Hong Kong: Oxford University Press, 1994).

12 Edward Friedman, "China's North-South Split and the Forces of Disintegration," *Current History*, Number 575 (1993), pp. 270-274; and Maria Hsia Chang, "China's Future: Regional, Federation, or Disintegration," *Studies in Comparative Communism*, Vol. 25 (1992), pp. 211-227.

13 Thomas Bernstein, "Changing American Concerns about China: From Human Rights to State Capacity," *In Depth*, Vol. 4 (1994), pp. 163-182.

14 Dorothy J. Solinger, "China's New Economic Policies and the Local Industrial Political Process: The Case of Wuhan," *Comparative Politics*, Vol. 18 (1986), p. 397.

15 Wang Shaoguang and Hu Angang's *Report on China's State Capacity* is representative of this school of thought.

16 Zhang Shuguang, "*Guojianenli yu Zhidubienge he Shihuizhuanxing*," *Zhongguo Shuping* (China Book Review), Vol. 3 (1995), pp. 5-22.

17 Deng Xiaoping, "On the Reform of the System of Party and State Leadership," *Selected Works of Deng Xiaoping (1975-1982)* (Beijing, China: Foreign Language Press, 1984), p. 302.

18 Diao Tianding, *Introduction to Chinese Local Government Structure* (Beijing, China: Law Publishing House, 1989), pp. 270-271.

19 For the ineffectiveness of the local people's congresses, see Zhao Baoxu (ed.), *Minzhuzhengzi yu Difangrenda* (Xian, China: Shanxi People's Publishing House, 1990).

20 See Zhao Suisheng, "China's Central-Local Relationship: A Historical Perspective."

21 *People's Daily* (Overseas edition), August 8, 1998, p. 8.

22 Author's personal Interview Project # 9806041.

23 "Ruhe Lushi Minzhu Jiandu Quan," *Xinchao* (Anhui Ribao Press, 1997), p. 84.

24 Author's personal Interview Project # 98060301.

25 *People's Daily* (Overseas Edition), July 26, 2000, p. 1.

---

*This article first appeared in *China's Challenges in the Twenty-first Century* edited by Joseph Y. S. Cheng and published by the City University of Hong Kong Press in 2002. The author is grateful for the permission from the City University of Hong Kong to be reproduced here.

CHAPTER 5

Rural Grassroots Organisations in China: Operating Mechanism and Internal Conflicts[1]

ZHAO SHIKAI,
Translator: YOW CHEUN HOE

Since the introduction of economic reform in 1978, the rural economy in China has experienced drastic changes in terms of its operating mechanism. The grassroots organisations, however, have not made obvious improvements in handling the rural affairs. To some extent, the grassroots organisations still operate under the old regime. There is grave disaccord between the organisations and peasants, as well as within the internal system of the organisations themselves. This chapter argues that the transformation of peasant organisations is a critical way to realising reform.

From their perspective, the rural grassroots organisations have completed their transformation. In practice, however, the old mechanism is still operating significantly and even playing the leading role in most aspects. Rural resources allocation has been increasingly determined by the market economy and the rural society has witnessed a diversification of interests. All these have brought about disharmony in the organisation system, essentially manifested in two aspects. First, the grassroots organisations have downplayed their role of supporting the development of the rural economy and the interests of peasants. Instead, they have more often infringed upon the peasants' interests, thus losing the identification by the peasants with them. Second, intensified structural conflicts have appeared within the grassroots organisation system itself as well as increased system clashes among the organisations. These, apparently, have caused them to be unable to function as expected.

Where the village-level administration is concerned, the main institutions in operation include village-level branches of the Chinese Communist Party, autonomous organisations, and economic organisations. What directly controls and governs the village affairs are actually the local governments in towns and villages. In the context of village, the town-and-village party committee and government are just two of an organic whole. The interconnections and interactions among these institutions have pushed forward the rural socioeconomic development move. During the course of socioeconomic development, however, this system itself is facing a series of impediments. This chapter attempts to examine the relationships among these institutions and analyse the problems that block grassroots organisations from operating effectively.

THE VILLAGE-LEVEL ECONOMIC ORGANISATIONS

Under subcontracting condition, peasant households rely most on the economic organisations that can offer public services pertaining to different parts and fields of processing lines. In the initial stage of the economic reform, these were called "local cooperative economic organisation." (*diquxing hezuo jingji zuzhi*).[2] Later on, they have been commonly called "community-based cooperative economic organisations" (*shequ hezuo jingji zuzhi*). Over the past two decades, the village-level economic organisations have been crucial in policymaking as far as rural economic affairs are concerned. They are defined as fundamental household-based institutions, carrying out both the centralised and decentralised administrations. The main task for them is to provide services for the production matters that individual households cannot handle themselves. They organised small-scale peasant households to realise "socialised massive production" (*shehuihua dashengchan*) and forge the connections between the individually weak peasant households and the complicated and uncertain "big market." The founding of these economic organisations was in consideration if the fact that the villages need not only organisations (such as village committees) to take care of social life, but also those that could provide for the economic activities.

While it was only in recent years that the central government started to emphasise autonomous organisations, the stress on the founding and functions of economic organisations has been repeated throughout the reform period. Even in a number of massive organisation rectifications, there was such emphasis and evaluations. These included the Rural "Party Rectification" in the mid-1980s, the "Rural Socialist Education" in the late 1980s and early 1990s, and the "Rectification of Rural Party Branches" that commenced in the mid-1990s initially for three years but ultimately lasting six years.

Nevertheless, over the past two decades, few village-level economic organisations have performed well, even with the high expectations of and active nurturing by the central government. To begin with, in most villages across China, the organisations are either only nominal or simply absent. In many localities, some signs, usually with the name of "village economic cooperative organisations" were put up but they did not operate as expected. As local peasants say, "three plates and a door, but nobody in the office". Elsewhere, one cannot even find a single sign, indicating that, in many localities, the organisations do not exist independently. Meanwhile, in places where the organisations have put up their plates and have been doing something, there are still some lingering problems. First, the operating boundaries of the organisations are ambiguous and the membership qualifications are unclear. Theoretically, they are supposed to be an institution for those involved in production lines. They, however, turn out to be an umbrella organisation sheltering all villagers; once born, the villagers automatically become members. Thus, the economic organisations overlap other autonomous organisations in villages. The village committees in their own right are autonomous organisations and they should not be confused with the cooperative economic organisations, the membership of which is voluntary. Defining the autonomous organisations as cooperatives will empower the village committees to make use of the identity of the cooperative economic organisation and fully control and govern the activities of the peasants within the given communities. As a result, the peasants would choose to take part in or withdraw from these organisations. In this sense, such organisations will be not much different from the ones in the commune system. Second, the cooperative organisations do not have legal status. Without their own regulations and membership requirements, they are organisations that nobody can delineate clearly. The question prompted here is whether or not at the village level such economic organisations should be allowed to exist. If they should be allowed, why are they hard to develop and how should they develop? If not, then we should reappraise the thinking behind the policy and the design of the organisations that have been around for such a long time.

Where agricultural activities are concerned, the peasants need, in their respective communities, these organisations that can provide services of economic activities. Not long after the introduction of the economic reform, the peasants already started to complain that while officials came to collect money, no one came to serve them. This resentment accelerated in the 1990s. The central government did notice the problem in the initial stage of the reform and has requested some measures to be taken. However, the progress made thus far has been very disappointing.

While public services have not yet fully developed in production fields, the centralisation of administration has increased obviously. Within the framework of the people's commune, the collective production activities were based and centered on production teams. The production teams were the core unit for every commune member in their daily lives, essentially responsible for the allocation of resources and jobs. The implementation of the household system brought about a shift in administration power from production teams to peasant households, a change from below. In other words, the early all-round contract system (*dabaogang*) was a contracting out from production teams to peasant households. After administration was separated from the party, the production teams became villager teams (*cunminzu*) in the new system. Compared to the past, the villager teams at present have lost the functions originally within the production teams. First, the villager teams do not have administrative power, which is now given to the peasant households. Second, the villager teams basically do not have power to govern villagers. According to the Organisation Laws of Village Committee, the villager teams are not first-rank autonomous units. Instead, what is autonomous is the so-called "administrative village" (*xingzhengcun*). The main task for the cadres in villager teams is to convey the requests from the top levels and help collect money and grain tax. In other words, the villager teams are no longer autonomous units among rural grassroots organisations.

Like the villager team as production team (*shengchandui*), the administrative villages as production brigades (*shengchan dadui*) also experienced changes over the past two decades when communes were dismantled and villages were founded instead. Many researchers focus on the historical changes of land contracting and administration delineation, but have ignored the changing features involved. As a matter of fact, the changes of the operation mechanism in the wake of outlook changes have been more profound and brought about more complicated and subtle implications, largely manifested in the increased administrative units in charge of the collective village properties.

First, land contracting power has shifted from villager teams to centralised administrative villages. In the early stage of the household responsibility system, land contracting was allocated within the scope of production teams, and the contracting power rested essentially on the production teams, which at present are called villager teams. Now the power has increasingly shifted upwards to the administrative villages. The Organisation Laws of Village Committee has determined that the villager teams, most of which were originally big production teams, have the power of contracting out land. From the perspective of rural public administration, the centralisation of the land contracting system will do something good for the effectiveness and justice in resources allocation, and it is the direction into which the villages should move. Nevertheless, we also have observed that, during the process of centralisation, collective conflicts accelerated as a result of lacking standards for the behaviour of village-level organisations. For instance, at times the village committees themselves sold the land out from under the villager teams, and in the land contracting cut at their will the boundaries of the land belonging to the villager teams. All these have led to the villager teams' discontent.

Second, the village collective property rights are centralised upwards to the level of administrative village. Presumably, the properties are managed by the village-level cooperative economic organisations. Nevertheless, in most localities, due to the absence of cooperative organisation, the village properties fall into the hands of village committees, which in reality are also incorporating the party branches. Now, with the complete overlap of village committee with cooperative economic organisations, the administrative villages not merely directly control the land contracting, but also have direct power over peasants in terms of administration and tax and fee collection. It is noteworthy that this new phenomenon has appeared.

As far as providing production services are concerned, the main problem confronting the village-level organisation is that it does not function the way it should and has not developed into a sound service-providing institution. In few places, particularly the coastal areas in South China, the organisations have been developing well. In some other places, the economic organisations swallowed up the autonomous organisations, typically reflected in those cases in which the village committees became only one of the departments of the village cooperative organisations. For the purpose of this analysis, there are some issues of particular importance: (1) We should examine the success and failures of the design and implementation of the policies concerning the village-level economic organisations over the past two decades. (2) Do the organisations have the internal logic to develop? If they do, what is the development route they should take on? (3) What are the public services needed by the peasant economically? What are the relations between the public services and autonomy that the peasants hope to see? The studies on peasant autonomy have so far ignored the peasants' need for economic services. For sure, the peasants are very concerned about how the cadres can be clean and how the village affairs can be fair. However, more often they pay more attention to such issues as to who is going to solve the production problems and how they can become well off. We are not sure that democratic elections and a democratic administration can resolve all of these problems. But from the peasants' viewpoint, these are the critical questions as far as the founding and operation of village-level organisations are concerned.

VILLAGE-LEVEL ORGANISATIONS AND VILLAGE-AND-TOWN GOVERNMENTS

If we mark 1985 as the year when the whole of China completed separating administration from the party, it was already 15 years since the people's commune system was abolished. However, a closer examination of the operating mechanism associated with the rural grassroots organisations reveals that the operating system of the people's commune is still prevalent in many aspects.

One of the remarkable features of the people's commune is its power centralisation, with all the activities at the low level having to follow orders from the top level. Both production brigades and production teams were under the direct control of the people's communes. As both administrative and economic organisation at the same time, the brigades were in charge of government departments, agricultural production organisations, and community affairs in villages. Indeed, the brigades were "small governments" with functions encompassing all political, economic, and social matters. Meanwhile, the production teams played a role as grassroots units in the people's communes, with considerable autonomy as far as the production administration and public properties are concerned.

The economic reform brought an end to the production teams and gave rise to peasant households as units responsible for production and commercial activities. With the increased marketisation of economic activities of the peasant households, the autonomy of rural society has expanded. Basically, the reform goal of grassroots organisations has shifted from an emphasis on "control" and "administration" to one of "service" and "support". For instance, in the early period of economic reform, the policies highlighted "double-level administration with centralisation and decentralisation concurrently". In the early 1990s, the focus shifted to "strengthen a servicing system to the society", the important tasks of which were to help fill the needs from the peasant households.

Nevertheless, the present situation shows that the effort made so far has been far less than substantial and fruitful. Compared to the drastic transformation in the rural economic system, the changes in the rural non-economic system have been less remarkable. Where the village-level is concerned, the plates of brigades were pulled down already and the structural functions of the village-level organisations did experience some change. However, in terms of the internal mechanism, the organisations are still an all-encompassing body in charge of party affairs and administrative tasks as well as economic matters. This is largely manifested in the fact that their predominant task has been to carry out and complete all the jobs assigned by the town-and-village governments. More often than not they are solely responsible to the town-and-village governments and become the "quasi-governments" under the latter. In other words, the village committees, which are autonomous with the participation of peasants, in fact have not yet changed the administrative nature of the production brigades. On the other hand, the servicing function towards community members has not yet been fully developed; many things that should be done either have not been done at all or have not been handled well. To use the peasants' words, these organisations "are only wanting money but do not want to work at all" and "the village cadres are increasingly inconsiderate towards the villagers." As a result, it is not surprising that they are losing the trust and support of the villagers. Meanwhile, the village-level organisations have their own difficulties. They defend themselves, saying that they "have done tough jobs that appeared not pleasing (the peasants)" and that "the jobs were not out of their willingness but were instead the assignments from the top level that they could not get away from". To the village committees, they were originally autonomous organisations and were supposed to serve the needs of the community members. However, now they seldom have autonomous affairs and have largely become the administrative instrument of the top-level government.

Why has there been functional failure and job misplacement as far as the village-level organisations are concerned? More specifically, why have they been eager to carry out the tasks assigned by the top level despite the villagers' resentment? The reason lies in the relationships between cadres at the village level (*cun*) and those at the township level (*xiang*). In order words, the town-and-village governments have effective measures to control the cadres in village organisations. To use the official terms of the leaders of towns and villages, the village-level cadres accept the "leadership" of town-and-village governments because "the clear and strict system of goals and responsibilities" has already been set up. The town-and-village governments' grip over the village cadres is reflected in a number of aspects as follows.

First, in terms of organisational structure, the town-and-village-governments attempt to effectively control the village-level organisations so that the village cadres can act as a useful instrument to help them carry out their own policies. More specifically, the governments endeavour to directly command the matters pertaining to the career and employment of the core cadres. In many places, this kind of control is a systematic control over income, adopting awarding and punishing measures that can greatly impinge on the cadres. The regulations involved are exceedingly detailed. For instance, upon the completion of a collective project assigned from the top level, one can receive a certain amount of bonus or deduction; upon achieving a targeted net per capita income, one can be given a monetary award; upon getting a private enterprise (*getihu*) established, one can be rewarded monetarily; within a year, each investment in an industrial project will bring about a certain quantity of award; each illegally-born child and each late attendance at a meeting of town-and-village government will lead to a fine of a certain amount; each complaint received from peasants will lead to fine of a certain amount; and the higher the level of government that receives the complaint that much more will be the fine.

Second, in terms of tasks, the town-and-village governments attempt to impose direct control over the village and demolish the peasant autonomy. It is common that each year the governments usually divide and label the socio-economic development tasks with a number of tangible indicators and assign concrete projects downwards to the villages. Apart from yearly projects, there are projects that need several stages to complete. These include collecting overall fees, purchasing food in both summer and autumn, and the propaganda month of family planning. Once implemented at the low level, some follow-ups will be taken to examine and evaluate the projects and decide awards and punishments. With the direct control operating, the ideal relations of "supervising and being supervised" are hard to establish among the villages. In some cases, the town-and-village governments have exploited the peasant autonomy as an instrument to directly control village-level affairs. For instance, in the elections of a village committee, if they think they need to do purge a cadre, they will hold a real an election. On the contrary, if they are afraid that a cadre will be dismissed in an election, they will make some manipulation in favour of him in the election process and procedures. Under this kind of "supervision", it is hard to imagine how the so-called autonomous organisations could truly be self-governed and have their own rights and power in policymaking.

Third, in some situations, a kind of non-systematic "conspiracy" relationship has been forged between the village-and-town governments and village cadres. This means that the leaders in the governments to some extent indulge the cadres to make use of their power for their own ends and tolerate their misbehaviour in doing their jobs, including coercive acts over the peasants. Without doubt, the cadres in the governments know best the problems associated with the village cadres' behaviour, but the misbehaviour is hard to correct at the grassroots level. The "conspiracy" relationship is firm and strong. Given the lack of internal corrective mechanisms among the village organisations themselves, the top-level departments will pay attention and try to give resolution only when the peasants make serious complaint and the situation becomes radical and critical. Under such circumstances, the social cost to solve the problems will be high for both peasant and government.

Why did some cadres in the town-and-village governments not agree to peasant autonomy? Why did they want to directly control the village-level organisations? They explained, "We have to complete the tasks," "we have our own responsibility system to achieve the goals," and "without the direct cooperation from the village cadres, the village jobs will never be done" and so forth. Compared to the situation in the 1980s and early 1990s, the town and village tasks have "increasingly generated heavy pressure" and "become more and more difficult." In the past, many cadres in the county and city government organs competed to take on positions in towns and villages, but they now consider such transfers disgusting.

The difficulties associated with the tasks in the town-and-village governments are manifested in many aspects such as: (1) to complete financial and tax jobs, which determine the normal operation of the government organs; (2) to achieve economic goals set by the top-level government, which are essential indicators of the accomplishments of the town-and-village governments; (3) to carry out orders from the top-level government to collect fees and accumulate capital; (4) to successfully implement family planning, which is regarded as a national policy; and (5) to collect three reserves and five levies (*san ti wu tong*).

In order to complete the financial and tax jobs so that the governments can go on operating, many governments at times misappropriated the three reserves and five levies collected from villages and even the money essential for the village-level organisations such as public reserve funds, public welfare funds, and administrative expenses. Generally speaking, the financial situation of villages and towns at present is tough and most in the central and western regions and many in the eastern region simply cannot pay wages. Many town-and-village governments' debts increased rapidly over the past few years and many are called "bankrupt governments". Some deputies to the National People's Congress who come from the grassroots organisations made appeals, "We should solve the village-level financial problems as soon as possible. Otherwise the organs are about to paralyse".[3] Some leaders of the town-and-village governments even publicly posed questions as to "How long could our grassroots governments survive?" The factors leading to the financial problems of the town-and-village governments are very complicated and an in-depth analysis cannot be conducted here. Nevertheless, these are the main obstacles confronting the current effort to establish the grassroots organisations.

Since the mid-1990s, the increased number of conflicts in villages have drawn serious attention to village-level democratic election and administration. As a result, village-level democracy has been exploited to solve conflicts that have increasingly caused headaches for the top-level governments. It is of course encouraging that the establishment of a democratic system has received particular attention. However, we should also take note that the accelerated conflicts, particularly those concrete ones confronting the village-and-town government, have deepened the financial crisis, shaken the foundation of trust of the village-level organisations and constituted critical constraints to the development of democracy. No matter how successful the village-level elections turn out to be, it is unlikely that the village-and-town governments' tremendous financial pressure will be lifted. Neither is it likely to reduce the tendency of leaders in towns and villages to pressure the low level for their own political ends. It is not hard to imagine how present village cadres utilise any means, whether appropriate or not, to make the village collective debts soar. Without resources, the newly appointed cadres will not only be unable to pay wages, but also will be worn out from dealing with the accumulated debts left by the former cadres. Under such circumstances, who among the villagers will stand up and take part actively in the elections of village heads? Or, what background will be associated with the ones who participate in the elections? Some places have witnessed a downgrading of the quality of village cadres. A closer investigation will reveal that this is largely due to the fact that the village-level organisations have been getting worse in terms of their behaviour and operation. Thus, we should take note of the economic problems and institutional constraints confronting the villagers' autonomy.

As the present situation shows, the rebuilding of village-level organisations through democratisation depends not only on the internal components of villages themselves, but also rests on how the top-level governments take action to deal with the problems. It is unpractical to think that a village-level democratic system can be established when the political institutions at higher levels (village-and-town governments and even county governments) are still operating the same way as before. Truly-elected village committees will definitely bring great impact to the operation of the grassroots governments, that is, the village-and-town governments. In the past, the village-and-town party committee directly controlled the village-level core cadres and they usually directly appointed the branch secretaries. Directly appointed by the top level, the village cadres are thus responsible for the top level. This is particularly noticeable when the top-level order conflicts with the villagers' needs. In daily administration, the villagers by no means can supervise the village cadres. Once real democratic election is implemented, the power of village cadres, largely the village committee members, will shift from being appointed by the top level to being given by the people. As a result, the behaviour of village cadres will be more in accordance with the villagers' wills. When there is a conflict between the top level and villagers, the village cadres will likely be on the side of the villagers and even resist the top-level governments.

Where the current village-and-town governments are concerned, there is still much restructuring and reform needed. At present, in many places efforts have been made to dismantle villages and merge towns. This will be effective in reducing the number of village-and-town cadres and thus reduce as well the peasants' burden. Nevertheless, this resolution will only change the ratio of the grassroots cadres to peasants, and will hardly alter the operating mechanism. What can be taken into consideration is the abolition of village-and-town finances and even restructuring the village-and-town government into the agencies of the country governments.

VILLAGE-LEVEL PARTY ORGANISATIONS AND AUTONOMOUS ORGANISATIONS

Generally speaking, in the village-level organisation system, the core component is the party branches, with the branch secretaries in charge of everything in the villages. The village-and-town governments will come and consult with the secretaries over everything. As a saying goes, "give award to the branch secretary when there is an achievement, and look the branch secretary up when there is a problem." Among the village cadres, in terms of wages, the branch secretaries receive the highest salary while the village committees and the committee heads get less and play only subordinate roles. In the majority of villages, the villagers take for granted that the branch secretaries are the leaders of the villages. The village heads (*cun zhuren*) need to be responsible for the branch secretaries and be cooperative to work with the latter. With the village cadres being directly governed by the top level, the branch secretaries are given the highest power. This has determined the clear supervisor-and-supervised relations: (1) between party branches and village committees; and (2) between branch secretaries and village heads. These relations have been working smoothly. However, when massive democracy mobilisation and direct elections took place in villages, and when the government attempted to hold elections so as to legitimise the power of the grassroots cadres, a new force from below began and created conflicts with the force from top. Within villages, representing the force from top are branch secretaries, while standing for the force from below are the heads of village committees. Thus, the conflicts between the two power systems at times have been taking place between the secretaries and heads.

With the emergence of village committees elected from below, the conflicts between the two forces are inevitable, though the government documents emphasise the core position of the party branches and secretaries. Even though nobody says the power of party branches should be reduced, the village committees, with the legitimacy based on the people's will, in one way or another interrupts the party-branch-dominated situation and poses a direct challenge to the existing power structure. The village committee members will always claim their own rights based on the laws. In the eyes of both the branch secretaries and village committee heads, there are many crucial things that need the extension of their respective power. For instance, there have been conflicts in the administrative power over properties such as lands and village-run enterprises. In the second round of land contracting, some localities witnessed cases in which the newly elected village heads ignored the party branches and handled their own contracting affairs. Where the administrative power over finance is concerned, the problems have revolved around the right to approve reimbursement. In the past it was the secretaries who signed to approve reimbursement. In order to solve the power conflicts over the question of who has the right to sign, some county governments released documents stating that all reimbursements have to seek approval from both branch secretaries and village heads. Meanwhile, over the human resource issue, the conflicts have increased, particularly concerning the arrangement of such important positions as accountant, storekeeper, and electrician. It appeared that there has been more conflicts in the villages that had more villagers participated in elections. In places where the collective economy is stronger and village-level economic organisations are more developed, the clashes have centered on who should be the leader of the economic organisations. The position can have different names, such as the chief manager of the agriculture, industrial and commercial company as well as the head of the village economic cooperative. Anyway, whoever takes up the position will have the greatest power over the village economy. In some localities, the outcome of the conflicts depends on such personal factors as foundation of power and family background. In some places, some top-level governments, in order to settle the conflicts, have made the decision that all positions should be uniformly taken up either by secretaries or village heads.

Recent years have witnessed the intensification and deepening of the conflicts between the party branches and village committees. They competed with each other on the village-level political stage, and their respective claims and requests reached the top-level departments that they were dealing with. Thus, operating in the system are two different kinds of logic. One is that "the party branch is the core of the leadership" and "the principle is for the party to govern the cadres". Another is that "the villagers have their autonomy based on the laws" and "the party branch should not intervene in the legitimate autonomy".

Based on these two different kinds of logic, there appeared two different forces trying to control the village-level organisation activities. In some places, the leading departments, in order to maintain the authoritative status of the party branches in villages, released documents stating, "The village committees should consult with and report to the party branches about important activities. Without the consent from the party branches, they cannot individually hold villagers meetings. The big events and issues in village should be determined by a joint meeting of the party branches and village committees, with the former chairing the meeting." On the other hand, the village committees strive for their rights based on the "laws." More often than not they have to follow the branch secretaries. As the current situation shows, the conflicts are inevitable regardless of the scale and place of the conflicts. This is an institutional problem and institutional reform is needed to solve an institutional problem.

In fact, many local leading departments have been trying to solve the conflicts between the party branches and village committees. Among others is the "two-vote system," in which the party members receive votes of confidence from villagers. The system was designed originally to strengthen the foundation of villagers' support of the branches and thus strengthen the branches' leading position in the village affairs. The system ended up with repercussions far more complicated than originally expected, which will not be discussed here. Another measure adopted is "one shoulder with all burdens," which combined two forces and appointed one particular person to represent two forces. Some places employed this measure. In Liaocheng *shi* in Shandong province, effort was made to let the branch secretary compete in the election of village head.[4] The argument is that, if the secretary have been given the trust by the villagers, he can "shoulder both secretary and village head jobs." If the votes he eventually obtained are few, it means that he not only cannot be the village head, but he also is not qualified for the secretary position. If the newly elected village head is a party member, then he will be appointed as the branch secretary through the organisation procedures. This measure can resolve the personalised conflicts, that is, eradicate the secretary-and-head conflicts that often happen because of the bad personal relations.

This approach, however, has two problems. First, while the combination of two different forces will, in some situations, enable the person to soundly coordinate both the top and low levels, in some situations he needs to have an inclination. In other words, some will incline to the top level whereas some will incline to the low level. Second, if the votes' supervision is weak or absent, a new "autocratic" leader will emerge. Some localities did witness this problem, where the peasants' discontent with the cadres ended up larger than before the election. Thus, we should continue to observe the concrete effect of this kind of power arrangement. It is more worth noting that, once this kind of election has been institutionalised or adopted more widely in China, it will tremendously impact the village-level party organisations. By then, within the party, grassroots organisations will emerge as a new kind of motivation, that is, the main task will be to ensure that their own candidates win the positions as leaders of the autonomous organisations. Part of the function of the party, thus, will be to transform into an election machine.

Thus, it appears that, in order to coordinate the relationship between party branches and village committees, we have to divide the powers and delineate clearly the activity scopes for them. This is so that the two forces will work effectively in their respective scope, but will never intervene into each other's field. More specifically, this is an institutional reform aiming to truly separate the party from the administration as far as the village-level is concerned. The party branches will retreat from village affairs and never directly participate in and control the process of handling the issues that only the village committees have the rights to address. The role of the party branches is merely to supervise or monitor the village-level organisations.

In the mid- and late-1980s, there was a considerably influential view that the party should be separated from administration only on the top level, but not on the grassroots level. This view was based on the argument that, with so few affairs and tasks in villages, the separation would increase the number of unnecessary officials and reduce efficiency. I have no intention to discuss the question from this angle. The problem does not rest on whether the separation is necessary in such a small scope as a village. Instead, it lies in the adverse implications engendered by the blurred responsibility delineation between the party branches and village committees, the continuity of which will certainly accelerate the conflicts that are now already prevalent and hence affect the village development as a whole.

DISCUSSION: GRASSROOTS ORGANISATIONS AND PEASANT ORGANISATIONS

Grassroots organisations in their own right should have their activities based in communities. However, the above examination of the operating mechanism in reality has shown that the village-level organisations appear more to represent and serve the top-level power institution. More specifically, the town-and-village governments have been adopting direct control over village affairs. During the course of this, the town-and-village leaders confronted with pressure from the top-level government have passed it on to the village-level organisations through constrictive administration. In the meantime, the leaders are pursuing their vested interests. Then, in carrying out the tasks assigned by the top level, the village-level organisations directly transfer the pressure to the villagers and the village cadres add in their own interests as part of the goals of the tasks. As a result, when problems arise in villages, it is hard to identify whether they are due to the organisation structure itself or the morality and behaviour of the cadres involved.

Facing the conflicts and exploitation from the grassroots organisations, the peasants cannot help but accept them. They are discontent and grumble, but most of the time they remain silent. When the time comes, the discontent will lead to individual and even collective resistance from the peasants. That the village tension and conflicts always burst out among the peasants mean that there are some institutional problems in the mechanism of expressing different interests in villages. Though they have autonomy over production and economic activities, the peasants do not have a new mechanism to make their requests heard and their rights protected. In other words, there is no institutional construction in getting their interests organised. Thus, facing the pressure from the top level, the peasants either just accept it and keep quiet, or resort to individual and collective resistance. The question is not whether there is conflict in the village, as conflict can take place under whatever social conditions. The question lies in the lack of institutional solutions to the conflicts. Since the introduction of economic reform in 1978, though the rural economy system has experienced profound transformation, changes have not substantial in the political regime and social administrative system, which are to some extent still similar to the ones of the era of people's commune.

The most effective resolution is to have organisations that can effectively protect the peasants' interests. This will enable the peasants not merely to act individually on the village social stage, but also found independent organisations to interact with other village institutions. As a result, there will be a mutual-balancing mechanism among various village-level forces, which will lead to the realisation of various interests through fair and systematic dialogues and negotiations. Many might not agree with this and instead suggest it would be better if the current grassroots organisations could be "the agency of the government and also the representative of the peasants". However, given the changes in the relations between village-level organisations and peasants since 1978, particularly the many conflicts that took place in villages, we have to admit that the "agency-and-representative" model is a failure, or just playing with words. The peasants need organisations of their own. Or, we should say, the peasants need to represent themselves, and this representation should be organised. This kind of organisation could be not only in the form of autonomous organisations within the community scope, but also should extend to peasant organisations. This is because only the peasant organisations with a broader scope have the leverage to negotiate or deal with other organisations and the capability to resist the clash with the peasants' interests by the organisations that are responsible for the top level. Only then can the peasants can truly protect their own interests in their interactions with other organisations.

ENDNOTES

1 Translated from a revised version of a paper written by the author, "Zhongguo nongcun jiceng zuzhi: biange he wenti", *EAI Working Paper* (Chinese Series), No. 25, 20 June 2000.

2 According the Document No. 1 (1984) by the Chinese Central Government, "In order to fully realise the cooperative system between the centralised and decentralised administrations, it is generally appropriate to set up local cooperative economic organisations based on shared lands. These organisations can be called agriculture cooperatives, economic joint organisations, or with other names chosen by the people. They can base their operation in villages as well as production teams. They can be either separated from village committees or have two names for one organisation. See *Xin shiqi nongye he nongcun gongzuo de zhongyao wenxian xuanbian* (The Important Selected Materials of the Agriculture and Rural Activities in the New Era)(Zhonggong Zhongyang Wenxian Chubanshe, 1992).

3 "The Appeals from the Grassroots Deputies to the National People's Congress", *Nongmin Ribao*, 13 March 2000.

4 *Nongmin Ribao*, 1 December 1999.

CHAPTER 6

Kinship, Village Elections and Structural Conditions in Zhejiang

HE BAOGANG

During village elections, lineage is sometimes used to challenge the party boss and force him to resign. Some villages nominate their own lineage members as candidates and a few of these candidates are even elected as heads of the village. Once in office, these village heads put up opposition to the township government, and will not cooperate with the village party branch.[1]

Worried about the detrimental effect of clan loyalties, some township leaders have pointed out that such lineage ties may undermine the rule of the Chinese Communist Party (CCP) in rural China and pose a serious problem in carrying out village elections. Their argument is that elections will intensify fighting between rival clans. It has been argued that big clans always win elections, and the interests of minority families are often ignored. For this reason, it is suggested by some that village elections should be delayed in villages characterised by the presence of different clans. In such villages, it is argued, elections should not be imposed from above.[2] Is such an argument convincing? Or is it an exaggerated statement? Does a strong clan force exist in all the villages? If so, does it really constitute a serious problem for village elections? Will village elections become an instrument of political control over small clans by big clans? What kind of relationship then does kinship and the village election have in rural China?

Scholars have offered different answers to these questions. Findings from observations made in different areas fall into three categories. First, in some villages, there is no palpable clan influence on the election. Second, in villages where kinship sentiments are strong and farmers are highly mobilised, the election for a village committee tends to be more competitive, as in such villages it is difficult for the township government to manipulate the election.[3] Field studies by Anne Thurston find that big clans tend to be dominant in election, and elections are more competitive in a pluralistic community where institutional and non-institutional bodies, including the clan, vie to play a more significant role in the election.[4] Third, in some other villages, kinship has a negative effect on the election, where candidates from the big clan take all the seats on the committee, much to the disadvantage of the smaller clans. With regard to the question of evaluating kinship impact, Xu Yong admits that kinship may "help village leaders with some of their work and promote a kind of self-restraint among clan members". Nevertheless Xu also believes that kinship would inevitably lead to the erosion of the institutional power.[5] Other scholars also think that the village head will "become a puppet controlled by someone from behind the scene, namely, the clan head".[6]

Answers to the question of how kinship influences elections are diverse and contingent. Different empirical cases tell us different stories, but they offer no conclusive views. Differences amid these findings and views have raised an interesting yet puzzling epistemological question: Which of the above represents a more general trend? It is true that each of the views can be backed up by some case studies and each may hold some partial truth. Yet what we need is an understanding of the general trend rather than a fragmented and incomplete knowledge from particular case studies. Accordingly, this will be the approach taken by this paper. Since most books and articles on village elections so far have focussed on case studies, which in terms of methodology could not possibly yield any solid generalisation, we have chosen to base our study on a number of surveys.

The paper draws on two sets of sources. The first is two surveys in which I organised a research team with the help of Zhejiang University and carried out our investigation within two months, in October-November 1998. We received 1,245 valid responses from the voters.[7] The makeup of the respondents is as follows: 629 from major clans (50.5 percent), 555 from minor clans (44.6 percent), and 61 from unspecified clan background (4.9 percent). We also obtained 111 valid responses from the village head group from 111 villages in Zhejiang province. The second source is the students' filed summer study reports. We organised some third and fourth year students from Zhejiang University to research different aspects of village elections for their summer investigation assignment. We have 40 student reports from 1998 and 1999. The two sets of sources are complementary to each other. The survey results provide a general knowledge but lack concrete examples, while the case studies provide concrete stories of real flesh-and-blood people but do not generate a reliable understanding of general characteristics and trends.

The paper has four sections. Section One describes the revival of kinship in rural China. Section Two presents empirical findings from various case studies on the various impacts of kinship on village election. Section Three describes a general trend through statistical analysis. Section Four examines the economic conditions under which kinship exercises its influence, and the structural determinants of the limit of kinship influence in village elections.

THE REVIVAL OF KINSHIP

It is common knowledge that traditional Chinese society was one with a prevalent clan culture. Clan power used to permeate the governance of the rural community. Some scholars hold that it is common in the rural south, particularly in some mountainous regions, for the majority or even the entire village to share one surname, a situation quite different from that in the north. For example, in his *Social and Cultural Changes in Modern Rural Northern Zhejiang*, Cao Jingqing pointed out that until the mid-1990s, with few exceptions, each of the 3,654 villages of the 23 townships in Haining, Zhejiang, had a common surname.[8] Similar cases can be found in a fairly large number of regions in Zhejiang.

During the reform era, there has been a re-emergence of the clan force.[9] Now, much to the concern of some people, the clan influences not only communal life but also local politics. Factors that have led to the revitalisation of the clan culture include the rural economic reform, the establishment of the responsibility system in production and the loosening-up of ideological control. With the return of the household production model, farmers once again have the land at their disposal, though the state still retains the nominal ownership of the land. On the other hand, the household production model has generated the need for mutual aid and cooperation among peasants. The first person a peasant would turn to for help is always someone of the same clan. Moreover, if he wants to get a job in the city, he may also need help from the family clan or other relations. As a result, kinship consciousness arises.

The revitalisation of a clan culture manifests itself in many ways. The first is the writing of the family or clan genealogical record, which has become popular as kinship relations prove to be important for daily affairs and as the official ideology declines. Overseas Chinese provide another driving force for the activity when they return to their mainland homes for a visit, for resettlement, or in search of family roots. Some township governments encourage the activity, believing that the record writing will help attract overseas investment and boost the local economy. According to a study, during the 1980s, the practice of record-writing was widespread in the rural areas of Yongkang, Zhejiang.

The second manifestation is the rebuilding or renovation of the ancestral hall, where clan activities are conducted and the authority of the clan elders exercised. The house is the symbol of kinship solidarity as well as a physical space for clan gathering. In the 1980s, travellers marvelled at the large number of ancestral houses and temples being built across the rural south of Zhejiang.

The third indication is the revival of clan rituals aimed at promoting clan identity and clan consciousness. One such example is Nanshan, a mountain village where most villagers share the surname *Lin*. Kinship sentiments are so strong there that even today, male offspring are still named in a genealogical order. The 315 *Lin* families constitute an absolute majority in the village. The *Lin* clan has an ancestral hall. At the start of spring, some elders will be elected as ritualists of the year. Major festivals also provide the occasions for ancestor worship.[10]

Finally the fourth indication is clan rivalry and clan fighting. Even top leaders of the CCP Central Committee have expressed their concern when in the early 1990s clan fighting broke out among several villages in Tiantai County, Zhejiang. In 1993, a dispute over the ownership of some woodland between two villages in Cangnan County, Zhejiang, also resulted in a clan fight, in which even explosives were used.[11]

The rise of clan forces has brought about an impact on many aspects of rural life, including the election of the village committee. Consensus on this point can be found in speeches by both central and local leaders, in official documents as well as in academic studies. Before 1994, the kinship issue had been referred to as a "serious problem" with regard to its meddling in and influencing village elections in the official documents of Zhejiang Province.

KINSHIP IMPACT ON VILLAGE ELECTION

Owing to China's large rural population and many differences among its numerous villages in terms of clan culture, economic development and economic structure, kinship impact on the election also varies from village to village. Clan forces have a greater impact on village elections in some villages than others. All field reports demonstrate diverse impacts.

Manifestations of kinship impact on the election are manifold. In the first place, clan culture may have a subtle influence on the villagers' value system. Where kinship sentiments are high, villagers attach great importance to kinship relations and will vote accordingly. Niujiao Village in Fangcun Township, Changshan County, presents such a case. The majority of the villagers there share the surname *Xu*. With a strong sense of clan identity, they think they are all descendants of one great grandfather and they still follow the custom of naming a child according to their own genealogical lineage. Data based on the responses to a questionnaire indicate that 73 percent of the people polled would vote only for those candidates who were from their own clan. The kinship impact had caused concern among some leaders, who thought in such cases "all important political qualifications plus competence for work have been lowered to second place", and "owing to the problematic standard the voters adopted, those elected are not necessarily the best". However, in the same township, a different case was found in Qianxi, a multi-surnamed village with many immigrant villagers. There was not much sense of kinship in that village. When polled, only 3 percent of the people said they would take into account whether the candidate came from the same clan, and no one put kinship as the most important factor in choosing a candidate.[12]

In some villages, clan or faction rivalry was intense and kinship was employed by all sides to seek voters' support. In such cases, the votes could be so scattered that the voting turned out to be ineffectual. Sometimes the election simply could not go on, or it became clan-manipulated.[13] During the 1993 village election, in the northern part of Jiaojiang, Zhejiang, campaigns by rival clans sometimes led to scuffles or even the use of knives. Elections in such villages had to stop.[14]

Kinship impact in Tiantai County was more palpable than in other counties. In some mountain villages there, "kinship sentiments were very strong and contenders vied by every means for votes". The result was that those elected were unable to reach agreement on division of work and responsibility. Some work was left unattended to. In other cases, campaigns ended in violence and elections suffered many setbacks or even came to nothing. Statistics showed that by May 1994, 91 village committees, or 10 percent of the village committees of the county, had only one or two members elected, while 12 villages did not have an election at all.[15]

In some villages of Chengzhou, the 1999 election had to be put off because of clan interference. The Anzai Village of Luxi Township, Lousan of Shihuang Township and Juezi of Ganling Township were some examples.[16] In other cases, strong clan forces made it possible for the clan elders to manipulate the election and hold veto power in the village committee, thus there was the "clanisation of power".[17]

Clan influence had also generated a disparity in the chance of winning between candidates from a major clan and those from a minor clan. During elections, either for membership of the village committee or for the position of village head, the presence of clan influences always favoured candidates from a major clan. According to a study, in the village of Wangzhai, Dongyang, where 90 percent of the villagers shared the surname Wang, all the members of the village committee had the Wang surname. Some villagers complained that voters with other surnames, even though they were permanent villagers, were denied the full rights of election and treated as a minority because their voting was negligible.[18]

In fact, bloodline and in-laws were important social resources in the election. Jing Zhongming's case study of a village in Zhejiang (Summer, 1999) showed how a candidate with a wide network of relations had advantages over those who were without such relations. Candidate A had three brothers and a sister, who was married in the village to a man, who in turn had four brothers. Candidate A also had an uncle, who again had three sons. The votes Candidate A got from his bloodline network and in-laws could be very substantial.[19]

The impact of kinship could be more powerful when backed by wealth. Dujia Village of Shangyu municipality, for instance, was noted for having a high proportion of its economy involved in the private sector. Many of its villagers were engaged in business or rural industry. Consequently the village depended on its wealthy members for the building and maintenance of its infrastructure. The village head elected in 1999 was himself from the wealthiest clan, which had made good money in running a business building. He exerted his influence on village affairs and on the election before deciding that it would be even better if he took the position of the village head himself.[20]

When the election was over, kinship influence could still be felt in the work of the elected body. For instance, in rural areas, it was considered to be of vital importance to have male off-spring to carry on the family name and bloodline. Hence the work of family planning and birth control could be very unpopular in some cases. Wary of a confrontation with their kinsmen, "village leaders would rather leave the work to the township".[21] In addition, some village leaders took sides in disputes between kin and non-kin. The former head of Yangban Village, Tiantai County, was an example. He had been elected mainly because he had money as well as the backing of his powerful clan. Once in office, he was negligent in his work and partial towards his kin. "He worked only for his kin and was unbearably partial", as was said.[22] Some other leaders, with the next election in mind, became hesitant when their work might involve a confrontation with kinsfolk.

So far we have reviewed the negative influence of the clan. Next, however, we will look at some limitations of kinship influence. First of all, some candidates from small clans did get elected, whereas some from major clans did not. This was because other factors, such as a candidate's competence, also contributed to the outcome of the election. Take for example Lizhang Village of Xunqiao Township, in which Zhang was a major surname. The party secretary of the village was a Zhang (the position of party secretary was not open to election), while the village head was a Xu, a non-majority surname. During the 1997 election for people's representatives, Secretary Zhang supported someone from his own clan as candidate, who had returned home as a wealthy man after years of doing business away. The candidate Zhang, however, lost the election though he had all the support from Secretary Zhang, offered many cigarettes to voters and exploited kinship sentiments.[23] Here the outcome of the election was not dictated by kinship.[24]

Kinship sentiments were not manifest in some villages. Even in villages where there was a strong sense of kinship identity, villagers did not necessarily put kinship as the most important factor. As shown in Zhu Genghua's study, in Niujiao Village, Fangcun Township, although 73 percent of those polled said they would take into account whether the candidate was from their own clan, only 9 percent took this as the most important factor. A study (Summer, 1998) by Zheng Rubing of Sanyuan Village indicated that most villagers there simply did not care about the candidate's surname, saying, "Why does his surname matter if he can do a good job?"[25] Here, kinship sentiments were hardly palpable and differences in surnames had little to do with the election.

A study of Xitang Village, Longyou County, indicated that voters put quality before their clan background when choosing a candidate. They would first look at the candidate's education and competence. Xitang consisted of six natural villages, with six major surnames. 87 percent of the respondents said they would choose those able to do good things for the village and that the candidate's surname and clan background would make no difference.[26] Two peasants in Xinqun Village, Kaihua County expressed similar views.[27] Moreover, in their observations of village elections in Fujian province, researchers of the American International Republican Institute did not find clan-related campaign activities.[28]

GENERAL TRENDS AS INDICATED BY STATISTICS

The above studies have presented contradictory findings, which may only lead to contradictory generalisations and conclusions. Yet contradictory situations and facts do exist, since the Chinese rural society is highly complex and full of contradictions and possibilities. Here we would like to determine which of the contradictory views is closer to the truth, or represents a more general trend. Data from two surveys may form a more solid basis for the description of the trend.

1) Criteria of voters in choosing candidates

The villager survey shows that the first two criteria (see Table 6.1) are "I know about the candidate and I will decide for myself" (38.6%) and "I will vote for candidates of righteousness and justice" (34.6%). On the other hand, only 1.5 percent of the respondents said they would "vote only for those from (their) own clan", one of the smallest percentages on the list. This points to the limited kinship influence on voter behaviour.

TABLE 6.1 HOW DID YOU DECIDE WHICH CANDIDATE(S) TO VOTE FOR?

Criteria/reasons	No. of people	Percentage (%)
1. Know about candidate and decide for oneself	480	38.6
2. Decide after briefing of candidate	64	5.1
3. Get others' opinions, then decide	88	7.1
4. Follow those around	21	1.7
5. Follow directions of leaders	14	1.1
6. Vote for those from my own clan	19	1.5
7. Vote for candidates of righteousness and justice	431	34.6
8. Tick in order of candidates' names	28	2.2
9. See no difference between candidates	79	6.3
10. No response	21	1.7
Total	1245	100.0

The results also indicate that the size of a clan does not make a difference in voters' attitude. 1.6 percent of those from large clans choose to "vote for someone of the same clan" and 1.3 percent of those from small clans choose to do the same. Similarly, voters of both major and minor clans put "impartiality" as one of the most important criteria. Voters of major clans put "I know about the candidate and I will decide for myself" (42.1%) and "I will vote for candidates of righteousness and impartiality" (33.1%) on the top. Only the order is slightly changed with those of the minor clans, who put "righteousness and impartiality"(38.2%) before "I know about the candidate and I will decide for myself" (34.1%). It is highly understandable that the latter put "righteousness and impartiality" above everything else (see Table 6.2, in which items 1-10 correspond to the questions in Table 6.1).

In choosing a village head, the first three criteria are "can lead villagers in developing local economy and welfare" (57.1%), "willing to speak for the common people" (54.5%) and "can do a good job for the party" (37.1%). Only 3.8 percent of the respondents ticked the criterion "will represent interest of (my) clan" (see Table 6.3).

TABLE 6.2 CLAN BACKGROUND AND VOTERS' CRITERIA IN CHOOSING CANDIDATES

Background	Major clan Number (%)	Minor clan Number (%)	Unspecified Number (%)	Total Number (%)
1	265 (42.1%)	189 (34.1%)	26 (42.6%)	480 (38.6%)
2	26 (4.1%)	31 (5.6%)	7 (11.5%)	64 (5.1%)
3	47 (7.5%)	33 (5.9%)	8 (13.1%)	88 (7.1%)
4	11 (1.7%)	10 (1.8%)		21 (1.7%)
5	6 (1.0%)	5 (0.9%)	3 (4.9%)	14 (1.1%)
6	10 (1.6%)	7 (1.3%)	2 (3.3%)	19 (1.5%)
7	208 (33.1%)	7 (1.3%)	11 (18%)	431 (34.6%)
8	17 (2.7%)	10 (1.8%)	1 (1.6%)	28 (2.2%)
9	32 (5.1%)	45 (8.1%)	2 (3.3%)	79 (6.3%)
10	7 (1.1%)	13 (2.3%)	1 (1.6%)	21 (1.7%)
Total	629 (100%)	555 (100%)	61 (100%)	1245 (100%)

TABLE 6.3 REASONS VOTED FOR HIM/HER AS VILLAGE HEAD

Reason/criteria	Answer	Number	(%)
It is my sacred duty	yes	1162	93.3
	no	83	6.7
Will speak for common people	yes	678	54.5
	no	567	45.5
Will do a good job for the party	yes	462	37.1
	no	783	62.9
Will lead in developing village economy and welfare	yes	711	57.1
	no	534	42.9
Will represent clan interest	yes	473.8	
	no	1198	96.2
Will speak for people in the same trade	yes	40	3.2
	no	1205	96.8
Is well respected	yes	119	9.6
	no	1126	90.4
For other reasons	yes	135	10.8
	no	1110	89.2
Total		1245	100

Here again there is not much difference between major and minor clans. For the former, the first three criteria are "can lead villagers in developing local economy and welfare" (58.3%), "will speak for the common people" (51.4%) and "can do a good job for the party" (34.1%). The latter's choices are: "will speak for the common people" (57.8%), "can lead villagers in developing local economy and welfare" (55.7%) and "can do a good job for the party" (55.7%). Only 3.7 percent of the majority group and 4.0 percent of the minority group chose "can work for the benefit of my clan" (see Table 6.4). Data here again support the idea that kinship is not an important factor in voting and clan influence on vote behaviour is not significant.

TABLE 6.4 CLAN BACKGROUND AND VOTERS' CRITERIA IN CHOOSING CANDIDATES

Clan background	Good for village economy and welfare	Will speak for common people	Will do good job for party	Good for clan interest
Major clan	58.3%	51.4%	34.3%	3.7%
Minor clan	55.7%	57.8%	55.7%	4.0%

We also surveyed village heads to find out why they think voters voted for them. Are their reasons similar to those of the voters? Our findings (see Table 6.5) are as follows: "because the villagers elected me" (55.0%), "I have the leading ability to develop village economy" (34.2%), "I had been village head before" (13.5%), "I have certain special quality" (7.2%), "I am well-respected" (4.5%), "I had been hand-picked by leadership above" (3.6%), "I represent the interest of my own clan" (2.7%) and "I don"t know" (2.7%). Note that only 2.7 percent thought they had been elected in the interest of his/her clan. If we compare the responses of the major clan group with those of the minor clan group, we will find the difference between them is not great. The former is in such order: "because the villagers elected me" (57.9%), "I have the leading ability do develop the village economy" (40.4%), "I had been village head before" (12.3%), "I have certain special quality" (8.8%), "I am well-respected" (5.3%), "I can represent the interest of my own clan" (3.5%), "I was hand-picked by leadership above" (1.8%) and "I don't know" (1.8%). The latter is in the order of "because the villagers had elected me" (51.1%), "I have the leading ability to develop village economy" (29.8%), "I had been village head before" (14.9%), "I have certain special quality" (6.4%), "I was hand-picked by leadership above" (6.4%), "I am well-respected" (4.3%) and "I can represent the interest of my own clan" (2.1%) (see Table 6.5).

TABLE 6.5 CLAN BACKGROUND AND REASONS GIVEN BY VILLAGE HEADS

Reasons and criteria	Major clans (%)	Minor clans (%)
People elected me	57.9	51.1
Special quality	8.8	6.4
Good for village economy and welfare	40.4	29.8
Well-respected	5.3	4.3
Former head of villages	12.3	14.9
Hand-picked	1.8	6.4
Clan interest	3.5	0.0
Unknown	1.8	

2) Values of the village heads

Among the newly elected village heads, 58.6 percent put in the first place the interest of the electorate, 19.8 percent put the interest of the state and 10.8 percent put the interest of the Communist Party. Only 1.8 percent put clan interest in the first place. There is little difference in the values between those from major clans and those from minor clans. The former respond in the following order: electorate interest (54.4%), state interest (21.1%), party interest (12.3%) and finally clan interest (3.5%). The latter responds in similar order: electorate interest (59.6%), state interest (21.3%), party interest (10.6%), but here none puts clan interest in the first place (see Table 6.6).

TABLE 6.6 CLAN BACKGROUND AND VILLAGE HEADS' VALUES "AS ELECTED VILLAGE HEAD, YOU WOULD FIRST CHOOSE TO REPRESENT..."

Choices	Head's clan background	Number	(%)
Voters' interest	major clan	31	54.4
	minor clan	28	59.6
	unspecified	6	85.7
Party interest	major clan	7	12.3
	minor clan	5	10.6
	unspecified		
State interest	major clan	12	21.1
	minor clan	10	21.3
	unspecified		
Clan interest	major clan	2	3.5
	minor clan		
	unspecified		

The priorities that newly elected village heads put on their agenda yield similar findings. In the order of importance, these are: "solve (urgent) problems in the village" (73.9%), "speak for the villagers" (69.4%), "often make investigation among the masses" (44.1%), "exercise supervision over the party secretary" (19.8%) and "do something for my own clan" (11.7%) (see Table 6.7).

TABLE 6.7 ONCE ELECTED, YOU WILL (MULTIPLE CHOICES)

Speak for villagers	Solve problems	Make investigation	Exercise supervision	Work for clan interest	Others
69.4%	73.9%	44.1%	19.8%	11.7%	9.0%

Most village heads, regardless of clan difference, put the clan factor as the last consideration for their future work (see Table 6.8).

TABLE 6.8 VILLAGE HEADS' CHOICES IN VIEW OF CLAN BACKGROUND

Clan back ground	Major clan No. (%)	Minor clan No. (%)	Unspecified No. (%)
Speak for villagers	39 (68.4)	36 (76.6)	2 (28.6)
Solve problems	44 (77.2)	47 (76.6)	2 (28.6)
Make investigations	22 (38.6)	27 (57.4)	
Exercise supervision	12 (21.1)	9 (19.1)	1 (14.3)
Work for clan interest	6 (10.5)	6 (12.8)	1 (14.3)
Others	6 (10.5)	4 (8.5)	

3) Does election favour those from the major clans?

When asked what they thought about the results of the election, 52.9 percent of the voters responded by saying that the latest election in their villages had produced an impartial leadership, while 19.9 percent said the outcome of the election favoured villagers of the major clans, 17.3 percent said it favoured the more wealthy in the village, and 6.7 percent said they felt that the interest of the minority clans was well guaranteed. We can see that more than half of the respondents said that the election was fair, though 19.9 percent of the respondents thought that the election favoured those from the major clan (see Table 6.9).

TABLE 6.9 VOTERS' ASSESSMENT OF THE ELECTION

	Favours those of major clans	Guarantees interests of those of minor clans	Has produced impartial leadership	Favours the more wealthy
Percentage (%)	19.9	6.7	52.9	17.3

How then do we view the above assessment in the light of clan background? Is there a difference in assessment between people from different clan backgrounds? Our data indicate such a difference does exist in some way. Among those from the major clans, 15 percent said the election favoured the major clans, while 26.1 percent of the minor clan group said it favoured the major clans. However, what is more significant is that between them more than half (54.5 percent of the major clan group, 50.8 percent of the minor clan group) thought the election had produced a fair leadership. 6.4 percent of major clan voters and 6.8 percent of the minor clan voters thought the outcome of the election would guarantee the interest of those of the minority clans. Besides, 20.5 percent of those from major clans and 13.2 percent of those from minor clans thought the election results favoured the more wealthy people in the villages (see Table 6.10).

TABLE 6.10 VOTERS' ASSESSMENT OF ELECTION IN TERMS OF CLAN BACKGROUND

Clan background	Favours those of major clans	Guarantees interests of those of minor clans	Has produced impartial leadership	Favours the more wealthy
Major clan voters (%)	15.4	6.4	54.5	20.5
Minor clan voters (%)	26.1	6.8	50.8	13.2

In Table 6.10, for the item (the election) "favours those of the major clans", there is a gap of 10.7 percent between the two groups of respondents. I use the Pearson chi-square method of statistical independence to test the null hypothesis that there is no difference between major and minor clans with regards to the result of election. The chi-square (c^2) value is 25.26, and the significance or "p" value with one degree of freedom is 0.00. I therefore reject the null hypothesis that such a gap is statistically meaningful. The gap may lead to two interpretations: that the election is to some extent really favourable to those of the major clans or those voters of the minority clans just feel or worry about the unfavourable implications of the election results.

The nature of the above figures is subjective, that is, the way people with different clan backgrounds offer their different opinions on elections is in favour of big family clan. We may examine some more objective data as an alternative approach to this question. The village head survey indicates that among the village heads, except those whose clan background were unspecified, 42.3 percent were from minor clans and 51.4 percent from major ones (see Table 6.11).

TABLE 6.11 CLAN BACKGROUND OF THE ELECTED VILLAGE HEADS

Clan background	Number of village heads	Percentage (%)
From major clans	57	51.4
From minor clans	47	42.3
Unspecified	7	6.3
Total	111	100.0

Other factors excluded, the number of village heads coming from minor clans is expected to be smaller when we take into account the smaller proportion of minor clans to the village population; thus that 42.3 percent of the village heads come from minor clans is significant, because it indicates that clan background is not a decisive factor in the election. This significantly disproves the assumption that big family clans always dominate village politics. There is thus no substantial evidence to support the view that village election would always favour large clans, who with majority numbers tend to dominate the electorate process at the expense of smaller clans. This finding can be supported by other studies. Shi Xuefeng finds that one village election in Huadong has changed the power balance based on family clan.[29] Hu Biliang, in his study of one village in Shanxi, also demonstrates that the posts of village power are not always distributed in favour of big clans.[30] In my field study, I observed in numerous cases that the party secretaries come from big family clans, while elected village heads come from small family clans.

4) Views about the fairness of the election

We found that 8.8 percent of the voters thought that the recent election in their villages was very fair, 44.7 percent thought it was fair, 35.3 percent thought it was unfair and 10 percent said they were not sure. Were voters influenced by their respective clan background in making the assessment? We found that 10.3 percent of the major clan voters thought the election was very fair, while 7.2 percent of the minority clan voters held the same view. 43.1 percent of the former and 46.5 percent of the latter thought it was fair. A rate of 35.3 percent of those who thought the election was unfair could be found in both groups. 9.9 percent of the former and 10.6 percent of the latter responded that they were not sure. A similar proportion of voters, who viewed the election as fair or very fair, can be found in both groups (53.4 percent of the former and 53.7 percent of the latter). Hence we can say that there was no presence of kinship influence in voters' assessments (see Table 6.12).

TABLE 6.12 CLAN BACKGROUND AND VOTERS' ASSESSMENTS REGARDING THE FAIRNESS OF THE ELECTION

Question	Clan background Number (%)	NO Number (%)	YES
Very fair?	Major clan	564 (89.7)	65 (10.3)
	Minor clan	515 (92.8)	40 (7.2)
	Unspecified	57 (93.4)	4 (6.6)
Fair?	Major clan	358 (56.9)	65 (43.1)
	Minor clan	297 (53.5)	40 (46.5)
	Unspecified	33 (54.1)	28 (45.9)
Unfair?	Major clan	407 (64.7)	222 (35.3)
	Minor clan	359 (64.7)	196 (35.3)
	unspecified	40 (65.6)	21 (34.4)
Unsure?	Major clan		62 (9.9)
	Minor clan		59 (10.6)
	unspecified		4 (6.6)

In addition, even when voters put the election as "unfair", they did not take kinship influence as the cause for the "unfairness". Rather, they put the cause as "vote-canvassing" (22.1 percent of the major clan group and 19.9 percent of minor clan group), "fraud and cheating" (4.6 percent:5.9 percent), "domineering leadership" (7.8 percent:7.6 percent) and "violation of the will of voters" (5.2 percent:7.6 percent). Thus there was not much difference in voters' assessments even though they had different clan backgrounds.

In conclusion, from the above data, it is clear that clan consideration only has some minor affect on voters' behaviour, in that the elected village heads do not think that their success depends on clan voters, the elected village heads do not take clan interest as the important strategy to maintain their posts, and that the clan factor does not influence the positive or negative assessment of the election. All of these indicate that villagers and village heads in Zhejiang, to a large degree, exercise rational interest calculations across kinship divides, and reveal that villagers and village heads are becoming modern citizens who are not overridingly obsessed by kinship identity. This finding casts doubt on the validity of the view concerning the persisting significance of kinship in rural China.[31]

STRUCTURAL CONDITIONS AND THEIR IMPACT

The conclusion we can draw at this stage is that kinship had but a limited impact on elections in rural Zhejiang. It did not pose a serious problem. Even in cases in which clan forces were involved, these forces were not the root of the problem. Therefore, township leaders have no solid reason based on clan influence for putting off or even calling off elections. Likewise, when academics cite the impact of clan forces as evidence for the lack of democratic ideas among China's peasants, their arguments remain unconvincing.

Nevertheless, two questions remain. First, why does kinship have different impacts on village elections in different areas? Second, why does kinship in general have only a limited impact on elections? Let us first address the question of the diversity of kinship influences.

First, village party organisation contributes to local variations. If the village party organisation is stronger, it is likely to contain the influence of kinship and vice versa. The seeming presence of lineage influence takes place when the village party secretary is incapable and incompetent, and as a result, one lineage or village chief is likely to challenge the party authority through kinship resource. Nevertheless, there is a subtle influence through a particular village power structure. Village power can be divided into public power represented by party organisation and village committees, and private power represented by kinship. In some villages, most members of formal organisations, such as party and village committees, come from the same lineage as a result of formal organisation and informal kinship structure overlapping. In such a case, though the party secretary and village committee members deny the influence of kinship, its latent influence is always there.[32]

Our case studies also found that all instances of kinship influence on elections took place in the poor mountainous or remote areas. During our interviews with local officials, they invariably located strong kinship influence in poverty-stricken areas. On the other hand, as indicated by studies conducted in the summers of 1998 and 1999 by students of the Department of Political Science, Zhejiang University, there was no kinship problem in economically developed villages, such as those in Wenzhou District. Kinship dispute and kinship manipulations of village affairs were rare in villages close to townships and busy in business. We also learned in an interview in Yuyao that kinship had a strong influence in villages with an under-developed economy, but had little influence on voters from well-to-do areas.[33]

Hence we can conclude that kinship influence is in counter proportion to economic development, because the development of the economy leads to the plurality of interests, which undermines the idea of a dominant clan interest. Now, among others, household and individual interests are highly valued. The implication for elections is that when there are different interest groups within a big clan, each group will have its own candidate in mind, with the result that votes are so scattered that a candidate from a major clan does not necessarily get elected. In addition, kinship influence varies with changes in the village economic structure. In an agricultural village, where market economy plays no significant part and villagers still share a common interest, the clan is able to maintain its influence. However, kinship influence declines in villages with a substantial collective economy, in which the rural enterprises are far more accountable for the ups and downs of the villagers' income than the non-institutional clan. We found in our survey that those who ticked the item "will vote for my family clan" were mostly from agricultural villages (73.7 percent). Another 21.2 percent who chose the same item were from villages with a dominant private economy. In contrast, none of those from villages with a dominant collective economy chose that item. It seems that the influence of family clan on electoral voting decreases in a dominant collective economy with a well-developed commercial life.

Now I would like to turn to the question of the limitedness of influence of kinship through examining the structural conditions, social and political, under which the influence of the clan is checked and constrained in many ways. First, let us examine the issue from the relationship between state and society. Unlike Indian society where the traditional caste system remains today and consequently the influence of kinship is significant in village elections,[34] the Chinese communist state has completely changed the rural social structure. After 1949, particularly after the agrarian collectivisation, the clan force was rendered insignificant despite its lingering influence. With the setting-up of the brigade, a social as well as administrative institution, the peasants were well under control. The brigade, with the communist party branch in leadership, became the most effective ruling body over the peasants. It held both the means of production and livelihood of the peasants. The state amassed all rural power. Peasants, like urban workers of the "unit" (*danwei*), became members of the people's commune, which was like a large rural unit. In contrast, the traditional clan and rural community elite had lost their social resources and the related power and privileges. The brigade was the only legitimate institution in the countryside, not to be challenged by the clan or any other institutions. The peasants, meanwhile, became "commune members" instead of clan members.[35]

It is true that since the economic reform, the Chinese state has withdrawn some of its power from the rural area and such a withdrawal has provided an opportunity for the family clan to revive. Nevertheless, one empirical study finds that the revival of clan forces has a structural limit: there is no permanent structure of kinship at the village level. The members of a clan often gather temporarily when needed. The traditional clan or lineage organisations have not been revived.[36] It is also important to recognise that though the Chinese state has undergone a transformation from a totalitarian state to an authoritarian state, the Chinese authoritarian state is still powerful enough to control clan forces. And the state does not rely on kinship to rule villages. The Chinese state is now far more powerful and effective in exercising control than it was historically, when clan forces were dominant in many parts of the country. The state has in its hand practically all the important resources and is powerful enough to curb kinship influence.

Second, family and kinship had enjoyed moral privileges in Confucian doctrine because the family was regarded as the foundation of a Confucian state. Traditional Confucian states had relied on kinship to exercise local rule. Under Mao's regime, however, the kinship structure was systematically attacked and lineages were defined as feudal relics.[37] Today, despite the revival of kinship, it lacks support from the official ideology. Few people would accept kinship's involvement in elections. Rather, governments at all levels would crush any clan attempt to manipulate elections, so as to keep the elections fair and just. As shown in various cases, local governments would punish any clan forces that attempted to manipulate elections, because politically the clans had no legitimacy.[38] The electoral Law of Zhejiang Province warrants prosecution against any one who involves kinship factionalism and uses kinship force to sabotage an election. Public opinion shows an even stronger objection to clan manipulation than to manipulation from institutional bodies such as township government. The clan, without recognition by the state and without social legitimacy, simply could not *openly* get involved in elections. Some clan leaders, while trying to manipulate elections, denied clan motivation. Kinship line, instead of being a blessing, in some cases became a curse to the candidate, for "an inner struggle is likely to occur when there emerge two rival contenders in the same clan, which will bring gains to neither of them but a third party".[39]

Third, a clan culture thrives in a traditional agrarian economy or natural economy. The replacement of traditional economic structures by modern ones has effectively destroyed that economic base. The modern version of clan culture has to base itself solely on lineage and clan relationships. After 1949, the materials as well as spiritual resources available to the clan were seriously limited. Gone was the land whose produce the clan could use for worshipping, schooling and charity. Gone also were the clan's charity grain stores. Politically, too, the clan elders lost almost everything, as power now lay in the village institutional bodies. They were even no longer the moral authority. In the reform and open-door era, more power and more social and economic resources have shifted to the young and the middle-aged. A society dominated by the old is only an image of the past. The younger generation is not as kinship-minded as its forefathers were. Kinship influence, when it does make itself felt on the election, is limited and fragile. In general, clan elders do not have the traditional resources to exercise their influence.

The production responsibility system is a double-edged sword for kinship and the role of kinship in family/kinship-run enterprises may change. A sizeable number of researchers have regarded the rural economic reform and the production responsibility system as a major prompt for the re-emergence of kinship. While there is truth in their view, we must point out another possibility, that is, the system may also serve as a check to kinship, because it promotes a sense of individuality by calling the peasants' attention to their own interest. Further, as Huang Xiyi remarks: "kinship re-emerges as important, while it is no longer a dominant element in the rural economy and politics; and kin networks extends, while this extension is accompanied by kinship division".[40]

Similar things can be said of the family-run enterprises, whose dramatic expansion in the 1980s was a milestone in the development of the rural economy. At the early stage, kinship did provide a driving force for many of the rural enterprises. However, as these enterprises develop and the social economy becomes more market-oriented, kinship becomes an obstacle instead of a driving force. The 1990s witnessed the growth of the occupational relationships and the decline of blood relations. That in the late 1990s, many family-run enterprises had to change or abandon their kinship feature is good proof.

Fourth, there has been increasing social mobility in China, which further weakens kinship identity and kinship relationships. The many comings and goings change the village composition and diminish clan power. Kinship consciousness grows only in a relatively closed society, where one meets the same circle of people daily. As social mobility increases, business and job relations become more important than relations established on lineage and locality. In Datang, Zhuji Municipality, for instance, a large portion of the rural population has moved into townships and taken up jobs there. Some villagers now have little to do with their kinsfolk, because they are always on the go, doing business away in other places.

Some peasants have gone as far as Guangzhou and Shenzhen in search of jobs. In Datang, many people feel it is a rare occasion when there is a reunion of kinsfolk.[41] Even when people do come together, they no longer feel as close to each other as they once did. On the other hand, migrations and travels have opened the peasants' minds. Their values change. They are more likely to value liberty and rights and to assert their individuality, both of which are alien to kinship sentiments.

Fifth, rural dwelling conditions have changed. The traditional rural housing model was conductive to a clan culture. Kinship households used to live so close by that they shared door-steps and gates. In the reform era, the rural economy has developed and people feel they need more and better houses. There are so many applications for housing grounds that one major function of the village committee is to check and approve these applications. Now houses are built separately. Some houses even look solitary. Tan Ke's study (1998) of a village in Keqiao Township, Shaoxing, is an example. The local authority had launched a project for building "new villages". Many peasants followed the project and left their old houses. Over the past ten years, there were more than 150 households that had built new houses. As a result, the makeup of the neighbourhood changed dramatically and kinship relations were deeply affected.[42] Another example is Hefu Village, Huzhou, where the formerly scattered houses now have been replaced by even more widely separate ones. Such a dwelling mode does not promote a sense of community among the villagers. In former days, the sense of community or sense of belonging could be generated not only by dwelling conditions but also by politics. The production brigade used to hold meetings for political study, or for political criticism, as in the 1970s. So did the production team. Now that there are no more of these kinds of political activities and the clan is unlikely to replace politics in generating a sense of belonging, villagers are left with little sense of clan difference and clan identity.[43]

Finally the functions of marriage and family have also changed. Marriage is no longer a means to strengthen kinship ties. Giving birth to a child no longer carries much significance for the clan. Rather, it is regarded as a human responsibility, a need for regeneration. In this sense, the Chinese rural concept of human reproduction is similar to that found both in Chinese urban society and in the West. According to one study of Shanshi Township of Wenling Municipal (1994), when asked about the number and sex they would desire of their children, most villagers replied that they would be happy with two children, preferably one boy and one girl, even without the state policy of birth control. The old idea that "fortune favours the man that has many off-spring" now sounds out of date, particularly among young couples. In another study in the same year of a rural area of Jin County, which was noted for its rural industry, we found that a considerable number of young couples prefer daughters to sons. The reasons they gave were interesting: "the son is not really dependable when you get old, because often a son forgets his mother once he marries his wife. In contrast, the daughter is good, because when she marries her husband, you are richer with a son-in-law, which is worth a son nowadays". Villagers with such changed values about family and marriage would not care much about kinship.

In light of all the changing conditions discussed above, village elections are less likely to provide a channel for the institutionalisation of the clan. Instead, they weaken the clan force by helping raise the villagers' consciousness of law, guarantee an equal opportunity for all candidates through regular process, and promote rationality among voters. Most importantly, under the one-party domination condition, given the fact that the CCP regards clan and kinship as illegitimate, it is unlikely that any political forces would mobilise clan forces openly. Clan forces might be strengthened only if different parties were able to compete for power by mobilising them openly and legally.

CONCLUSION

While acknowledging the influence of kinship on village elections, this paper argues that kinship and clan forces do not constitute a serious problem for village election nor does they undermine the CCP significantly. It has demonstrated the limitedness of the influence of kinship on village elections in general terms. The limitedness of the influence of kinship can be explained by the powerful domination of the state over rural society, the hostility of Marxism towards kinship, the decline of the economic basis of kinship, and the change in marital relationships and living conditions in rural life.

ENDNOTES

1 Department of Civil Affairs of Ningbo Municipality, "Guanyu cunweihui jiangshe qingkuang de diaocha baogao" (A Report on the Building-up of Village Committee), 27/05/1994.

2 For example, in view of clan influence on elections, the Organisation Department of Zhejiang Committee of the CCP and the Civil Affairs Department of Zhejiang province jointly issued a directive in the name of the provincial Party Committee in 1992. The directive "On the Work of Village Elections in Rural Area" warned to "not press for elections in villages, and where feudal clan forces are strong, villagers have little sense of law and order, relations between cadres and the rank and file may be strained besides other problems that may arise. Much work needs to be done before embarking on any election".

3 Li Lianjiang and Xiong Jingming (1998) "Cong zhengfu zhudao de cunmin zizhi maixiang minzhu xuanju" ("From Government-guided Village Autonomy to Democratic Election"), *Ershiyi shiji* (21st Century) 50:153.

4 Anne F. Thurston (1998), "Muddling toward Democracy: Political Change in Grassroots China", United State Institute of Peace, p. 2.

5 Xu Yong (1997), *Zhongguo Nongcun cunmin zizhi* (*Village Autonomy in Rural China*), Huazhong shifangdaxue chubanshe (Central China Normal University Press), p. 363.

6 Qian Hang & Xie Weiyang (1995),*Chuantong yu zhuanxing: Jiangxi Taihe nongcun zongzu xingtai* (Heritage and Transformation: Clan Conditions in Rural Taihe, Jiangxi Province) (Shanghai Shehui Kexue Chubanshe (Shanghai Social Science Press), pp.49-52.

7 They were from two villages in Tangxia Township, Reian Municipal (Wenzhou District), seven in Luao Township, Sanmen County (Taizhou District), three in Shuige Township, Lishui Municipal, four in Wuyun Township, Jingyun County (Lishui District), and five in Chengdong Township, Shaoxing Municipal (Shaoxing District).

8 Classic analyses of clan, kinship and lineage are presented by M. Weber in *Weber: Selections in Translation*, W. G. Runciman (ed.), translated by Eric Mathews (Cambridge Press, 1978), pp.315-330; Hugh D. R. Baker, *A Chinese Lineage Village: Shung Shui* (Stanford: Stanford University Press, 1968); Maurice Freedman, *Lineage Organisation in Southeastern China* (London: Athlone, 1958); Maurice Freedman, *Chinese Lineage and Society: Fukien and Kwangtung*, (London: Athlone); Rubie S. Watson, *Inequality among Brothers: Class and Kinship in South China*, (Cambridge: Cambridge University Press, 1985); Sulamith Heins Potter and Jack M. Potter, *China's Peasants: The Anthropology of a Revolution* (Cambridge: Cambridge University Press, 1990), Chap. 12; and Cao Jingqing *et al* (1995) *Dangdai zhebei xiangcun de shehui wenhua bianqian* (Social and Cultural Changes in Modern Rural Northern Zhejiang) (Shanghai: Far East Press).

9 On the revival of clan forces, see Tang Jun, "Dangdai Zhongguo nongcun jiazu fuxing de beijing", (The Background of the Revival of Clan Forces in Contemporary Rural China), *Shehuixue Yanjiu* (Studies in Sociology), No. 2, 1996; Sulamith Heins Potter and Jack M. Potter, *China's Peasants: The Anthropology of a Revolution* (Cambridge: Cambridge University Press, 1990), Ch. 12.

10 When any of the off-spring succeeds in passing the national college entrance examination, there will be grand ancestor-worshipping rituals presided over by the clan head. Each of the sub-divisions will have only some representatives at the ceremony, while all of the family members of the successful candidate get the honour of an invitation. When the worshipping is over, the candidate, bearing honour flowers, will take a glorious walk around the village amid cheers and congratulations. This reminds one of the historical glories the successful candidate and his kinsmen enjoyed when he passed the imperial examination. Lin Zhaohuang, who was doing his field study there in the summer of 1999, witnessed the whole worshipping process and the glorious walk, which took place after the results of the entrance examination were released. Lin Zhaohuang (enrolled in 1997, School of Political Science, Zhejiang University), "Yige daibiao, liangzhong yizhi de jiyue" (Representing Two Wills: Case Study of the People's Representatives of Dayu Township)(1999 summer study).

11 Department of Civil Affairs of Wenzhou municipality, "Guanyu dangqian wenzhou nongcun shehui zhian zhuangkuang de diaocha baogao" ("A Report on Current Social Order and Security in Rural Wenzhou"), 23/05/1994.

12 Zhu Genghua (graduate student enrolled in 1996, School of Political Science, Zhejiang University), "minzhu fengxian yu zhengfu xingwei" (The Risk of Democracy and Governmental Behaviour: Case Study of Village Elections in Fangcun Township, Changshan County, June 1997).

13 For example, in the Jiangbei region of Ningbo, there were two remote mountain villages notorious for clan rivalry. In one village, rivalry campaigns made it impossible to elect the leading body. In the other village, the election did bring out a committee, but its members were so divided in opinion that it could not really accomplish anything. Pan Youge, Wang Shihao and Huang Yushun (investigation team from the Ministry of Civil Affairs), "Zhejiangsheng cunji zuzhi zhangkuang diaocha" (Investigation on Village Institutions in Zhejiang Province), 10/06/1994.

14 Dept. of Civil Affairs of Jiaojiang municipality, "Guanyu cunweihui huanjie xuanju gongzuo qingkuang de baogao"("Report on the Work in Village Election"), 15/01/1994.

15 Department of Civil Affairs of Tiantai County, "Jiaqiang dong dui cunweihui de lingdao, gaibian luohou mianmao" (Make improvement through the Strengthening of Party Leadership over Village Committee), 20/05/1994.

16 Qiu Zhengjun (enrolled in 1996, School of Political Science, Zhejiang University), "'Cunguan' zhijie xuanju, gai xi hai shi you?"(Direct Election of Village Head: Good or Bad? On the 1999 Village Election in Chengzhou Municipality) (1999 summer study).

17 Jing Yan (enrolled in 1994, School of Political Science, Zhejiang University), "Cong huanjie xuanju kan xian jieduan nongmin zhengzhi canyu" (Village Election and Current Political Participation of the Peasants) (MA thesis, 1998).

18 Cao Liwei (enrolled in 1996, School of Political Science, Zhejiang University), "Renzhongdaoyuan kan cunminweiyuanhui xunju de wenti jiqi wanshan" (A Long Way to Go: Problems in the Election of Village Committee and Solutions) (1998 summer study). Similarly, a case study of Shaoyou Village, Paitou Township, Zhuji Municipal, indicated that whether a surname was shared by a majority or a minority and whether it was indigenous or brought by later settlers had important implications in local elections. For one thing, a candidate with a majority surname could turn it to an advantage. As Wang was the majority surname in this village, a Wang candidate had a much better chance than his otherwise surnamed contenders did to win support from other Wangs. For another thing, a clan dominated the village, holding five seats out of nine in the village committee, including the village head. The five members were all in-laws and cousins among themselves. As a result, the clan held the veto power in the committee. Bian Wei (enrolled in 1997, School of Political Science, Zhejiang University), "Guanyu cunminweiyunhui xunju de diaocha baogao" (A Report on the Village Election) (1998 summer study).

19 Jing Zhongming (enrolled in 1997, School of Political Science, Zhejiang University), "Cunweihui xunju ying zou shang zhenggui" (Village Election: Don't Go Astray) (1999 summer study).

20 Xu Ming (enrolled in 1997, School of Political Science, Zhejiang University), "Getijinji xia de cunmin zizhi" (Village Autonomy under Private Economy: Case Study of Dujia Village)(1999 summer study).

21 Xu Yong (1997), *Zhongguo nongcun cunmin zizhi*, p.361.

22 Department of Civil Affairs of Tiantai County, "Jiaqiang dong dui cunweihui de lingdao, gaibian luohou mianmao" (Making Improvement through the Strengthening of Party Leadership over Village Committee), 20/05/1994.

23 Xu Wei (enrolled in 1997, School of Political Science, Zhejiang University), "Cunninweiyuanhui minzhu xuanju jincheng" (Process of the Democratic Election of Village Committee: Case Study of Sancun Village, Taizhou") (1998 summer study).

24 Another interesting case was Tao-Xu-Feng Village of Hemudu Township, Yuyao. Consisting of three natural villages, the village had Tao, Xu and Feng all as major surnames. Yet Tao was the largest of the three as indicated by its foremost position in the compound name of the village. Of an electorate of 752, 70 percent were surnamed Tao. The election for the village committee was held in March 1999. Feng Jirong, the former village head, won candidature with 102 votes while his contender Tao Guofu did so with 87 votes. In the final voting for the village head, Feng, in spite of his lesser surname, won with 387 votes and was re-elected village head. The candidate Tao lost with 367 votes. Song Peihua (enrolled in 1997, School of Political Science, Zhejiang University), "Cunminweiyunhui minzhu xuanju wenti diaocha" ("Democratic Election of Village Committee: Case Study of Tao-Xu-Feng Village in Hemudu") (1999 summer study).

25 Zheng Rubin (enrolled in 1997, School of Political Science, Zhejiang University), "Guanyu sanyuancun cunminweiyuanhui xuanju de diaocha" ("Report on the Village Election of Sanyuan Village Committee") (1998 summer study).

26 Sun Xiao (enrolled in 1997, School of Political Science Zhejiang University), "Longyouxian huzhengzheng xitagncun cunmin xuanju diaocha" ("A Study on the Village Election in Xitang Village, Huzheng Township, Longyou County") (1998 summer study).

27 Wang Jie (enrolled in 1997, School of Political Science, Zhejiang University), "Guanyu cunminweiyuanhui xuanju de diaocha" ("A Study on the Election of Village Committee") (1998 summer study).

28 International Republican Institute, "People's Republic of China Election Observation Report", 15-31/03/1994, p.27.

29 In the past, the posts of village power were distributed proportionally according to the relative strength of three big family clans in one village. Shi Xuefeng, "Between Tradition and Modernity: the Village Power under Strong Family Clan Background", working paper, 2000, Beijing.

30 Hu Biliang, *Institutional Changes of Chinese Village and Power Distribution*, Taiyuan: Shanxi Economic Press, 1996, pp. 168-9. Nevertheless, Zhao

Litao observes that a family clan has dominated village power in the 1970s in one village in Hebei. Zhao Litao, "Family Clan and Village Politics 1950-1970", *Twenty-first Century*, No. 55, October Issue, 1999, pp. 45-52.

31 On this point, see Sulamith Heins Potter and Jack M. Potter, *China's Peasants: The Anthropology of a Revolution*, Cambridge: Cambridge University Press, 1990, pp. 256-67.

32 Guo Zhenglin provides a detailed analysis - "A Political Analysis of the Triangle Relationship between Kinship, Party Branch and Village Committee", *Strategies and Management*, No. 2 (2000), pp. 94-104.

33 Talks of Lang Youxing & Xiang Hui with cadres of Party Organisation Department of Yuyao municipality.

34 One study reveals kinship considerations constitute the highest factor influencing villagers' choice of candidates (60 percent of the respondents), the next is caste considerations (55 percent), advice by elders (52 percent), social services done by the candidate (37 percent), candidate's influence on officials (37 percent), personal virtues of the candidate (27 percent), seniority in age (21 percent), wealth (18 percent), and education (13 percent). See S. L. Chopra, "Village Elections", *Kurukshetra*, April 1966, p. 23.

35 However, Zhao Litao dismisses the view that the family clan was declining before economic reform and has been reviving after economic reform. Drawing on his field study in one village in Hebei, he demonstrates that one family clan has been dominating village power since the 1970s and that village leaders felt more secure in his private clan circle. See Zhao Litao, "Family Clan and Village Politics 1950-1970", *Twenty-first Century*, No. 55, October Issue, 1999, pp. 45-52. The continuity and persistence of kinship structure is also stressed by Sulamith Heins Potter and Jack M. Potter, *China's Peasants: The Anthropology of a Revolution* (Cambridge: Cambridge University Press, 1990), pp. 256-67.

36 Qiang Hang, "Reconstructing of Contemporary Clan and Reconstructing Environment in China", *Chinese Social Science Quarterly* (Hong Kong), Winter Volume, February Issue, 1994, pp. 76-88.

37 Sulamith Heins Potter and Jack M. Potter, *China's Peasants: The Anthropology of a Revolution*, (Cambridge: Cambridge University Press, 1990), pp. 255-6.

38 China's situation contrasts with the development of chieftaincy in Ghana. Under the British colonial rule, a minimal state was introduced and chieftaincy remained powerful. During the 1950s under an expansionist state, the national Native Authorities were replaced by elected local councils, in which chiefs held no position after 1954. By the time of the 1966 coup, under an incredible shrinking state, traditional authority of chieftaincy was reasserted in the face of state paralysis. See Paul Nugent, "An Abandoned Project? (The Nuances of Chieftaincy, Development and History in Ghana's Volta Region), *Journal of Legal Pluralism*, Nos. 37-38 (1996), pp. 203-225.

39 Jing Zhongming (enrolled in 1997, School of Political Science, Zhejiang University), "Cunweihui xuanju ying zoushang zhenggui" (Village Election: Don't Go Astray) (1999 summer study).

40 Huang Xiyi, "Two-way Changes–Kinship in Contemporary Rural China", in Flemming Christiansen and Zhang Junzuo, (eds.), *Village Inc. Chinese Rural Society in the 1990s* (Surrey: Curzon Press, 1998), p. 191.

41 Jing Yan (enrolled in 1994, School of Political Science, Zhejiang University), "Cong huanjie xuanju kan nongmin zhengzhi canyu" (Village Election and Current Political Participation of the Peasants) (1998 thesis).

42 Tan Ke (enrolled in 1997, School of Political Science, Zhejiang University), "H cun minzhu guanli tiaojian de diaocha" (Study on Conditions for Democratic Management in H Village) (1998 summer study).

43 Wang Ying (enrolled in 1997, School of Political Science, Zhejiang University), "Hehu cun cunmingweiyuanhui xuanju diaocha" (Study on Election of Village Committee in Hehu Village)(1998 summer study).

PART 2

Damage Control and Response: Struggle for Relevance

CHAPTER 7

The Age Factor in Chinese Politics

ZHENG SHIPING

All political systems face the problem of "political exit" and leadership renewal. Great achievements in scientific research have yet to enable political leaders of any type of regime to slow down the biological clock. In democracies with or even without term limits for public officials, elections are often the only viable ways to satisfy the need of "political exit" and leadership renewal of the regime. Under the political systems without a regular electoral process, however, most political leaders tend to overstay or are unwilling to step down of their own volition. And even if they are, many still face the problem of retiring/stepping down gracefully. Leadership renewal is an equally challenging issue for regimes without regular elections: how to select and promote younger leaders to succeed ageing leaders.

In Chinese politics, several factors directly affect one's political career. For many members of the older generation, their revolutionary credentials of guerrilla warfare and mass mobilisation were basic requirements. It helped if they were able to read and write well. And sometimes, luck also had a lot to do with it: managing to physically survive many battles and power struggles by being present at the right place at the right time or absent at the wrong place at the wrong time. But most significantly, one needed to develop and maintain close relationships with their political patrons.

For the younger generation today, the credentials of guerrilla warfare and mass mobilisation have been replaced by the credentials of education and work performance, especially in project management and economic development. Other than that, the factors of patron-client relationships and luck still matter greatly. In recent years, however, a new factor of age has emerged to shape the political process in China.

The leadership of the Chinese Communist Party (CCP) started off young in 1949. Yet because there was no retirement system, the leadership began to look like a "gerontocracy" three decades after taking over power. After Mao Zedong died in 1976, the Chinese regime under Deng Xiaoping began to experiment with a retirement system for party and government officials in the early 1980s. The Deng regime had also been calling for the promotion of officials who were "more revolutionary, better educated, younger, and more professionally competent." Of all the criteria, however, only the "age limit" seems to be manifestly an objective criterion, non-political, and non-ideological, which the Chinese leadership could use openly and effectively to speed up leadership renewal at various levels of the party and government. The mid-1980s thus saw a massive generational change of the party and government leadership.

After Deng, Jiang Zemin further consolidated the retirement system and used age limit as a convenient political instrument to force his political rivals to step down on the one hand and to promote younger leaders on the other. Since 1992, the retirement age of 65 has been set for central ministers, provincial governors, and commanders of military regions. Upon approaching this retirement age, one has to assess his or her chance of "going up" above the level of minister/provincial governor or accept the reality of "going out." Recently, age limits have also been set for officials below the level of central minister and provincial governor. For instance, section chief, division chief, and bureau chief are now expected to step down from their leading posts at the age of 52, 55, and 58 respectively.

If age limits do exist in other countries, they usually stipulate how old one has to be in order to be qualified for running for certain public offices. For instance, in the United States, one has to be 25 years old to run for a seat in the House of Representatives and 30 for a seat in the Senate of the U.S. Congress, and 35 for the office of the presidency. Japanese government does require civil servants to retire at the age of 55, but there is no age limit for the retired government bureaucrats to enter politics. And many of them do and have become prime ministers or cabinet ministers. While it seems to be a universal trend (with many exceptions, of course) that government officials and political leaders are getting younger and voters generally do not like ageing statesmen, there are not many countries where one is denied a chance for taking a public office because he or she is not young enough. In China, however, whether one can move up or has to step down along the ladder of political hierarchy now depends on how young or how old one is, before anything else. The age limits being enforced and institutionalised have therefore begun to shape China's political process in some interesting and unpredictable ways.

FROM GERONTOCRACY TO YOUNGER GENERATION

Until recently, age hardly mattered in Chinese politics. Most of the revolutionaries that took over power in 1949 were in their late 40s and early 50s. For instance, the average age of provincial party and government chiefs in 1950 was 45 years. In 1949, when Mao Zedong declared the founding of the People's Republic, he was 55 years old. Zhou Enlai was 50 years old when he became the Premier of China's central government in that year. Among the oldest members of the Long March generation, Zhu De was 62 years old in 1949. Among the youngest members of the Long March generation, Deng Xiaoping was only 46 years old in 1949. The average age of the ten most senior military leaders of the CCP was 57.2 years in 1955, the year when they were promoted to the rank of marshal.

However, despite the regime ageing over the ensuing decades, neither a retirement system for senior leaders nor an age limit for holding office was put in place. Three decades after it established the People's Republic, the CCP regime began to look like a "gerontocracy." Mao Zedong had held on to power until he died at the age of 83 in 1976. Marshal Zhu De and Premier Zhou Enlai who died in the same year were 89 and 77 years old respectively.

The ageing problem continued after Mao died. By the time the Politburo of the 11th Central Committee was formed in 1977, five of its 23 members were over 70 and two over 80. When Deng Xiaoping returned to the power center in 1978 he was already 75 years old. By the time the Politburo of the 12th Central Committee was formed in 1982, 11 of its 25 members were in their 70s and five were over the age of 80. The party leadership even looked octogenarian when a few revolutionary veterans in their 80s and 90s still wielded enormous political power.

The early 1980s also saw millions of ageing officials returning to power below the level of top leadership. Like Deng Xiaoping, they had physically survived the Cultural Revolution and were now rehabilitated. By the end of 1982, about three million previously purged officials had been rehabilitated. Political rehabilitation, while necessary and justified, created a new problem: the party organisation and government agencies were soon filled with a disproportionately high number of ageing officials.

It came as no surprise that while rehabilitating many ageing officials, Deng also stressed the need to select and promote younger officials. In 1982, Deng Xiaoping introduced "age limits" and abolished the "life tenure" for senior leaders as a means to force his ageing colleagues to retire without losing face; they would also not stand in the way of Deng's selected younger leaders. Massive political rehabilitation in the early 1980s was subsequently followed by an equally massive generational change of leadership in the mid-1980s.[1] Many rehabilitated ageing officials stayed in office for an average of two to three years before they were replaced by much younger officials. By the end of 1986, 1.37 million ageing officials who joined the CCP before 1949 had retired. Between 1982 and 1987, 550,000 younger and middle-aged cadres assumed leading positions at the county level and above.[2]

GENERATIONAL CHANGE OF CHINA'S PROVINCIAL LEADERSHIP

At the start of the People's Republic of China (PRC) in 1949, the average age of China's provincial chiefs was about 46 years: 45 for provincial party secretaries and 47 for provincial governors. Over time the regime naturally aged. The provincial party and government leadership was seriously disrupted during the initial years of the Cultural Revolution of 1967-1970. When the rehabilitated ageing officials returned to their leadership positions at the provincial level after the Cultural Revolution, the ageing trend continued until 1983-85 which saw a dramatic decrease in the average age of the provincial leaders, as many ageing provincial leaders were replaced by much younger ones.

For instance, among the outgoing provincial party secretaries and governors, 20 were succeeded by those who were at least 15 years younger. Six outgoing provincial leaders were succeeded by those who were more than 20 years younger. The average age of the incoming provincial leaders was 13.6 years lower than that of their predecessors. By 1985, the average age was 57.3 for provincial party secretaries and 56.1 for provincial governors, still higher than the average age of provincial chiefs in the early 1950s, but much lower than the average age of 66 of provincial chiefs in 1982 (see Figure 7.1).

FIGURE 7.1 AVERAGE AGE OF PROVINCIAL LEADERS (1949–2001)

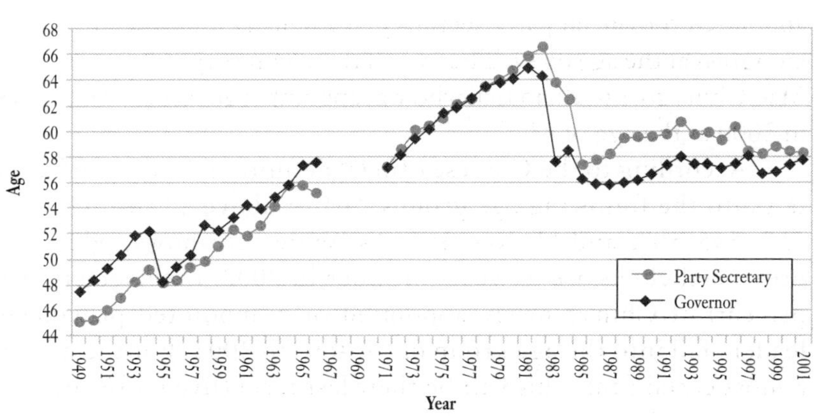

During the next 15 years or so (1985-2000), China's provincial leadership has been gradually ageing again. It is the recent round of provincial leadership change before and after the CCP's 16th Party Congress that has brought the average age of China's new provincial leaders to a level comparable to that of 1985. The average age of the 59 newly appointed or reappointed provincial party secretaries and governors for the 31 provincial administrative units (22 provinces, 5 autonomous regions, and 4 municipalities)[3] was 57.4 years in 2002.[4] The average age of 28 provincial governors/mayors is 56.6 years and the average of provincial party secretaries is 57.9 years, about one year higher. Most provincial party secretaries tend to be older than their government counterparts because the political career path in post-Mao China is that younger leaders often serve as provincial government chief before becoming a provincial party chief.

As Table 7.1 indicates, among the 31 newly appointed or reappointed provincial party secretaries, the oldest are Zhang Lichang, party secretary of Tianjin, who is also a member of the new Politburo, and Xu Youfang, party secretary of Heilongjiang. Both are 63 years old in 2002. Among the 28 newly appointed or reappointed provincial governors, the oldest is Niu Maosheng, Governor of Hebei, also 63 years old. The youngest provincial party secretary is Xi Jinping who became a full member of the 16th CCP Central Committee and was appointed provincial party secretary of Zhejiang after the 16th Party Congress at the age of 49. The title of the youngest governor in post-Mao China goes to Zhao Leji who was appointed governor of Qinghai in 2000 at the age of 43.

According to the Chinese official definition, leading officials fall into the following age groups: "61 or above", "56-60", "51-55", "45-50", and "below 45". As Table 7.1 shows, while 11 provincial chiefs are 61 years or older in 2002, the majority (63 percent) of China's newly appointed or reappointed provincial leaders fall into the age group of "56-60" in 2002. For them, it is almost certain that this will be their last term (five more years at most) in office because of the official retirement age of 65 for provincial chiefs, unless they can manage to move one step up above the level of provincial governor.

TABLE 7.1 NEWLY APPOINTED/REAPPOINTED PROVINCIAL LEADERS (2002)

Age	Name	Position	15th CC	16th CC
63	Niu Maosheng	Governor, Hebei	Full	Full
	Xu Youfang	Party secretary, Heilongjiang	Full	Full
	Zhang Lichang	Party secretary, Tianjin	Full	Full
62	Hong Hu	Governor, Jilin	Full	Full
	Liu Zhenhua	Governor, Shanxi	Alternate	Full
	Wen Shizhen	Party secretary, Liaoning	Full	Full
61	Cao Bochun	Party secretary, Guangxi	Full	Full
	Chen Kuiyuan	Party secretary, Henan	Full	Full
	Huang Zhendong	Party secretary, Chongqing	Full	Full
	Song Zhaosu	Party secretary, Gansu	Alternate	Full
	Yang Zhengwu	Party secretary, Hunan	Full	Full
60	Liu Qi	Party secretary, Beijing	Full	Full
	Abul'ahat Abdurixit	Governor, Xinjiang	Full	Full
	Huang Zhiquan	Governor, Jiangxi	Alternate	Full
	Shi Xiushi	Governor, Guizhou		Full
	Song Fatang	Governor, Heilongjiang	Alternate	Full
	Uyunqimg	Governor, Inner Mongolia		Full
	Wang Yunkun	Party secretary, Jilin	Full	Full
	Xu Rongkai	Governor, Yunnan		Full
	Zhang Zhongwei	Governor, Sichuan		Full
	Zhou Yongkang	Party secretary, Sichuan	Full	Full
59	Bai Kemin	Party secretary, Hebei		Full
	Ma Qizhi	Governor, Ningxia	Alternate	Full
	Xu Zhonglin	Party secretary, Jiangsu		Full
58	Chu Bo	Party secretary, Inner Mongolia	Alternate	Full
	Legqog	Governor, Tibet	Alternate	Full
	Li Zhaozhuo	Governor, Guangxi	Full	Full
	Qian Yunlu	Party secretary, Guizhou	Alternate	Full
	Wang Lequan	Party secretary, Xinjiang	Full	Full
	Wang Xiaofeng	Governor, Hainan	Full	Full
57	Chen Jianguo	Party secretary, Ningxia	Alternate	Full
	Ji Yunshi	Governor, Jiangsu	Alternate	Full
	Tian Chengping	Party secretary, Shanxi	Full	Full

TABLE 7.1 NEWLY APPOINTED/REAPPOINTED PROVINCIAL LEADERS (2002) (cont'd)

Age	Name	Position	15th CC	16th CC
	Yu Zhengsheng	Party secretary, Hubei	Full	Full
	Wang Hongju	Mayor (acting), Chongqing		Full
	Wang Jinshan	Governor (acting), Anhui	Alternate	Full
	Wang Taihua	Party secretary, Anhui	Alternate	Full
56	Bai Enpei	Party secretary, Yunnan	Full	Full
	Chen Liangyu	Party secretary, Shanghai	Alternate	Full
	Huang Huahua	Governor (expected), Guangdong	Alternate	Full
	Jia Zhibang	Governor, Shaanxi	Alternate	Full
	Li Jianguo	Party secretary, Shaanxi	Full	Full
	Li Shenglin	Mayor, Tianjin	Full	Full
	Luo Qingquan	Governor (acting), Hubei		Full
	Song Defu	Party secretary, Fujian	Full	Full
	Zhang Dejiang	Party secretary, Guangdong	Full	Full
	Zhang Gaoli	Party secretary, Shandong	Alternate	Full
	Zhang Yunchuan	Governor, Hunan		Full
55	Lu Hao	Governor, Gansu	Alternate	Full
	Guo Jinlong	Party secretary, Tibet	Alternate	Full
	Meng Jianzhu	Party secretary, Jiangxi	Alternate	Full
54	Su Rong	Party secretary, Qinghai	Alternate	Full
	Wang Qishan	Party secretary, Hainan	Alternate	Full
53	Bo Xilai	Governor, Liaoning		Full
50	Lu Zhangong	Governor (acting), Fujian	Alternate	Full
49	Xi Jinping	Party secretary, Zhejiang	Alternate	Full
48	Han Zheng	Mayor (expected), Shanghai		Full
47	Li Keqiang	Governor, Henan	Full	Full
45	Zhao Leji	Governor, Qinghai		Full

Sources: *China Directory 2001* (Tokyo: Radiopress, Inc., 2001); *Zhonggong Yanjiu* (Study of Chinese Communist Problems) (Taipei: The Institute for the Study of Chinese Communist Problems), various issues of 2000-2002.
Note: At the time of writing, the mayor of Beijing, governor of Zhejiang, and governor of Shandong are yet to be appointed.

It is especially worth noting that the composition of the 16th CCP Central Committee has further institutionalised the pattern of local representation, according to which all the provincial party and government chiefs are guaranteed a seat as full member in the central committee. Table 7.1 shows that of the 59 newly appointed or reappointed provincial party secretaries and governors/mayors, 24 were full and 23 were alternate members of the 15th Central Committee, but 12 have entered the CCP Central Committee for the first time. The latter includes, among others, six relatively old leaders: Shi Xiushi (aged 60), governor of Guizhou; Uyunqimg (aged 60), governor of Inner Mongolia; Xu Rongkai (aged 60), governor of Yunnan; Zhang Zhongwei (aged 60), governor of Sichuan; Bai Kemin (aged 59), party secretary of Hebei; and Xu Zhonglin (aged 59), party secretary of Jiangsu. Because of the official retirement age of 65, most of them will not be expected to sit on the 17th CCP Central Committee in 2007.

The most promising are those who are aged between 45 and 55, including: Su Rong, party secretary of Qinghai; Wang Qishan, party secretary of Hainan; Bo Xilai, governor of Liaoning; Lu Zhangong, acting governor of Fujian; Xi Jinping, party secretary of Zhejiang; Han Zheng, the expected mayor of Shanghai; Li Keqiang, governor of Henan; and Zhao Leji, governor of Qinghai. Barring the unexpected, they can reasonably expect to be active in Chinese politics for another ten years or more. Indeed, some of China's new rising political stars may very well emerge from this group.

NEW AGE LIMITS, NEW RULE

Age limits have not only shaped the lineup of provincial chiefs, but also the officialdom below the level of provincial governor. In 2002, Chinese leaders conducted several top-level meetings, with a heightened sense of urgency, to discuss the issue of training and promoting young cadres.[5] Since the second half of 2000, the Organisation Department of the CCP Central Committee and State Ministry of Personnel have required that officials at the level of section chief, division chief, and bureau chief step down from their leading posts at age 52, 55, and 58 respectively. The so-called "258" rule has lowered the age limit from 55 to 52 for section chief, from 58 to 55 for division chief, and from 60 to 58 for bureau chief.

Until this new rule was implemented, the retirement age for Chinese officials from section chief up to vice minister was 60. Barring promotions or transfer, most officials would stay in their current posts until they retired at age 60. This was the so-called "life tenure before retirement." Following the new rule officials have to leave their posts upon reaching certain age limits, even though they have not yet reached their official retirement age of 60, thus "leaving but not retiring" (*ligan bu tuixiu*).[6] For lack of a better term, we shall call the new age limits as the "stepping down"(*ligan*) age. This helps to distinguish the age (52, 55, or 58), at which an official at a certain level must step down, from the retirement age of 60 (see Table 7.2).

TABLE 7.2 AGE LIMITS FOR PARTY AND GOVERNMENT OFFICIALS

Retirement Age	Party Position	Government Position
70*	Party general secretary Member of Politburo	State president Premier/vice-premier
65	Provincial party secretary	Minister Provincial governor
60	Deputy provincial party secretary	Vice minister Vice provincial governor
58	Prefectural party secretary	Bureau/department chief Prefectural government head
55	County party secretary	Division chief County government head
52	Township party secretary	Section chief

*** The retirement age for the highest-ranking Chinese party and government officials has yet to be institutionalised.**

The new age limits have not only affected the incumbent, but also the officials in waiting. In line with the new age limits, those who are above 50 will not be considered for appointment to the level of bureau chief, those above 45 to the level of division chief, and those above 40 to the level of section chief.

Meanwhile, the Organisation Department of the CCP Central Committee has also launched the so-called "6080" Project, which calls for special attention to be given to those who were born in the 1960s and completed college education and started to work in the 1980s, that is, those young officials below the age of 40. More specifically, the "6080" Project requires that the leadership team at the division/county level have at least two members who are around the age of 30, that at the bureau/prefecture level one or two members below the age of 40, and that at the ministerial/provincial level one member in his/her early 40s.[7] At the end of 2000, there were 333 prefectures and 2,074 counties in China.[8] According to *Xinhua* news reports, by February 2001, there were about 1,500 cadres at the prefectural level who were under 45 years old and more than 2,300 cadres at the county level who were under 35 years old.[9]

IMPACT OF AGE LIMITS ON CHINA'S TOP LEADERSHIP

While age limits for officials at or below the level of central minister/provincial governor are very specific and even mechanical, age limits for China's top leaders are also being institutionalised. Months before the 16th Party Congress was convened, there had been a lot of speculation about whether Jiang Zemin would retire from any or all of the posts he held–the party secretary, the state president, and the chairman of the Central Military Commission that commands the military in China. The controversy surrounding Jiang's retirement originated from the "gentleman's agreement" reached at the 15th Party Congress in 1997, which requires members of China's highest decision-making body–the Politburo Standing Committee–to retire after the age of 70. By the same token, those leaders above 70 would not be eligible as candidates for membership in the new Politburo Standing Committee. This informal rule of retirement for China's top leaders is consistent with the historical trend. The number of Politburo members over the age of 70 has been decreasing since it jumped to 16 (64 percent of the total) in the 12th Central Committee in 1982: six in the 13th Central Committee in 1987, two in the 14th Central Committee in 1992, and finally down to only one (Jiang Zemin) in the 15th Central Committee in 1997.

At the 16th Party Congress, six of the seven members of the previous Politburo Standing Committee ultimately stepped down from the pinnacle of the political power. Five of them are at or above the age of 70, including Jiang Zemin (age 76), Li Peng (age 74), Zhu Rongji (age 74), Wei Jianxing (age 71) and Li Lanqing (age 70). The collective retirement of the powerful six has helped institutionalise the informal rule that the retirement age for China's top leaders is 70. Indeed, with the retirement of Li Ruihuan, the youngest retiree of the six, at the age of 68, it may further lower the retirement age for China's top leaders in the future.

Table 7.3 presents a comparison of the age structures of the CCP Politburo from 1956 to 2002. It shows that the age gap–the age difference between the oldest member and youngest member of the Politburo–has been narrowing from a high of 50 years in 1973 to 36 years in 1982, 29 years in 1987, 26 years in 1992, 18 years in 1997, and now 12 years in 2002. This means that the almost all of the members of the new Politburo belong to the same generation.

Jiang Zemin, of course, is not entirely retired from the power center. In view of the composition of the new Politburo and its Standing Committee, it is quite an understatement to say that in the next few years the new Party General Secretary Hu Jintao will live in the political shadow of Jiang Zemin. Indeed, with Jiang keeping his post as the chairman of the powerful Central Military Commission for at least a few more years, Hu will continue to live in the physical presence of Jiang.

TABLE 7.3 CHANGING AGE STRUCTURES OF THE CCP POLITBURO (1956-1997)

Central	Year	Average Age	Oldest	Youngest	Age Gap Committee (Years)
Eighth	1956	58.3	71	47	24
Ninth	1969	62.7	83	37	46
Tenth	1973	63.6	87	37	50
Eleventh	1977	65.6	85	44	41
Twelfth	1982	72.4	85	49	36
Thirteenth	1987	64.4	80	51	29
Fourteenth	1992	62.5	76	50	26
Fifteenth	1997	63.4	71	53	18

Sources: Compiled by the author from the information available in *China Directory*, various editions from 1990-2001 (Japan: Radiopress, Inc.); *Zhongguo gongchandang renming da cidian* (Who's Who of the Chinese Communist Party 1921-1991) (Beijing: China International Broadcasting Press, 1991); *Zhonggong yanjiu* (Study of Chinese Communist Problems) (Taipei: The Institute for the Study of Chinese Communist Problems), various issues of 1990-2001.

Hu Jintao's most important political asset remains his young age. The average age of the 24 members of the new Politburo is 61 years, about four years lower than that of the members of the Politburo formed in 1997. Whereas in the Politburo of the 15th Central Committee, Jiang was both the highest ranking and oldest member, in the Politburo of the 16th Central Committee, Hu Jintao is now the highest ranking and the second youngest member.

The average age of the nine members of the new Politburo Standing Committee is 62 years, about three years lower than that of the members of the Politburo Standing Committee formed in 1997. Of these nine members, five will either reach their retirement age or be very close to it when the next party congress convenes in 2007, including Luo Gan (b. 1935), Huang Ju (b. 1938), Wu Guanzheng (b. 1938), Zeng Qinghong (b. 1939), Jia Qinglin (b. 1940), and perhaps Wu Bangguo (b. 1941). Only Hu Jintao (b. 1942), Wen Jiabao (b. 1942), and Li Changchun

(b. 1944) are likely to serve one more term in the Politburo Standing Committee in 2007.

The Communist Party in China has been undergoing a massive leadership change and renewal in recent years. While informal power politics is still relevant in deciding who gets what official position, formal rules and regulations have become increasingly important. Never before in the history of the PRC and indeed in the history of China has the age of top leaders become such a relevant and key factor in politics. Almost all of a sudden, Chinese leaders and officials need to check their birthdays and ponder over their political careers on the basis of how old they already are or how young they still remain. As age limits become institutionalised and more forcefully implemented, they have begun to impact the behaviour of individual officials and shape China's political future.

ENDNOTES

1 For studies of the generational changes of China's leadership in the 1980s, see Hong Yung Lee, *From Revolutionary Cadres to Party Technocrats in Socialist China* (Berkeley: University of California Press, 1991); John P. Burns (ed.), *The Chinese Communist Party's Nomenklatura System: A Documentary Study of Party Control of Leadership Selection, 1979–1984* (Armonk, NY: M. E. Sharpe, 1989); Melanie Manion, "The Cadre Management System, Post-Mao: The Appointment, Promotion, Transfer, and Removal of Party and State Leaders", *The China Quarterly* (June 1985), pp. 203–33; Li Cheng and Lynn White, "Elite Transformation and Modern Change in Mainland China and Taiwan: Empirical Data and the Theory of Technocracy", *The China Quarterly* (March 1990), pp. 1–35; and Zang Xiaowei, "Provincial Elite in Post-Mao China", *Asian Survey*, June 1991, pp. 512–25.

2 *Zuzhi renshi xinxibao* (The Gazette of Organisation and Personnel), 180 (10 November 1988), p. 1.

3 This does not include Hong Kong Special Administrative Region, Macau Special Administrative Region, and Taiwan.

4 At the time of writing, the mayor of Beijing, the governor of Zhejiang, and the governor of Shandong had yet to be decided.

5 In a Politburo meeting in early 2000, Jiang Zemin mentioned that leaders of major powers in the world were only in their 50s and China needed to promote young leaders in their 50s and 40s. On 8-9 January 2000, a national conference of party organisation department chiefs concluded that the age structure of ministers, vice ministers, and provincial party and government leaders was not desirable. On 27-28 April 2000, at a

two-day national workshop, Vice President Hu Jintao urged greater efforts to be given to training and selecting younger officials. In June, in a speech at a national conference of party schools, Jiang Zemin called for redoubled efforts to select and train a great number of young leading officials. *People's Daily*, 29 April and 10 June 2000.

6 *Mingpao* (Hong Kong), 4 August 2000, p. B15.

7 Ibid.

8 Of 333 prefectures, 259 were cities at prefectural level and of 2,074 counties, 400 were cities at county level. *China Statistical Yearbook* (Beijing: National Bureau of Statistics of China, 2001), p. 3.

9 *Xinhua* news report, 11 May 2001.

CHAPTER 8

Party Recruitment: From Crisis to Private Entrepreneurs

IGNATIUS WIBOWO

In order to retain its vitality, any organisation needs to pay serious attention to recruitment–how many new members are to be recruited each year, and what kind of persons are to be admitted, etc. These new members will, eventually, determine the character of the organisation in the years to come. This is especially true with the Chinese Communist Party (CCP) which–in Leninist tradition–must be an elite party that draws its members from a specific social group in society. For a communist party, therefore, the recruitment of new members is crucially important.[1]

Against this background, the announcement of permission to recruit private entrepreneurs into the CCP cannot but take everybody by surprise. Jiang Zemin announced this on the occasion of the 80th anniversary of the CCP, on 1 July 2001, and in the 16th Congress of the CCP a year later, enshrined it into the Party Constitution. People, both inside and outside China, are raising questions as to the adoption of this policy because the CCP was established to be the vanguard party of the working class.

This chapter seeks to address one simple question: why did the CCP adopt such a policy? Is it a desperate attempt to increase the numbers through recruitment? Or, is it dictated by a calculation of broadening the support base? I will argue that the policy of recruitment of private entrepreneurs is determined by various factors, three of which are: (1) the crisis of recruitment; (2) the pressure by private entrepreneurs; (3) Jiang's sheer desire for personal glory.

IMMINENT CRISIS OF RECRUITMENT

The propaganda machine of the CCP always declares the constant increase of the total number of party members. Thus, it is declared that party members have increased from 4.5 million in 1949 to about 65 million in 2001, or an increase of about 60 million in 52 years. (Table 8.1) The fastest increases took place three times:

(1) 1954 to 1955: 7,859,473 – 9,393,394
(2) 1965 to 1966: 18,100,00 – 18,710,000
(3) 1972 to 1973: 20,000,000 – 28,000,000

There is no official explanation for these large increases but the three occasions reflect three critical turns in Chinese political history, each characterised by a new ideology or policy.[2] Under Jiang Zemin, party recruitment statistics also report a steady increase. Party membership increased from 50 million in 1990 to 64 million in 2000, up by 14 million. There were reports of expulsion of party members, but the number is apparently so small that it can be neglected.[3] The propaganda machine of the CCP, obviously, gives the impression that the CCP has been doing well in recruiting new members.

TABLE 8.1 ANNUAL CCP MEMBERSHIP GROWTH 1949-2000

Year	Total Number	Gross Change	% Change
1949	4,488,000	1,488,00	49,6
1950	5,000,000	512,000	11.4
1951	5,800,000	800,000	16.0
1952	6,001,698	239,405	4.2
1953	6,369,000	367,302	6.1
1954	7,859,473	1,490,473	23.4
1955	9,393,394	1,533,921	19.5
1956	10,730,000	1,336,606	14.2
1957	12,720,000	1,990,000	18.5
1958	12,450,000	-270,000	-2.1

TABLE 8.1 ANNUAL CCP MEMBERSHIP GROWTH CCP 1949-2000 (cont'd)

Year	Total Number	Gross Change	% Change
1959	13,960,000	1,510,000	12.1
1961	17,380,000	na	Na
1964	18,010,000	na	Na
1965	18,710,000	700,000	3.9
1966	20,000,000	na	Na
1969	22,000,000	na	Na
1971	17,000,000	na	Na
1972	20,000,000	3,000,000	17.6
1973	28,000,000	8,000,000	40.0
1976	35,070,000	na	Na
1977	35,000,000	na	Na
1979	37,000,000	Na	na
1980	38,000,000	1,000,000	2.7
1981	38,923,569	923,569	2.4
1982	39,657,212	733,643	1.9
1983	40,950,000	1,292,788	3.3
1984	41,000,000	50,000	0.1
1985	42,000,000	1,000,000	2.4
1986	44,000,000	2,000,000	4.8
1987	46,011,951	2,011,951	4.6
1988	48,000,000	1,988,049	4.3
1989	49,000,000	1,000,000	2.1
1990	50,000,000	1,000,000	2.0
1991	50,320,000	320,000	0.6
1992	51,956,000	1,636,000	3.3
1993	52,800,000	844,000	1.6
1994	54,000,000	1,200,000	2.3
1995	56,781,000	2,781,000	5.2
1996	57,000,000	2,190,000	3.9
1997	58,000,000	1,000,000	1,7
1998	61,000,000	3,000,000	4,4
1999	na	Na	Na
2000	64,510,000	Na	Na

Source: Zheng Shiping, *Party vs. State in Post-1949 China. The Institutional Dilemma* (Cambridge: Cambridge University Press, 1997), p. 268; from Jiang Zemin's Speech at the 15th Party Congress, 12 September 1997, *Beijing Review*, Vol. 40, No. 40 (October 6-12, 1997), p. 31; 1998: from *Renmin ribao* (28 June 1999), p.1; 2000: from *Renmin ribao* (4 June 2001), p.1.

Despite these positive reports, at the same time, there were also reports of difficulties in recruiting new members. Rosen's study shows that in the late 1980s, students of prestigious universities in China were more eager to follow the "black path" (studying abroad) than the "red path" (joining the party). The margin is overwhelmingly large: 73.8 percent for the former, and 5.5 percent for the latter.[4] To the students, joining the party is considered to be "a game of snakes and ladders" where people can rise and fall all of sudden, and consequently does not offer certainty. Similar responses, also in the late 1980s, came from the workers. Only 16.68 percent of them expressed "strong desire" to enter the party, while the rest did not. Some "hoped to join, but didn't think that they have qualifications" (29.7 percent), some "hoped to join, but the party spirit is not correct" (29.1 percent), and some simply "had not given any thought to it" (22.46 percent).[5] In the countryside, a survey conducted in Gansu Province revealed only 6.1 percent of rural youth below the age of 30 expressed their interest in the party membership.[6]

About ten years later, another survey on peasant attitudes toward the party in Ning County, also in Gansu Province, reveals that recruitment to party membership is still a problem. There are fewer and fewer young peasants who would like to join the party, leading to a reduction in young party members. Out of 8,932 party members in that county, only 24 percent was below the age of 35. One of the reasons cited is that they did not get any economic benefit from joining the party. "In addition, by entering the party, you are put under strict discipline, you have to go to meetings, and the organisation can influence your way of earning money."[7] A survey on workers at a state-owned enterprise in Hunan Province shows that out of 7,548 workers there were only 710 party members or 9.4 percent. But what is striking is that out of 695 units, there are 284 units that do not have any party members. In addition, in these units only 283 workers (out of 2,519) applied for party membership.[8] Workers who are supposed to form the main body of the party have apparently lost interest in the party.

Rosen's study of ten years ago is further confirmed by some other surveys on students and intellectuals in the late 1990s. For instance, one report from Henan Province says that high-school students, especially those at the lower level, have no interest in joining the party. Up to now, there were still a good number of students sitting at a high level who are party members, but it is feared that in the coming years there will be no student party members.[9] A survey conducted of a group of typical intellectuals, Beijing's intellectuals, does not deviate too far away.[10] Among the intellectuals who are not party members, 45.2 percent of them who "hope to join the Chinese Communist Party." The rest either "join the democratic parties" (3.5 percent), or "don't want to join any party" (27.9 percent), or "simply give no thought to it" (23.5 percent). The report adds: "To be noted, the number of those who hope to join the party tends to decline, whereas those who do not want to join any party tend to rise."[11]

Given this contrary evidence, the official statistics of the rise of party members should be interpreted with scepticism. These recent surveys and that of ten years ago both indicate that there were fewer and fewer people interested in joining the party, be they peasants, workers, or intellectuals. The party seemed to receive a very low appreciation from the groups who traditionally formed the core of the party. The poor and the educated tended to avoid the party for a variety of reasons. The peasants simply thought that party membership did not bring immediate benefit, especially economic benefits. The workers, equally, found that joining the party would not bring any economic benefit, and, furthermore, it also did not give them a sense of pride because nowadays the party members were not much different from other ordinary people, indeed most of them were involved in corruption. The intellectuals saw that there was a big gap between theory and practice, so big that they tended not to believe all the theories presented by the party.

To overcome this crisis, the best available option is to open the door of the party as widely as possible to everybody. The party can no longer afford to recruit members originating from only one or two particular social groups of society if it wants to survive.

THE PRESSURE TO TAKE PRIVATE ENTREPRENEURS

While the CCP is facing a crisis of recruitment, there is a social group in China which has appeared to be eager to join the party. Yet, this group has long been a stigma in the socialist society of China during Mao's era; they are the private entrepreneurs. With the progress of the liberalisation of Chinese economy, their presence in society is also becoming more and more conspicuous.[12] According to one estimate, the number of private entrepreneurs in China in the year 2000 was ten times higher than it was in 1956. There were only 160,000 private entrepreneurs then, compared to 20,110,000 now.[13] Another author, relying on the "Almanac of Private Entrepreneurs in China, 2000," suggests that in 1999 there were 20,220,000 private entrepreneurs who controlled capital as high as 1,028.7 billion *yuan*.[14]

Why are the private entrepreneurs happy to join the party? If they are already wealthy, why bother to join the party? The motivation of private entrepreneurs to join the party is complex, consisting of various calculations, which are different from one location to another. But, in China, private entrepreneurs are seeking not only wealth but also power which they can use to increase their wealth.[15] In a country governed by a single party, power is concentrated in the hand of the party–in our case the CCP–such that private entrepreneurs must be able to make use of it. Instead of supporting a new political party to further their interests (like those in democratic countries), they choose to take advantage of the readily available political party that rules with absolute power. Although even without having joined the party they have already enjoyed some benefit,[16] they will have even greater advantages if they join the party.[17]

Jiang Zemin has long been known for his negative view of private entrepreneurs. For instance, in 1989 he made a statement of banning private entrepreneurs from joining the party. He stated: "What is discussed in this conference is that private entrepreneurs are not allowed to join the party."[18] A document of the Central Committee confirmed Jiang's statement: "Our party is the vanguard of the working class. The relationship of private entrepreneurs and the working class is one of the exploiters and the exploited. Thus, it is not allowed to recruit private entrepreneurs into the party."[19] But, evidently, he can no longer defend this view as he cannot ignore a social group that forms 10 percent of the population in China and controls such a big sum of money.

He may reason that, given the crisis of recruitment, it is better to accept the private entrepreneurs into the party. Their membership will not only increase the numbers of the party but will also strengthen the position of the CCP that it is desperately in need of support for economic development programme. If the CCP wants to continue to develop the economy, the best way to get the entrepreneurs' support is by openly recruiting them and acknowledging that they are part of the ruling party.

Thus, there is a reciprocal need. The private entrepreneurs need power and influence from the party, whereas the party needs their strong support for their programme. It has to be noted that Jiang did not elaborate further on the meaning of recruiting private entrepreneurs. They may be recruited to the party, but it does not necessarily mean that they can hold leadership positions, such as Party Secretary, in the party.

JIANG'S PERSONAL DESIRE FOR GLORY

The recruitment of private entrepreneurs into the party has actually been going on for quite some time. For instance, in 1988, there was a report revealing that 200,000 (or 0.4 percent) of the 50 million party members were private entrepreneurs.[20] But, the party did not want to acknowledge this fact until Jiang Zemin announced it on the occasion of the celebration of the 80th anniversary of the CCP, on 1 July 2001. The critical question is: why did it take so long for Jiang to make it a formal policy? Why did he not spell it out some years ago (for instance, at the 14th Congress, 1992)? The timing certainly must have been carefully chosen.

Commentators from abroad were quick to take the statement by Jiang as an attempt on his part to leave his mark on history.[21]

Whether he is a great pretender or not, the fact is that he cannot hide his desire to be recognised as "paramount leader" of China. This desire was clearly manifested during the celebration of the 50th anniversary of China's National Day, 1 October 1949. First, his huge portrait was paraded in line with that of Mao Zedong and Deng Xiaoping. Secondly, he inspected the military in a posture identical to that of Mao and Deng, namely standing in an open jeep and receiving a salute from the military.[22] By doing this, no one can fail to see that Jiang has tried to put himself on a par with Mao and Deng.

Jiang's desire can be realised both by staying in power for good and by issuing a new teaching. The first and the second goals are separate but they are connected. If Jiang would like to stay in power for good, it means that he must produce a new body of teaching. But, the second goal can be achieved independently if the first goal cannot be achieved. As to the first goal, Jiang is certainly aiming at being re-elected again at the 16th Congress in 2002. This has been an open secret that since the year 2000 Jiang was trying hard to be re-elected as the General Secretary of the CCP.

But Jiang is no Mao or Deng, who were truly paramount leaders. Jiang did not have such charisma that he could say a few words and everybody would obey (in Chinese: *shuo le suan*). He is the General Secretary, but he actually is a *primus inter pares* who needs a consensus from his colleagues at the Politburo before he issues a decision.[23] As such, to achieve the first goal, Jiang had to be able to persuade his colleagues by providing credentials.

Ideology is the field which Jiang sees as an opportunity not to miss.[24] Mao Zedong has long been known for his contribution to China in the form of "Mao Zedong Thought," and Deng Xiaoping in the form of "the theory of Deng Xiaoping." In 1999, Jiang made attempts by launching an ideology of "three emphases" (*san jiang)*, similar to campaign movements during the Mao era where cadres had to engage in study sessions, criticisms and self-criticism, etc. But it ended miserably because no one was impressed by this ideology as it was "so out of tune with the daily pursuits of the people in China's bustling capitalistic market economy."[25] He made his last attempt in the year 2000 when he launched the "three represents" (*san ge daibiao*).

As time was short, early in the year 2000, Jiang made a tour to Guangdong, and there he propagated his teaching about "three represents" that the party represents "the most advanced productive forces, the most advanced culture, and the fundamental interests of the broad masses of the Chinese people".[26] Since then, also taking the style of campaign movements, the "three represents" dominated the mass media and discussion groups in China. From February to mid-November 2000, the *People's Daily* (the CCP's mouthpiece) alone published more than 300 papers on the "three represents" and various reports on how the concept had spread throughout the country.[27] About a year and a half year later, at the occasion of the 80th anniversary, Jiang repeated this new teaching and at the same time also made it clear that private entrepreneurs were allowed to join the party. Despite the debate, Jiang was successful in implanting the teaching of "three represents" into the Party Constitution during the 16th Party Congress in 2002.

This achievement is indeed impressive. Now, Jiang has not only overhauled the ideology of the party but also introduced a new element in the rank and file of the party, namely the private entrepreneurs. Mao Zedong had made a breakthrough by recruiting peasants into the party and changed the party into a peasant-based party. Similarly, Deng Xiaoping also has introduced a major change by allowing the intellectuals to join the party, indeed by taking them into the working class. Jiang must have felt that he could now compare himself with Mao as well as Deng in terms of contribution to the party.

It is also becoming clear why Jiang chose the occasion of the 80th anniversary of the CCP in July 2001 to announce the policy of permitting the recruitment of private entrepreneurs. It was a kind of "pre-emptive strike" on the part of Jiang who calculated that by announcing the teaching a year before the 16th Party Congress there would be enough time for his colleagues to evaluate him. Jiang must know well that his colleagues will not easily give him a free ride. But, Jiang may also want, through the massive campaign of "three represents," to convince the whole population that he still deserves another term as General Secretary. The acceptance by the population is another credit to him.

A BROADER CONTEXT

The recruitment of private entrepreneurs has to be understood in a broader context, namely the steady shift of party membership as a whole. Is it something so extraordinary, or something irresistible? The debate on the recruitment of the private enterprises gives an impression that it is something ordinary, such that it will lead to the demise of the party. Take the example of the argument put forward by Lin Yanzhi, the Vice Party Secretary of the Party Committee of Jilin Province. In his article published in a leading journal, *Zhenli de zhuiqiu* in Bejing, he argues against the recruitment of private entrepreneurs into the party, claiming that capitalists have the potential to damage the party. "Only when there is the purity of the organisation, will there be a thorough understanding, a unity of guiding thought, and then the party will have a coagulation power as well as a fighting capacity."[28]

That same journal actually has published more articles on the topic, all arguing against the recruitment of "private entrepreneurs" into the party.[29] Another journal, *Zhongliu*, since early 2000, has published articles discussing the problem of letting private entrepreneurs join the Party. One article reports the influx of private entrepreneurs who joined the Party, and warns of the danger of such a policy.[30] Some articles question the future of the party. "Can the CCP Change into Socialist Party?"[31] or "Actually, the Party Wants to Change into What Type of Party?"[32] One author has gone so far as to suggest the expulsion of all capitalists from the party![33]

The view of those who were labelled as "leftists" actually has overlooked the fact that recruitment, in the past ten years, has seen a radical shift. Due to the difficulties of recruiting young men and women, the party has adapted the criterion of recruitment to the new realities. Workers and peasants slowly lose their predominance within the party; there are more and more party members who are not coming from "good class background."

One can see this trend in *Zhongguo baike nianjian* (Annual Encyclopaedia of China) which started publication in 1990 and ended in 1995. This encyclopaedia provides data not only on the annual increase of members, but also on education, on age, and for the first time on gender. From Table 8.2, one can immediately observe that the majority of party members are male, over the age of 36, and primary school graduates.

TABLE 8.2 DETAILED DESCRIPTION OF PARTY MEMBERS, 1990-1994 (IN THOUSANDS)

	1990	1991	1992	1993	1994
Total Party Members	50,320	51,510	52,000	54,000	55,400
New members	1,300	1,630	1,760	1,760	1,870
Gender					
Male	43,010	43,930	44,9 00	45,900	46,900
Female	7,310	7,580	7,800	8,100	8,500
Age					
Below 25	2,030	1,990	2,040	2,100	2,260
26-35	23,760	24,160	9,250	9,200	9,400
36-45			15,250	15,500	15,700
46-60	18,230	18,390	S18,600	18,800	19,090
Over 60	6,300	6,970	7,600	8,20	8,950
Education					
High school or over	5,180	5,650	6,190	6,800	7,430
Primary school	19,070	18,710	18,330	17,800	17,450

Sources: *Zhongguo baike nianjian* (Annual Encyclopaedia of China) *1990-1994*, (Beijing: Zhongguo da baike quanshu chubanshe, 1990-1994).

The encyclopaedia provides further details regarding the distribution of social groups, starting from the year 1992 (Table 8.3). We can observe that the decline of peasants in its ranks has been rapid, even though in absolute terms the peasants still make up a sizeable force within the party. Gone are the days when the majority of party members were peasants. The number of workers, however, showed a slight increase from 8 million to 9 million. Both peasants and workers combined together form 50 percent of all party members. The other half comprises various groups, like administrators, technicians, managers of state-owned enterprises and collective enterprises, and military personnel. This new distribution shows a diversity of social background of party members; the CCP no longer comprises peasants, workers, and army men as indicated in the Party Constitution. Almost all social groups in Chinese society can join the party (interestingly, intellectuals have not been mentioned in this encyclopaedia).

TABLE 8.3 PROFILE OF PARTY MEMBERS, 1992-1994 (IN THOUSANDS)

	1992		1993		1994	
	Number	%	Number	%	Number	%
By Profession						
Workers	8,680	16.5	8,700	16.1	9,810	17.7
Peasants	18,700	36.0	18,700	34.6	18,850	34.6
Administrative	4,600	8.9	4,600	8.5	4,810	8.7
Technicians	6,550	12.6	n.a.	-	7,700	13.9
Managers of SOEs and Collective enterprises	4,290	8.3	4,400	8.2	5,200	9.4
Others	4,000	7.7	4,800	8.9	2,100	3.8
Unaccounted for	-	7.1	-	23.7	-	11.9
Total Party members	52,000	100	54,000	100	55,400	100

Sources: *Zhongguo baike nianjian* (Annual Encyclopaedia of China) 1990-1994, (Beijing: Zhongguo da baike quanshu chubanshe, 1990-1994).

These statistics demonstrate that since the early 1990s the majority of the members of the CCP have no longer been workers or peasants. In other words, the CCP has diversified its membership from one exclusively consisting of workers and peasants to one consisting of various social groups. This trend has not been publicy acknowledged. The party leadership–both at the national and local levels–simply takes it as unthinkable that the party should include social groups other than workers or peasants.

Viewed from this context, it is understandable that the party must allow the recruitment of private entrepreneurs, even if it is not supported by legal documents. Thus, for instance, the admission of private entrepreneurs into the party has actually taken place since as early as 1980. As recorded by Rosen, the party made "a major effort to attract new rich peasants, the so-called 'specialised households' and 'ten-thousand-*yuan* households.'"[34] In Jiangsu Province, the journal *Qunzhong*, from June to November 1988, carried articles debating the question "In the primary stage of socialism, should the party raise or lower its demands on members?"[35] In Liaoning, similar debates appeared in the journal *Dangjian wenhui*, arguing the suitability of recruiting a millionaire who ran a private enterprise.[36] In the1980s recruiting private enterprises took place, ignoring the objections raised by those who did not agree.

This trend seemed to go unabated. For instance, in April 2000, an article mentions that 158 private entrepreneurs in Qingfu County (Shanghai) had joined the party.[37] This statistic is confirmed by Liu Changfa, three months later, who reports that until the end of 1998 Qingfu County had 158 private entrepreneurs who became party members, adding that it accounted for about 15 percent of all party members who were in private enterprises in the whole county.[38] Liu provides even more interesting data. In a "certain city" on the eastern coast, from 1994-1996, the party had recruited 61 new members, 36 of which were private entrepreneurs (59 percent). Liu also reports that in three cities in Jiangsu Province (Qinshuqian, Lianyungang, Zhunyangsan), 858 private entrepreneurs applied and were admitted to join the party. This number forms 42 percent of the total applicants.

It is very difficult to arrive at an exact number of how many private entrepreneurs in all of China joined the party. Quoting the *Almanac of Private Economy in China 2000*, Li Qiang estimates that some 19.8 percent of the 20.2 million private entrepreneurs in China were party members in 1999.[39] In other words, there are currently about 4.3 million private entrepreneurs who are party members. But, it has to be qualified that these 4.3 million private-entrepreneurs-cum-party-members are not all the result of recruitment because they could have been party members who turned private entrepreneurs. (For example, one report discloses that in one locality, 36 out of 52 party branches within private enterprise are run by party secretaries, effectively making them private entrepreneurs).[40]

Thus, it is becoming clearer that the policy of recruiting private entrepreneurs only reflects a national trend of diversifying party members. The CCP is adopting, to overcome the crisis, a new strategy of recruitment in which anybody can now join the party, including private entrepreneurs. Thus the announcement made by Jiang in 2001 was not something new, but one that had actually been going on for at least a decade. What Jiang has done is only to give a formal justification or legitimatisation to the actual practice.

CONCLUSION

As mentioned in the beginning of the chapter, recruitment is crucially important for the survival of an organisation. In our discussion, I have started by pointing out how the crisis of recruitment has forced the leadership to invite anyone to join the party. The private entrepreneurs, theoretically, are not permitted to join the party. But, with their growing important role in the economy, the leadership (in this case, Jiang Zemin) was ready to soften its rigid stance on the matter. To prevent an ideological gap, Jiang developed a new ideology (three represents) where the presence of the private entrepreneurs could be accommodated. The private entrepreneurs themselves are more than happy to accept the offer as they realise that money without power is like walking with one foot.

But, it is also clear that behind this accommodating attitude, Jiang also would like to secure a special place in the Chinese history as a "paramount leader" similar to Mao and Deng. Hence, the teaching of "three represents" is basically a means to salvage the party from its crisis, and at the same time, to enhance the stature of Jiang Zemin. Jiang's opponent must have known this and it is not surprising that they (the leftists) attacked Jiang's policy fiercely, despite the fact that the recruitment of private entrepreneurs had been going on for more than a decade.

As we know, Jiang did not get the extension for a leadership position in the party. In the 16th Party Congress (November 2002), his colleagues in the Politburo might have opposed the idea of giving him another term as General Secretary. To save face, however, they allowed Jiang's teaching about "three represents" to be enshrined in the Party Constitution. In addition, Jiang was also allowed to plant five of his friends to become members of the powerful Standing Committee of the Politburo.

Jiang's defeat aside, three conclusions can be drawn in terms of party recruitment. First, the party is indeed facing a crisis of recruitment. The statistics released by the party show a steady increase of party members, yet at the same time, there are also reports of widespread apathy among the population toward the party. The diversification of party members is also a case in point where the party has yielded to the pressure of recruiting any body. For outsiders, one can only speculate upon the exact number of party members; it may not be as high as 65 million. Until there is an independent study by non-party researchers, it will be impossible to know the reality.

Secondly, recruiting private entrepreneurs into the party will not affect the party partly because private entrepreneurs account for a small portion of party membership and partly because those who join the party will certainly not be able to occupy a decision-making position (such as Party Secretary). Will senior members give way to newcomers and allow them to become their leaders? Only in very special cases can it happen, but in general, the senior members of the party will occupy the leadership positions. If private entrepreneurs can become only ordinary members, then the leftists; worry is rather misplaced; they should, actually, direct their criticisms towards party members who become entrepreneurs.

Thirdly, due to widespread apathy towards the party among the population, the party opens its door to everybody; there is no longer a special group to be targeted for recruitment of new members. Workers and peasants, in terms of numbers, may still dominate the party, but members of the CCP are now more diversified, consisting of different sorts of social groups. Consequently, it is becoming difficult for the party to claim it is the "vanguard party of the proletariats." The teaching of "three representatives" is actually an honest recognition of the radical shift from Lenin's concept.

What will happen if the party can only recruit people of little talent? If the best and the brightest opt to go to private sector, there is a real possibility that the party will be full of people who only care about their career but do not have much ability. In other words, the party will consist of people who have poor educational background. It is true that the party provides training to new members as well as other members through various "party schools," but these schools still function more as an indoctrination ground than as education providers. In the longer term, party members will find it difficult to compete with those in the private sector, and this will further aggravate the problem of recruitment. Eventually, the party will consist of uneducated people who are holding great power.

ENDNOTES

1 There are numerous works that deals with Lenin's idea of the vanguard party. For a brief introduction, see R.N. Carew Hunt, *The Theory and Practice of Communism. An Introduction* (New York: The Macmillan Co., 1961), pp. 163-170.

2 In 1954 Mao decided that the party should take more members from among the peasants. In 1965 the radicalisation of ideology became more and more acute every day. In 1972 Deng Xiaoping made the first come-back. Roberta Martin, *Party Recruitment in China: Patterns and Prospects*, Occasional Papers (New York: East Asian Institute, Columbia University, 1981).

3 Reports can be found under the heading "Zhongguo gongchandang", in *Zhongguo baike nianjian* (Annual Encyclopaedia of China) *1990-1994*, (Beijing: Zhongguo Da Baike Quanshu Chubanshe, 1990-1994).

4 Stanley Rosen, "The Chinese Communist Party and Chinese Society: Popular Attitudes toward Party Membership and the Party's Image", *The Australian Journal of Chinese Affairs*, N0. 24 (July 1990), p. 63.

5 Ibid., p. 70.

6 Ibid., p. 71.

7 Zhonggong zhong ninxian wei zuzhibu, *Gongchandang ren*, No. 12 (December, 1998), pp. 7-9.

8 *Gongren ribao* (26 June, 2000), p. 7.

9 *Henan daxue xuebao (shehui kexue yuan)*, Vol. 39, No. 2 (March 1999), pp. 100-101.

10 This survey is conducted in two phases: from December 1996 to March 1997, and again from March to June 1999. In the first phase, 3,031 questionnaires were returned (89.1%) and in the second phase 367 were returned (87.3%). See, NN, "*Shehui jingji guanxi xin bianhua zhong de zhishi fenzi yu zhizheng dang jianshe*" [The Intellectuals and the construction of the party in the midst of new changes of social and economic relations], in *Dangdai zhongguo yanjiu* (Beijing), No. 1 (January, 2000), pp. 117-126.

11 Ibid., p. 145.

12 Studies on private entrepreneurs in China are numerous, see, for example, Margaret M. Pearson, *China's New Business Elite: The Political Consequences of Economic* Reform (Berkeley, CA: University of California Press, 1997); Li Qiang, *Dangdai zhongguo shehui fenceng yu liudong* (Beijing: Zhongguo jingji chubanshe, 1993), pp. 313-331; Zhang Houyi and Ming Lizhi (eds.), *A Report of the Development of Private Enterprises in China* (Beijing : Social Sciences Literature Press, 1999); Tian Xiaowen, *The Private Economy in China: Will the Ugly Duckling Become a Swan*, paper presented at the conference on "The Challenges to China's Fourth Generation Leadership", 8-9 November 2001, organised by East Asian Institute, National University of Singapore.

13 Lin Yanzhi, "Gongchandang lingdao he jiayu xin zichan jieji", *Zhenli de zhuiqiu*, No. 5 (May, 2001), p.3.

14 Li Qiang, "Guanyu siying jingji de ruogan ziliao" (Several Materials on Private Economy), *Zhenli de zhuiqiu* (In Pursuit of Truth), No. 5 (May, 2001), p. 17.

15 The penetration of businessmen into politics has been taken up by a number of scholars, the classic one is that of Charles E. Lindblom, *Politics and Markets. The World's Political-Economic Systems* (New York: Basic Books, 1977); the penetration by global capitalists, see Noreena Hertz, *The Silent Takeover. Global Capitalism and the Death of Democracy* (London: William Heinemann, 2001).

16 Pearson, *op.cit.*; David Wank, "Private business, bureaucracy and political alliance in a Chinese city" in *The Australian Journal of Chinese Affairs*, No. 33 (January 1995), pp. 55-71. *Idem*, "The Institutional Process of Market Clientelism: *Guanxi* and private business in a South China city", *The China Quarterly*, No. 147 (September 1996), pp. 820-838.

17 This proposition needs to be tested by systematic research on the motivation of private entrepreneurs to join the party.

18 Jiang Zemin, speech at the conference of national organisation department, 21 August, 1989, in *Shisan da yilai zhongyao wenxian xuanbian* (Selected Important Documents since the 13th Party Congress), Vol. II (Beijing: Renmin Chubanshe, 1991), p. 584.

19 Central Committee of the CCP, "Announcement on strengthening the construction of the Party", 28 August, 1989, in Ibid., p. 598.

20 *Ming Pao*, 4 August 1992; quoted in John D. Friske (ed.), *China. Facts & Figures Annual Handbook*, Vol. 17, (Academic International Press, 1993), p. 42.

21 *International Herald Tribune* (2 July 2001), p. 1; John Pomfret, "China Allows Its Capitalists to Join Party", *Washington Post* (2 July 2001), p.1.

22 Joseph Fewsmith, *China since Tiananmen. The Politics of Transition* (Cambridge: Cambridge University Press, 2001), p. 221.

23 This situation has been assessed by Parris H. Chang, Lucian Pye, Lowell Dittmer, Frederick Teiwes, David Bachman, Joseph Fewsmith, David Shambaugh, etc., in a special issue of *The China Journal*, No. 45 (January 2001).

24 On the importance of ideology in China, see Franz Schurmann, *Ideology and Organization* (Berkeley, CA: University of California Press, 1968).

25 Lance L.P. Gore, "Dream On: Communists of the Dengist Brand in Capitalistic China", in John Wong and Zheng Yongnian (eds.), *The Nanxun Legacy and China's Development in the Post-Deng Era* (Singapore: Singapore University Press and World Scientific Publishing, 2001), pp. 197-219.

26 On this campaign, see, for instance, Fewsmith, *op.cit.*, pp. 229-230.

27 See Zheng Yongnian, "China's Politics in 2000: Preparing the Ground for Power Transition", *EAI Background Brief*, No. 79 (Singapore: 26 December 2000), p. 6.

28 Li Yanzhi, *op.cit.*

29 Li Yongqiang et al., "Guanyu siying qiyezhu nengfo dang laomo dang gongchandangyuan de diaocha baogao" (Report of an Investigation on the Question whether or not Private Entrepreneurs Can Become Worker Model and Members of the CCP), *Zhenli de zhuiqiu*, No. 3 (March, 2001), pp. 21-26); Xiang Qiyuan, "Gongren jieji de zhengdang qi neng xishou zibenjia" (How Can the Ruling Party of the Working Class Admit Capitalists?), *Zhenli de zhuiqiu*, No. 1 (January, 2001), pp. 27-34.

30 Liu Changfa, "Huashuo 'laoban dangyuan', 'laoban shuji'" (Just Say 'Party Member Boss', 'Secretary Boss'") *Zhongliu*, No. 7 (July, 2000), pp. 10-11.

31 Wang Xiangguang, "Gongchandang qi neng gaiming wei shehuidang" (Should the CCP Change its Name into Socialist Party?) *Zhongliu*, No. 4 (April, 2000), pp. 2-5.

32 Huang Rutong, "Jiujing yao jiangcheng yi ge shenme dang?" (Actually It Would Like to Change into What Type of Party?), *Zhongliu*, No. 3 (March 2000), pp. 16-19.

33 Lu Fashun, "Qingchu siying qiyezhu, weihu dang chunjiexing" (Expel the Private Entrepreneurs, Preserve the Purity of the Party) *Zhongliu*, No. 4 (April, 2000), pp. 6-8.

34 Rosen, *op. cit.*, p. 61.

35 "Zai shehui zhuyi chuji jieduan, dang dui dangyuande yaoqiu jinggai gao yixie haishi di yixie".

36 Almost all issues of *Dangjian wenhui* (Shenyang) in 1988.

37 Lu Fashun, “Qingchu siying qiyezhu, weihu dang chunjiexing”, pp. 6-8.

38 See, Liu Changfa, *op.cit.*

39 Li Qiang,, *op.cit.*, p.26.

40 Liu Changfa, “Huashuo ‘laoban dangyuan, laoban shuji’” , pp. 10-11.

CHAPTER 9

China's Cadres and Cadre Management System

KJELD ERIK BRODSGAARD

WHO ARE THE CADRES?

There are currently 40.5 million cadres in China (see Table 9.1). Of these, 47.5 percent or 19.2 million work in the so-called *shiye danwei* (service units), 35.2 percent or 14.3 million in production enterprises and 17.2 percent or 7.0 million in government and party organs. Women account for 35 percent of the total number of cadres and national minorities for 6.8 percent.[1] Almost all leading cadres from the county level and above are party members, whereas lower level cadres need not be party members. The Chinese Communist Party (CCP) currently has 64.5 million members.[2]

The term "cadre" was first developed during the Russian revolution and then translated into Chinese as *ganbu*. In this original sense, the cadres are the leaders of the revolution, the masses and the followers. They are the vanguard of the revolutionary class that Lenin, in his important "organisational manual", *What is to Be Done*, said should be created and trained to lead the revolution.[3] Lenin made it quite clear that the party should create a veritable class of professional revolutionaries, who would act as the central nucleus of the party and would "devote to the revolution not their free evenings but their whole life."[4]

The cadres in China can be regarded as the post-revolutionary successors of the imperial bureaucracy. The emperor made sure the bureaucracy served him loyally and did not develop its own interests and power base. In the same way the present regime makes sure that the cadres serve the party and its leader ("emperor") – whether it is Mao Zedong, Deng Xiaoping or Jiang Zemin – and do not develop local or institutional power bases that may undermine central control.

After the 1949 revolution in China, cadres usually referred to persons in responsible or leading positions within an organisation or those who assumed responsibility for specific political tasks. Accordingly a person's status as cadre does not necessarily involve membership of the CCP although in practice this would often be the case, especially for leading cadres (i.e., cadres above the county-level).

TABLE 9.1 SECTORAL DISTRIBUTION OF CADRES IN CHINA, 1981-1998

Year	Total (million)	Govt. organs		Service Units		Enterprises	
		million	%	million	%	million	%
1981	19.8	3.5	17.9	8.5	43.0	7.7	39.0
1982	21.0	3.9	18.5	9.1	43.5	8.0	37.8
1983	22.0	4.1	18.5	9.4	42.7	8.5	38.8
1984	25.1	4.6	18.2	10.1	40.1	10.5	41.8
1985	26.5	5.0	18.8	11.4	42.8	10.2	38.4
1986	27.7	5.3	19.2	12.0	43.2	10.4	37.5
1987	29.1	5.5	19.0	12.7	43.9	10.8	37.1
1988	30.5	5.7	18.8	12.8	42.0	12.0	39.3
1989	32.1	5.9	18.4	13.3	41.7	12.8	39.9
1990	33.2	6.1	18.5	13.8	41.4	13.3	40.1
1991	35.0	6.5	18.7	14.2	40.5	14.3	40.8
1992	35.9	6.6	18.5	14.6	40.7	14.7	40.8
1993	37.0	6.7	18.0	15.3	41.2	15.1	40.8
1994	38.0	6.8	17.9	15.8	41.6	15.4	40.6
1995	38.3	6.8	17.8	16.4	42.9	15.1	39.4
1996	39.3	6.9	17.3	17.5	44.4	15.0	38.3
1997	40.2	7.0	17.2	18.4	45.9	14.8	36.9
1998	40.5	7.0	17.2	19.2	47.5	14.3	35.2

Source: Zhonggong Zhongyang Zuzhibu, Zhonggong Dangshi Yanjiushi, and Zhongyang Dang'an Guan, *Zhongguo gongchandang zuzhishi ziliao, 1921-1997, fujuan 1* (Material on the Organisational History of China's Communist Party, 1921-1997. Appendix Volume 1) (Beijing: Zhongyang dangxiao chubanshe), p. 1332.

ORIGINS OF CADRES

During the 1950s there was a regularisation of the cadre corps. A full-fledged wage system was set up and a more detailed ranking system was introduced. According to a handbook published in 1958, cadres included the following personnel: (1) employees from clerical personnel and above; (2) industrial technicians; (3) agro-technicians; (4) maritime technicians; (5) public health technicians of middle level and above; (6) scientific technicians; (8) news and publishing personnel; (8) teaching personnel; (9) personnel in culture and the arts; and (10) translators.[5] In short, cadres were defined by simple bureaucratic distinction according to their education and whether or not they were employed by the state.

Since then there has been no fundamental change in this categorisation. However, all along, an undercurrent of doubt has existed as to whether such a purely bureaucratic distinction would suffice and therefore regular ideological campaigns have been conducted to ensure the continuous political and ideological education and training of the cadres.

Official Chinese sources report a figure of 40.5 million cadres in 1998. The percentage of cadres in government organs has not changed much since the onset of the reform period. But the share of cadres in *shiye danwei* (service units) had grown from 40.1 percent in 1984 to 47.5 percent in 1998, whereas the category of cadres in production enterprises had fallen from 41.8 percent in 1984 to 35.2 percent during the same period (Table 9.1).

In Chinese political terminology there is a distinction between ordinary cadres and leading cadres (*lingdao ganbu*). Leading cadres are defined as cadres at county (division) level and above. Numbering 508,025, they constitute only about 8 percent of the cadre corps in government organs. Ninety-two percent or 466,355 of them, are cadres working at the provincial level and below such as local city and county party secretaries (Table 9.2). Only 34,221 of the leading cadres work in the central organs in Beijing.[6]

TABLE 9.2 THE NUMBER OF CADRES ABOVE COUNTY-LEVEL IN GOVERNMENT ORGANS IN CHINA, 1979-1998

Year	Total	*Bu* or Ministerial Level	*Ju, si, ting* or Department Level	*Xian* or County Level
1979	159,065	1,646	22,450	134,969
1980	167,650	1,882	23,483	142,285
1981	183,927	1,791	23,875	158,261
1982	198,229	1,849	25,123	171,257
1983	199,826	2,179	26,058	171,589
1984	230,776	2,143	26,294	202,339
1985	259,596	2,150	27,906	229,540
1986	287,809	2,197	28,899	256,713
1987	305,646	2,156	29,623	273,867
1988	317,123	2,316	30,322	284,485
1989	335,018	2,280	30,699	302,039
1990	344,885	2,261	30,259	312,265
1991	361,512	2,285	31,881	327,346
1992	376,773	2,258	33,148	341,367
1993	398,189	2,590	34,498	361,101
1994	406,119	2,465	33,451	370,203
1995	445,286	2,459	35,620	407,207
1996	468,274	2,317	37,011	428,946
1997	492,328	2,406	39,181	450,741
1998	508,025	2,562	39,108	466,355

Source: Zhonggong Zhongyang zuzhibu, Zhonggong Dangshi Yanjiushi, and Zhongyang Dang'an Guan, *Zhongguo gongchandang zuzhishi ziliao, 1921-1997, fujuan 1* (Material on the Organisational History of China's Communist Party, 1921-1997. Appendix Volume 1) (Beijing: Zhongyang Dangxiao Chubanshe), p. 1357.

The most important of leading cadres are those at the ministerial (provincial) level and above. There are only 2,562 of these (Table 9.2), including provincial governors and party secretaries, and they all belong to the Central Committee's nomenklatura. However, as argued elsewhere in this paper, the next lower level, the department (*ju*, *si*, *ting*) level, is increasing in importance and there have been inter-agency fights as to whether the party or the government has the power to appoint these officials. Currently all provincial *ting*-level positions are on the nomenklatura controlled by the provincial party committee, while the central *ju*-level positions are on the Central Committee's nomenklatura.

The 40 million or so cadres reported in Chinese sources seem to equal the number of people who belong to the *bianzhi*, i.e., the system of established posts fixed centrally in Beijing. This is probably the reason why many analysts confuse the term cadre with the concept of *bianzhi*.[7] However, a number of people on the *bianzhi* have never been classified as cadres. These include typists, support officers, and drivers. It can also be argued that middle and primary school teachers should not be viewed as cadres. Due to these considerations the two concepts need to be analytically separated.

Except in 1957 and 1962, the number of cadres has risen steadily since 1949. The most significant increases occurred in the 1950s when the party was expanding its grip on Chinese society (Table 9.3). The 36.2 percent increase in the number of cadres between 1955 and 1956 seems to be related to the nationalisation of industry and trade that took place during this period. The 2.4 percent reduction of cadres in 1957 is probably related to the anti-rightist campaign of that year, which saw significant purges of suspected right-wing leading personnel. The 1962 reductions were the result of the administrative reforms during the economic crisis years of 1961-1962. Statistics are not available for the Cultural Revolution, but since there was a growth of only 8.4 percent from 1965 to 1971, it seems safe to assume that at the height of the Cultural Revolution the number of cadres in fact declined. Since 1978 the number of cadres has grown every year without exception and now constitutes 3.3 percent of the total Chinese population.

TABLE 9.3 THE GROWTH OF CADRES IN CHINA, 1950-1998

Year	Number of Cadres	Yearly Change (%)
1950	908,000	n.a.
1955	7,170,500	8.1
1956	9,768,000	36.2
1957	9,535,600	-2.4
1958	9,550,800	0.2
1958	10,470,900	9.6
1960	11,326,500	8.2
1961	11,551,500	2.0
1962	10,606,600	-8.2
1963	11,031,400	4.0
1964	11,512,900	4.4
1965	11,923,400	3.6
1971	12,928,300	n.a
1972	13,766,300	5.4
1973	14,510,900	4.4
1974	15,148,200	4.4
1975	15,617,000	3.1
1977	16,158,100	2.6
1978	17,402,000	4.9
1979	18,138,700	4.2
1980	18,951,000	4.5
1981	19,771,600	4.3
1982	21,010,500	6.3
1983	21,954,600	4.5
1984	25,082,500	14.3
1985	26,553,600	5.9
1986	27,674,200	4.2
1987	29,032,000	4.9
1988	30,454,700	4.9
1989	32,056,900	5.3
1990	33,180,600	3.5
1991	34,971,700	5.4
1992	35,891,100	2.6
1993	36,996,500	3.1

TABLE 9.3 THE GROWTH OF CADRES IN CHINA, 1950-1998 (cont'd)

Year	Number of Cadres	Yearly Change (%)
1994	37,961,800	2.6
1995	38,316,900	0.9
1996	39,322,000	2.6
1997	40,191,100	2.2
1998	40,488,600	0.7

Source: Zhonggong Zhongyang Zuzhibu, Zhonggong Dangshi Yanjiushi, and Zhongyang Dang'an Guan, *Zhongguo gongchandang zuzhishi ziliao, 1921-1997, fujuan 1* (Material on the Organisational History of China's Communist Party, 1921-1997. Appendix Volume 1) (Beijing: Zhongyang dangxiao chubanshe), pp. 1329-1330.

The regional distribution of cadres varies considerably. In Beijing the cadre force accounts for about 11 percent of the population (Table 9.4). The proportion of cadres is also relatively high in Tianjin (7.5 percent) and in Shanghai (6.9 percent). Beijing's case can be explained by its special status as the capital. Tianjin and Shanghai are important political and educational centres, and so clearly will have a larger proportion of cadres.

The provinces of Liaoning, Jilin and Heilongjiang are also overrepresented in terms of cadres. A plausible explanation is that these provinces are traditionally the locations of large state-owned enterprises, especially in the heavy-industry sector. This usually entails a considerable number of cadres subordinated to central ministries and organs in Beijing and national party organisations. Conversely, the comparatively lower proportion of cadres in Jiangsu, Zhejiang and Anhui seems to be related to the stronger focus of these provinces on foreign-funded enterprises and a growing private sector. In these economically less centralised sectors, the party and its cadres play only a minor role and in many instances are not present at all.

TABLE 9.4 REGIONAL DISTRIBUTION OF CADRES IN CHINA, 1998

Province	Population (million)	Cadres (thousand)	As % of population
National	1,248.10	40,488.60	3.25
Beijing	12.46	1,474.10	11.83
Tianjin	9.57	724.70	7.57
Hebei	65.69	1,826.00	2.77
Shanxi	31.72	1,194.40	3.76
Inner Mongolia	23.62	893.20	3.78
Liaoning	41.57	2,152.20	5.18
Jilin	26.44	1,308.30	4.95
Heilongjiang	37.73	1,736.20	4.61
Shanghai	14.64	1,027,80	6.97
Jiangsu	71.82	2,304.20	3.20
Zhejiang	44.56	1,274.80	2.86
Anhui	61.84	1,297.50	2.09
Fujian	32.99	955.80	2.89
Jiangxi	41.91	1,114.20	2.72
Shandong	88.38	2,238.80	3.21
Henan	93.15	2,135.80	2.29
Hubei	59.07	2,167.70	3.67
Hunan	65.02	1,725.40	2.65
Guangdong	71.43	2,341.20	3.28
Guangxi	46.75	1,225.00	2.62
Hainan	7.53	223.50	2.96
Chongqing	30.60	1,036.90	3.39
Sichuan	84.93	1,934.50	2.27
Guizhou	36.58	903,70	2.47
Yunnan	41.44	1,182.40	2.85
Tibet	2.52	79.20	3.14
Shaanxi	35.96	1,225.30	3.41
Gansu	25.19	773.30	3.06
Qinghai	5.03	212.40	4.22
Ningxia	5.36	219.70	4.09
Xinjiang	17.47	973.10	5.57

Sources: Zhonggong zhongyang zuzhibu, Zhonggong dangshi yanjiushi, and Zhongyang dang'an guan, *Zhongguo gongchandang zuzhishi ziliao, 1921-1997, fujuan 1* (Material on the Organisational History of China's Communist Party, 1921-1997. Appendix Volume 1) (Beijing: Zhonggong dangshi chubanshe, 2000) p. 1344-1347; *Zhongguo tongji nianjian 1999* (China Statistical Yearbook 1999), p. 113.

The educational level of cadres has improved dramatically during the reform period. While the share of cadres with Junior Middle School education and below was almost 50 percent in 1979, it nosedived to 7.8 percent in 1998. Now more than 44 percent of the cadre force has a university degree compared to only 17.9 percent in 1979 and 6.9 percent in 1950. In addition to becoming more professionally qualified, the cadre corps has undergone a process of rejuvenation. In 1979 only 29 percent of the cadres were younger than 35 years of age. Now the proportion has increased to 49 percent (see Table 9.5).

TABLE 9.5 AGE DISTRIBUTION OF CADRES IN CHINA, 1979-1998

Year	Total	Below 35		36 to 45		46 to 54		55 and Above	
	Number	Number	%	Number	%	Number	%	Number	%
1979	18.1	5.2	28.6	6.8	37.5	5.1	27.9	1.1	5.8
1985	26.5	10.4	29.2	7.6	28.9	6.9	26.3	1.5	5.6
1990	33.2	14.4	33.3	8.8	26.6	7.8	23.7	2.1	6.3
1995	38.3	18.2	47.4	10.2	26.7	7.3	19.1	2.5	6.7
1996	39.3	18.9	48.1	10.4	26.5	7.4	18.9	2.5	6.3
1997	40.2	19.8	49.4	10.5	26.2	7.3	18.2	2.4	6.0
1998	40.5	20.1	49.5	10.9	27.1	7.3	18.1	2.2	5.3

Sources: Zhonggong Zhongyang zuzhibu, Zhonggong Dangshi Yanjiushi, and Zhongyang Dang'an Guan, *Zhongguo gongchandang zuzhishi ziliao, 1921-1997, fujuan 1* (Material on the Organisational History of China's Communist Party, 1921-1997. Appendix Volume 1) (Beijing: Zhonggong dangshi chubanshe, 2000) p. 1344-1347; *Zhongguo tongji nianjian 1999* (China Statistical Yearbook 1999), pp. 1355-1356.

THE ORGANISATION DEPARTMENT AND THE NOMENKLATURA

Organisationally the cadres are managed by the Organisation Department of the party committees at central and local levels. The work of the organisation departments at these levels is supplemented by the personnel departments that are established at all levels of government and which belong to the Ministry of Personnel. However in 1998 the Ministry of Personnel had to shift most of its management functions to the party, which now is in exclusive control of the cadre corps.[8]

The Organisation Department of the Central Committee has always been an important department in the communist political system. Before 1949, Chen Duxiu, Mao Zedong, and Chen Yun had headed this department. Since 1949, important leaders such as Peng Zhen, Deng Xiaoping, Hu Yaobang, Qiao Shi, and Song Ping have all served as head of the Department.[9] In March 1999 Jiang Zemin's right-hand man Zeng Qinghong was appointed to this important position. During his two years in office he has managed to turn the Department into a major platform for strengthening the role of the party in organisational as well as ideological work.

The Organisation Department's principal instrument of power is its management of the nomenklatura system. This system consists of a list of positions (and a list of reserves for these positions) over which the party committees have the authority to make appointments.[10] The most important part of the nomenklatura is the list of 4,000 posts to be filled and managed by the Central Committee.[11] As the Chinese governing structure applies a system where the higher level takes charge of the lower, the Central Committee and its Organisation Department also control the nomenklatura of ministerial-level and provincial-level leading cadres. In the 1970s and early 1980s the Organisation Department actually managed two levels down, which meant that in addition to the ministerial level, it also had control over the important *ju*-level in the Chinese administrative hierarchy.

From 1984 the Organisation Department's direct management power was limited to one level down. This move seems to be related to Deng Xiaoping's attempts to give more power to the provinces.[12] It also conformed with Zhao Ziyang's attempt to limit the reach of the Organisation Department and to upgrade the State Council's Ministry of Personnel. Thus, in September 1988 Zhao transferred management of 54 enterprises and *shiye danwei* from the Organisation Department's control to the State Council.[13] Zhao

Ziyang saw this as part of his plans to create a merit-based civil service system.

According to these plans, put forward at the 13th Party Congress in 1987, in the future, state and party cadres should be classified into two categories, a political-administrative category (*zhengwu gongwuyuan*) and a professional work category (*yewu gongwuyuan*).[14] Only the former category comprising some 500,000 of the 6-million-strong cadre corps was to be managed by the party. The rest were to be managed by the newly-formed Ministry of Personnel.

The Organisation Department led by Song Ping fought back by refusing to transfer the cadre files to the Ministry of Personnel, a necessary first step for implementing Zhao Ziyang's personnel reform. The Department also tried to block the move to abolish party core groups (*dangzu*) in government offices and departments.

The Organisation Department was further weakened in 1989 when Song Ping was appointed to the Standing Committee of the Politburo and Lu Feng, a deputy director since 1983, became head without belonging to the Central Committee. Lu Feng only became a member of the Central Committee at the 14th Party Congress in 1992. In 1994, a deputy director, Zhang Quanjing, replaced Lu Feng and headed the Organisation Department until 1999. At the time of appointment, Zhang Quanjing was also not even a Central Committee member. Neither of the two made it to the Politburo.

In short, during the 1990s, the Organisation Department was headed by relatively junior political figures who did not belong to the top policymaking bodies of the party. This is a pattern quite unlike the 1970s and 1980s when the leaders of the Department were usually Politburo members with considerable political clout. This seems to indicate that although Zhao Ziyang was toppled in 1989, his personnel reform continued to exercise influence. The new civil service reform of 1993 is another indication of the weakening of the Organisation Department's role in personnel management.

However, from 1998 the process was reversed and the Organisation Department took back its appointment authority of the *ju*-level leaders at the central level,[15] a move clearly signifying that the government's role in cadre personnel work was being reevaluated. The appointment of Jiang Zemin's close aide and confidant Zeng Qinghong as Director of the Department in March 1999 further signalled that the Organisation Department would increase its influence.

Currently, the civil service system which was implemented from 1993 onwards is in reality controlled by the Organisation Department. The Department regards all civil servants from the level of *ke* (section) and above as cadres. On this basis it seems difficult to establish an independent civil service system. In fact, the very notion of the civil servants serving the state and not the party fundamentally runs counter to the very idea of the leading role of the party.

Throughout the 1990s, especially from 1993 onwards, most party documents issued to guide the work of leading personnel referred to civil servants (*gongwuyuan*) rather than cadres (*ganbu*). From 1999 the usage of the term "cadre" again gained prominence, indicating the shift in emphasis mentioned above.

The CCP has been regarded as "the post-revolutionary successor to the gentry." In a similar vein one could argue that the cadres are the post-revolutionary successors to the imperial bureaucracy, following a governing system Max Weber called "bureaucratic patrimonialism."[16] The emperor made sure that the bureaucracy served him loyally. He did this through stringent criteria (the examinations) for entering the bureaucracy and having a set of policies that ensured officials were constantly rotated and that they would not serve in their home province. In the same way the CCP has made use of the cadre corps to serve the emperor (Mao, Deng, Jiang Zemin). However, post-Deng China has seen the bureaucracy growing stronger. In fact the whole idea behind Zhao Ziyang's civil service reform was to create a professional bureaucracy which operated according to fixed rules and regulations with clear procedures for recruitment, advancement and career exit. Such a process, however, tended to erode the power of the party leadership, which is why, to reassert itself, the party has given increased importance to the cadre system in recent years.

EFFORTS TO IMPROVE CADRE MANAGEMENT

As the noted French political scientist Maurice Duverger claims, in every human community the organisation of power is the result of two opposed forces: beliefs on the one hand, practical necessities on the other.[17] In China the Chinese Communist Party (CCP) has tried to combine the two forces in governing the country through a professionally competent and ideologically correct cadre corps.

Cadres are managed by the party according to detailed regulations relating to recruitment, appointment, performance evaluation, training, etc. The objective of cadre management is to make sure that professionally competent people are recruited and promoted and that these remain loyal to the party's ideological and political line.

During the 1950s there was a regularisation of the cadre corps. A full-fledged wage system was established and a more detailed ranking system was introduced. Since then cadres have in general been defined by simple bureaucratic distinction according to their educational background and whether or not they are employed by the state. However, all along there has been an undercurrent of doubt as to whether bureaucratic position and a state-salary would be enough to satisfy the definition of cadre.

In fact, party documents are increasingly stressing that cadres are supposed to possess both virtue (*de*) and ability (*cai*). In general virtue is viewed as the fervour with which a cadre carries out the ideological line of the party. Ability is generally interpreted as professional competence and performance in one's job. "Virtue and ability" represents a view of the role of the cadres which is also found in the concept of "red and expert." It implies that cadre management is not just a question of personnel management; it is also a question of upholding the correct ideological line.[18] Whereas Mao stressed redness (*de*), Deng tended to stress expertness (*cai*). Jiang Zemin's "three represents" (*sange daibiao*) campaign can be seen as an attempt to close the distance between the two polar views of the role of the cadres.

APPOINTING AND SELECTING CADRES

Cadre management is an instrument used by the Chinese leadership to maintain control over the political and administrative system. It is especially important to keep control over the leading cadres, who form the backbone of the system. Formally, the leading cadres in China at and above the county level are managed according to the Interim Regulations on Selection and Appointment of Party and Government Leading Cadres issued in February 1995.[19]

The General Provisions of these regulations emphasise that when selecting and appointing leading cadres in China it is important to follow a number of basic principles. These include openness, equality, competition, and the selection of the best. Although their selection and appointment are based on meritocratic principles, it is also stressed that cadres should have both political integrity and ability (*de cai jianbei*) and that the party should manage the cadres.

The chapter on Selection and Appointment Conditions stipulates that candidates to be promoted to leading party and government posts higher than the county (division) level must have held at least two posts at lower level organs and that candidates who are promoted from deputy post to a head post (*zheng zhi*) generally must have worked at the deputy post for more than two years. Also party and government cadres should be promoted one grade at a time. These stipulations have apparently been included to avoid the kind of "helicoptoring" which some cadres experienced during the Cultural Revolution. Finally, the chapter also stipulates that an educational level higher than vocational school is generally required and leading cadres at minister or provincial-leader level should have a college education or equivalent.

Candidates to be considered for selection and appointment to leading posts should be proposed by so-called democratic recommendation by the party committee at the same level or by the higher-level organisation or personnel department. At the time of an official's change of term, various people and personnel are consulted such as party committee members, leading members of government organs, leading members of the discipline inspection commissions and people's courts, and leading members of lower-level party committees and governments. Members of democratic parties and representatives of people without party affiliation should also be consulted.

Candidates that have been nominated will have to undergo evaluation according to elaborate procedures, which may include interviews for a number of leading offices or when an official is nominated to a new position in his or her own department. Evaluation is not confined to the end of the term of office. Leading members of party committees and government departments are also evaluated in the middle of their term. Any promotion or dismissal arising from the evaluations must undergo a process of deliberation (*yunniang*) and be reported to the party committee at the higher level.

The Interim Regulations also carry intricate provisions concerning how to make decisions through discussion in party committees and party core groups (*dangzu*). For example, it requires a two-thirds quorum of the members of a given committee when appointment and dismissal of cadres are being discussed.

Chapter 7 clearly underlines the power of the party in appointing leading officials in state and government organs. Much of this power rests in the right to recommend candidates for leading positions. However, in certain circumstances the party has to take into account dissenting views on its recommendation of candidates. If, for example, a recommended candidate twice fails to get the approval of the standing committee of the People's Congress for a government position, he shall not be recommended for the same post in the same locality again.

Chapter 8 deals with job exchange/transfer and avoidance (*huibi*). As a general rule, any leading member of a local party committee or government who has served in the same post for ten years must be transferred to a new post.

These are clearly the authoritative measures for cadre management. In 1998 these measures were supplemented by a development programme for establishing a national party and government leadership for 1998-2003, which among other things stressed the necessity to develop a reserve contingent for leading positions.

THE CADRE DEVELOPMENT PROGRAMME

According to the "development programme" of the Central Organisation Department, by the year 2003 every administrative level from central down to county and town (*zhen*) level should have a leadership line-up consisting of different age groups, ranging from leaders in their 60s to young cadres in their 40s.[20] This is to ensure a flexible cadre corp with a so-called rational age composition in the leadership (*lingdao banzi*).

The formal requirement at the central ministerial (*bu*, *wei*) level is that in addition to leaders in their 60s, there should be "a number of" leaders around 50 and "at least" one member of this leadership group should be of no more than 45 years of age. It is stipulated that there must be "a number of" formal leaders of ministries and commissions (*zheng zhi*) who are in their 50s.

At the provincial level there must also be a leadership group composed of different age groups. Requirements related to party leadership at this level are that there should be at least three leaders below the age of 50, whereas two cadres below this age would suffice for state organs at a similar level. For both party and state organs at least one member of the leadership group should be no more than 45 years old. "A number of" formal party and government leaders should be no more than 50 years of age.

At bureau-level (*ju*, *si*, *ting*), the next lower level in the administrative hierarchy, similar rules established by the Organisation Department apply, but in general age requirements are lowered by an additional five years in each category. For example, there must be "a number of" bureau directors and department leaders who are around 45 years of age.

As a general rule the development plan emphasises that there should be at least one female member in the party and state leadership groups from provincial down to county level. This appears to be a very minimalist solution to the problem of under-representation of women in leading organs; in general, one cannot escape the impression that the organisational department is more concerned with rejuvenating the leading organs rather than tackling the question of gender representation.

Minorities and people from non-CCP groups should be represented in leading organs according to the development plan. Thus party and government organs above county level should be allocated cadres of national minority origin who possess both ability and political integrity. Government organs from provincial level and below should include non-CCP cadres, and plans for the inclusion of such cadres in leadership organs at central levels should be worked out. At lower levels, province, city and county should at least have 10, 15 or 20 percent representation, respectively, of non-CCP cadres. This has paved the way for non-CCP cadres to make careers in the civil service. However, in general these cadres will not assume the very top post (*zheng zhi*) in the administrative organs, but only the deputy position.

According to the development plan it is necessary to establish a group of reserve cadres (*houbei ganbu*). These are the people who should be groomed to take over leadership positions. At county level and above there should be two persons listed on the reserve list for every head and one for every vice-head of a ministry, bureau or department.

Finally, the development plan stresses the need to constantly upgrade the cadres through education and training. This has been restated recently in a major party document concerning cadre education and training for 2001-2005.[21] The document stipulates that all cadres at the county (division) level and above must attend at least three months of training in a party school during the period. In addition cadres should also attend at least 12 days of collective study a year organised by the party committee.

At the ministerial (*bu*) and provincial (*sheng*) level, 400 cadres each year will receive training and refresher courses on a rotational basis, so that altogether 2,000 cadres at this level will have undergone further study and training in the Central Party School, the Central School of Administration, or in the Defence University at the end of the period. The same number of party secretaries at the county level will receive further training in the planning period. The new training programme also acknowledges the need to expose leading cadres to the outside world in order to broaden their horizons and make them more qualified to lead. About 200 ministerial (*bu*) and department (*ting*) level cadres will be sent abroad on a yearly basis to conduct studies and inspection.

CADRE TRANSFER

The 1998-2003 development plan reinforces the sense of stronger party control, which was already evident in the 1995 regulations. An instrument of further control which is often used in order to prevent "local fiefdoms" from developing is the so-called cadre transfer system. For lower-level cadres the rules are that leading cadres have to be transferred after their second term, i.e., after a maximum period of ten years. For top-level cadres this rule is perhaps even more important and often takes place at the discretion of the ultimate powerholders in Beijing.[22]

Transfers can occur in two principal ways. One is interprovincial transfer where cadres are transferred from one province to another. Examples include the transfers of party secretaries Wu Guangzheng of Jiangxi to Shandong in 1997 and Li Changchun of Henan to Guangdong in 1998 to replace the local party leader Xie Fei.[23]

A second way of transfer is from provinces to the centre or from the centre to the provinces. In some cases the transfer indicates promotion, as when Zhu Rongji was transferred from Shanghai to Beijing in 1992 or when provincial party secretary Jiang Chunyun was transferred from Shandong to the centre in 1995; but in other cases transfer to Beijing could mean a demotion, as was true in the cases of former Hainan provincial leaders Liu Jiangfeng and Deng Hongxun in 1993. Transfer from the centre to the provinces can also indicate attempts to reassert central control, as when politburo standing committee member Wei Jianxing replaced Chen Xitong as head of the party in Beijing in 1997 or when minister of labour Ruan Chongwu replaced both Liu Jianfeng and Deng Hongxun in Hainan in 1993.

In fact there is much more mobility and flexibility in the provinces than these examples would indicate. The legally specified term of office for a governor is five years. In reality, since 1979, the average tenure length for governors is only 2.85 years and 3.44 years for party secretaries.[24] Thus, tenure patterns for top provincial officials do not seem to indicate considerable administrative localism in China in the reform era, as has been argued by some scholars.[25]

At lower levels there are also considerable rotations. In 1996 the Ministry of Personnel disseminated the Provisional Measures of Position Change among Civil Servants. Following the decision to adopt these measures, in the 1996-1998 period, 400,000 civil servants were rotated.[26] The measures stipulate that, normally, rotation should affect no less than 30 percent of the civil servants from section level and above. The mechanism is considered an important instrument to prevent localism and corruption.[27]

IDEOLOGICAL WORK

An additional mechanism for ensuring control over the cadres is ideological work. The ideological dimension of cadre behaviour appears again and again in the post-1949 period. It is epitomised in the concepts of "red" and "virtue" (*de*). At times this dimension took over so that the cadres' political and moral credentials became more important than their professional and technical abilities. This was especially evident during the Great Leap Forward (1958-1960) and the Cultural Revolution (1966-1976).

During Deng's era one notes a certain de-ideologisation. Deng favoured pragmatism and empirical work and downgraded lofty ideological debates and campaigns. The result was a weakening of the party's legitimacy.

In tandem with the strengthening of cadre work and the Organisation Department's role in cadre management, Jiang Zemin has focussed on developing a stronger ideological orientation for the party and its cadres. Thus Jiang introduced the "three talks" (*san jiang*) campaign in 1999 and recently the "three represents" (*sange daibiao*). This campaign, begun in February 2000, has assumed major proportions and now forms the core of the CCP's current propaganda work. Very recently Jiang has introduced the notion of "rule by virtue" (*yide zhiguo*) in an attempt to bolster the party's authority.[28]

For the cadres this chain of events means a re-emphasis on "red" and "virtue" in the "red-expert" and "virtue-ability" dichotomies. For the party it is a way of ensuring that its instrument of power-the cadres-do not transform into purely civil servants who only care about their work in a bureaucratic sense and forget their larger mission of ensuring the legitimacy of the party and its continued rule.

DEEPENING CADRE WORK

Recently, cadre management has received new attention. This is related to the leadership change that took place at the Party Congress in 2002, as the third generation of Chinese leaders prepares to leave the scene. This change of guard will necessitate that new cadres be trained at lower levels so that there will be a pool of young leaders (fifth or sixth generation) to move up, when the time is ripe.

The recently published Programme to Deepen the Cadre Personnel System outlines the actions that will be taken in order to create a competent and more professional cadre corps.[29] In recruiting cadres, key measures include open appointment and selection. Within the next three to five years all positions below provincial *ting*-level will be filled according to a public notification system (*gongshi zhi*) and there will be experiments with multi-candidate elections for leading government and party posts. In supervising the cadres, clear measures for evaluation (*kaohe*) are to be introduced and combined with public feedback on the quality of the work done, which involves soliciting public opinion on the performance of the cadres.

The Programme also envisages a further strengthening of the principle of work exchange between different departments and regions, so that cadres from the eastern provinces would work for a while in western provinces and vice versa. The programme also introduces other measures to ensure the flexibility and mobility of the cadre corps such as flexible remuneration based on performance and clear guidelines for removing incompetent leaders. Finally, a number of other measures will be adopted to strengthen the supervision and monitoring of the cadre personnel system, including pecuniary rewards for good job performance.

To be sure, many of these measures are already in effect and have been discussed through the 1990s and even earlier.[30] But it has certain significance that they are now restated in a comprehensive form and discussed in a number of important editorials in the press. The programme has been worked out by the Organisation Department under Zeng Qinghong rather than the Ministry of Personnel, implying that the "deepening cadre personnel system" is the responsibility of the party. The measures taken by the party are expected to run parallel to Zhu Rongji's institutional reform as worked out by the State Council. This common long-term goal is a more efficient use of cadres and civil servants in the Chinese political system.

ENDNOTES

1 *Renmin Ribao*, 2 July 2000.

2 Ibid.

3 See Lenin, *What is to be Done?: Burning Questions of Our Movement* (Beijing: Foreign Languages Press, 1973, originally published 1902).

4 Ibid., p. 225.

5 See Ezra F. Vogel, "From Revolutionary to Semi-Bureaucrat: The 'Regularisation' of Cadres," *The China Quarterly*, No. 29 (January-March 1967), pp. 36-60.

6 See Zhonggong Zhongyang Zuzhibu, Zhonggong dangshi yanjiushi, and Zhongyang dang'an guan, *Zhongguo gongchandang zuzhishi ziliao, 1921-1997, fujuan 1* (Material on the Organisational History of China's Communist Party, 1921-1997. Appendix Volume 1) (Beijing: Zhonggong Dangshi Chubanshe, 2000) p. 1357.

7 For a discussion of this phenomenon, see Kjeld Erik Brodsgaard, "China's Civil Service Reform: Changing the Bianzhi," *EAI Background Brief No. 81*, East Asian Institute, National University of Singapore (14 February 2001).

8 See "Liao Wang" Zhoukan Bianjibu (ed.), *Guowuyuan jigou gaige gailan* (General Survey of the Institutional Reform of the State Council) (Beijing: Xinhua Renmin Chubanshe, 1998), 85-92.

9 See Thomas Kampen, "The CCP's Central Committee Departments (1921-1991): A Study of Their Evolution," *China Report*, Vol. 29, No. 3 (1993), pp. 299-317.

10 John Burns, *The Chinese Communist Party's Nomenklatura System* (Armonk, New York: M.E. Sharpe, 1989), pp. ix-x.

11 There is also a secondary list, the "List of Cadre Positions to be reported to the Center," which actually extends the party's control into many of

the organisations mentioned in the first list and also covers economic enterprises and *shiye danwei*. See "Zhongyang zuzhibu guanyu xiuding 'zhonggong zhongyang guanlide ganbu zhiwu mingchengbiao' de tongzhi" (Notice of the CCP Organisation Department on Revision of the "Job Title List for Cadres Managed Centrally by the Chinese Communist Party"), 10 May 1990, in Renshibu Zhengce Fagui (ed.), *Renshi gongzuo wenjian xuanbian* (Selection of Documents Concerning Personnel Work) (Beijing: Zhongguo renshi chubanshe, 1991), Vol. 13, pp. 35-53. See also John Burns, "Strengthening CCP Control of Leadership Selection: The 1990 Nomenklatura," *The China Quarter*ly, No. 138 (June 1994), pp. 458-491.

12 Ibid., p. 464.

13 "Zhongyang zuzhibu guanyu biandong wushiwuge qishiye danwei lingdao ganbu zhiwu guanli quanxiande tongzhi" (Notice of the Central Organisation Department on Changing the Management Jurisdiction for Leading Cadre Positions of 55 Enterprises and Service Units), 24 September 1988, in Renshibu Zhengce Fagui (ed.), *Renshi gongzuo wenjian xuanbian* (Selection of Documents Concerning Personnel Work) (Beijing: Xuefan Chubanshe, 1989), Vol. 11, pp. 6-9.

14 See Zhao Ziyang, "Yanzhe you Zhongguo tese de shehuizhuyi daolu qianjin" (Advance along the Road of Socialism with Chinese Characteristics), *Renmin Ribao*, 4 November 1987.

15 On the importance of bureau-level cadres, see also Yasheng Huang, *Inflation and Investment Controls in China* (Cambridge: Cambridge University Press, 1996).

16 See Max Weber, *Economy and Society*, Vol. 1 (Berkeley: University of California Press, 1978), p. 231-235.

17 See Maurice Duverger, *Political Parties* (New York: John Wiley & Sons, 1954), p. 133.

18 For a discussion of the concept of Party cadre, see also Franz Schurmann, *Ideology and Organisation in Communist China* (Berkeley: University of California Press, 1968), pp. 162-172.

19 "Zhonggong zhongyang guanyu yinfa 'dang zhengfu lingdao ganbu xuanba renyong gongzuo zanxing tiaoli' de tongzhi (Notice of the Central Central Committee of the CCP Concerning "Interim regulations on Selection and Appointment of Party and Government Leading Cadres"), 9 February 1995, in *Renshi gongzuo wenjian xuanbian* (Selection of Documents Concerning Personnel Work), Vol. 18 (Beijing: Zhongguo renshi chubanshe, 1996), pp. 13-26.

20 Zhongyang Zuzhibu (Organisation Department of the CCP), "1998-2003 nian quanguo dang zheng lingdao banzi jianshe guihua gangyao" (Development Programme Concerning the Establishment of a National Party and State Leadership for 1998-2003), June 24, 1998, in *Renshi gongzuo wenjian xuanbian*, Vol. 21, pp. 90-100.

21 "2001-2005 nian quanguo ganbu jiaoyu peixun guihua" (The 2001-2005 Education and Training Plan for All Cadres), *Renmin Ribao*, 11 May 2001.

22 See also "Zhongong zhongyang guanyu yinfa 'dang zhengfu lingdao ganbu xuanba renyong gongzuo zanxing tiaoli' de zongzhi" (Notice of the Central

Committee of the CCP Concerning "Interim Regulations on Selection and Appointment of Party and Government Leading Cadres"), 9 February 1995, pp. 13-26.

23 See also Zheng Yongnian, "China's Incremental Political Reform: Lessons and Experiences," in Wang Gungwu and John Wong (eds.), *China: Two Decades of Reform and Change* (Singapore: Singapore University Press, 1999), pp. 11-40.

24 Huang Yasheng, *Inflation and Investment Controls in China: The Political Economy of Central-Local Relations During the Reform Era* (Cambridge: Cambridge University Press, 1996), p. 115.

25 See, for example, Li Cheng and David Bachman, "Localism, Elitism, and Immobilism: Elite Formation and Social Change in Post-Mao China," *World Politics*, Vol 42 (October 1989), pp. 64-94.

26 See *People's Daily Online*, 16 August 16 2000.

27 For a discussion of these measures in relation to the issue of corruption in China, see Zou Keyuan, "Why China's Rampant Corruption Cannot be Checked by Laws Alone," *EAI Background Brief No. 74*, East Asian Institute, National University of Singapore (2 November 2000).

28 See Zheng Yongnian and Lai Hongyi, "Rule by Virtue: Jiang Zemin's New Moral Order for the Party", *EAI Background Brief No. 83*, East Asian Institute, National University of Singapore (March 2001).

29 "Shenhua ganbu renshidu gaige gangyao" (The Programme to Deepen the Cadre Personnel System), *Renmin Ribao*, 21 August 2000.

30 See Thiagarajan Manoharan, "Basic Party Units and Decentralised Development," *Copenhagen Papers in East and Southeast Asian Studies*, No. 5 (1990), pp. 137-146.

CHAPTER **10**

Reforming China's Judicial System: New Endeavour Towards Rule of Law

ZOU KEYUAN

CHINA'S JUDICIAL SYSTEM

The judicial system is a necessary component of state machinery to govern the country. It can be defined as an "entire network of courts in a particular jurisdiction".[1] The word "judiciary" may carry a broader meaning when it is used in conjunction with the term "judicial system"; it refers to the branch of government invested with the judicial power to interpret, construe and apply the law.[2] There are two different views in China about the definition of "judicial system": one defines it as the system of organising the people's court, people's procuratorate, the public security organ and judicial administrative organ and their function of judicial enforcement;[3] and the other narrows it to only include the organisation and activities of the court and the procuratorate.[4] The scope of this chapter is limited to the judicial reform relating to the court and the procuratorate. However, such a limitation does not mean that this author endorses the narrower definition of the judicial system. Rather, based on the practice of China's legal system, the definition of judicial system should be broader.

After the founding of the People's Republic of China (PRC) in 1949, communist China began to establish its own judicial system based on communist ideology and the Soviet model. Unlike the political structure of separation of powers (in which the judicial system is mainly the system of adjudication), China's existing judicial system broadly comprises the People's Court, the People's Procuratorate, the Department of Public Security and the Department of Justice and other governmental departments having the function of judicial administration, such as the Ministry of State Security and the Notaries. Such broad composition may cause confusion, but it is a reality in China. Some departments, such as the Department of Public Security, have more judicial power than the court and the procuratorate, though the Department of Public Security is under the State Council.[5]

Both the People's Court and the People's Procuratorate are founded in accordance with the Chinese Constitution.[6] The Court, as mandated by the Constitution, is the judicial organ of the state courts (including the Supreme Court), at various local levels, military courts, and other special courts such as the maritime and railway transport courts. It has four levels: the Supreme Court, the higher courts at the provincial level (total of 31), intermediate courts at the prefectural level (389), and primary courts at the county level (3,067). The Supreme Court,[7] which is the highest judicial organ, supervises the administration of justice by local and special courts. Courts at a higher level supervise courts at lower levels. A two-level trial system is applied in Chinese courts whereby a case should be finally decided after two trials, first by a lower court, then by a higher court when there is an appeal. In criminal cases, the procuratorate may present a protest to the higher court when it is dissatisfied with the decision made by the lower court.

The internal organisation of the Court is guided by the Organic Law of the People's Courts.[8] Within each court, there are usually several divisions, such as civil, economic, criminal, administrative, and enforcement. A court has one president and several vice presidents, and a division has one chief and several associate chiefs. Each court also has a judicial committee that is composed of the presidents, division chiefs and experienced judges. The members of the committee are appointed by the standing committee of the people's congresses at the corresponding level. The judicial committee is the most authoritative body in a court, and it is responsible for discussing important or difficult cases, giving direction concerning other judicial matters and reviewing and summing up judicial experiences. Its direction usually guides judges and collegial panels to deal with cases, particularly difficult and complicated ones.

Inside the Supreme Court, there are the Adjudicative Committee, the Court Conference, adjudicative divisions, respectively, in charge of "cases of administrative matters", "cases concerning communications and transport", "economic cases", "civil cases", and "criminal cases". Recently, a new division in charge of maritime and foreign-related cases was established within the Supreme Court.[9] The Supreme Court can handle cases: (a) of first instance assigned by laws and decrees; (b) of appeals and of protests lodged against judgements and orders of higher people's courts and special people's courts; and (c) of protests lodged by the Supreme Procuratorate in accordance with the procedures of judicial interpretation.[10] In addition, the Supreme Court has the power to interpret questions concerning application of specific laws and regulations in judicial proceedings.

According to the Chinese Constitution, the Procuratorate is the "State organ for legal supervision". Article 5 of the Organic Law of the People's Procuratorates defines the functions and powers of the people's procuratorates at all levels as the following:

1. to exercise procuratorial authority over cases of treason, cases involving acts to dismember the state and other major criminal cases severely impeding the unified enforcement of state policies, laws, decrees and administrative orders;
2. to conduct investigation of criminal cases handled directly by themselves;
3. to review cases investigated by public security organs and determine whether to approve arrest, and to prosecute or to exempt from prosecution;
4. to exercise supervision over the investigative activities of public security organs to determine whether their activities conform to the law;

5. to initiate public prosecutions of criminal cases and support such prosecutions;
6. to exercise supervision over the judicial activities of people's courts to ensure they conform to the law; and
7. to exercise supervision over the execution of judgments and orders in criminal cases and over the activities of prisons, detention houses and organs in charge of transformation through labour to ensure such executions and activities conform to the law.[11] In a word, the procuratorate has two main functions: (a) legal supervision; and (b) public prosecution for criminal cases.

Like the organisation of the court, within the structure of the procuratorate, the Supreme Procuratorate is the highest, and the local procuratorates are divided into three levels and include procuratorates at the provincial level; branches of the procuratorates in prefectures and cities directly under the provincial governments; and procuratorates of counties, cities, autonomous counties and municipal districts. Procuratorial committees are created inside the procuratorates at different levels. They apply, according to Article 3 of the Organic Law, "the system of democratic centralism and, under the direction of the chief procurator, hold discussions and make decisions on important cases and other major issues".[12] Procuratorates at all levels have a chief procurator, a number of deputy chief procurators and procurators. The chief procurators exercise unified leadership over the work of the procuratorates. The term of office of the chief procurators is the same as that of the people's congresses at corresponding levels.

Though very similar in terms of organisation, there is a difference between the court and the procuratorate. According to the Constitution, within the judicial branch, the higher level courts supervise the work of the lower courts and the courts at various levels are responsible to the respective people's congresses that created them. But within the structure of the procuratorate, the higher procuratorates direct the work of those at lower levels. The procuratorial organs at the lower level are responsible to both the corresponding people's congresses that created them and the people's procuratorates at higher levels.

LAUNCHING THE JUDICIAL REFORM

The judicial reform is part of the overall legal reform in China.[13] The communiqué of the Third Plenary Session of the 11th Central Committee of the Chinese Communist Party (CCP) held in December 1978 set forth the goals of the legal construction and reestablishment of the legal system in China. It stated that:

> To safeguard people's democracy, it is imperative to strengthen the socialist legal system so that democracy is systematised and written into law in such a way as to ensure the stability, continuity, and full authority of this democratic system and these laws; there must be laws for people to follow, these laws must be observed, their enforcement must be strict, and law breakers must be dealt with. From now on, legislative work should have an important place on the agenda of the National People's Congress (NPC) and its Standing Committee. Procuratorial and judicial organisations must maintain their independence as is appropriate; they must faithfully abide by the laws, rules, and regulations, serve the people's interests, and keep to the facts; they must guarantee the equality of all people before the people's laws and deny anyone the privilege of being above the law.[14]

These statements since then have become the guidelines to re-establish the legal system as well as to reform the judicial system.

It is recalled that during the Cultural Revolution, the judicial system was totally demolished. In 1968, Mao was quoted as saying that China should "depend upon the rule of man, not the rule of law", and courtrooms were condemned as "bastions of bourgeois justice".[15] After Mao's era, the judicial system was re-established with the construction process of the Chinese legal system. However, the judicial reform has very much lagged behind the legal reform in other areas, such as legislation. Judicial reform in the 1980s focused mainly on training the judges, most of whom were retired military servicemen. Only recently has China realised that it is necessary to carry on a large-scale judicial reform so as to improve the enforcement of its laws; this is regarded as a major and necessary step towards the rule of law.

The major step was taken after Deng Xiaoping's southern China tour in 1992, which led to the development of the market economy in China and the catching-up with international standards. The fundamental change on the economic front inevitably impacted the legal reform as well as the judicial reform. In 1995 China enacted its laws on judges and on procurators. The purpose of the enactment was to professionalise the judicial personnel. The Judge's Law aims to ensure that the "people's courts independently exercise their judicial authority in accordance with the law; judges carry out their duties in accordance with the law; judges' quality is upgraded; and scientific control over judges is implemented".[16] The Procurator's Law has similar objectives for the procuratorate and its personnel.[17]

The year 1998 witnessed rapid development in judicial reform. First, China began to enhance its judicial system by stressing quality and efficiency in handling cases. The judicial reform was expected to include the improvement of a lay assessor system in which laypersons will assist judges in making court judgements.[18] Such an assessor group can be regarded as a first endeavour to establish a system similar to the jury system. Second, the Supreme People's Court formulated rules to rework China's 17,411 township court outposts to strengthen the judiciary's role in rural areas to help maintain rural stability. In the last five years, township court outposts handled 50.3 percent of all first-instance cases in China.[19] Third, in October 1998 ten senior judges were appointed as superintendents to be responsible for offering advice in handling major, difficult or misjudged cases. They were also authorised to investigate major issues concerning judicial corruption in the courts.[20] Not only were senior judges appointed as superintendents, but in Beijing, some law professors were also appointed as members of the "Advisory and Supervisory Committee of Law Experts" for the procuratorate of the East City District. It was the first time that type of practice was carried out in China.[21] Fourth, court trials and hearings began to be opened to the public, except those involving privacy, minors and State secrets. This new practice was first initiated in Beijing from 1 December 1998 and expanded nation-wide in 1999.[22] Fifth, in September 1998, the Supreme People's Court issued a regulation on the investigation of judicial officers who violate laws relating to trials and misjudged cases. The Supreme People's Procuratorate issued a similar regulation two months before the above regulation. Both regulations are helpful for building up a system for investigating misjudged cases.[23] Sixth, the basic legal rights of Chinese citizens were better protected. Victims, witnesses and suspects in criminal cases were advised of their legal rights by a simple card listing fundamental rights when they came into contact with the procuratorial system.[24] Finally, the recruitment system of judges was changed. Various legal workers, such as senior lawyers and law professors, were recruited to be judges.[25] Judges were divided into four levels: chief justice, justice, senior judge and judge.[26] Similarly, the procurators are also divided into several levels.[27] Through these efforts, the ranking systems for judges and procurators have been established in China.

Based on the previous achievements, the judicial reform marched forward significantly in October 1999 when the Supreme People's Court prepared and distributed the Five-Year Reform Programme of the People's Courts to the courts at all levels for implementation. The Programme sets forth the aims for the period from 1999 to 2003: (1) to further deepen the reform of adjudicating forms centred on the principle of open trial; (2) to establish the adjudicating management mechanism focusing on strengthening the responsibility of judges and the collegiate bench; (3) to reform the internal institutions of the courts and to reasonably equip the forces of adjudicating personnel and judicial administrative personnel; (4) to establish a team of judges with high quality; (5) to modernise the office of the courts and to improve the efficiency of the adjudicating work and the level of management; (6) to improve the supervisory mechanisms to safeguard the fairness and cleanness of the judicial personnel; and (7) to explore the reforms of the organisational system of the courts, the management system of the court cadres, and the management system of the courts' funds. For the purpose of safeguarding the judicial fairness and cleanness, the Reform Programme stressed the importance of establishing the internal checking mechanism, including the strengthening of the adjudicating supervisory system, the implementing of the (Trial) Measures in Dealing with the Liability of the Adjudicating Personnel of the People's Courts for Violations of Laws in Adjudication and the (Trial) Measures on Adjudicating Disciplinary Punishment of the People's Courts, and the improving of the inspector system.[28] As part of the Reform Programme, the Certain Opinions on Strengthening the Grass-roots Construction of the People's Courts were issued in 2000.[29]

Likewise, the Supreme People's Procuratorate in January 2000 adopted the Implementing Opinions of the Three-Year Procuratorial Reform. Accordingly, from 2000, procuratorates at all levels should carry out a new responsibility system under the chief procurator to handle cases. In addition, reform will be made for the prosecuratorial working mechanism to reinforce the function of legal supervision; for an institutional mechanism to reinforce the direction of the lower procuratorates by the higher procuratorates; for a procuratorial personnel system to raise the quality of the procurators and other personnel working in the procuratorates; for an internal and external supervisory mechanism to safeguard justice, honest and high efficiency; and for a financial management system to provide the procuratorates with material security.[30]

REALISING JUDICIAL INDEPENDENCE

To realise the aims set forth in the Reform Programme above needs great effort and the sincerity of the CCP and the Chinese government. The foremost aspect for successful judicial reform is the realisation of judicial independence. It is generally acknowledged that "an independent judiciary is the best means for protecting the rule of law".[31] The goal of the rule of law requires "the development of a judicial system that is relatively autonomous of the executive and legislative powers of government".[32] Judicial independence is an essential element of the "separation of powers" in the Western liberal notion. It is "an essential aspect of democratic government following on necessarily from the essential presence of judicial power within the powers of the state"; it "allows for a system of mutual checks and balances against the excesses of one branch of government"; and it "ensures that judges are free to do justice in their communities".[33] According to the standards adopted by the International Bar Association, judicial independence comprises personal independence (adequate guarantee that judges are not subject to executive control, adequate salaries and pensions, and security of the job), substantive independence (a judge is subject to nothing but the law and commands of his conscience), internal independence (a judge is independent vis-à-vis his judicial colleagues and superiors in the decision-making process), and collective independence (the judiciary as a whole enjoys autonomy vis-à-vis the executive).[34]

China has attempted to make the judiciary work independently within the stipulation in the Chinese Constitution that "the people's courts exercise judicial power independently in accordance with the provisions of the law, and are not subject to interference by any administrative organ, public organisation or individual".[35] Such independence was reaffirmed in the Organic Law of the People's Courts.[36] It allows the courts to exercise state judicial power independently, free from interference from any organisations or individuals including the CCP itself and its members.

According to a scholarly explanation, the word "court" contained in the above stipulation is of pivotal importance and it means that the individual judges do not have the judicial power but the courts where the judges perform their duties do. The collegial panels are the trial units not the individual judges, and the judgments by the collegial panels are made in the name of the courts. Therefore, the independent power of adjudication is vested in courts and not in judges.[37] In this sense, only collective independence is realised. Because of this collectiveness, in practice, presidents and/or division chiefs have the power to review and suggest changes in draft judgments prepared by collegial panels, thus constituting an internal interference with the independent adjudication of collegial panels.[38]

Second, it is generally understood that judicial independence means the extent to which judges handling cases can be independent. However, in China, judicial personnel are actually nominated and appointed by people's congresses at the corresponding levels and the budgets of the courts are also decided and provided by governments at the corresponding levels. Therefore, it is hard for judicial personnel to ward off the influence of the administrative organs.[39] Interference often occurs when a court handles a case which involves the interests of a local government or a department. According to a survey, judges in China confirm the existence, sometimes serious, of illegal interference in judicial independence.[40] There is a case reported in the *People's Daily* on interference in the judicial investigation involving Zhao Yuming, a legal person of a branch company of the Guiyang Chemical and Construction Company located in Dujun City, Guizhou Province. Zhao was suspected of embezzlement and subject to an arrest approved by the Guiyang People's Procuratorate in December 2000. However, due to the interference of the local government, the enforcement of the arrest warrant could not be carried out.[41] Because of their dependence on the local government for financial and other necessary support, judges and/or courts, even knowing that some cases are not fairly handled, tend to subordinate themselves to the instructions of the local government or party leaders.[42] Thus the independence of the Chinese judiciary is still limited and it may take a long time to reach genuine judicial independence. What is more problematic for judicial independence is the fact that China is still a one-party-rule regime which is different from Western democracy.

THE IMPACT OF THE PARTY ON JUDICIAL INDEPENDENCE

As we know, China is a one-party-rule country and the CCP is the ruling party. There has been a long debate on which is prevailing, the party or the law (*dang da haishi fa da*) in the Chinese society. Under the Chinese Constitution, any organisation, presumably including the CCP, should act in accordance with the law and no one is above the law. From this legal norm, the party should be subject to the law. However, the legal reality is more complicated that the statutory legal norm. Since law is made by the legislature, those who control it can make the law to reflect their will and to reach their goal. In China, as the NCP is under the hands of the CCP, then in principle there should be no law which could be in conflict with the party's interest and/or inconsistent with the party's policy. For example, during the Tiananmen Square incident in June 1989, China hastily passed the Martial Law for Beijing so as to pave the way of the crackdown on the student movement. On the other hand, due to the objectiveness of the law, a Frankenstein phenomenon may occur once a law has been enacted, particularly concerning human rights and social equality. For example, the Administrative Procedural Law gives the right to the ordinary citizens to bring party members or organisations to court, thus at least to some extent curbing the party's interest, or the interest of some party members. In order to march towards the rule of law, the party bears certain degree of tolerance. But if somebody uses the law to threaten the ruling status of the party, the party may not tolerate it.

The relationship between the judicial system and the CCP is a common topic in academia as well as in the mass media. Since the judicial system is a main institution to enforce law, it is extremely important to the party. The loyalty became a principal requirement of recruitment for the judiciary. This can explain from one aspect why so many retired military servicemen were recruited simply because they were the most loyal people to the party. Although the Chinese Constitution stipulates that "no organisation or individual may enjoy the privilege of being above the Constitution and the law", the CCP often interferes in judicial affairs, as reported from time to time. The Political-Legal Committee of the CCP is a very powerful organisation, usually giving instructions to the relevant court on how to handle cases. The Political-Legal Committee has the power to jointly issue legal documents together with the Court and/or the Procuratorate. For example, on 29 March 1983, the Political-Legal Committee of the Central Committee of the Party, at the request of the Shaanxi Provincial Political-Legal Committee, issued a ruling regarding the criteria for initiating prosecutions for corruption offences involving less than RMB 2,000, which was officially circulated to all courts and procuratorates to follow.[43] Related to this is the so-called "double restraint" (*shuanggui*),[44] a CCP internal practice which usually applies to high ranking corrupt officials within the Party. The case is handed over to the judiciary only after it has been through the Discipline Inspection Committee. Many cases come within this practice, even if criminal acts are obvious and should be subject to the penal code. This internal practice is criticised as "entirely arbitrary", and has shown that it is "improbable that China will move towards a depoliticised legal system as long as the Party treats its own members without reference to any legal process".[45] In addition, it is noted that most of the court cadres are CCP members[46] and they are usually inclined to obey party decisions or policies when they decide on cases, particularly those which have political implications. It is commonly recognised that party affiliation produces an impact on a judge's decision. It occurs even in the United States where the separation of powers is known to be firmly established; as has been acknowledged, "a judge's party affiliation may have a feedback reinforcement on his value system which in turn determines his decisional propensities".[47] However, in China's case, the impact of party affiliation is extremely salient. Some of the impact may be attributed to the Chinese Constitution: on one hand, it affirms judicial independence, but on the other, it expressly provides that the four basic cardinal principles should be followed by all in China.[48] Since judicial independence is acted within the ambit of law, the above constitutional requirement must be fulfilled by the court and the procuratorate when they handle cases.

It is recalled that as early as 1979, the Central Committee of the CCP issued the Instruction on Strictly Implementing the Criminal Law and the Criminal Procedure Law in which the system of review and approval of cases by the Party Committee should be annulled.[49]

Unfortunately, in practice, the influence of the CCP over China's judiciary is still great.

Since China has pledged to follow international rules and standards to build its own legal system, it should consider absorbing the general judicial principles and rules for its judicial reform.[50] The United Nations has adopted a series of political and legal documents guiding the development and improvement of its member States' judicial systems. The most important one is the Basic Principles on the Independence of the Judiciary,[51] which sets forth the rules and standards for the independence of the judiciary and the qualifications of judges. In terms of judicial independence, it stipulates that:

1. The independence of the judiciary shall be guaranteed by the State and enshrined in the Constitution or the law of the country. It is the duty of all governmental and other institutions to respect and observe the independence of the judiciary.
2. The judiciary shall decide matters before them impartially, on the basis of facts and in accordance with the law, without any restrictions, improper influences, inducements, pressures, threats or interferences, direct or indirect, from any quarter or for any reason.
3. The judiciary shall have jurisdiction over all issues of a judicial nature and shall have exclusive authority to decide whether an issue submitted for its decision is within its competence as defined by law.
4. There shall not be any inappropriate or unwarranted interference with the judicial process, nor shall judicial decisions by the courts be subject to revision. This principle is without prejudice to judicial review or to mitigation or commutation by competent authorities of sentences imposed by the judiciary, in accordance with the law.
5. Everyone shall have the right to be tried by ordinary courts or tribunals using established legal procedures. Tribunals that do not use the duly established procedures of the legal process shall not be created to displace the jurisdiction belonging to the ordinary courts or judicial tribunals.

6. The principle of the independence of the judiciary entitles and requires the judiciary to ensure that judicial proceedings are conducted fairly and that the rights of the parties are respected.
7. It is the duty of each Member State to provide adequate resources to enable the judiciary to properly perform its functions.[52]

It is clear that there are a number of defects existing in China's judicial system which have negatively affected judicial independence, in addition to the interference from the CCP. Compared to the above UN standards, the way leading to a full realisation of judicial independence in China is a long march. Only when China closely follows the UN standards could it realise full judicial independence.

IMPROVING PROFESSIONAL QUALITY

How to upgrade the quality of judges and other judicial personnel is an unavoidable issue that judicial reform faces. The initial personnel of the PRC courts were military servicemen. Even today, the courts, particularly local courts, are staffed with many retired military servicemen. Because of the low prestige and low salary of judges, law students are reluctant to work in the courts, especially the local ones.[53] According to a 1997 statistic, among 250,000 court cadres, those with a bachelors degree accounted for 5.6 percent, and those with a master's degree 0.25 percent, while in the procuratorate the figure was 4.0 percent and 0.15 percent respectively among 180,000 personnel.[54] At present, there are about 280,000 adjudicating personnel throughout the country, but the actual number of qualified judges is small.[55] Largely due to the poor quality of judges, mishandled cases have been reported frequently. In Heilongjiang Province, for instance, between 1993 and 1996, sentences given in 438 court cases were found to be erroneous and 460 judicial officials were punished for malpractice.[56]

In addition, there is one big worry in the current phenomenon. On the one hand, graduates from law schools who are willing work in the judiciary cannot be properly recruited by the court or the procuratorate, but those laid off from the government departments can work in the court.[57] Under such circumstances, it is extremely difficult to improve the professional quality of the judges and procurators despite the efforts made. Another interesting thing is that the military has rebutted the criticism of the recruitment of retired military servicemen to be judges, asking why retired military servicemen cannot become judges.[58]

The Law of Judges is the first legislation to govern the system of judges, and it contains a number of principles: (1) competition in selection and employment of judges; (2) merit measured on performance; (3) integrity and ability in the discharge of judicial functions; and (4) the administration of judicial functions according to law.[59] The Law identifies "obligations" and "rights" for judges. Its counterpart law for the personnel of the procuratorate is the Law of Procurators which was promulgated in 1995 as well and contains similar provisions.[60]

The provisions on the qualifications of judges in the Law of Judges cannot be fully implemented, particularly in the local courts because of various interferences as well as the loophole of flexibility left in the law. For that reason, the NPC decided to amend these two laws. At the 16th Session of the Ninth NPC held in July 2000, two draft amendments to the existing laws regarding judges and procurators which were designed to improve the quality of the judiciary by raising qualification standards were discussed. According to the draft laws, those who are appointed judges or procurators must be college graduates and have practised law for at least two years, or must be postgraduates who have practised law for at least one year. Those who do not major in law must be confirmed as having the same level of knowledge of the law.[61] The new amendments were adopted in June 2001 and will enter into effect as of 1 January 2002. They are hailed as playing an important role in strengthening the calibre of China's judiciary and ensuring that justice be served, and dramatically lifting the benchmarks for entrance to the legal professions.[62] For the first time, the amended law of judges required that the president and vice-president of a people's court should be chosen from judges or those with legal practice background.[63]

In accordance with the above two amended laws and for the purpose of meeting the professional requirements, the Supreme Court, the Supreme Procuratorate and the Ministry of Justice jointly issued a circular to unify the judicial examination from 2002 for entry-level judges, procurators as well as for the qualifications to become lawyers.[64] This measure may improve the quality of judges and procurators, but it is not clear why the examination for judges and procurators is combined with the examination for lawyers. In addition, the procuratorate prepared a training programme for procurators from 2001 to 2005. Accordingly, by the end of 2005, 90 percent of the procurators should have college qualifications, of whom about 100 should possess a PhD degree and 4,000 a master's degree, and 40 percent a bachelor's degree.[65] A recent selection of judges in the Beijing Municipality showed that the educational level of judges has been raised: among 252 presiding judges and 329 sole judges selected, one has a PhD, 25 have a master's degree, 307 have a bachelor's degree and 215 are junior college graduates.[66]

With China's entry into the World Trade Organisation (WTO), the training of judges on WTO rules has become a pressing task in China. It is reported that the National Judges College has already started to provide Chinese judges with a series of WTO-related training courses.[67] The judiciary also tries to upgrade the standards of professional ethics for judges and procurators. For instance, in October 2001 the Supreme Court issued a circular requiring courts at all levels across China to improve judges' self-discipline and efficiency in accordance with the Chinese Judges' Professional Ethics, including improving judicial justice, working efficiency, honesty, judicial management and self-improvement.[68]

It is worth mentioning that the United Nations has prepared some guidelines for judges' qualifications, selection and training. The Basic Principles on the Independence of the Judiciary adopted in 1985 requires that "Persons selected for judicial office shall be individuals of integrity and ability with appropriate training or qualifications in law. Any method of judicial selection shall safeguard against judicial appointments for improper motives."[69] Judges should maintain independence when they handle the cases. They have the right of freedom of expression, but they should always conduct themselves in such a manner as to preserve the dignity of their office and the impartiality and independence of the judiciary. Judges shall be free to form and join associations of judges or other organisations to represent their interests, to promote their professional training and to protect their judicial independence.[70]

In addition, the Guidelines on the Role of Prosecutors are also important reference for China's judicial reform.[71] They require states to make sure that:

(a) Selection criteria for prosecutors embody safeguards against appointments based on partiality or prejudice, excluding any discrimination against a person on the grounds of race, colour, sex, language, religion, political or other opinion, national, social or ethnic origin, property, birth, economic or other status, except that it shall not be considered discriminatory to require a candidate for prosecutorial office to be a national of the country concerned;
(b) Prosecutors have appropriate education and training and should be made aware of the ideals and ethical duties of their office, of the constitutional and statutory protections for the rights of the suspect and the victim, and of human rights and fundamental freedoms recognised by national and international law.[72]

IMPROVING WORK EFFICIENCY

The other important aspect in judicial reform is the transparency and efficiency of the court adjudication. China has some 280,000 judges–the highest number in the world–but suffers a bad image of its judiciary's low efficiency in handling cases.[73] Recently, open trials and hearings, except for those involving privacy, minors, or state secrets, have been undertaken in big cities, such as Beijing. Chinese citizens who intend to attend the court trial or hearing, and reporters who want to cover the trials will have to apply to the court for valid identity certificates.[74] Open trial is a litigation principle that attempts to maximise the fairness and transparency of the judicial system. It is commented that "[t]he publicity of trials can have a far-reaching impact on ensuring the integrity of the legal system, because it is the most direct, widespread, and forceful form of oversight".[75]

Although open trial is a kind of procedure, it involves a number of key aspects in judicial reform. It requires transparent and just court procedures and high quality judges. It also requires the reform of the internal operation in the court, such as the review and approval system of the adjudicative committee. Thus, open trial, as part of the judicial reform, can facilitate the overall judicial reform. However, the biggest problem in open trial, as Xiao Yang, President of the Supreme People's Court once admitted, is the quality of judges.[76]

In June 2000, the Supreme People's Court decided to make public verdict documents which would be published in major media, courts' publications and/or on the Internet. It would increase the credibility of court rulings and public trust in the judiciary.[77] This is an additional move that is significant to the court's implementation of the open trial system.

The efficiency of court work is another problem in law enforcement. Recently, cases which have not been handled or handled but not yet enforced have increased dramatically. According to a high court statistic, the national incidence of unenforced cases stands at 30 percent a year. In some courts, the backlog of adjudicated but unresolved cases has risen to 60-70 percent of the annual caseload.[78] In 2000 at a national meeting on civil trials, Xiao Yang urged all the judges to enhance trial efficiency and handle cases in due time set by the law. According to him, people were not satisfied with some aspects of court work and the majority of their complaints were centred on injustice and low efficiency in handling cases. For the interest of the people, "cases that can be concluded in the remaining days of this year should not be delayed to the 21st century".[79] The efficiency of case handling has been increased in recent years. According to a figure, in 1989, with 120,000 adjudicating personnel, the number of closed cases was 3,182,194, accounting for 26.5 closed cases per person per year; and in 1998, with 170,000 adjudicating personnel, the number of closed cases was 5,864,274, accounting for 34.5 closed cases per person per year. The average amount for one judicial person handling the closed cases increased to 30.19 percent.[80] However, despite the efforts, the problem of low efficiency still remains.

The issue of work efficiency can be traced to the internal operation of the court, particularly the result of having a judicial committee to make a final decision on a case after a legal proceeding. In addition, when a case is considered complicated or important, the final decision may be concluded by the judicial committee of a court rather than the designated collegial panel. This mechanism is said to be designated to safeguard the correct and impartial exercise of judicial powers, but in practice it may also be used as a device by some committee members to interfere improperly with the collegial panel's function and to favour one side of the litigation.[81] This mechanism of separating trial process from decision-making is clearly a deficiency in China's judicial system. For that reason, it is advocated that "the responsibility for the proper handling of cases should rest with the presiding judge. This will reduce the need for multiple judges, lower the number of procedural steps, and shorten the time of litigation, thereby lowering procedural costs and increasing procedural efficiency".[82]

One way of improving the efficiency and transparency of court work is through the people's assessors system. The people's assessors system was first stipulated in the 1954 Constitution, but it was not retained in the 1982 Constitution. In practice, the standing committee of local people's congresses may select people's assessors and provide a list of them to the courts at the corresponding level. Courts may select people's assessors from the list and invite them to participate in the case of first-instance trial. Collegial panels for the first-instance trial may be composed of judges and people's assessors or exclusively of judges. The people's assessors system is different from the jury system in common law jurisdiction in that the people's assessors are not selected on the basis of citizenship; they function as judges, and have the authority to decide both issues of facts and law. Although this system is praised as a form of judicial democratisation and of direct involvement of the ordinary people in judicial activities, there remain a number of problems (e.g., assessors with little legal knowledge; assessors sitting but doing nothing in the legal proceedings; no operative regulations to select assessors). To improve the system, it has been suggested that more precise regulations be provided, particularly those concerning the qualifications and treatment of the assessors, rights and duties of the assessors, the clear selection procedure, and the scope of the system application so that some, if not all, of the problems can be eliminated.[83]

The withdrawal system is an important part of the litigation procedure. It is provided for in the Chinese procedure laws in that :

> If a party to a case considers that a member of the judicial personnel has an interest in the case or, for any other person, cannot administer justice impartially, he has the right to ask that member to withdraw. The president of the court shall decide whether the member should withdraw. If a member of the judicial personnel considers that he should withdraw because he has an interest in the case or for any other person, he should report the matter to the president of the court for decision.[84]

The term "judicial personnel" in the above provision is not very clear: it can naturally include judges and other adjudicating persons, but it is not clear whether all the persons assisting in handling the case are included. Second, the provision does not mention whether the withdrawal system applies to the work of the adjudicating committees. Third, the provision does not mention whether the president should withdraw from a case in which he may have an interest. Finally, it does not mention whether it applies to the enforcing personnel of court judgements. Due to these shortcomings, improvement to the withdrawal system is necessary. Some scholars suggest "three opens" in the withdrawal system as the key to its improvement: (1) open to the public the relevant regulations and rules; (2) open to the public the resume of the relevant judges; and (3) open to the public the resume of the judges in particular cases. Meanwhile, the existing regulations should be amended.[85] Clearly, China has realised this necessity. Last year, two sets of new regulations on the withdrawal system were introduced: the Certain Provisions on the Strict Implementation of the Withdrawal System of Adjudicating

Personnel (31 January 2000),[86] and the Provisional Measures on the Withdrawal of Office of the Procurators (4 July 2000).[87] According to these two regulations, the withdrawal system has been further improved, and some shortcomings are remedied by new provisions. For example, a judge or procurator who has retired from his office for less than two years is not allowed to be a legal representative or defence counsel.

The "wrong verdict liability" system (*zuo an zui jiu zhi*) functions as an effective measure to improve the quality of adjudication as well as to curb judicial corruption. It aims to punish judicial personnel who infringe substantive or procedural law in the adjudicating process and make wrong decisions causing harmful consequences. In June 2001, three judges at the Huanggu District Court in Shengyang, Liaoning Province, were held liable under this system for their wrong decision on a case involving a dog's injury claim.[88]

In addition, the Procuratorate has taken several measures to improve its work. In October 1998, the Supreme Procuratorate made a decision on the implementation of the open procuratorial work throughout the country. In early 1999, detailed measures were prepared. Procuratorial work can be reported to the public through regular or occasional press conferences, or in the mass media.[89] In May 2001, the Supreme Procuratorate adopted six measures on handling cases: (a) all clues of cases should be managed collectively and no one should handle them in private; (b) statutory procedures must be strictly complied with to place a case on file for prosecution; (c) investigation and arrest must be carried out in strict accordance with law; (d) change or cancellation of arrest must be undertaken in strict accordance with law; (e) prosecution must be undertaken strictly under the law; and (f) appealing cases must be handled by more than two persons in accordance with law.[90] It is envisioned that through these efforts, the work of the procuratorate can be substantially improved.

CURBING JUDICIAL CORRUPTION

It is widely reported that judicial corruption is the most corrupt phenomenon in China. Judicial corruption is manifested in the following respects: (1) judicial local protectionism and department protectionism; (2) adjudication in violation of statutory procedures or overdue adjudication; (3) abuse of power to detain interested parties or lawyers or limit their personal freedom; (4) abuse of judicial power to extort property, services, or collect fees at random; and (5) breach of the law to protect private interests or protection of the interest of relatives or friends at the expense of the interests of others.[91] Cases involving judges' abuse of power have been frequently revealed in the mass media. Through the recent "Intensified Educational Rectification Movement" within the judiciary in 1997 and 1998, some 177 courts at provincial, prefectural and county levels have been reshuffled and unqualified leaders were removed. Nearly 5,000 judges and prosecutors in the first eight months in 1998 were disciplined.[92] In 1999, 1,886 unqualified prosecutors were transferred, 2,156 officials in 1,062 local procuratorates were laid off and replaced.[93] In 2001, 22 judges in Hainan Province were removed due to their corruption.[94]

Some recent major cases include such judicial personnel as: Cheng Guiqing, President of the Qiaoxi District Court of Zhang Jiakou City, Hebei Province; and Li Yongqing, vice-president of the Intermediate Court of Lhasha, Tibet.[95] In May 2000 the intermediate court of Hechi Prefecture, Guangxi Autonomous Region, rendered 18-year and 12-year prison sentences respectively to Hu Yaoguang, former head of the Luo Chen Prison, and his accomplice Wei Zeguang, former president of the second tribunal of the intermediate court of the Hechi Prefecture, for their bribery and malfeasance. This was the first case of judicial corruption handled in Guangxi.[96]

In general, corruption sows the seeds for social and political tensions, threatens the very fabric of society and undermines the effectiveness of the state and the political legitimacy of government.[97] The negative impact resulting from judicial corruption on society is more damaging than corruption in other government agencies due to the nature and functions of the judiciary. The courts, procuratorates and departments of public security are direct law enforcement organs of the state in China. Judicial corruption could turn the rule of law to a rule of individuals pursuing their private interests. It undermines public confidence in judicial organs' ability to implement laws and regulations, weakens the viability and effectiveness of the legal system and finally destabilises the social order. Second, judicial personnel are those who are supposed to be most familiar with the law and if they break the law, their misconduct will definitely give ordinary people the impression that the law is not something important and serious, or even to perceive it as equivalent to nothing, leading to the possibility of defiance by the people, and even the destruction of the authority of the law.

There are a number of factors causing judicial corruption. The factors outside the judiciary are:

(1) inconsistency with the judicial system provided in the Chinese Constitution and with the market economy;
(2) the previous system of a planned economy still plays a negative role in the current transitional period of economic reform;
(3) little legal conscience of the leaders and the masses at this preliminary stage of building up a culture of the rule of law;
(4) dominance of administrative departments over the judiciary and dependence of the judiciary and its judges on them;
(5) the political idea that the judiciary serves politics is still strong; and
(6) absence of institutions established by the people's congresses to monitor the judiciary.

For the factors within the judiciary, they include:

(1) the system of appointing judges is backward, the quality of the judges poor, and the judges have no personal independence;
(2) complexity of the court's internal organisations which limit the display of judges' initiatives;
(3) difficulty to realise the functions of the court due to the influence of the political system;
(4) appointment power belongs to the organ of personnel of the local government;

(5) the financial state of the court is dependent on the local government;
(6) little right of discretion of judges, and adjudication is affected by internal and/or external influences on many occasions;
(7) heavy dependence of the judges on the adjudication committee because of the internal disciplinary system for misjudged cases, thus making the low efficiency of case handling;
(8) low salary of the judges which makes it difficult to keep every judge clean; and
(9) the internal institutions of the court and the judges have the same working environment as any administrative department.[98]

How to overcome these factors, particularly the internal ones, depends to large extent on the success of judicial reform.

China has promulgated many laws and regulations to fight corruption. However, such anti-corruption laws and regulations may not be effective in the absence of honest and efficient investigative and judicial bodies. Thus, to fight corruption in China is to first fight judicial corruption. Only when judicial corruption is curbed and greatly reduced to a controllable extent can the goal of the overall anti-corruption campaign be achieved.[99]

For that purpose, the judicial bodies have taken a series of measures. In February 2000, the Supreme People's Court issued the Regulations on Strictly Implementing the Withdrawal System of the Adjudicating Personnel to curb corruption among judges and to maintain judicial justice. The Regulations clarified the meaning of the words "other relations" between adjudicating persons and litigants contained in the withdrawal system provided for in the Organic Law of the People's Court, Law of Criminal Procedure, Law of Civil Procedure and Law of Administrative Procedure. According to the above Regulations, "the other relations" refer to:

(1) relative relationship between the adjudicating person and litigant agent or defendant of the case;
(2) private meeting of the adjudicating person with plaintiffs, defendants or their lawyers without the court's permission;

(3) accepting money or gifts from litigants, or attending banquets and other activities sponsored by them;
(4) recommending lawyers, or referring cases to lawyers; and
(5) borrowing money, vehicles or communications equipment from litigants, or accepting financial support when shopping or decorating houses. For any of the circumstances above, the adjudicating person should withdraw himself from handling the case.[100]

According to Xiao Yang, the Supreme Court has established various internal regulations regarding reporting of judges' violation of laws or disciplines, disciplinary punishment on adjudicating personnel for misjudgement, and adjudicating inspection.[101] The Supreme People's Procuratorate formulated the Standards for Case Review by the Committee of Procuratorate in 1999.[102] It also has the Ten Disciplines of Honesty for Prosecution.[103] In order to prohibit spouses and children of high-ranking officers (at or above bureau level) within the procuratorate, rules were issued in late 2000 to the effect that such spouses and children should not open law firms at places which are under the jurisdiction of the procuratorate, or represent clients in cases filed with the procuratorate.[104]

SUPERVISION OF THE JUDICIARY

Supervision of judicial functions is regarded as one of the measures to curb judicial corruption and to improve judicial justice. Although supervision can come from various sources, such as the mass media, the CCP and other democratic parties, the masses (e.g., by letter of accusation), or the procuratorate which is the statutory organ supervising the work of the court and the superior court, the main supervision is provided by the people's congress. The people's congress may have the power to supervise the work of the court and the procuratorate. There are some successful supervision cases reported in the mass media. On 30 August 2000, the Standing Committee of the People's Congress of Hefei City, Anhui Province, passed a resolution on the case of Wang Renchai (who was wrongly charged for assault and sentenced six months of custody), demanding the investigation of the responsible persons involved in the case and asking the city government, the intermediate court and the city procuratorate to report to the people's congress the result of the investigation and the handling of the case.[105] Another case occurred in Shandong Province: three peasants were sentenced to imprisonment of 12 and 14 years for robbery in 1996. After being put in jail, they appealed many times. In December 1999 the Standing Committee of the Provincial People's Congress received the letter of appeal and found many doubts on the case. In December 2000, the People's Congress sent a Notice of Supervising Individual Case, asking the Provincial Court to retry the case. On 29 December 2000, the Provincial Higher People's Court declared the innocence of the three inmates and released them.[106] Undoubtedly, appropriate supervision can facilitate judicial justice and fairness.

There is a regular reporting system between the people's congress and the court/procuratorate. It is reported that for the first time in Chinese history the work report of a court addressed to the People's Congress was rejected. In February 2001, the Work Report of the People's Intermediate Court of Shenyang (capital city of Liaoning Province) was rejected by the Shenyang People's Congress. It was hailed as "a benchmark event in China's democratic politics".[107] The Work Report was finally adopted six months later after it had been revised. The rejection by the People's Congress is an indication of the exercise of supervisory power by the people's representatives in the Congress. On the other hand, it raised a number of legal issues such as: under what circumstances can a work report of a court be rejected, how to revise it when it is rejected, and by what means? To solve such issues, the call was to enact the law on supervision.[108]

The law on supervision of important and egregious cases under the judiciary was drafted in 1999 and is still under review in the NPC. The draft law grants the right of supervision to the people's congress over important and egregious cases handled by the judiciary in three aspects:

(1) judgements with mistakes;
(2) cases going far beyond the prescribed time limit; and
(3) cases involving violation of law or torture by the adjudicating organ or the procuratorate.[109]

While the supervision from the people's congress is recommendable,[110] there is some fear that the normal and independent work of the judiciary could be unreasonably and excessively interfered with by possible abuse of the supervisory power. In particular, some judges fear the negative repercussions of this kind of supervision and are worried about whether the people's congress would become "a court above the court".[111] In addition, some scholars consider the supervision by the people's congress a case of legislative power overstepping judicial power, and a potential threat to the improvement of the judicial system. The reporting system to the people's congress is a barrier to the independence of the judiciary and judges.[112] In order to avoid possible abuse of the supervisory power, there should be a balance between judicial independence and judicial supervision.[113] It is suggested that the people's congress should not review directly any case, or propose and/or decide how to handle any case, or support one party of the case to resist the valid court decision, or supervise a case under the influence of a particular individual or group, or pass a resolution to revoke or change the judgement of the court.[114] In considering this, the draft law sets forth five principles for the people's congress to comply with when it exercises the power of supervision: (1) supervision should be conducted within the authorisation and procedure stipulated in the Constitution and the law; (2) supervision should be conducted only after the court decision has been made; (3) the power of supervision should be exercised collectively; (4) the people's congress should not exercise the power of adjudication or prosecution, or directly handle a case, or interfere with the normal judicial proceedings; and (5) the judiciary should accept the supervision of the people's congress.[115]

As a positive response, the Supreme People's Court has prepared Certain Opinions on Acceptance by the People's Court of Supervision from the People's Congress and Its Standing Committee.[116] In recent years, supervision over the work of judicial organs has been further strengthened. The CCP Central Committee decided in August 2001 to send inspection teams to examine the work of judicial and law enforcement organs to see whether the 1999 Decision on Further Strengthening the Cadre Team of Law Enforcement has been effectively implemented.[117]

PROBLEMS AND PROSPECTS

Judicial reform is actually not new in China. As we recall, as early as the 1950s, China launched a judicial reform movement nationwide. However, its purpose was quite different from that of the current one: it was aimed to "insure the political reliability of court personnel and to solidify the foundation for 'socialist legality'".[118] At that time, many of the judges were former judges under the Kuomintang regime and their loyalty was suspected, though the communists abolished the old judicial system.[119] As a result, many old judges were expelled from the judiciary, and some were even put into jail. To fill the vacancies, communist cadres were brought into judicial work. The judicial reform at that time was hailed as a victory, having consolidated the socialist judicial organ of all levels, established communist ideology as guidelines for judicial work, and laid a solid foundation for the People's Democratic Dictatorship.[120] It is seen in the practice that the judicial reform in the 1950s carried a different purpose from the current reform: for the former, due to the distrust of the old legal system, the communist power had to reform it to serve its own interest since the judiciary, in the eye of the communists, is an important instrument of the People's Democratic Dictatorship; while for the latter, it is part of China's attempt to modernise its judicial system to meet present and future needs. It is a process of quality improvement.

Judicial reform may be interfered with by other adverse factors from the outside. Recently President Jiang Zemin put forward a doctrine of so-called "rule by virtue" (*yide zhiguo*) in parallel to the rule of law, and wanted the CCP to govern the country by combining the rule of law with the rule by virtue.[121] Virtue, linked with the

Confucian classics, can help to prevent and curb corruption, including judicial corruption. Some courts began to implement the so-called "rule the court by virtue" (*yide zhiyuan*).[122] At present, there is no doubt that party policy continues to be the guiding principles for the work of the court and the procuratorate, as is manifested in a recent call by Xiao Yang, who requested the court personnel to study Jiang Zemin's "three represents" carefully so as to improve the quality of law enforcement.[123]

While many scholars have commended Jiang's doctrine,[124] there may be a downside in that emphasising too much the rule by virtue would undermine the implementation of the rule of law, since the term "rule by virtue" implies "rule by man" as it requires rule by virtuous people, which could be seen to place emphasis on the personality of leaders rather than on law.[125] Recent cases have shown that the CCP is still disregarding the rule of law and is allowing political will to dominate their decisions (rule by man rather than rule of law): the spy plane crash in April 2001, the Gao Zhan case, and the Lai Changxing case.[126] From these events, people have reasons to doubt whether the judicial reform could succeed.

China's WTO entry will no doubt bring big challenges to the Chinese judiciary, and will force China to deepen its judicial reform.[127] As observed outside China, China's legal system is inadequate for the needs of foreign companies trying to do business there and the volume of business–and therefore the likely number of commercial disputes–is growing well beyond the system's capacity. There are three obstacles: (a) the CCP remains supreme in China, not the law; (b) lack of trained judges; and (c) corruption.[128] The current judicial reform aims to remedy the above inadequacies. According to one commentator, "China's economy will not mature until there is a judicial system that produces a modicum of accountability among government and party officials".[129] In this sense, the WTO entry can produce a very positive impact on the development of judicial reform and China's road towards rule of law. On the other hand, the development of the market economy depends on a sound judicial system. Before economic reform, there were mainly two functions for the court: (a) punishing the enemy;

and (b) dealing with family matters such as divorce. Nevertheless, since economic reform the court has been deeply involved in economic development. With the development of the market economy, the judicial system can play a greater role than before. As predicted by Chinese government officials, more cases relating to investment and trade will increase after China's entry into the WTO.[130] As pledged, the judiciary must ensure that its judicial work is of a high quality, efficient and impartial, both procedurally and substantially, in providing services for economic development.[131] In this context, the success of judicial reform is critical.

Although judicial reform based on the Reform Programme of the Supreme People's Court and the Programme of the Supreme People's Procuratorate has begun and also achieved some progress, it is "a long-term matter", as conceded by the President of the Supreme People's Court,[132] and there are a number of problems to be resolved. The tasks at the next stage would be painstaking, and may involve political reform as well, i.e., aiming at judicial independence and neutrality of the judges. The most important matter is how to give true independence to the Chinese judiciary. There are two main obstacles to realising this: (1) the Communist Party's interference, illustrated by the presence of the political and legal committees within the Party which have power to decide the judgement of some cases; and (2) the current financial and human resources in support of the judiciary which come from the relevant governmental departments and party units; thus the operations of the judiciary are constrained by the providers. In addition, judicial corruption is another major problem which should be tackled in the judicial reform. Thus, how to realise judicial justice is one of the key tasks for China to attain the rule of law. In particular, three main issues which remain to be fully resolved are: judicial localisation (scope of court territorial jurisdiction is determined along with the local administrative zoning such that the court becomes part of the local government); judicial administration (a higher court is the leader of a lower court and lower courts make decisions based on the instructions from the higher courts. Within a court, there is an administrative hierarchy among the judges and other judicial personnel); and bureaucratisation of judges (judges are treated as civil servants).

The 1999 Programme on court reform and the 2000 Programme on procuratorate reform refrained from addressing the issue on how to adjust the power between the judiciary and the ruling party, the people's congress or the government. They also avoid touching on any power adjustment between the judiciary (the court and the procuratorate) and other judicial administrative organs.[133] This indicates that the judicial reform at present is not bold enough. Any substantial change in power structure will depend on future political reform. The success of the overall judicial reform also relies on the necessary reform of the systems regarding police, lawyers and notary, which is not addressed in this paper. It is recommended that a unified institution of judicial reform be established to coordinate the judicial reform in different organs.[134] Some scholars even suggest changing the name of the court, and deleting the word "people".[135] On the other hand, it should be noted that the success of the judicial reform depends not only on the reform of the judicial system *per se*, but also on the supporting legal infrastructure based on other major laws such as the Criminal Procedure Law, Civil Procedure Law, Administrative Procedure Law, Arbitration Law, State Compensation Law, Administrative Punishment Law, Lawyer's Law, Police Law, and Law of Prison.

In July 2001, the Supreme Court set forth five reform areas for the coming years: (a) to push forward the reform of adjudication and supervision, to prepare standards for re-trial cases, and to regulate the procedure of opening and handling re-trial criminal cases; (b) to further improve the system of litigation evidence; (c) to cooperate with other departments to simplify the criminal procedures; (d) to experiment with the arrangement of having separate ranks for law clerks working in courts; and (e) to experiment with the equipment of assistants to judges and the number of judges in some courts.[136]

It can be concluded that although the current judicial reform is positive and can be regarded as a link to the chain of the overall political reform, it is not a prerequisite to push forward a fundamental change in China's political structure since it centres only on the improvement of the work of the court and the procuratorate as well as the quality of the judicial personnel, rather than addressing seriously the judiciary's independence. It is believed that judicial reform will be still ongoing, though slowly and sometimes not smoothly, towards the rule of law. An American legal scholar describes China's legal reform as "a bird in a cage".[137] This is true as long as legal reform, including judicial reform, is carried out under the restraint of the CCP leadership. However, the cage would be too small when the bird has grown up. The bird would finally fly away, just as what the country experienced in its economic reform.

ENDNOTES

1 *Black's Law Dictionary*, Sixth Edition (St. Paul, Minn: West Publishing Co., 1990), p. 849.

2 Ibid.

3 See Yuan Hongbing and Sun Xiaoning, *Chinese Judicial System* (Beijing: Peking University Press, 1988)(in Chinese), p. 3.

4 See Chen Yehong and Tang Ming, *Comparison of Chinese and Foreign Judicial Systems* (Beijing: Commercial Press, 2000)(in Chinese), 4-6. Another extreme view limits the judicial system only to "courts", see Li Fucheng, "A Special Conference on China's Judicial Reform", *Peking University Law Journal* (in Chinese), Vol.12 (6), 2000, p. 718.

5 There is a saying in China that "big public security, small court, and optional procuratorate" (*da gongan, xiao fayuan, keyou kewu jianchayuan*), see Cui Shixing, "Make Firm the Basis of Just Law Enforcement", *People's Daily* (in Chinese), 28 March 2001, p. 10.

6 Articles 123-135 of the 1982 Constitution, reprinted in Bureau of Legislative Affairs of the State Council of the PRC (ed.), *Laws and Regulations of the People's Republic of China Governing Foreign-Related Matters*, Vol. I (Beijing: China Legal System Publishing House, 1991), pp. 299-300.

7 The People's Supreme Court was established in October 1949 just after the founding of the PRC, see He Lanjian and Lu Mingjian (eds.), *Judicial Work of Contemporary China*, Vol.1 (Beijing: Contemporary China Publisher, 1993), pp. 23-24.

8 Organic Law of the People's Court was promulgated in 1979 and amended in 1983. English text is available in Ronald C. Brown, *Understanding Chinese Courts and Legal Process: Law with Chinese Characteristics* (The Hague: Kluwer Law International, 1997), pp. 150-157.

9 "Supreme Court newly establish the fourth division of civil cases", *China Ocean News* (in Chinese), 11 August 2000.

10 Art. 32 of the Organic Law of the People's Courts.

11 The Organic Law of the People's Procuratorate was adopted in July 1979 and took effect as of 1 January 1980. English text is available in Legislative Affairs Commission of the Standing Committee of the National People's Congress of the People's Republic of China (comp.), *Laws of the People's Republic of China* (Beijing: Foreign Languages Press, 1987), pp. 80-87.

12 Ibid.

13 For an overview of China's legal reform, see Zou Keyuan, "Towards Rule of Law in China: Experiences in the Last Two Decades", *China Report*, Vol.36 (4), 2000: 491-509.

14 "Quarterly Chronicle and Documentation (October-December 1978)", *China Quarterly*, No.77 (March 1979), p. 172.

15 See Jasper Becker, *The Chinese* (New York: The Free Press, 2000), p. 326.

16 Art.1 of the Judge's Law.

17 See Art.1 of the Procurator's Law.

18 Shao Zongwei, "Judicial reform outlined", *China Daily*, 3 December 1998.

19 "Legal reform touches on township courtrooms", *China Daily*, 30 November 1998.

20 Shao Zongwei, "Reform brings new supervisory judges", *China Daily*, 31 October 1998.

21 See *People's Daily* (in Chinese), 3 December 1998.

22 See *Mingpao* (in Chinese), 3 December 1998.

23 See Zhao Zongwei, "New rules improve judicial safeguards", *China Daily*, 4 September 1998.

24 Zhao Zongwei, "A historic first: rights listed on cards", *China Daily*, 27 October 1998.

25 See *Lianhe Zhaobao* (in Chinese), 9 November 1998.

26 See *People's Daily* (in Chinese), 18 November 1998.

27 "Our Country Will Establish Prosecutorial Ranking System", *People's Daily* (in Chinese), 26 November 1998.

28 See Circular of the Supreme People's Court Regarding the Print and Distribution of Five-Year Reform Programme of the People's Courts, in *Gazette of the Supreme People's Court of the People's Republic of China* (in Chinese)(1999), No.6, pp. 185-190.

29 Text in *Legal Daily* (in Chinese), 14 August 2000, p. 2.

30 Text in *Legal Daily* (in Chinese), 23 February 2000.

31 See Michael Herz, "Rediscovering Francis Lieber: An Afterword and Introduction", *Cardozo Law Review*, Vol.16, 1995, p. 2107. This view is concurred by other jurists, such as Calvin R. Massey, "Rule of Law and the Age of Aquarius", *Hastings Law Journal*, Vol.41, p. 760 (quoting Geoffrey de Q. Walker for the proposition that "an independent judiciary is an indispensable requirement of the rule of law"); and Frances Kahn Zemans, "The Accountable Judge: Guardian of Judicial Independence", *Southern California Law Review*, Vol.72, 1999, p. 631 (arguing that "an independent judiciary" is a "necessity" for the rule of law).

32 Eric W. Orts, "The Rule of Law in China", *Vanderbilt Journal of Transnational Law*, Vol.34, 2001, p. 99.

33 Mark Findlay, "'Independence' and the Judiciary in the PRC: Expectations for Constitutional Legality in China", in Kanishka Jayasuriya (ed.), *Law, Capitalism and Power in Asia: The Rule of Law and Legal Institutions* (London and New York: Routledge, 1999), p. 297.

34 See Li Yuwen Li, "Judicial Independence: Applying International Minimum Standards to Chinese Law and Practice", *China Information*, Vol.15 (1), 2001, pp. 68-70.

35 Article 126 of the Chinese Constitution. The English version is available in *Laws and Regulations of the People's Republic of China Governing Foreign-Related Matters*, Vol.1 (Beijing: China Legal System Publishing House, 1991), p. 299.

36 Article 4 of the Organic Law provides that the courts should conduct adjudication independently and subject only to the law, and shall not be interfered with by administrative organs, social organisations or individuals.

37 See "People's Courts", in http://www.chnlaw.com/LegalForum/Legalsystem/Courts/Courts.htm (accessed: 29 June 2001).

38 It is interesting to note that according to some scholars, due to the poor quality of judges, too much emphasis on judicial independence would possibly exacerbate judicial corruption. See Guo Chunming & Liu Zhigang, "Judicial Justice: A Summarisation of the Seminar on the Goals of the Judicial Reform", *Chinese Legal Science* (in Chinese)(2000), No.4, p. 156.

39 See Song Bing, "Assessing China's System of Judicial Review of Administrative Actions", *China Law Reporter*, 1994, VIII/1-2, p. 17.

40 See Gao Qicai *et al*, "Procedure, Judges and Adjudicating Impartiality", *Legal Science* (in Chinese) (2000), No.8, p. 9.

41 According to Mayor of Dujun, the case should be handled by Dujun. See "Behind the Unenforced Arrest of a Criminal Suspect", *People's Daily* (in Chinese), 2 August 2001, p. 4.

42 See Cai Dingjian, "Development of the Chinese Legal System Since 1979 and Its Current Crisis and Transformation", *Cultural Dynamics*, Vo.11 (2)(1999), p. 161.

43 See Anthony R. Dicks, "Compartmentalised Law and Judicial Restraint: An Inductive View of Some Jurisdictional Barriers to Reform", *China Quarterly*, No.141 (1995), p. 97.

44 It refers to the practice that a suspected corrupt official must report within the prescribed time and at the prescribed location to the Party Discipline Inspection Committee during the preliminary investigation prior to the intervention of the judiciary.

45 Becker, *supra* note 15, p. 340.

46 A recent official report acknowledged that 95 percent of judges and other legal administrators are Party members who are carefully selected for being politically loyal to the Party line, see Xin Ren, *Tradition of the Law and Law of the Tradition: Law, State and Social Control in China* (Westport, Conn.: Greenwood Press, 1997), p. 60.

47 Stuart S. Nagel, "The Relationship between the Political and Ethnic Affiliation of Judges, and Their Decision-Making", in Glendon Schubwert (ed.), *Judicial Behavior: A Reader in Theory and Research* (Chicago: Rand McNally & Company, 1964), p. 246.

48 The four basic cardinal principles are: (a) leadership of the CCP; (b) adherence to Marxism, Leninism, and Mao Zedong Thought; (c) adherence to the people's democratic dictatorship; and (d) adherence to the socialist road. See Preamble of the Chinese Constitution.

49 See Jiang Huiling, "Judicial Procedure and Judicial Reform", *People's Judicature* (in Chinese), No.7, 1999, p. 24.

50 The Chinese like to use the jargon "getting on track with the international community" (*gen guoji jiegui*).

51 It was adopted by the Seventh United Nations Congress on the Prevention of Crime and the Treatment of Offenders held at Milan from 26 August to 6 September 1985 and endorsed by General Assembly resolutions 40/32 of 29 November 1985 and 40/146 of 13 December 1985.

52 See Principles 1-7 of the Basic Principles, available in " http://www.unhchr.ch/html/menu3/b/h_comp50.htm (accessed: 2 July 2001).

53 Song Bing, *supra* note 39, pp. 16-17.

54 See Tan Sigui (ed.), *Study on China's Judicial Reform* (Beijing: Law Press, 2000)(in Chinese), p. 23.

55 See Li Hanchang, "A Perspective of Judges' Quality and Training against the Background of Judicial System Reform", *Chinese Legal Science* (in Chinese), 2000, No.1, pp. 48-49.

56 Liu Junhai, "Legal Reforms in China", in Jean-Jacques Dethier (ed.), *Governance, Decentralisation and Reform in China, India and Russia* (Boston: Kluwer Academic Publishers, 2000), p. 395.

57 See "How China's Judiciary Faces the New Century", *Democracy and Legal System Monthly* (in Chinese), No.2, 2000, p. 80.

58 See Yi Yanyou, "A Bibliographical Note on Judicial Reform Studies", *Peking University Law Journal* (in Chinese), Vol.12 (6), 2000, p. 749.

59 The text is reprinted in Peng Liming (ed.), *Compendium of the Current Laws of the People's Republic of China* (Beijing: China Building Materials Publishing House, 1998) (in Chinese), pp. 132-140.

60 Text in Peng, *ibid.*, 140-148.

61 See "Amended Laws Raise Qualifications of Judges", *Beijing Review*, 7 August 2000, p. 6. For reference, see Zhuang Huining, "How to Revise the Laws of Judges and Prosecutors?" *Outlook Weekly* (in Chinese), 24 July 2000, 26-27.

62 "China adopts amendments to laws on judges, prosecutors", *China Daily*, 1 July 2001.

63 "China's legislature examines 8 draft laws", *China Daily*, 27 June 2001. It should be noted that even before the adoption of the amended laws, the new selection process first took place in Beijing in March 2001 perhaps experimentally, through which a batch of 252 presiding judges (who

oversee the operation of a court) and 329 sole judges (who preside alone over simple cases) were selected. Presiding judges, formerly appointed by the chief judge, or by the court president, or by the administrative official of a court division, are selected via a two-way process that includes authorisation from the court president and the chief judge of the court division. See "New Selection Process to Improve Judicial System", *China Daily*, 31 March 2001.

64 Ibid.

65 "Five-Year Education and Training Programme for Procuratorate", *People's Daily* (in Chinese), 14 March 2001, p. 6. The court also has its training programme for the year of 2001 to 2005, see Xiao Yang, "Work Report of the Supreme People's Court", *People's Daily* (in Chinese), 22 March 2001, at 2.

66 "New selection process to improve judicial system", *China Daily*, 31 March 2001.

67 "Supreme court gets ready for WTO entry", *China Daily*, 22 February 200. The whole text is available in *Legal Daily* (in Chinese), 22 October 2001, p. 4.

68 See "New Codes of Conduct for Judges", *China Daily*, 19 October 2001.

69 See Principle 10 of the Basic Principles, available in http://www.unhchr.ch/html/menu3/b/h_comp50.htm (accessed: 2 July 2001).

70 See Principles 8-9 of the Basic Principles, available in .htm" http://www.unhchr.ch/html/menu3/b/h_comp50.htm (accessed: 2 July 2001).

71 Both were adopted by the Eighth United Nations Congress on the Prevention of Crime and the Treatment of Offenders, Havana, Cuba, 27 August to 7 September 1990.

72 Art. 2 of the Guidelines, available in http://www.unhchr.ch/html/menu3/b/h_comp45.htm (accessed: 2 July 2001).

73 "How China's Judiciary Faces the New Century", *Democracy and Legal System Monthly* (in Chinese), No.2, 2000, p. 80.

74 Tang Min, "Trails to Open to Public in Beijing", *China Daily*, 20 September 1998. For the Beijing Municipality, there are three regulations governing this practice: the Decision of Beijing Higher People's Court on Implementing Public Trial at All Beijing Courts; the Regulations on Citizens' Overhearing of Publicly Tried Cases; and the Regulations on Reporters' Overhearing of Publicly Tried Cases.

75 Liu Junhai, *supra* note 55, p. 397.

76 See Yang Zhejing and Cheng Xingsheng, "Principle of Open Trial", *People's Judicature* (in Chinese), No.4, 1999, p. 35.

77 Feng Qihua, "Judicial transparency", *China Daily*, 28 June 2000. See also "Supreme People's Court Publicises Its Adjudicating Documents to the Public from Today", 19 June 2000, available in http://www.court.gov.cn/channel7/xinwen_1.htm (accessed: 15 June 2001).

78 Liu Junhai, *supra* note 55, p. 403.

79 "Top Judge Urges Trial Efficiency", Xinhua 30 October 2000, available in http://www.china.org.cn/english/3306.htm (accessed: 2 March 2001).

80 Tong Ji & Wang Liwen, "How to Further Raise the Adjudicating Efficiency from the Pace of Court's Case Handling", *People's Judicature* (in Chinese), No.5, 1999, p. 19.

81 See "People's Courts", in http://www.chnlaw.com/LegalForum/Legalsystem/Courts/Courts.htm (accessed: 29 June 2001).

82 Cai Dingjian, *supra* note 42, p. 162.

83 See Sun Jungong, "The Status and Improvement of Our People's Assessors System", *People's Judicature* (in Chinese), No.9, 1999, 29-30.

84 For example, Article 16 of the Organic Law of the Court.

85 See Cheng Xiaobing and Wang Yonghe, "Thinking of Improving Our Judge Withdrawal System", *People's Judicature* (in Chinese), No.4, 1999, p. 31.

86 It is cited in Jianfu Chen, "Judicial Reform in China", *CCH's China Law Update*, May 2000, 3-4.

87 Text in *New Law Monthly* (in Chinese), No.5, 2001, 21-22.

88 See "Three judges were held liable due to their wrong decision in Shenyang", available in http://www.peopledaily.com.cn/GB/shehui/44/20010622/495403.html (accessed: 23 June 2001).

89 "Detailed Measures on Open Procuratorial Work of the People's Procuratorate", 4 January 1999, available in http://www.spp.gov.cn/jwgk/jwgk02.htm (accessed: 15 June 2001).

90 "Six Provisions Which Must Be Strictly Enforced by Procuratorial Organisations Made by the Supreme People's Procuratorate", *Communiqué of the Supreme People's Procuratorate of the People's Republic of China* (in Chinese), No.3, 2001, p. 28.

91 Guo Chunming & Liu Zhigang, *supra* note 38, p. 158.

92 See "Courts Correcting Misjudged, Mishandled Cases", *China Daily*, 15 September 1998.

93 Jin Zeqing, "Prosecutor vows corruption fight", *China Daily*, 11 March 2000.

94 See *Ming Pao* (in Chinese), 3 October 2001.

95 See Zhuang Huining, "To Use Heavy Punishment against Crime of Misconduct in Office", *Outlook Weekly* (in Chinese), 8 May 2000, p. 26.

96 "The First Case of Judicial Corruption in Guangxi", Xinhua News Agency, 29 May 2000, available in ily.com.cn/GB/channel1/11/20000529/81108 http://www.peopledaily.com.cn/GB/channel1/11/20000529/81108 (accessed: 26 August 2000). They got the money from prisoners' families to parole the prisoners or reduce their length of sentence illegally.

97 See S. Rose-Ackerman, *The Political Economy of Corruption - Causes and Consequences* (World Bank, Viewpoint Note No.74, 1996); cited in Ibrahim F.I. Shihata, "Corruption – A General Review with an Emphasis on the Role of the World Bank", *Dickinson Journal of International Law*, Vol.15, 1997, p. 461.

98 Guo Chunming & Liu Zhigang, *supra* note 38, p. 158.

99 For details, see Zou Keyuan, "Judicial Reform Versus Judicial Corruption: Recent Developments in China", *Criminal Law Forum*, Vol.11 (3), 2000: 323-351.

100 See "The Supreme Court issued the Regulations on Strictly Implementing the Challenge System to safeguard judicial justice", *People's Daily* (in Chinese), 1 February 2000; and "China tightens rules for judges", *The Straits Times*, 2 February 2000.

101 Xiao Yang, "Firmly Eliminate Corruption among Judicial Personnel and Work Hard to Maintain Judicial Justice - Report on Carrying out Centralised Education and Rectification among People's Courts", *Gazette of the Standing Committee of the National People's Congress of the People's Republic of China* (in Chinese), 1999, No.1, p. 13.

102 Text in *Communiqué of Supreme People's Procuratorate of the People's Republic of China* (in Chinese), 2000, No.2, 22-24.

103 Han Zhubin, "Work Report of the Supreme People's Procuratorate", *Communiqué of Supreme People's Procuratorate of the People's Republic of China* (in Chinese), 2000, No.2, p. 19.

104 "The Supreme People's Procuratorate Hammers out Business Activities Prohibited from Engaging in by Spouses and Children of Officers at or above Bureau Level within Its Own System", *China Law*, February 2001, p. 106.

105 See "Maintaining judicial justice", *People's Daily* (in Chinese), 18 October 2000, p. 9.

106 See "Maintaining judicial justice", *People's Daily* (in Chinese), 14 February 2001, p. 12.

107 See Wang Lijie, "Progress in Ruling by Law", *Beijing Review*, 24 May 2001, p. 18; and "Vetoing a Court Report – Milestone in the Democratic Process", available in http://www.china.org.cn/english/7765.htm (accessed: 2 March 2001).

108 See Zhou Qingju *et al*, "Legal Thinking of the Rejected Report of the Zhenyang Intermediate Court", *Outlook Weekly* (in Chinese), No.37, 10 September 2001, 26-27.

109 See *People's Daily* (in Chinese), 25 August 1999, p. 3.

110 For details, see Yu Xiaoqing & Li Yonghong, "Necessity and Feasibility of the People's Congress to Supervise the Individual Cases in the Judiciary", *Legal Science* (in Chinese), 1999, No.1, 25-28; and Cheng Xianqing, "Thinking on the Supervision of Individual Cases", *People's Daily* (in Chinese), 28 July 1999, p. 9.

111 See Li Xiuyuan, "Rational Thinking of the Phenomena of Judicial Interference", *People's Judicature* (in Chinese), No.10, 1999, at 15. Li is President of the Jiangxi Higher People's Court.

112 Li Fucheng, *supra* note 4, at 717, and Yi Yanyou, "A Bibliographical Note on Judicial Reform Studies", *Peking University Law Journal* (in Chinese), Vol.12 (6), 2000, p. 748.

113 For details, see Wang Chengguang, "Conflict between Independent Adjudicative Power by the Court under the Law and the Supervisory Power of the People's Congress over Individual Cases before the Court and Its Mechanism of Adjustment", *Law Science Monthly* (in Chinese), No.1, 1999, 18-24.

114 See Wang Chenguang, "The Conflict", p. 23.

115 See *People's Daily* (in Chinese), 25 August 1999, p. 3.

116 See Xiao Yang, "Firmly Eliminate Corruption among Judicial Personnel and Work Hard to Maintain Judicial Justice – Report on Carrying out Centralised Education and Rectification among People's Courts", *Gazette of the Standing Committee of the National People's Congress of the People's Republic of China*, 1999, No.1, 8-9.

117 See *People's Daily* (in Chinese), 17 August 2001, p. 6.

118 Shao-chuan Leng, *Justice in Communist China: A Survey of the Judicial System of the Chinese People's Republic* (Dobbs Ferry, New York: Oceana Publications, Inc., 1967), p. 39.

119 See James P. Brady, *Justice and Politics in People's China: Legal Order or Continuing Revolution?* (London: Academic Press, 1982), p. 107.

120 See Shih Liang, "Achievements in the People's Judicial Work during the Past Three Years", *People's Daily* (in Chinese), 23 September 1952.

121 On 10 January 2001, at a meeting with officials in charge of propaganda, Jiang highlighted the concept of rule by virtue. For details on Jiang's "rule by virtue", see Zheng Yongnian and Lai Hongyi, "Rule by Virtue: Jiang Zemin's New Moral Order for the Party", *EAI Background Brief* No.83, March 2001.

122 For example, there is a report on the court of Xingdu County of Sichuan Province. See Xie Meikun and Chen Xiaoyu, "Actively Explore the New Ways of 'Rule the Court by Virtue'", *People's Court Newspaper* (in Chinese), 9 June 2001, available in http://www.china-judge.com/sfgg/sfgg410.htm (accessed: 15 June 2001).

123 See *People's Daily* (in Chinese), 1 August 2001, at 2. The "three represents" refer to Jiang's recent doctrine that the CCP should represent the advanced productive forces of the society, an advanced culture and the interest of the majority of the Chinese people.

124 For example, rule by virtue can guide the behaviour of judicial personnel. See Qiao Xingsheng, "Relationship between 'Govern the Country by Virtue' and 'Govern the Country by Law' and Its Significance", *Economy and Law* (in Chinese), April 2001 (Serial No.96), at 46. For further reference, see Hao Tiechuan, "On Governing the Country According to Law and by Virtue", *Social Sciences* (in Chinese), Shanghai Academy of Social Sciences, No.4, 2001, 2-4.

125 Tony Lau, "Jiang's appeal to virtue harks back to Confucius", *South China Morning Post*, 20 February 2001, p. 8.

126 If the CCP or the Chinese government had enough legal consciousness, it should submit the crash case to the International Court of Justice for settlement. The late event proved that China lost face as well as substance in dealing with this case. For the Gao Zhan case, if Gao was not a spy, she should not be subject to criminal trial; if she was a spy, she should not be released just one day after her sentencing. The Communist leadership thereby totally disregarded China's law and judiciary. In the Lai Changxing case, Zhu Rongji had no authority to promise that Lai would not be sentenced to death. Whether there is a death penalty or not fully depends

on the decision to be made by a court. According to the Chinese criminal procedure law, no one is guilt, until proved so that the principle of presumption of innocence applies.

127 Chinese scholars have begun to discuss the impact of the WTO entry on the judicial reform, see, for example, Guan Baoquan, "WTO Entry and Innovation of China's Judge System", *People's Judicature* (in Chinese), No.12, 2000, 29-32.

128 "Asian Legal System Inadequacies", *Asian Intelligence*, No.585, 30 May 2001, p. 5.

129 Shai Oster, "Jiang's Biggest Gamble", *Asiaweek*, 19 October 2001, p. 34.

130 See "Long Yongtu predicts more litigations during the early period of China's entry into WTO", *Lianhe Zaobao* (in Chinese), 14 July 2001, p. 26.

131 See "Opinions on Playing Fully the Role of Adjudication to Provide Judicial Protection and Legal Services for Economic Development", Supreme People's Court, 3 March 2000, cited in Jianfu Chen, *supra* note 81, p. 7.

132 Zhao Zongwei, "People's Congresses to Monitor Court Work", *China Daily*, 26 September 1998.

133 See Gu Peidong, "A Macro-study on the Judicial Reform in China", *CASS Journal of Law* (in Chinese), Vol.22 (3), 2000, p. 12.

134 For details, see Pan Jianfeng, "Looking at the Existing Problems in Our Judicial Reform from the Angle of Japan's Third Judicial Reform", *Legal Science* (in Chinese), 2000, No.8, 14-17.

135 See Hu Xiabing, "Restructuring the Name of the Court", *Law Science Monthly* (in Chinese), No.8, 2000, 21-22.

136 "China's Supreme Court determines five reform areas", available in "http://www.chineseinternetnews.com.cn/node2/node3/node100/userobject6ai13021.html" http://www.chineseinternetnews.com.cn/node2/node3/node100/userobject6ai13020.html (accessed: 30 July 2001).

137 See Stanley B Lubman, *Bird in a Cage: Legal Reform in China After Mao* (Stanford: Stanford University Press, 1999), p. 297.

CHAPTER 11

Party-Army Relations under Jiang Zemin

ZHENG SHIPING

By the time the Chinese Communist Party concluded its 16th Congress in November 2002, Jiang Zemin had already spent 12 years as the commander-in-chief of the People's Liberation Army (PLA). Jiang's tenure is in no way comparable to that of Mao Zedong who had commanded the Communist armed forces since 1935 and until he died in 1976. Nor can Jiang's record be on parallel with that of Deng Xiaoping who had commanded China's military force from 1981 and until 1994, three years before he died. That may not be a fair comparison, though. As veteran revolutionaries, Mao and Deng had organised armed uprisings and conducted major wars both before and after 1949. They were Communist army generals as much as Communist party leaders. Jiang, on the other hand, has never served in the army and did not have any network of supporters in the military before becoming China's commander-in-chief in 1990. An engineer by training, Jiang is indeed the first civilian leader to command the army in the history of the People's Republic of China (PRC).

This is particularly extraordinary in view of the fact that other party leaders before Jiang either finished the tenure prematurely or failed to become the commander-in-chief in the first place. Hua Guofeng, who had at least some experience in guerrilla warfare before 1949, became China's commander-in-chief after Mao died in 1976. Hua, however, proved to be a nominal commander only as the army was firmly controlled by senior military leaders like Marshal Ye Jianying. Hua had stayed in his post for no more than five years before he was replaced by the strongman Deng Xiaoping. During the Deng era, party chief Hu Yaobang never managed to get a seat on the party's

Central Military Commission (CMC), let alone be the commander-in-chief. After Hu Yaobang was ousted, new party general secretary Zhao Ziyang did become the first vice chairman of the CMC in 1987. Nevertheless, overshadowed by Deng Xiaoping and his protégé, CMC executive vice chairman Yang Shangkun, Zhao turned out to be largely powerless as far as military decisions were concerned; this was tragically demonstrated by the events in 1989.

After Mao and Deng, the biggest challenge to Jiang Zemin was how to command the army in an era of no strongman. In view of others' failures, Jiang's stable tenure must have surprised many observers. Under his reign from 1990 to 2002, the PLA has become more professionalised, modernised, and regularised. In the meantime, Jiang has also succeeded in establishing himself as the actual commander-in-chief of the military. And it is certain that Jiang will be able to finish his tenure through retirement, not other ways. Despite his unprecedented success as the first civilian leader to command China's military, however, Jiang has not attempted to resolve the paradox in party-army relations or to restructure China's military command system created by Mao Zedong and preserved by Deng Xiaoping.

THE PARADOXICAL PARTY-ARMY RELATIONS

China's armed forces today are composed of the PLA, the People's Armed Police (PAP) and the militia.[1] The 2.5 million-strong PLA includes the Navy, the Air Force, the Second Artillery Force (missile force), and the ground force of 21 group armies deployed among seven military regions, which in turn oversee 27 military districts in 27 provinces (including four autonomous regions of Xinjiang, Tibet, Inner Mongolia), four military garrisons in four municipalities (Beijing, Tianjin, Shanghai, and Chongqing), and two PLA garrisons in Hong Kong and Macao Special Administrative Regions respectively. Managing and commanding such a large and complex organisational force is obviously no small challenge.

Mao Zedong's ideas regarding party-army relations can best be summarised by what Mao wrote in 1938: "Political power grows out of the barrel of a gun. Our principle is that the Party commands the gun, and the gun must never be allowed to command the Party. Yet, having guns, we can create Party organisations, as witness the powerful Party organisations which the Eight Route Army has created in northern China. We can also create cadres, create schools, create culture, create mass movements. Everything in Yenan has been created by having guns. All things grow out of the barrel of a gun."[2] This long quote is necessary because many analysts tend to focus on one maxim–political power grows out of the barrel of a gun" or the other–"party commands the gun." But when we read Mao's statement in its entirety, it is not difficult to see that Mao's statement hardly defines the party-army relations one way or the other. Mao would perhaps call this ambivalent party-army relationship a dialectic one, but in reality it was only up to Mao to decide whether and when the principle of party commanding the gun should be stressed or the army needed to be brought in to rebuild party organisations.

Because of Mao's ideas about party-army relations and due to the fact that before 1949 the Chinese Communist Party was by default a military organisation, there has emerged an interlocking power-sharing relationship between the CCP and the PLA after 1949. In many ways, the army is in the party and the party is in the army. The party's presence in the military has been maintained through a complex system. First, a political commissar exists at all unit levels down to that of platoon and squad. Second, at the regiment level and above, there is a political department responsible for carrying out the party's directives and rules pertaining to political work in the military. Third, there are party committees set up at the battalion level and above, the party branch existing at the company level, and the party small group present below the company level. Finally, the discipline inspection committee has existed since 1978 at the regiment level and above: it is responsible for enforcing party discipline and rules within the military. All the political commissars, political departments, party committees, and party discipline inspection committees are tightly controlled by the PLA General Political Department.[3]

While the party has existed and functioned at various levels in the army, the army is also heavily represented in the party leadership. For instance, at the Eighth Party Congress in 1956, the first party congress held after 1949, the PLA marshals and general controlled more than one-third (35 percent) of the total seats in the newly-formed central committee and in the Politburo. During the Cultural Revolution, when Mao needed the army to "create Party organisations," the military representation in the Ninth CCP Central Committee and the Politburo in 1969 climbed to 45 percent and 52 percent respectively.

The party-military relations during the Mao years had thus evolved to be a paradox: The military was structurally involved in party politics, yet it posed little danger of overthrowing the CCP regime. This paradox not only differentiated China from most Western countries where the military is expected to be politically neutral and civilian control over the military is valued, but also set China apart from many developing countries where army officers often attempt to take over power from civilian governments in military coups. The mutually dependent relationship between the party and the military in China makes it seemingly unnecessary for the military as a whole to seize political power from the CCP leadership.

This, however, does not always apply to individual military leaders who have lost the power struggle in party politics and therefore decide to take actions against the party leadership. Marshal Lin Biao's alleged plan to use force against Mao Zedong in 1971 might be one such example. Here the system of internal control, checks, and intelligence in the military plays a pivotal role in detecting and deterring any military coup attempt. Without prior authorisation from the CMC, for instance, a division commander in peace time can only move a platoon (about 30 men), a group army commander can only move a company, and a military regional commander can only move a battalion. Any attempt to move PLA units, without prior authorisation, will be checked by the political commissar, political department, and party committee in the same PLA unit. Moreover, the Third Department (in charge of domestic military intelligence) of the

PLA General Staff Department maintains listening posts and agents throughout the country, and "any unsanctioned movement of PLA units in China can be very rapidly detected" and immediately reported to the highest military authority–the PLA General Staff Department and the CMC in Beijing.[4]

Again, Lin Biao's case is a good example. Even as the second most powerful man in the Chinese military at that time, Marshal Lin Biao could only rely on his son to organise a secret unit in the military, not the regular troops, to carry out his alleged coup plan. The secret plan was detected by Mao before it was fully carried out and Lin Biao's failed attempt eventually led to his terrible death. Military coup attempts in China, therefore, are not only difficult to organise, but also stand little chance of success.

THE INSTITUTIONAL DILEMMA OF THE MILITARY COMMAND SYSTEM

Institutionally, Mao in the early 1950s decided to continue the pre-1949 military command system of the PLA general department/headquarters, namely, the PLA General Staff, the PLA Political Department, and the PLA General Logistics Department. As it wouldn't have seemed appropriate for the new Chinese state to be without a ministry of defence, such a ministry was indeed set up in 1954. The newly established Ministry of Defence was a shell organisation only and no special functional departments were set up to manage the military affairs.[5] Under this institutional arrangement, the PRC's Ministry of Defence has little command and control authority over the army, even though it has been consistently ranked second (after the Ministry of Foreign Affairs) in the Chinese central government. It was only during the tenure of Defence Minister Lin Biao in 1959-1971 that the Ministry of Defence gained some control authority over the military mainly due to Marshal Lin's personal prestige. Since the 1970s, the Ministry of Defence has again turned into a shell organisation, consisting of only a few dozen staff personnel and performing primarily a ceremonial role such as hosting foreign military delegations or arranging for Chinese military delegations to visit foreign countries.[6] This makes the PLA command system institutionally different not only from that in Western nations, but also from that in the former Soviet Union.

The institutional dilemma is easy to spot. For instance, a recently published official white paper on national defence describes the working relationship between the Ministry of Defence and the PLA general departments in the following way, "The routine work of the Ministry of National Defence is handled, respectively, by these four general headquarters/departments."[7] One has to wonder that if it is the routine work of the Ministry of Defence, why it should be handled by the PLA general departments which are not part of the Ministry of Defence and do not report to the Minister of Defence.

Despite the institutional gap between the prestige and power of the Ministry of Defence, neither Deng Xiaoping nor Jiang Zemin has touched the Maoist command system of the PLA general department/headquarters. Today all the military affairs of China's armed forces are managed by the PLA General Staff Department. This department directly oversees the seven military regions and through them the military districts at the provincial level, and the PLA service branches of the Navy, the Air Force, and the Second Artillery Force. As such it is responsible for organising and commanding the military operations of all the military units of the PLA.

The PLA General Staff Department is not only much more powerful but also several times larger than the Ministry of Defence. As Table 11.1 shows, whereas the PLA General Staff Department is a huge organisation consisting of many key offices and bureaus, the Ministry of Defence looks like a mini-Ministry of Foreign Affairs for the military. It is also worth noting that while other ministries in the Chinese central government have between three and seven vice ministers, the Ministry of Defence does not have a single vice minister.

TABLE 11.1 ORGANISATIONAL UNITS OF MINISTRY OF DEFENCE AND GENERAL STAFF DEPARTMENT

PRC Ministry of Defence	**PLA General Staff Department**
Minister	Chief of General Staff
No Vice Minister of Defence	Six Deputy Chiefs of Staff
Foreign Affairs Bureau	General Office
Division of American and Oceanic Affairs	Political Department
Division of Asian Affairs	
Division of European Affairs	Operation Department
Division of West Asian and African Affairs	
	Mobilisation Department
	Signal Department
	Armaments Department
	Arms Department
	Military Training Department
	Military Affairs Department
	Second Department*
	Third Department*
	Bureau of Guards
	Management Bureau
	Surveying Bureau

*** The Second Department is in charge of foreign military intelligence and the Third Department is in charge of domestic military intelligence. The First Department is the Operation Department. See Michael D. Swaine, *The Military & Political Succession in China: Leadership, Institutions and Beliefs* (Santa Monica, CA: RAND, 1992), pp. 122-3.**

Apart from the PLA General Staff Department, the PLA General Logistics Department is responsible for PLA's supplies and transportation while the recently established PLA General Armaments Department is responsible for PLA's weapons procurement. Finally, the continuing existence of the PLA General Political Department represents another powerful political and institutional legacy of Mao's revolution. This department, which is in charge of the political commissars, political departments, party committees, and party discipline inspection committees in the PLA, is literally the extension of the party in the military.

All four general departments are directed and coordinated by a relatively small but powerful staff (about 100 people) serving the leadership of the CMC, the pinnacle of the military high command in China.[8] On the other hand, the Chinese central government –the State Council–and its Ministry of Defence cannot issue military orders to the PLA.[9] Not only is the CMC not under the command of the Chinese state, it is also largely independent of the CCP's organisational control. First, members of the CMC are procedurally elected by the CCP Central Committee, but the composition of the CMC membership is often preordained before the election.

Second, although within the hierarchy of the party, the CMC is elected by the Central Committee and within the hierarchy of the state, the CMC (same people as in the party's CMC) reports to the National People's Congress, the CMC actually enjoys equal status as the CCP Central Committee, the State Council, and the Standing Committee of the National People's Congress. The most important announcements in China are often made jointly by the four power centers, for instance.

Through the CMC, the military has acquired a high degree of organisational autonomy from the CCP Central Committee. The four PLA general departments are generally free from intervention from various functional departments of the CCP Central Committee. For instance, the management of military officers and non-combat cadres in the military is the responsibility of the PLA General Political Department, not the Organisation Department of the CCP Central Committee. Political education in the military is the responsibility of the PLA General Political Department, not the Propaganda Department of the CCP Central Committee. Although major military decisions and policies have to be approved by the Standing Committee of the CCP Politburo, matters concerning the PLA are generally left to the generals in the CMC.

JIANG ZEMIN AS COMMANDER-IN-CHIEF

Upon becoming the chairman of the powerful CMC in 1990, Jiang must have felt uncomfortable and worried. Jiang was uncomfortable because as the only civilian on the CMC, he was surrounded by the PLA generals who were both older and more senior than he was. Jiang was worried because neither he nor anyone else knew for sure how long he would be able to sit on the CMC. In the first four years of his tenure, Jiang had by and large lived in the political shadow of the paramount leader Deng Xiaoping. Indeed, in early 1992, Jiang barely survived a succession crisis before the 14th Party Congress. When Deng's confidence in Jiang was decreasing, Jiang almost lost his job. It is perhaps not until 1994, when Deng's worsening heath condition rendered him essentially incapacitated, that Jiang began to assert himself as the supreme leader in his own right. Jiang's actual tenure as commander-in-chief of China's military is almost eight years so far.

Jiang's first move was to expand the membership of the CMC so that he would be able to put a few new faces on the CMC. In 1995, General Zhang Wannian and General Chi Haotian became the new vice chairmen of the CMC and both have served Jiang well since then. While it is not quite accurate to characterise them as Jiang's "yes-man" because at least General Zhang Wannian is known to have disagreed with or even criticised Jiang on certain policy issues, it is impossible for Jiang to be the commander-in-chief without the help and support from these two men.

Jiang of course needed to seek support and loyalty from many more PLA leaders. One institutional resource that Jiang has as the chairman of the CMC is the power of promoting military leaders to the rank of general, the highest rank in the PLA. Not surprisingly, Jiang has used this power as frequently as one can imagine. Between 1993 and 2002, Jiang has made seven such promotions (see Table 11.2) and a total of 63 generals owe their promotions to Jiang, at least procedurally. It is worth noting that most of the top military leaders in active duty today were promoted to the rank of general in 1998, 1999, 2000, and 2002.

TABLE 11.2 MILITARY PROMOTION (1955-2002)

CMC	Chairman Year	Number of Promotions
Mao Zedong	1955	10 Marshals 10 Senior Generals 55 Generals
Deng Xiaoping	1988	17 Generals
Jiang Zemin	1993	6 Generals
	1994	19 Generals
	1996	4 Generals
	1998	9 Generals
	1999	2 Generals
	2000	16 Generals
	2002	7 Generals

Sources: *Zhongguo Renwu Nianjian 2000* [China's Who's Who Yearbook 2000] (Beijing: China's Who's Who Yearbook Press, 2000; *China Directory*, from 1990 through 2002 (Tokyo: Radiopress, various years of 1990-2002).

While promoting younger military leaders, Jiang has also pushed for more military leadership changes by enforcing the retirement system effectively to his advantage. Either by accident or by design, during Jiang's tenure, a new precedent seems to have been established in the military in which one's seniority and biological age must be compatible. Since the established age limits stipulate that military regional commanders cannot be older than 65, group army commanders cannot be older than 55, and division commanders cannot be older than 50, military officers have to be younger than their superiors or face retirement. By late 1997, all the military generals who had more seniority than Jiang had retired, making it less challenging for Jiang to consolidate his power base in the military. By the same logic, not only are the military generals more junior than Jiang, they cannot be older than Jiang because Jiang is the chairman of the CMC. For instance, the highest-ranking military leader before the 16th Party Congress, CMC Vice Chairman Zhang Wannian (born in 1928), was the oldest of the all the military leaders in active duty. But General Zhang is still two years younger than Jiang.

Besides utilising the institutional power resources regarding promotion and retirement to consolidate his command of the military, Jiang has also resorted to political and legal means. Politically, Jiang in September 1995 specifically called on the leading cadres to "talk politics" [*jiangzhengzhi*]. For the military leaders, to talk about politics means the military must accept the "absolute leadership of the party" [*dang de juedui lingdao*], which in turn means the military must resolutely obey the command of the CMC with Jiang as the chairman.

On the legal side, Jiang has, since 1996, made special efforts to promote the concept of "ruling the army by law" [*yifazhijun*]. Among the many military regulations and laws amended or adopted since 1996, the most noticeable are *The Law of the People's Republic of China on National Defence* (adopted in 1997), *The Law of Military Service of the People's Republic of China* (amended in 1998), *The Regulations on Military Service of Active-Duty Soldiers of the Chinese People's Liberation Army* (amended in 1999), and *The Regulations on Military Service of Active-Duty Officers of the Chinese People's Liberation Army* (amended in 2000).

Jiang's efforts to consolidate his command of the military do not necessarily mean that the PLA generals will always listen to him. According to some sources, military generals, both retired and in active duty, have had disagreements with Jiang over policies toward Taiwan and the United States. Recently, military leaders had also been slow to show their support for Jiang's handling of the U.S. Ep-3 spy plane incident. Nevertheless, to think that Jiang could control the military the way Mao or Deng did is perhaps expecting too much.

NEGOTIATED PARTNERSHIP BETWEEN THE PARTY AND ARMY

Party-army relations during Jiang's years look more like a negotiated partnership. The military generally accepts the principle of "party commands the gun," which means accepting Jiang as the commander-in-chief. The military can also be expected to stand behind the CCP leadership's decisions on major political, ideological, and economic issues. On specific policies concerning defence budget, security, intelligence, military exercises, Taiwan, relations with the United States, etc., the military can actively voice its positions through many formal as well as informal channels. The civilian leadership not only has to take into consideration the inputs from the military, but also has to offer concessions and rewards to seek compliance or support from the military.

Defence Spending

Over the years, China's defence spending has been a key concern and controversy among China's neighbouring countries and in the West. Many military analysts believe that China's officially published defence budget figures are much lower than the actual defence spending figures. However, due to lack of reliable information on how much money is generated by the extrabudgetary sources such as direct subsidies, local government support, revenues from arms sales, and the army's business activities (at least until 1998), there has been a wild guessing game as to how much the PLA actually spends. For instance, China's officially published defence spending for 1994 was RMB55 billion, about 1.18 percent of China's GNP of that year, or close to US$6.4 billion. Estimates about how much the PLA actually spent, however, have ranged from the U.S. Central Intelligence Agency's estimate of US$20 billion, the Pentagon's estimate of US$40 billion, the U.S. Arms Control and Disarmament Agency's estimate of US$50 billion, to a RAND estimate of US$196 billion, about 3.25 percent of China's GDP in that year.

Defence budget changes can reflect changing domestic politics as well as security concerns and needs for military modernisation. As Table 11.3 indicates, in post-Mao China, the defence spending saw its largest increase in 1979 when China launched a "punitive war" against Vietnam. Since then, Deng Xiaoping, who had considered fast economic growth as the top priority, managed to cut the defence spending twice: 12.9 percent in 1980 and 13.3

percent in 1981. Between 1982 and 1988, the average annual increase of defence spending was 4.5 percent. Adjusted for inflation, China's defense spending actually decreased during the 1980s. It is hard to imagine that any party leader other than Deng Xiaoping would be able to persuade the military to live with defense budget cuts for so many years. And even a strongman like Deng had to make deals with the military. Deng's permission, if not open encouragement, for the PLA to engage in business, was one such a compromise meant to supplement the army for what it lost from the defence budgets.

Since 1989, however, not only has the PLA not faced a cut in defence spending, it has also seen spending on defence increasing at a double-digit rate every year. The PLA's pivotal role in helping resolve the Tiananmen crisis gave the military leaders legitimate reasons to ask for economic rewards for political loyalty. The U.S.-led Gulf War created a heightened sense of urgency on the part of China's leaders for military modernisation. If a large portion of the defence budget increase was used to purchase military hardware from foreign countries, then the devaluation of the RMB against the U.S. dollar (for as much as 30 percent in 1994) also pushed for more defence spending. Meanwhile, PLA generals kept reminding the central government to fulfill Deng Xiaoping's promise made in the early 1980s that when the Chinese economy recovered and grew, the defence spending would also increase accordingly.

Equally significantly, since he succeeded Deng as the new chairman of the CMC, Jiang has presented himself to the military as someone who attends to the interests and concerns of the military. Jiang has called for improving the living standards of the soldiers and increasing the salaries and benefits of the PLA officers. Not surprisingly, in recent years, military officers have received bigger pay raises than their civilian counterparts in the government. Jiang has also advocated development of high-tech combat units and rapid-response units as top priorities, and supported military weaponry upgrading. While all these were politically wise moves by Jiang to win the support from the military, they pushed the defence budgets upward.

TABLE 11.3 CHINA'S DEFENCE SPENDING (1976-2002)

Year	Spending in RMB (100 Million Yuan)	% Change Over Previous Year	Spending in U.S. Dollars	As % of GDP (100 Million)
1976	134.5		73.5	4.57
1977	149.0	9.7	81.4	4.65
1978	167.8	12.6	101.1	4.63
1979	222.6	32.7	144.6	5.51
1980	193.8	-12.9	114.0	4.29
1981	168.0	-13.3	98.9	3.46
1982	176.4	5.0	93.3	3.33
1983	177.1	0.4	89.5	2.98
1984	180.8	2.1	77.6	2.51
1985	191.5	5.9	65.1	2.14
1986	200.8	4.9	58.2	1.97
1987	209.6	4.4	56.3	1.75
1988	218.0	4.0	58.6	1.46
1989	251.5	15.4	66.7	1.49
1990	290.3	15.4	60.7	1.57
1991	330.3	13.8	62.1	1.53
1992	377.9	14.4	68.6	1.42
1993	425.8	12.7	73.9	1.23
1994	550.7	29.3	63.9	1.18
1995	636.7	15.6	76.3	1.09
1996	720.1	13.1	86.6	1.06
1997	812.6	12.8	98.0	1.09
1998	934.7	15.0 1	12.9	1.19
1999	1,076.4	15.2	130.0	1.31
2000	1,207.4	12.2	45.5	1.35
2001	1,410.0	16.8	170.3	1.56
2002	1,662.0	17.9	200.7	1.66

Sources: China's defence spending figures in U.S. dollars are based on the exchange rates at the time. Defence spending figures and exchange rates are from *China Statistical Yearbook*, from 1980 to 2001 (Beijing: China Statistics press); *China Statistical Abstract 2002* (Beijing: China Statistics Press, 2002). Percentage changes of China's defence spending figures and defence spending figure as a percentage of China's Gross Domestic Product (GDP) are calculated by the author.

Finally, when Jiang and other leaders like Premier Zhu Rongji decided in 1998 that the army had to separate itself from the numerous businesses it had been running since the early 1980s, defence budget increases would seem to be the only way to compensate the army for giving up the lucrative commercial activities.[10]

Thus, while military analysts outside China are concerned about the double-digit increases of China's defence spending, Chinese military leaders may very well believe that the defence budget increases in the recent decade are not only necessary, but are far from adequate. No matter who is the commander-in-chief in China now or several years later, it would seem politically impossible, if nothing else, for China's defence spending to grow slower than a double-digit rate.

Military Representation

During Jiang's tenure, the PLA has continued to play a significant role in China's policymaking process. For instance, at the legislative sessions of the National People's Congress, PLA delegates, representing 2.5 million servicemen and servicewomen, constitute the largest group, larger than the delegation from China's largest province of Henan whose population exceeds one hundred million. Whenever a cast of votes is needed, either to approve the work report and budget of the central government or to elect the new cabinet members of the State Council, the PLA delegation as the biggest voting block carries a lot of political weight and bargaining power.

While the percentages of military representatives in the party Central Committee varied greatly during the Mao and Deng era, Jiang has, between the 15th Party Congress in 1997 and the 16th Party Congress in 2002, managed to set the percentage of military representation to be at about one-fifth of the full members in the Central Committee and below one-tenth of the members of the Politburo (see Table 11.4).

TABLE 11.4 MILITARY REPRESENTATION IN THE CCP CENTRAL COMMITTEE (1956-2002)

Year	Party Congress	Central Committee (%)	Politburo (%)
1956	Eighth	35.2	35.0
1969	Ninth	45.0	52.0
1973	Tenth	24.0	40.0
1977	Eleventh	29.5	57.0
1982	Twelfth	21.5	43.0
1987	Thirteenth	18.6	11.1
1992	Fourteenth	22.7	10.0
1997	Fifteenth	21.1	9.0
2002	Sixteenth	22.2	8.0

Sources: Michael D. Swaine, *The Military & Political Succession in China: Leadership, Institutions and Beliefs* (Santa Monica, CA: RAND, 1992), p. 159; *China Directory 1999* (Tokyo: Radiopress, 1998); *Zhonggong Yanjiu* [Study of Chinese Communist Problems] (Taipei: The Institute for the Study of Chinese Communist Problems), various issues of 1997-2002.

In the 16th CCP Central Committee of 198 full members, the military representatives take up 44 seats. This seems to be a good number of central committee seats needed to maintain a balanced representation in the central committee by all major PLA units. Indeed, like that of the 15th Central Committee, the list of military representatives on the 16th Central Committee reads like a "who's who" of China's military force. For instance, all four departments of the PLA general headquarters (General Chief of Staff, General Logistics Department, General Political Department, and General Equipment Department) have three full members on the new Central Committee. Moreover, commanders and political commissars of the PLA Navy, Air Force, Second Artillery Force, seven military regions (with the exception of the commander of Nanjing Military Region), and the People's Armed Police are full members of the new central committee (see Table 11.5). It is worth noting that 17 of China's new military leaders have entered the CCP Central Committee for the first time.

TABLE 11.5 MILITARY LEADERS IN THE 16TH CENTRAL COMMITTEE

Military Unit	Name	Post	15th CC	16th CC
Central Military Commission	Jiang Zemin	Chairman	Full	Full
	Hu Jintao	Vice Chairman	Full	Full
	Guo Boxiong	Vice Chairman	Full	Full
	Cao Ganchuan	Vice Chairman	Full	Full
	Xu Caihou	Member	Full	Full
	Liang Guanglie	Member	Full	Full
	Liao Xilong	Member	Full	Full
	Li Jinai	Member	Full	Full
General Staff Department	Liang Guanglie	Chief of Staff	Full	Full
	Ge Zhenfeng	Deputy Chief		Full
	Qian Shugen Deputy	Chief	Full	Full
General Political Department	Xu Caihou	Director	Full	Full
	Tang Tianbiao	Deputy Director	Full	Full
	Yuan Shoufang	Deputy Director	Alternate	Full
General Logistics Department	Liao Xilong	Director	Full	Full
	Zhang Wentao	Commissar		Full
	Sun Zhiqiang	Deputy Director		Full
General Armaments Department	Li Jinai	Director	Full	Full
	Chi Wanchun	Commissar		Full
	Li Andong	Deputy Director		Full
Navy	Shi Yunsheng	Commander	Full	Full
	Yang Huaiqing	Commissar	Full	Full
Air Force	Qiao Qingchen	Commander		Full
	Deng Changyou	Commissar		Full
Second Artillery Force	Jing Zhiyuan	Commander (expected)		Full
(Missile Force)	Sui Mingtai	Commissar	Full	Full

TABLE 11.5 MILITARY LEADERS IN THE 16TH CENTRAL COMMITTEE (cont'd)

Military Unit	Name	Post	15th CC	16th CC
Shenyang Military Region (4 Group Armies)	Qian Guoliang	Commander	Full	Full
	Jiang Futang	Commissar	Full	Full
Beijing Military Region (5 Group Armies)	Zhu Qi	Commander		Full
	Fu Tinggui	Commissar (expected)		Full
Jinan Military Region (3 Group Armies)	Chen Bingde	Commander	Full	Full
	Liu Dongdong	Commissar		Full
Nanjing Military Region (3 Group Armies)	Zhu Wenquan	Commander		Alternate
	Lei Mingqiu	Commissar	Full	Full
Guangzhou Military Region (2 Group Armies)	Liu Zhenwu	Commander	Alternate	Full
	Liu Shutian	Commissar	Full	Full
Chengdu Military Region (2 Group Armies)	Wang Jianmin	Commander		Full
	Yang Deqing	Commissar		Full
Lanzhou Military Region (2 Group Armies)	Li Qianyuan	Commander	Alternate	Full
	Liu Yongzhi	Commissar		Full
People's Armed Police	Wu Shuangzhan	Commander		Full
	Li Dongheng	Commissar (expected)		Full

Sources: *Zhongguo Renwu Nianjian 2000* [China's Who's Who Yearbook 2000] (Beijing: China's Who's Who Yearbook Press, 2000), pp. 121-3, 132-40; *Zhonghua Renmin Gongheguo Nianjian 2000* [PRC Yearbook 2000] (Beijing: PRC Yearbook Press, 2000), p. 436; *China Directory 2001* (Tokyo: Radiopress, 2001), pp. 158-207; *Zhonggong Yanjiu* [Study of Chinese Communist Problems] (Taipei: The Institute for the Study of Chinese Communist Problems), various issues of 2000-2002; *The People's Liberation Army as Organisation: Reference Volume*, V. 10, eds., by James Mulvenon and Andrew N. D. Yang (RAND: Santa Monica, CA 2002).

In the new Politburo, the military has only two representatives, as it is the case in the Politburo of the 15th Central Committee. New Politburo members, General Guo Boxiong and General Cao Ganchuan, who are also the new vice chairmen of the party's CMC, are expected to succeed retiring general Zhang Wannian and General Chi Haotian.

At the 15th Party Congress in 1997, Jiang succeeded in having General Liu Huaqing retired from the Politburo Standing committee and General Liu was conspicuously not replaced by another military general. Until then, military leaders had always been present in the Standing Committee of the Politburo, the party's highest decision-making body. In the newly formed Standing Committee of the Politburo of 16th CCP Central Committee, even with an expanded membership from seven to nine people, there is no military general. Apart from stabilising the percentage of military representatives in the Central Committee, establishing the rule that no military representative shall be present in the Politburo Standing Committee is perhaps the most significant achievement Jiang has made in redefining or fine-tuning the power-sharing relationship between the party and army.

Jiang's personal success and institutional achievement not withstanding, it is fair to say that Jiang has not made any substantial progress in reforming the PLA command system and restructuring the party-army relations. In recent years, before or on the first day of August, the official birthday of the PLA, the military newspaper routinely publishes front-page editorials reaffirming the "fundamental principle and system of party's absolute leadership over the army" and criticising the ideas of "making the military separate from the party" [*jundui fei danghua*], "de-politicising the military" [*jundui fei zhengzhihua*], and "making the military part of the state" [*jundui guojiahua*]. This suggests that the long-existing debate in China over whether the party or the state should command the gun is far from over.

China, however, faces no danger of military coups against the civilian leadership of the party. If the party leadership is united, it is almost impossible for the military to challenge the party. But even if the party leadership is divided and there may be more room for the military to maneuver, it is difficult to imagine that the military will be tempted to become the king-maker by supporting its favourite candidate for the party's top leadership position against the wishes of the majority of the members of the party central committee and its Politburo. It is equally hard to believe that the military will necessarily support the chairman of the CMC against the wishes of the majority of the members of the party central committee and its Politburo. Thus the same paradoxical party-army relations can be expected to continue.

CHINA'S COMMANDER-IN-CHIEF AFTER JIANG

Whether Jiang Zemin steps down as the chairman of the CMC a few years after the 16th Party Congress, it seems that in the remaining time of his tenure, Jiang has no intention or sufficient time to restructure the party-military relations, thus leaving some challenging issues to his successor Hu Jintao.

Like Jiang, Hu was also an engineer by training and has no experience in the army. However, after becoming the vice chairman of the CMC in September 1999, Hu has been offered opportunities to attend the CMC meetings and the legitimacy to develop working relationships with the PLA generals. Hu has therefore had at least several years preparing for the job of the commander-in-chief while other civilian leaders (Hu's rivals, if any) are not even allowed to get involved in military affairs. If the Chinese ruling elites finally decide that Hu will be the next commander-in-chief after Jiang Zemin, Hu's chance for having a successful tenure as the chairman of the CMC is better than Jiang's or anyone else's, for that matter.

Apart from the initial endorsement from Deng Xiaoping and broad consensus among the party elite on his status as the successor to Jiang, Hu's most valuable asset is his age. Born in December 1942, Hu is 60 years old when he succeeds Jiang Zemin in 2002-2003. Conceivably, he may have ten years to establish and consolidate his power base in the military. The biggest uncertainty, of course, is when exactly Jiang will decide to give the CMC chairmanship to Hu Jintao.

In the Chinese political system, the CMC chairmanship is a powerful post, even more powerful than the other two top posts– the party general secretary and state president. For one thing, the CMC chairman has the power to appoint or remove military officers from the level of PLA general departments, military regions, armed services, to the level of principal division commander. To be sure, mere assumption of the CMC chairmanship does not necessarily translate into actual control over the military generals, but becoming CMC chairman will make available to Hu Jintao both the political legitimacy and institutional resources to build his power base in the military. Any delay in Hu's assumption of the CMC chairmanship only makes it more difficult for him to develop an effective working relationship with the new generation of the PLA top brass, let alone to make any serious efforts to restructure China's military command system and the party-military relations.

ENDNOTES

1 According to China's defense white paper, the PAP of one million troops is responsible for maintaining China's domestic security and social order. The 1.5 million-strong militia is established to assist the PLA by performing combat readiness support and defensive operations and to help the PAP maintain social order. *China's National Defence in 2000* (Beijing: Information Office of the State Council of the People's Republic of China, October 2000).

2 *Selected Works of Mao Zedong*, Vol. II (Beijing: Foreign Language Press, 1975), pp. 244-5.

3 Michael D. Swaine, *The Military & Political Succession in China: Leadership, Institutions and Beliefs* (Santa Monica, CA: RAND, 1992), pp. 134-5.

4 Ibid., p. 125.

5 Jiang Jianhua, Feng Wanqin, and Ji Hong (eds.), *Zhonghua remin gongheguo zhiliao shouche 1949-1999* [Handbook on the People's Republic of China, 1949-1999) (Beijing: Social Science Documents Press, 2000), p. 193.

6 Kenneth W. Allen and Eric A. McVadon, *China's Foreign Military Relations* (Washington, D.C.: The Henry L. Stimson Center, 1999), pp. 11-13. Select Committee, U.S. House of Representatives, *U.S. National Security and Military/Commercial Concerns with the People's Republic of China*, Vol., 1 (Washington, D.C.: Government Printing Office, 1999), p. 8.

7 *China's National Defence in 2000.*

8 Kenneth W. Allen and Eric A. McVadon, *China's Foreign Military Relations*, p. 12.

9 *PRC Law on National Defence*, Xinhua News Agency (Domestic Service) 18 March 1997.

10 For an analysis of the military-business relations in China, see James Mulvenon, *Soldiers of Fortune: The Rise and Fall of the Chinese Military-Business Complex, 1978-98* (M.E. Sharpe, 2001).

PART 3

A Party in Transition

CHAPTER **12**

The Chinese Communist Party Under Jiang Zemin: Politics of Adaptation

CHEN WEIXING

Although a distinctive and coherent new pattern of Chinese politics has not emerged in the reform era in China, Chinese domestic politics has undergone two distinctive periods before the 16th CCP National Congress: "Politics of transformation" under Deng Xiaoping from 1978 to 1992 and "politics of adaptation" under Jiang Zemin from 1992 to 2002. Deng's "politics of transformation" concerns transforming the CCP for economic growth, while Jiang's "politics of adaptation" concerns attuning the CCP to the conditions of the CCP's decay and the erosion of China's social solidarity that resulted from Deng's politics. Deng Xiaoping Theory which encapsulates "politics of transformation" was written into the Constitution of the Chinese Communist Party (CCP) at the 15th CCP National Congress, and Jiang's "three represents" (the CCP representing the most advanced culture, the most advanced forces of production, and the interest of the overwhelming majority of the Chinese population), the capstone of Jiang's politics, will be written into the CCP Constitution at the 16th CCP National Congress. "Politics of transformation" and "politics of adaptation" reflect the fluctuation of the CCP politics within the parameters of continuing reform and upholding the CCP leadership, and point to different directions in Chinese politics in the reform era.

In discussing Jiang's "politics of adaptation" and putting it in perspective, this chapter examines Deng's effort to deconstruct Mao's "Party of Politics" first, then analyses the context of the "politics of adaptation", next discusses Jiang's "politics of adaptation", and finally, highlights the prospect of Jiang's "politics of adaptation".

POLITICS OF TRANSFORMATION UNDER DENG XIAOPING

Mao left a difficult legacy for Deng Xiaoping, but Deng rose to the challenge by transforming Mao's "Party of Politics" into a "Party of Economics."[1] The major features of China's Leninist state socialism under Mao's "Party of Politics" were a monolithic and all-pervasive party, an enforced official ideology, highly personalised and concentrated power, a planned economy and state and collective ownership of property and resources. To promote economic development, Deng Xiaoping managed to change the "totalistic" functions of the Chinese state associated with Mao's "Party of Politics." Class struggle was rejected, Communist ideology was reinterpreted, and the Chinese polity, economy and culture were depoliticised.

Promoting economic growth and introducing market-oriented reform in China involved depoliticising the Chinese polity, economy and culture. As Deng Xiaoping noted, if we do not institute a reform of our political structure, it will be difficult to carry out the reform of our economic structure.[2] The essence of Deng's reform effort was to transform China's planned economy and carry out different forms of capitalist experiment in China. Well aware of the political risk of creating space for innovative ideas and local initiatives in the process of depoliticising the Chinese polity, economy and culture, Deng made it clear at the beginning of the reform that the sanction and patronage by the CCP to the reform were a matter of principle. Not long after Deng's economic program was adopted at the 1978 Third Plenum of the 11th CCP Central Committee in December 1978, the "Four Cardinal Principles" (upholding Marxism-Leninism and Mao Zedong Thought, Socialism, the CCP leadership, and the proletarian dictatorship) were affirmed as the guiding political principles for China's economic reform. The essence of the principles is to uphold the CCP leadership,[3] as Deng Xiaoping himself defined them. Deng's contribution to China during this period lay in his ability to successfully depoliticise the Chinese polity, economy and culture and steer China out of ideological interruption to promote economic growth while at the same time uphold the CCP leadership. Tsou Tang was right when he used "the middle course"[4] to describe what emerged following the death of Mao and the ascendancy of Deng in the 1980s. But when we look back now, we can see that Deng was not even a moderate ideologue; he simply pushed ideology to the side.

Deng was a pragmatist, as reflected in his well-known saying "black cat or white cat, it is a good cat as long as it can catch mice." Unlike Mao Zedong who had favoured ideological values over developmental values and tried to move China toward communism, Deng tried to modernise China first. The primary difference between Maoist orthodoxy and that of Deng Xiaoping, as Brantly Womack correctly observed, is that Mao's politics was structured by a future-oriented revolutionary mission while Deng was oriented toward maximising the opportunities at hand.[5] It was evident to Deng that, after two decades of too much ideology, the priority for China after the Cultural Revolution was to develop China's economy at all cost.

Liberal economic policies that would promote economic development obviously contradicted Communist ideology in the immediate post-Mao China and thereafter. As the ideological conflict between capitalism and socialism could not be easily compromised in the wake of the Cultural Revolution after two decades of too much ideology and thereafter, Deng chose to simply abandon ideological questions, which had the effect of discarding the practical utility of Communist ideology in China's economic development. Deng believed, probably incorrectly, that all political and ideological questions would eventually be resolved once China achieved great economic success and prosperity under the CCP leadership. Despite the fact that there were significant movements from both the left and the right throughout the 1980s and in the early 1990s, such as the 1983-84 anti-spiritual pollution campaign, the 1986 political structural reform attempt, the 1989 Tiananmen Incident, and the 1990-92 socialist ideology education campaign, none of these movements was able to interrupt China's economic reform. Ideological questions were abandoned at the 1978 Third Plenum in favour of an agreement on the primacy of economic development when they resulted in violent struggle within the CCP. "The presumption," as Joseph Fewsmith pointed out, "was that with economic development, both the urgency and the divisiveness of ideological questions would be reduced."[6] Questions of political reforms were also abandoned when they resulted in violent struggle within the CCP in 1986 and 1989. It took four rounds of ideological debate before the "surname" (between Mr. *She*–socialism and Mr. *Zi*–capitalism) debate was settled and capitalism was endorsed as a means of economic development in China after Deng's Nanxun (tour of the South) in 1992.

The first round of debate about "practice is the sole criterion of truth" accompanied the ascendancy of Deng Xiaoping in the late 1970s. The second and third rounds were closed-door debates within the party, which were each marked by the party documents – "the Resolution on Certain Questions in the History of Our Party since the Founding of the PRC," passed at the Sixth Plenum of the 11th CCP Central Committee in June 1981 and the thesis of "the primary stage of socialism" declared by Zhao Ziyang, General Secretary of the CCP at that time, at the 13th CCP National Congress on October 25, 1987. The fourth round ended with Deng Xiaoping's 1992 Nanxun.

The formula, "seek truth from facts", was in fact Mao's motto. Using Mao's motto to attack Mao was meant to serve the double purpose of denouncing Mao's approach to development and justifying Deng's effort to depoliticise the Chinese polity. It was important that during the first debate, the late Mao himself was hardly directly attacked or criticised, as the question of Mao was not merely a personal matter. In the wake of the Cultural Revolution, both Deng and other senior CCP leaders recognised the political necessity of preserving Mao as a symbol of revolutionary legitimacy,[7] for the Deng leadership could not afford to throw out Mao with Mao's Party. After all, Mao symbolised the power of the CCP collective leadership, which was still the political guarantee for the reform. The "Resolution on Certain Questions in the History of Our Party since the Founding of the PRC", as passed at the 6th Plenum of the 11th CCP Central Committee in June 1981, attempted to separate Mao's errors from Mao Zedong Thought by stating that Mao's errors derived from his own thought. Such an assessment of Mao fulfilled the purpose of reorienting policy and legitimising Deng leadership. If the 1978 Third Plenum of the CCP Central Committee opened the door for Deng's economism, the 1981 "Resolution" closed the door on ideological interference because it, instead of officially beginning the criticism of Mao, ended it. The criterion became economic performance since then, and even the conservative victory of 1988-89 was based on it.

The thesis of "the primary stage of socialism" was first proclaimed by Zhao Ziyang at the 13th CCP National Congress on 25 October 1987. According to this thesis and its official interpretation, China's preconditions for economic development were unique, in that the pre-1949 Chinese economy was extremely underdeveloped and China's productive forces were still very low. As such, China was destined to go through a very long "primary stage" to accomplish the task of socialist modernisation in order to move on to a fully developed "socialism with Chinese characteristics." The fundamental task of socialism in the primary stage was to develop the productive forces by all means, including developing a market economy in China. It was of the utmost importance, however, to balance economic development and stability in this stage, for without stability, nothing could be achieved. Therefore, the CCP leadership had to be upheld, and efforts had to be made to eliminate factors jeopardising stability. The thesis of "primary stage" discarded the relevance of Communist ideology in China's reform without rejecting it. This would enable the CCP to develop productive forces through reform by adhering to the "two basic points" of upholding the "Four Cardinal Principles" and of persevering in reform and opening to the outside.

The 1989 Tiananmen Incident triggered a new debate within the CCP. The immediate cause for the Tiananmen Incident was the death of Hu Yaobang, the ousted CCP secretary general. To a large extent, the Incident reflected the popular resentment against the regime at that time. The causes were justified, but the chaos created by students in the Incident did not help the reformers within the CCP. Tiananmen reformers lost their case within the CCP. For a while, it seemed that the course of the reform would be reversed. We all know now what happened in 1992. Deng Xiaoping managed to rally the party behind his calls for faster and bolder reform after his Nanxun in January-February 1992, leading to the CCP Politburo's endorsement of his call at its meeting on 10-11 March 1992. The significance of Deng's Nanxun was that the CCP endorsed capitalism as a means of economic development in China and thus ended the "surname debate" within the CCP between socialism and capitalism that had accompanied China's economic reform. Deng's two possible considerations were: (1) realising the possibility that the course of China's economic reform could be reversed, Deng made a bold move to legitimise capitalism as a means of economic development in China, which, he believed, would end the ideological debate within the Party concerning the nature of China's economic reform, thus making sure that the course of economic reform would never be reversed no matter what happened in the process of the reform; and (2) ending the ideological debate between socialism and capitalism within the party would indefinitely postpone a very divisive issue ideologically and politically for his successors despite the fact that different forms of capitalism had been experimented with in China in practice.

With the official endorsement of capitalism as a means of development in China, Deng's effort to depoliticise the Chinese polity, economy and culture was finally completed. There should be no doubt that Deng Xiaoping did the right thing in the special historical context of China after two decades of political chaos by making economic growth China's top priority and by redefining the relationship between politics and economic and the role of ideology in China's development. There should also be no doubt that China's great economic success in the 1980s and 1990s was closely associated with Deng's effort to depoliticise the Chinese polity, economy and culture, which later became an important part of the so-called Deng Xiaoping Theory that was written into the CCP constitution at the CCP 15th National Congress in 1997. The essence of Deng Xiaoping Theory is its political utility that endorses capitalist practice in China's economic development on the one hand and emphasises the legitimacy of the CCP leadership in the reform on the other. Economic liberalism and political authoritarianism may not be a good combination, but it was a practical approach to economic development from 1978 to 1992 in China. The end result of Deng's reform was that the CCP was transformed from a "Party of Politics" into a "Party of Economics" although the fundamental contradiction between market economy and CCP dictatorship remained unresolved. The post-Deng leadership was to face the social and political ramifications of the contradiction resulting from the bewildering combination of one-party state socialism with competitive capitalism.

THE CONTEXT OF THE "POLITICS OF ADAPTATION"

Two consequences resulted from Deng's politics: The CCP's decay and the erosion of China's social solidarity.

Party decay can be described on two levels: institutional and individual. Party decay on both levels is associated with the demise of Communist ideology and depoliticisation of the Chinese polity, economy and culture. On the institutional level, a "Party of Economics" could not be monolithic, because when CCP politics became politics of economics, political power was shifted from the center to the localities, which dissipated the very source of CCP political power derived from the official CCP ideology. Under the "politics of economics," interest, defined in economic terms, became diverse, which diluted the center's unified political leadership. With the change of the CCP's mission in the reform, economic growth became the sole criterion for evaluating both the performance of party and government organisations and the performance of party and government officials. Increasingly, party organisations had come to resemble industrial corporations and party officials had come to behave as if they were hard-driving business executives vitally concerned with profitability and market share.[8] Unlike political interest, there could neither be shared economic interest between provinces and regions nor shared economic interest between higher party authorities and lower party authorities. Given the differentiation and diversity created since the economic reform, the center found it harder and harder to define the collective good for the whole country, because provinces, regions, and locales were each becoming "special zones" on their own ways and terms. The development of "dukedom economies" (*zhuhou jingji*)[9] is an example. In its extreme, provinces, regions and locales not only competed with each other but also "blockaded" each other".[10] Vertically, the more money the higher authorities got in terms of revenues, the less money the lower authorities would have left. Horizontally, the more market shares one province, region, or locale got, the less the other province, region, or locale had. In any case, party organisations and officials no longer had shared interests with the party authorities above and with each other when politics became politics of economics.

If excessive centralisation was to blame for the economic stagnation before the reform, it became necessary to encourage local initiatives and innovations in policy and organisational terms. The necessary condition for local initiatives and innovations was autonomy and independence from higher party authorities. Promoting economic growth was a local endeavour as nobody could depend on higher party authorities for their own prosperity and for their own organisational revenues and personal well-being. Economic activities such as mobilising investment funds, targeting enterprises for growth, gathering and providing information about market opportunities, acting as brokers for contracts, etc. were the individual efforts of local governments and government officials. As economic success was closely associated with market localism, the attempt to secure private advantage, politically, challenged the CCP's unified leadership. Deng's reforms, indeed, acted to strengthen the regions at the expense of the center and to solidify the political importance of economic capital and market position.[11] The central government was losing control [12] and becoming increasingly remote to the provinces in many ways. First, the center was losing its general regulatory capacity. According to one study, between 1978 and 1992, the central government's tax base had shrunk from 31.2 percent of GNP to 14.2 percent, even though China's GNP was growing at an annual rate of 9.5 percent.[13] Next, central government policies and regulations were often ignored. "Those who are supposed to have high authority cannot always command the actions of those who ultimately implement state policies," as Lucian W. Pye described it.[14] Finally, the center could no longer regain the control over the provinces it had before the economic reform without severe economic consequences. The provinces, however, were facing the same rising demands from their localities within their provinces. The dilemma for the CCP is that the CCP's new legitimacy after the demise of Communist ideology depended, to a large extent, upon the improvement of the Chinese welfare and standard of living, while the same imperative was becoming a challenge for the CCP's unified political leadership and a source of social instability. When party organisations and officials cannot depend on the higher party authorities for prosperity and revenues, the center naturally becomes increasingly unimportant and remote. When party organisations and officials have to compete with each other to promote their own interests on the market,[15] the Chinese party state becomes increasingly uncoordinated politically. In such a context, party organisations and officials are all seeking more power and freedom from higher authorities to conduct their own business and pursue their own interest and fight each other for opportunities and market shares. As a result, the CCP, as a political organisation in terms of its unified political leadership, political control, and mobilisation capability, decayed.

On the individual level, the party decay is reflected in the party disintegration. Party disintegration is exhibited in two ways: structural corruption within the CCP and the loss of the CCP members and the Chinese psychological attachment toward the CCP.

Communist ideology used to be an integrative force between the elites and between the elites and the masses for the CCP. With the demise of Communist ideology, the ideal of Communism was replaced by the pursuit of immediate economic and materialistic interests, the rules of politics and society based on ideology-related conventions gave way to the rules governed by material interests. Consequently, the party members' loyalty, commitment, dedication and sacrifices were lost in the process. As party officials and members were no longer constrained by conventions and clearly stated principles derived from the ideology and beginning to benefit materially and prosper from the economic reform, they tended to regard their institutional power as a tool for material interests and wealth. Institutionally, the structure from which party and state officials derive their power did not change much before and after the economic reform. Party officials and members, institutionally unchecked, tended to obey political conventions associated with the party ideology before the reform, partly because they had faith in the ideology and partly because they were constrained by the conventions associated with the ideology. With the demise of Communist ideology and loss of conventions derived from the ideology, party officials and members, institutionally unchecked, neither believed in any ideology nor felt constrained by any ideological conventions. Corruption within the party therefore became rampant.

The impact of the demise of Communist ideology and depoliticisation on the population was also profound. The cohesion of Chinese society and the integration among elites and between the elites and the masses in China had always been contingent upon an official ideology. Order and unity for 2,000 years in traditional China had, in part, been maintained by cultural conventions and virtues derived from traditional Chinese ideology rather than by religion or law, which had been a unique characteristic of the Chinese society.[16] The intellectual, psychological and moral void that resulted from the erosion of the traditional ideology, Confucianism, early in the 20th century created a political crisis for China, which generated a need for a new ideology and paved the way for the CCP's triumph in China. The intellectual, psychological and moral void that resulted from the demise of Communist ideology and Deng's depoliticisation once again generated a need for a new ideology for the post-Deng leadership. China fell into a severe and widespread "crisis of faith, trust and confidence" after the Cultural Revolution, which could be attributed to the ideological excesses of 1957 to 1978 and to the failure in policies associated with the ideology during the same period. The CCP rose to the economic challenge by making China the fastest-growing economy in the world but lost the psychological attachment of the masses it once enjoyed. On the one hand, the ideological excesses of 1957 to 1978 had indeed created an aversion and resistance to ideology among the masses, but on the other hand, the masses did have strong desire for spiritual satisfaction in the reform, which the demise of Communist ideology and depoliticisation were unable to satisfy. With the loss of the CCP's ideological appeal, the moral fabric of the Chinese society in an environment of money worship was also severely eroded. Some Chinese found spiritual sanctuaries in Falun Gong, others in religion, and still others in the pursuit of money. The majority, however, have not found any spiritual sanctuaries yet. With the fallouts of the Chinese welfare system in the 1990s, the Chinese population is neither psychologically nor materialistically attached to the CCP. The CCP has lost those who have found their own spiritual or monetary sanctuaries. Those without any sanctuaries are alienated from the CCP as they do not have any sense of social purpose. If the party members are corrupt and the masses no longer identify themselves with the CCP, the CCP will be lost unless it can rise to the challenge.

Related to the specific problem of party decay is the larger issue of social solidarity. The ideology-based social solidarity collapsed with the demise of Communist ideology and depoliticisation, but no new social solidarity has been established in its wake. An ideology-based social solidarity under the "Party of Politics" was one in which there were, arguably, shared beliefs, unchallengeable party authority, and tight political control. With the transformation of the CCP from a "Party of Politics" into a "Party of Economics," the social order based on the authority of ideological beliefs and tight political control changed. What took place in the process, if we could use Emile Durkheim's characterisation, was a historical shift from a form of social order based on shared belief and tight communal control (mechanical solidarity) to one based on the mutual interdependence of relatively autonomous individuals (organic solidarity).[17] In the process of the transformation of the CCP from a "Party of Politics" into a "Party of Economics," a historical shift has certainly taken place in China, and the form of social order is no longer "mechanical".

According to Durkheim, the mechanical solidarity of traditional societies was dependent upon the likeness of its members, whose common life circumstances made for shared beliefs and values. Under conditions of mechanical solidarity, individuality was nil, for the individual conscience was dependent upon the collective type and followed all of its movements. The organic solidarity produced by the division of labour depended on individual difference–the difference which developed with occupational specialisation. Specialisation created the conditions for the development of personal difference, opening up spheres of action which were not subject to collective control. Rejecting the view that industrialisation necessarily led to a breakdown in social order, Durkheim maintained that specialisation increased dependence on society, for with occupational specialisation the exchange of services became a condition of survival.[18] In the case of China, individual difference has developed in the process of the party transformation, opening up spheres of action which are not subject to collective control, as discussed above. Nevertheless, the exchange of services, the condition of survival which, according to Durkheim, contributed to "organic solidarity", is not based on the occupational specialisation but on the institutional linkage with the CCP. The institutional linkage as a condition of survival in China means that: (1) exchange of services and pursuit of personal interest depend on the linkage with the CCP apparatus; (2) the linkage with the CCP apparatus serves as the main axis around which economic and social activities revolve and upon which the Chinese society operates; and (3) the linkage with the apparatus constitutes the core of connection networks that help lubricate tensions and maintain the dominant position of the CCP. Without the institutional linkage, the exchange of services, the pursuit of personal interest, and the operation of connection networks and Chinese society will be disrupted, and the CCP's dominant position will be shaken.

The increased solidarity that Durkheim associated with the division of labour was not to be found in any actual, existing industrial society. In explaining why the increased solidarity did not occur in industrial society, Durkheim identified two main causes: the first was the absence of a body of rules appropriate to the changing circumstances of economic life, which left markets unregulated and workers without any sense of social purpose and the second was structured inequality. He argued that the spontaneous division of labour on which organic solidarity was based could only occur if society was constituted in such a way that the social inequalities exactly express natural inequalities. Interestingly, the abnormality identified by Durkheim does exist in China despite the fact or because of the fact that the institutional linkage has become a condition of survival in China today. With respect to the first anomie, "a body of rules appropriate to the changing circumstances of economic life" has not been fully developed in China. There cannot be fair competition and equal opportunities on the market under the current semi-planned and semi-market economy in China, because the privileged make and break the rules and control the opportunities. Workers and the average Chinese are certainly left without any sense of social purpose. Wide gaps between the rich and the poor and between the privileged and unprivileged are created and are becoming wider and wider. To a large extent, it is the institutional linkage as a condition of survival that favours those privileged and powerful that has contributed to the inequality in China. If Durkheim's central problem, as Beryl Langer pointed out, was not the a historical question of how social order is possible, but the historically specific one of how a modern industrial society, in which the traditional ties that bound individual to society have been weakened, might provide its members with a sense of social purpose and belonging,[19] this is also the challenge facing the post-Deng leadership after the depoliticisation of the Chinese polity, economy and culture.

Evidently, the Chinese system has functioned. How shall we account for the fact that China has indeed achieved impressive economic success under the leadership of the CCP and the CCP is still at the helm of the reform despite the fact that the CCP has decayed and new social solidarity is badly needed? There are four possible explanations. First, the CCP is still indispensable to the maintenance of order in China as the CCP has enormous physical force at its disposal. It showed clearly in the 1989 Tiananmen Incident, in its handling of Falun Gong, and in the recent detention of scholars that it would not hesitate to use physical force when the CCP authority and order were challenged and threatened. The CCP as a party of public order cannot be replaced at present as there is no alternative. Any possible alternative will immediately be cracked down upon by the CCP with force, while the cost of disorder is too big for the Chinese to bear. Second, the CCP has changed its modes of control in the reform era. Ideological control has given way to punitive campaigns and punitive management, and petitioner access and non-oppositional public participation have been introduced.[20] Third, the CCP has indeed achieved impressive economic success under the bewildering combination of socialism with competitive capitalism, which has provided temporary new legitimacy for the CCP. But this new legitimacy is eroding due to the lack of new social solidarity, structured corruption, uneven development and widening gaps between the privileged and unprivileged. Fourth, "special interest groups" arising from the reform are benefiting enormously from the system and want to maintain the system. As party officials in power and their families, those individuals who have connections with the CCP apparatus, and the new rich have become prosperous, the necessity to maintain and prolong the system become evident. They are "special interest groups" because they share the common interest of maintaining and prolonging the system under which they have prospered. The majority of the population is excluded from the privileged group not because their standard of living on average has not been improved since the reform but because opportunities have been unequal. Indeed, "interest" provides an exit for many average Chinese, which, to a certain extent, transforms people's "public action" (demands for political reform) to "private interest" (economic activities).[21] However the irony is that the "interest" has been a myth for the majority of the Chinese population. For those within the system, opportunities depend on how well one can play the political game, while for those outside the system, opportunities are contingent upon the links one has with those within the system. The privileged always have opportunities. It seems to many that opportunities and the road to wealth through linkage with the CCP apparatus are accessible and open. Many people do not resent the system as much as they do their lack of connection and luck. They do resent the privileges and unequal opportunities that those in power or those who have connections have, but they would not mind those privileges and those unequal opportunities if they could get them. Many are, in fact, fighting hard for those privileges and opportunities instead of against the system that creates these privileges and unequal opportunities. Desperately trying to find access and opportunities, they are forgetting that the cause for unequal opportunities and unnatural inequalities in China lies in the system and not in their inability to find access and opportunities. Evidently, the myth serves the interest of the privileged, but more importantly, it serves as a system stabiliser.

JIANG'S "POLITICS OF ADAPTATION"

This is the social and political context of Jiang's succession. The legacy that Deng left Jiang is different from that which he inherited from Mao but not less difficult. Deng left Jiang a robust economy, but also a party in a state of decay and the difficult task of building new social solidarity after the deconstruction of Mao's "Party of Politics" and the collapse of ideology-based solidarity. If Deng's legacy lies in his success in depoliticising the Chinese polity, economy and culture, Jiang Zemin's legacy will lie in how successfully he can attune the CCP to the new conditions in post-Deng China. Specifically, the historical task of building "socialism with Chinese characteristics" for Jiang is to build a new political order by providing prosperity for all (the basis of the new social solidarity) on the basis of sustained economic growth, incorporating the majority of the Chinese into the socio-economic structure of the reform, and instilling a new moral spirit into the party and the Chinese population.

Jiang's politics is encapsulated in the "three stresses" (stressing politics, political study, and political moral spirit), the combination of "rule by law" with "rule by virtue," and the "three represents".

Deng's advantages when he set China's reform in motion included: The outcry for order and economic growth, his own reputation, image and charisma which could be translated into trust and confidence, and his clients in the party and military. Deng was also able to use the power shaped by Mao's politics to change Mao's politics and the very nature of the Chinese state in the process. Deng was able to use all these to shift the CCP's priority from politics to economics and transform the CCP in the process. The era of the paramount leader ended with the death of Deng Xiaoping. The Jiang leadership is faced with "unprecedented challenges of governance."[22] The center has been severely handicapped in its reach, and it is the local government that is exercising power in many ways today in China. The center lacks the necessary clout with the local governments even though the center is still exercising organisational control over personnel matters. Jiang and his associates certainly do not enjoy Deng's reputation, image and charisma. To consolidate his power and establish his legitimacy within the CCP in post-Deng China, Jiang must resort to politics. The "three stresses" was first advocated by Jiang Zemin before the CCP's 15th National Congress in 1997. Following the CCP's 15th National Congress, a political campaign of "three stresses" was carried out within the party and government, which did not end until 2001. The political consideration for Jiang to put forward the "three stresses" was to use politics to consolidate his own power within the party and strengthen his unified leadership. Deng was able to transform Mao's "Party of Politics" into a "Party of Economics" and make his "Party of Economics" function, partly because Deng was able to use the power shaped by Mao's politics and use the power with finesse. The power shaped by Deng's politics has not proven to be as convenient for Jiang, as party decay has made it more difficult for Jiang Zemin, who did not enjoy the charisma and image of paramount leaders like Mao Zedong and Deng Xiaoping, to impose his politics. Stressing politics was to stress Jiang's politics and unified political leadership within the CCP and the political cohesiveness of the CCP around him. Stressing political study was to stress the CCP members' political consciousness of the CCP's new leadership and leadership role under the new conditions in post-Deng China and to improve the CCP members' loyalty and self-cultivation. Stressing political moral spirit was to warn CCP members against corruption and mischiefs and to ask them to show restraint.

The idea of "rule by virtue" was advanced by Jiang Zemin on January 11, 2001 at a national conference attended by heads of propaganda departments. Jiang stressed at the conference that the CCP must govern the country by combining "rule by law" with "rule by virtue." "Rule by virtue" resembles the Chinese aphorism: *xiushen qijia zhiguo pingtianxia*. That is, to cultivate and make one useful to the society (*siushen*), look after the family and have a strong sense of family responsibilities (*qijia*), look after the country (*zhiguo*), and peace and harmony under heaven (*pingtianxia*). China's economic reform started in an environment of moral and ideological decay following the Cultural Revolution, while the traditional Chinese culture, which had been severely devastated by years of revolution and political campaigns, was further devastated by money worship in the economic reform. The power of culture is important for the post-Deng leadership primarily because: (1) the means of political control has almost been exhausted; (2) party and government officials have not been constrained by the CCP's own rules; and (3) a code of conduct for party members and for the population is badly needed in the absence of an official ideology.

If economic growth was a way out of the difficult situation and the CCP's legitimacy could be temporarily based on the CCP's ability to deliver economic goods for Deng in post-Mao China, the CCP's legitimacy can only partly depend on China's economic growth in post-Deng China as social and political problems resulting from Deng's depoliticisation are piling up and discontent against the party is widespread. Jiang and his associates will be blamed if they fail to maintain sustained economic growth in China. The post-Deng leadership must try to clean up the CCP, accommodate and balance the demands of different social-economic classes, address the issue of the widening gaps between the rich and the poor and between the privileged and the unprivileged without compromising economic growth, and redefine central-local relations in the process of establishing a new political order in China. In response, Jiang Zemin put forward the "three represents" in February 2000.

"The most advanced culture" means that the CCP should serve as an integrative force that represents the positive things in China's reform and development. On the defensive side, it means what an advanced culture is not, rather than what it is, in response to the moral decay and the influence of Western culture. The most advanced forces of production reemphasise the priority and importance of economic growth in post-Deng China. Representing the interest of the overwhelming majority of the Chinese population, for the first time, raises the question of development for whom and what in China as well as the question of the CCP's political base in a post-Communist era. First of all, it is a response to the emergence of the wide gaps between the rich and the poor and between the privileged and the unprivileged. Representing the interest of the majority of the people is not just a matter of letting the wealth of the rich trickle down to the poor, which may or may not happen, but to make sure that the overwhelming majority of the Chinese population is the beneficiary of China's economic growth. Secondly, it redefines the CCP's political base and tries to accommodate the demands of the intellectuals, entrepreneurs, and other emerging social-economic classes that are the engines of China's economic development and incorporate them into China's political order. Jiang Zemin showed his intention in his speech on the occasion of the CCP's 80th anniversary that the emerging capitalists in China should be allowed to join the CCP. Thirdly, it emphasises the importance of the traditional leading classes of the CCP–the workers and peasants and the importance of reincorporating them into China's changed social and political order. Representing the advanced forces of production tells us that the CCP will stick to economic reform as advanced forces of production must be reflected in economic growth and the interest of the people must be measured economically. "Representing the interest of the overwhelming majority of the people" is the core of the "three represents" which is of direct relevance to the survival of the CCP and social stability in China. The "three represents" was written into the CCP Constitution at the 16th CCP National Congress in the fall of 2002. The essence of Jiang's politics is to adapt the CCP to the new conditions in post-communist China. The direction that the "three represents" points to is to build a new political order in China on the basis of sustained economic growth with the "three stresses" as the political instrument and the "rule by virtue" as the moral and cultural complement even though building a new political order is still not a clearly defined goal. Jiang's politics of adaptation now has a thesis, but it remains to be seen whether the CCP under Jiang's "three represents" can adapt itself to the new conditions in China.

THE PROSPECT OF JIANG'S "POLITICS OF ADAPTATION"

The CCP was able to sustain its economic growth and maintain order and stability during the ten years under Jiang Zemin from 1992 to 2002. However, it is also during these ten years that the wealth gap between the rich and the poor widened to a dangerous point, popular grievances and resentment further developed, and corruption became even more rampant. Given the challenges and leadership change at the forthcoming 26th CCP National Congress, what is the prospect of Jiang's politics of adaptation?

First, repoliticisation is more difficult than depoliticisation, because depoliticisation and marketisation are complementary in tone, while repoliticisation and marketisation are contradictory in nature. If economic growth is still the top priority of the CCP, the prospect of repoliticisation does not look good. Could the "three represents" constitute the core of a new ideological discourse in the post-Deng era, and could it resonate with the Chinese sense of crisis which has their roots in the fallouts of Communist ideology? The answer to these questions is probably "no."

Secondly, the political instincts of Jiang and his associates are still those appropriate to the "mechanical solidarity" although the mechanical solidarity associated with a traditional and highly homogeneous society has collapsed. As a result of the creation of great space and differentiation and development of individualism over the last 23 years in China, the Chinese society today is more diversified economically and pluralised politically. It is hard to imagine that the Chinese population will accept the collective good defined by the Jiang leadership and what the Jiang leadership has judged to be good for them unless their demands are met.

Finally, Jiang's successor may depart significantly from Jiang's politics in post-Jiang era. The 15th CCP National Congress was devoted to Deng Xiaoping as the theme of the 15th National Congress "hold high the great banner of Deng Xiaoping Theory for an all-round advancement of the cause of building socialism with Chinese characteristics into the 21st century" indicated. Deng Xiaoping Theory was written into the CCP Constitution at the Congress. In his report to the CCP 15th National Congress, Jiang Zemin stated that Deng Xiaoping is a great Marxist, and his greatest contribution to the party, to the Chinese people and to Marxism, and the precious legacy he left us is Deng Xiaoping Theory.[23] Yet, Jiang tried to define his own leadership and distinguish himself from Deng after the Congress even though Jiang was dependent on Deng after the succession. The 16th CCP National Congress will be partly devoted to Jiang as Jiang's "three represents" will be written into the CCP Constitution at the Congress. While Jiang stepped down at the 16th CCP National Congress in the fall of 2002, however Jiang will continue to play a role in Chinese politics after the Congress. But Jiang is not Deng, and he has not been able to establish himself as a paramount leader. If Deng could call all the shots without occupying any institutional position in his late years, Jiang may not be able to do so. Probably for this reason, Jiang wants to stay on the political scene officially after the Congress and put his clients in important institutional positions within the CCP and government, which has complicated the power struggle within the CCP surrounding the succession before the 16th CCP National Congress.[24] The fourth generation of the CCP leadership will be produced at the 16th CCP National Congress even if Jiang manages to stay, and Jiang's presence will be short-lived. To consolidate his power and establish his legitimacy, Jiang's successor, just like Jiang, must try to distinguish himself from Jiang in terms of personnel and politics.

If changes in politics and policies are always associated with the CCP leadership change, the leadership change at the 16th CCP National Congress would imply the coming of a new era of politics and policies in China. The direction that Jiang's politics of adaptation points to, as indicated above, is to build a new political order in China. Democratisation is certainly not the goal of Jiang's politics of adaptation, but it may be an indispensable part of any successful effort to build a new political order in post-communist China. Given the magnitude of change and the population's resentment toward inequality, corruption within the CCP, etc., the CCP is relying more and more on physical coercion to crack down on disobedience and dissidence. But the CCP's legitimacy and China's problems require much more than just physical power. It is hard to see successful adaptation effort in post-Jiang China simply as a top-down process launched for reasons of Party transformation and state stability in post-Jiang China. In the ultimate solution to the search for new bases of social solidarity and the CCP's political legitimacy, the organised force of the state will probably have to meet the unorganised and transformed citizen-masses halfway, either through institutions or on the street. Here lies the opportunity for the fourth generation of the CCP leadership to depart significantly from the Chinese normal politics. In this sense, the 16th CCP National Congress will set a new road sign for Chinese politics.

ENDNOTES

1. Chen Weixing, *The Political Economy of Rural Development, 1978-1999* (Westport, Connecticut: Praeger, 1999), pp. 29-33.
2. Deng Xiaoping, "On Reform of the Political Structure," *Selected Works of Deng Xiaoping*, vol.III (Beijing: Foreign Languages Press, 1994), p.179.
3. Deng Xiaoping, "*Deng Xiaoping Wenxuan, 1975-1982*," (Selected Works of Deng Xiaoping, 1975-1982) (Beijing: renmin chubanshe, 1984), p. 369.
4. Tsou Tang, *Cultural Revolution and Post-Mao Reforms* (Chicago: University of Chicago Press, 1987), pp. 219-258.
5. Brantly Womack, "The Problems of Isms: Pragmatic Orthodoxy and Liberalisation in Mainland China," a paper delivered at the 23rd Sino-American Conference, Institute of International Relations, National Chengchi University, Taipei, Taiwan.
6. Joseph Fewsmith, "The Dengist Reforms in Historical Perspective," in Brantly Womack, ed., *Contemporary Chinese Politics in Historical Perspective* (Cambridge: Cambridge University Press, 1991), p.23.
7. Maurice Meisner, *Mao's China and After* (London: Collier Macmillan Publishers, 1986), p. 463.
8. Andrew G. Walder (ed.), *Zouping in Transition: The Process of Reform in Rural North China* (Cambridge, Mass.: Harvard University Press, 1998), p. 17.
9. See Shen Liren and Dai Yuanche, "Formation of Dukedom Economics and Their Causes and Defects," *Chinese Economic Studies*, vol.25, no.4 (Summer 1992), pp.6-24 and Christine Wong, "Central-Local Relations in an Era of Fiscal Decline: The Paradox of Fiscal Decentralisation in Post-Mao China," *China Quarterly*, no.128 (December 1991), pp.691-715.
10. Zhu Rongji, premier of China's State Council, issued an order prohibiting economic blockade in provincial, regional, or local economic activities on 21 April 2001. See Renmin Ribao (People's Daily) (April 30, 2001), p.5.
11. Jeremy Paltiel, "Jiang Talks Politics -Who Listens? Institutionalisation and Its Limits in Market Leninism," *The China Journal*, no.45 (January 2001), p.113.
12. For instance, the loss of fiscal control caused the decline of state capability. According to Wang Shaoquang and Hu Angang, between 1978 and 1992, the central government's tax base had shrunk from 31.2 percent of GNP to 14.2 percent, even though China's GNP was growing at an annual rate of 9.5 percent. See Wang Shaoguang and Hu Angang, *Report on China's State Capacity* (Hong Kong: Oxford University Press, 1994).
13. See Wang Shaoguang and Hu Angang, *Report on China's State Capacity*.
14. Lucian W. Pye, "Jiang Zemin's Style of Rule: Go for Stability, Monopolise Power and Settle for Limited Effectiveness," *The China Journal*, issue 45 (January 2001), p.47.
15. See Kenneth Lieberthal and David M. Lampton (eds.), *Bureaucracy, Politics and Decision Making in Post-Mao China* (Berkeley: University of California Press, 1992).
16. Xu Ming (ed.), *guanjian shike jidai jiejuode 27ge wenti* (Twenty-Seven Pressing Issues at a Crucial Moment) (Beijing: jinri zhongguo chubanshe, 1997), p.452.

17. This is the thesis of Durkheim's *The Division of Labor in Society*. See Emile Durkheim, *The Division of Labor in Society* (New York: Free Press, 1964).
18. Emile Durkheim, *The Division of Labor in Society*, p.130. Also see Beryl Langer, "Emile Durkheim" in Peter Beilharz (ed.), *Social Theory* (Sydney, Australia: Allen & Unwin, 1991), p. 73.
19. Beryl Langer, "Emile Durkheim," p.74.
20. See Chen Weixing, "Control from the Center in the Reform Era in China: The Changing Modes," in Liu Guoli and Chen Weixing Chen (eds.), *New Directions in Chinese Politic for the New Millennium* (Lampeter: The Edwin Mellen Press, 2002), pp.1-18.
21. Zheng Yongnian, "Ideological Decline, the Rise of an Interest-Based Social Order, and the Demise of Communism in China," p, 12), a paper delivered at the Conference on Deng Xiaoping's Nanxun Legacy and China's Development at East Asian Institute of National University of Singapore, Singapore, 11-13 April 2000.
22. David Shambaugh, "The Chinese State in the Post-Mao Era," in David Shambaugh, ed., *The Modern Chinese State* (Cambridge: Cambridge University Press, 2000), p.162.
23. Jiang Zeming, "Hold High the Great Banner of Deng Xiaoping's Theory for an All-Round Advancement of the Cause of Building Socialism with Chinese Characteristics into the 21st Century", *Beijing Review*, Vol.40, No. 40 (October 6-12, 1997), p.1.
24. The 16th CCP National Congress is originally scheduled to be held in October 2002. It is postponed because of that.

CHAPTER 13

The "China Democratic Party" Event and Political Trends in Post-Deng China[1]

XIAO GONGQIN
Translator: YOW CHEUN HOE

In June 1998, a number of grassroots dissenters in China attempted to found the "China Democratic Party," triggering a political storm that spanned 11 provinces and lasted as long as six months. Suppressed by the Chinese government in late December 1998, the main activists were respectively imprisoned for a period that varied from 10 to 13 years. The China Democratic Party Event offers an essential angle with which to look into the Chinese politics in the post-Deng period, particularly with regard to the method and attitude adopted by the Chinese government in handling the event. This fundamentally helps us understand the Chinese political trends at the turn of the century and how they will develop in the two decades to come. More specifically, this sheds light on the views, reaction models and political choices that were held and will be held by the Chinese post-totalitarian regime towards political opposition.

The China Democratic Party Event took place in a small number of localities and involved some marginal groups within the Chinese communities; it therefore did not bring about profound nationwide impact. Though leaving no written materials substantial enough for analysis, the event occurred at a time when the usage of the Internet already prevailed in China. In their endeavour to establish the party, the people concerned made use of the Internet to expand their political influence. This makes possible an investigation based on the information retrieved from the Internet. This chapter attempts to examine some of the important issues pertaining to the event, including its social background, the political characteristics and mentality of the activists, the dilemma facing the Chinese government, the change in strategy adopted by the government, and the responses from Chinese society. It also conducts a historical examination of how politics in China changed at the turn of the century and, from the perspective of political science in China, investigates the fundamental features associated with the authoritarian regime in post-Deng China.

A NEW CHANGE IN THE CHINESE POLITICAL ATMOSPHERE

In the late 1990s the political atmosphere in Chinese society became more open and non-restrictive than compared to any other time since the Tiananmen Incident in 1989. The political openness happened in a period in which Deng Xiaoping and the revolutionary senior statesmen stepped down from the political stage and the regime under Jiang Zemin gradually moved into consolidation and stability. The thinking of the intellectuals increasingly became more vigorous and the space became larger for them to be concerned with and react to the current political situation. This is particularly evident in Beijing, the most important and concentrated site for intellectuals, where some civilian societies and organisations began to emerge. Many activities, such as book launches, book review awards, and seminars, were held by civilian bookshops and intellectuals. Targeting ordinary residents, these activities were financed with civilian resources, the major resource of which was intellectual-type entrepreneurs.

For sure, compared to the June Fourth period in which the Tiananmen Incident happened, the aforementioned academic activities, organised by popular initiatives and resources, were coloured considerably with rationality and moderation and posed no challenge to government authority. During the decade from the June Fourth Incident to 1998, a new kind of game rule gradually took shape between the intellectual communities and the government–the government would not intervene in the intellectuals' activities as long as the intellectuals did not challenge its authority.

The question prompted here is why did a limited expansion of freedom for popular activities appear? Why did this phenomenon emerge in the Jiang Zemin period and why did the government not intervene much? Basically, we can look at these questions at on two levels–one at the level of the ruling regime and the other at that of the populace.

First, General Secretary Jiang Zemin has been in power for more than a decade since the June Fourth Incident and his political base has been greatly consolidated since Deng Xiaoping passed away. As I pointed out in my article "The Political Attitudes and Prospects of the Chinese Social Strata at the Turn of the Century" (*Zhanlue he Guanli* No. 6, 1998), with the retreat of Deng Xiaoping and revolutionary senior statesmen from the political stage, the Leftist Fundamentalists lost their own perceived political backing as well as the power to manipulate leftist ideology and language hegemony to challenge the faction centered around Jiang. On the other hand, the majority of intellectuals who once tended to be radical and aggressive in the June Fourth period, had become moderate, resulting from what they had observed as the social cost that the former Soviet Union and East Europe had to pay for "revolutionary drastic change". Most Chinese intellectuals have now abandoned the "revolutionary model" and instead advocate the "reform model." Since they cooperate and work together with the government, mainstream intellectuals no longer constitute a direct political challenge to the government.

Without challenges and pressure from the leftist faction and without intervention from the revolutionary senior statesmen as in the Deng Xiaoping period, Jiang Zemin's decision-making power has become greater than that of Hu Yaobang and Zhao Ziyang in the past. Where the international political stage is concerned, his successful visit to the United States made Jiang increasingly realise that his having a liberal image, as well as the Chinese government doing so, will help China gain more resources and greater recognition and thus benefit

China in resolving unification issues with Taiwan. Take for example China's recent signing of two international conventions concerning human rights. And, during the United States' President Clinton's visit to China, live television broadcasting was permitted, during which President Clinton openly criticised the Chinese government's handling of the June Fourth Incident. For this openness, the Chinese government received tremendous applause from abroad and, within the country, the liberalists did not take this opportunity to rise and act against the government. This made the Jiang regime further realise that the adoption of limited political openness would not threaten political stability.

Indeed, in recent years, Chinese leaders could sense the moderation in the political attitudes of the mainstream intellectuals. In addition, they also came to realise that a limited amount of space for intellectuals constituted no real threat to national security and political stability, but helped the leaders expand their own presence on the international political stage and win over many more hearts within the country, which reinforced the legitimacy of the authority of the government.

Second, the Chinese leaders also increasingly realised how widespread and serious corruption has become. To some extent, whether consciously or not, they viewed the expanded popular freedom as a kind of effective monitoring mechanism initiated from the bottom-up over corrupt practices. Two decades of reform witnessed a rise and spread of corruption that now reached a severe stage. With the many internal reports "reflecting the situation" accumulating daily, the leaders were more aware than the ordinary people and intellectuals of the severity of the corruption problem. They also, to some extent, realised that little would come of "clean politics and self-discipline" if operated only by the government itself. Monitoring by the populace could, as the leaders perceived it, be a resolution to the corruption among government officials and servants.

What should be pointed out is that loosened political control is neither an initiative nor an encouragement from the Chinese leaders. Instead it is a tacit compromise, as opposed to the thorough restrictions and bans in the immediate few years after the June Fourth

Incident. The government no longer seriously supervises and controls activities initiated by the intellectuals, thus expanding the population's freedom. Without interference, these activities will grow like a tree within the society.

There is, however, another side of the story. The central government headed by Jiang Zemin in the post-Deng period went through a political crisis following the June Fourth Incident and there remained political insecurity. They realised that the problems of the June Fourth Incident–bureaucratic corruption, laid-off workers, and domestic financial crisis–could trigger discontent from the lower classes and might even lead to political turbulence. Any outbreak of discontent from the lower classes could prompt political requests from the intellectuals. From the historical lessons of the June Fourth Incident, the combined force of the lower class and intellectuals could possibly lead to the loss of political control. This is what the leaders worry about. At any rate, this worry remains theoretical and has not yet been translated into real experience and clear judgment. This ambiguity poses a certain degree of warning and restriction as to the question of loosening and liberalising of political control.

Thus, the collective attitude of the leaders in the post-Deng era is that they, on the one hand, wish to implement relatively liberal politics and, on the other, worry about the potential risk that might lead to their losing political control. This dilemma is a kind of unique mentality confronting the post-Deng high-rank technocratic leaderships. They are no longer eager nor stubborn about political indoctrination as are the old leftists in the party. The technical and professional training they received enables them to see practical results as more important than doctrine. For them, the iconography of the ideology will become important only when political security is threatened and when they want to attempt to deprive the opposition. However, when they feel political security is not affected, they do not resort much to the ideological propaganda. More or less, these technocratic leaders were, during their youth, influenced by the democratic trends of the 1930s and 1940s. As long as political stability is secure, they are not necessarily unhappy to see China more open and liberal in the future. However, they have no clear idea of how China will move into a more liberal society. The advantages as well as the disadvantages generated by a liberal image, including those in international affairs and associated with their historical position in the future, are somewhat contradictory and possibly impose a kind of tension in Chinese politics.

More specifically, they will tacitly carry on with this kind of attitude towards democratic trends as long as this does not lead to political risk and challenge. On the one hand, they continually, on formal political occasions and in official newspapers, assert the legitimacy of the ideology. On the other hand, they adopt a looser attitude towards the activities among the people. This can be regarded as a gesture of "touching stones to cross the river" in the political arena, following the one in the economic sector.

It is this contradictory mentality that has caused remaining ambiguity about where the line between political freedom and political control is. There is still a gray area between political control by the government and political freedom of the people. Without doubt, the gray area that emerged in the post-totalitarianism period is historically a step forward, as compared to the Maoist era in which the Chinese government imposed absolute control on society and the population's activities. This is an inevitable stage for post-totalitarianism in the long transition to democratic politics.

THE POLITICAL ATTITUDES OF THE PRESENT MAINSTREAM INTELLECTUALS

Before examining the people involved in the founding of the China Democratic Party, let us first look at the political situation of the mainstream intellectuals.

Basically, Chinese intellectuals in the first decade after the June Fourth Incident reflected a trend of secularisation (non-conviction) and moderation.

In fact, in the first decade after the June Fourth Incident, a rather clear social stratification took place among contemporary

Chinese intellectuals. As a whole, in the transition period from the planned economy to the one driven by the market, it became easier for intellectuals to "capitalise" on their knowledge to obtain such scarce social resources as wealth, fame, status, and power. Compared to other strata, they have constituted a stratum that benefits from the process of social differentiation. The majority of them hold a view that economic development under the present system not only benefits them but also facilitates progress for the whole nation. Besides, the secularisation driven by the market economy further dismantled the high political fervor and moral enthusiasm that appeared during the June Fourth period. They do realise that in the process of economic differentiation there is a considerable number of laid-off workers living in hardship and that the government is increasingly corrupt. They also realise that after entering the "deep water zone" of the reforms there is a group of lower class people who have increasingly intense conflicts with the political leaders. Nevertheless, intellectuals as a whole agree with the direction of the current policies and their criticism of social problems is no longer as great as in the 1980s. In fact, any foreigner who has a chance meeting with Chinese intellectuals would easily find that their social attitudes have drastically changed. Those intellectuals who, in the 1980s, were concerned about "the sounds of wind and rain and indeed everything" are fewer and fewer. On the other hand, tightened control of public opinion after the June Fourth Incident caused the intellectuals to lose their voice and interest in politics.

Essentially, based on the nature of the relationship, we can divide the intellectuals with close ties to politics into four categories.

The first category comprises those who agree with the current regime and who are absorbed by and directly serving the regime. They include those in the think tanks for the technocratic bureaucracy as well as those economists in colleges and research institutes who "like to write reports and proposals".

The second category is the "liberal-autocratic group" that contend to implement more liberal policies under the current regime. Included in this category are a considerably large number of intellectual-type entrepreneurs, professors and intellectuals in colleges, lawyers, engineers, and technicians, who became well-off financially. They have become rather independent economically and increasingly constitute part of the middle class. They have stayed outside of the political system and maintain relative autonomy in their own professions and academic fields. As a result of the economic benefits they have received, they hope China will democratise in future. However, due to the close ties they have with the present order and stability, they, whether consciously or not, are rather in agreement with the present policies. In fact, these intellectuals were of the radical groups of the June Fourth period. Ten years later, however, they became a new supporting base to the government.

The third category is composed of the liberal group that espouses democratisation from below. The ideal for them is the realisation of a democratic system in China. They express their political ideas mainly in academic discussions, talks, and writing, but do not translate them into political campaigns and movements. Unlike the previous groups, they are inclined to incremental and moderate progress to reform the political system and implement democracy. On the moral ground, they are critical of the corruption among the government officials. However, politically they are what can be called the "constitutionalism" group in China, which is indeed not much different from the previous "liberal-autocratic group."

The fourth category refers to the new socialists in colleges, which are called the "new leftist" intellectuals. They received and accepted the ideas of Western postmodernism and the economic theories of the Western "new left wing." They are disillusioned about the capitalist market economy in the West and thus criticise the problems and conflicts associated with the economic reform in China. They are more inclined to the leftists in Western Europe. They have strong criticism for economic polarisation and injustices arising with the economic reform. In newspapers they have harshly attacked the liberal group, which is the mainstream among intellectuals, for losing their spirit of criticism as intellectuals should have and for being a mouthpiece of the groups that benefit from the reform. Between these new leftists and the freedom group exist small-scale academic polemics that do not have much influence. The new leftists do not wish to participate directly in politics. As a whole they can be regarded as a group formed during the course of differentiation among the intellectuals and they do not influence the society.

To sum up, the advantage of having the knowledge to gain benefits from economic reform, as well as the secularisation and utilitarianism in the market economy, have caused the majority of intellectuals to become more politically moderate a decade after the June Fourth Incident. To varying degrees, they adopt an attitude that is cooperative with the government. As indicated previously in this chapter, the government's loosening of control towards the intellectuals has been mainly due to the leaders coming to realise the political moderation of the intellectuals. Though having different ideas and attitudes, the aforementioned intellectual categories do not constitute a political challenge to the ruling system.

In fact, during the two decades of the economic reform, we can notice considerably drastic changes in the relations between the government and the intellectuals and also in the measures of control by the former on the latter. In the period of totalitarianism, the government demanded that the intellectuals follow the party and system without condition. The leaders tried to make use of the ideology of totalitarianism to translate the intellectuals into the "new people" of socialism. However, in the period of post-authoritarianism or post-totalitarianism, the government no longer insisted that the intellectuals should, with any reservation, "listen to what the party says and follow where the party goes." Before the China Democratic Party Event took place, a kind of tacit understanding had already existed between the government and the mainstream intellectuals–as long as the intellectuals could behave themselves, did not translate their ideas into political demonstrations on the street, and did not challenge the present order and system, the government would tolerate and give more freedom to the intellectuals. With this, they hoped the government and the intellectuals could achieve a situation "with no conflict and fight" and that "the well water did not intervene into the river water."

Although there is a gap between the political goals of the current system and those of the intellectuals, they are not different in viewing the development of the market economy and the maintenance of the political order in the short- and mid-terms. Since the founding of the People's Republic of China, a new political trend has now emerged where the intellectuals and the government are mutually tolerant and inclusive.

How should we look at these new "game rules" formulated in the decade after the June Fourth Incident between the Chinese government and intellectuals? From one perspective, the mainstream intellectuals no longer pose an open and harsh challenge to the government, whether or not voluntarily, and this will undoubtedly give more room to the government to implement policies and even to maneuver should there be any failure in policies. In fact, according to the modern histories of many countries, the rapid expansion of the political participation of intellectuals has led to the collapse and disintegration of many traditional autocratic regimes.

From the foregoing analysis of the social situation and mentality of the mainstream intellectuals, we can essentially conclude that economic reform and social transformation have led to the moderation of the mainstream intellectuals. (To use to the words of the radical-liberal group, these intellectuals "have accepted amnesty".) The government, no longer facing tremendous pressure from the mainstream intellectuals and students as in the June Fourth Incident, has unconsciously loosened political control and brought about a relatively open political environment. Theoretically, the relatively open environment, social pluralism that emerges in the economic development, and continuous expansion of freedom of the people, will all possibly lead to a new compromise mechanism between intellectuals and the population on the one hand, and the government, on the other. These interactions, coupled with contract relations between different interest groups and social strata in economic development, are the social conditions for China to realise democracy in true sense. Under these conditions, the political transformation to democracy will gradually unfold. It is likely that China will, in this way, transit from totalitarianism to post-totalitarianism and on to a pre-pluralistic democratic period, and finally to a pluralistic democratic society with Chinese characteristics. There are a considerably large number of mainstream intellectuals who positively view the political pluralism and a multi-party system. However, they do not insist on implementing a multi-party system now as they realise the conditions are not yet mature. The changes in China in the last decade have caused them not to refute the implementation of a "liberal-autocratic regime." What they hope for is limited political reform, including the further monitoring of popular opinion on government.

THE RADICAL GROUPS AMONG THE MARGINAL INTELLECTUALS

However, in order for China to realise democracy through this incremental method, the fundamental condition is that social conflict does not become intense. When social conflicts become increasingly severe and mainstream intellectuals no longer challenge government authority, the marginal intellectuals will play a role as social critic and a mouthpiece of the masses, taking over as their voice from the mainstream intellectuals. Their social consciousnesses is increasingly provoked by government corruption, layoff problems, economic depression, deprivation of villagers by officials, decay in the judicial system, and social injustice. In addition, their inferior status and background cause their political participation and action to be more "revolutionary" and radical than the mainstream intellectuals.

From the viewpoint of these marginal intellectuals, they have a special social mission, which is to fill in the gap created by the mainstream intellectuals who voluntarily gave up their moral voice and monitoring system, which has led to negative social development. This social corruption and decay, as a result of the lack of monitoring system, are a kind of new trap of modernisation. From their viewpoint, the conflicts arise where "there is no one in the top level who can be trusted, and ones have to be tasked from the below." And from these conflicts, we can understand clearly the emergent new political power of the radical group in the mid-1998.

In fact, those participating in the founding of the China Democratic Party are not from the aforementioned mainstream intellectuals. Their existence has never drawn attention from the mainstream intellectuals, and they are totally excluded from the political and social mainstreams. Basically, they are marginal intellectuals somewhere between the mainstream intellectuals and labour. Based on the analysis of the activists in the founding of the China Democratic Party, we can draw a general picture about who they are and what they think.

First, activity scope. Basically, the dissenters in China can be divided into two groups. In the first group are those old democracy activists who lost their jobs and educational opportunities because of their participation in the June Fourth Incident, including Wang Youcai, Liu Lianjun, Zhao Xin, and Wang Linhai. The second group includes those middle-age workers with a considerably high educational level and experience of democracy movements. Fundamentally, there is not much of a relationship nor contact between the marginal and mainstream intellectuals. Almost none of the marginal intellectuals hold high positions, such as associate professor or assistant research fellow. The masses do not know about their activities. Before the China Democratic Party Event, most Chinese intellectuals and the general public had never heard of them. Even after the event and until now, their influence and activity scope are not large. They have long taken part in dissention and have been observed by the Security Department. Thus, some intellectuals and civilians, though knowing about them, try to keep their distance from them. The ordinary people are more concerned about their daily lives and thus do not contact them.

On the other hand, these marginal intellectuals know each other very well. They communicate with each other by telephone, fax machine and e-mail. Their interchanges and discussions transcend provinces, providing information and support to those dissenters detained by the Security Department. However, because they seldom contact people in other social strata, they are actually exclusive to others while constantly interacting among themselves. Where their activities are concerned, aside from distributing their own propaganda sheets on streets in different provinces, their main gestures include negotiations with the government. They made a request to the government to disseminate through the Internet the information about their attempt to found the China Democratic Party, with the hope of soliciting the support of foreign democracy activists. We can even say that their contacts with overseas democracy activists through the Internet are more intensive than those with the ones in China. Basically, they position themselves as political activists or political participants rather than scholarly intellectuals.

Second, political experience. Most are old democracy activists. Only Xu Wenli (in Beijing), who participated in the April Fifth Movement in 1979, was born in the 1940s. The majority of the rest were born in the 1960s and participated in the June Fourth Incident, including Wang Youcai (Zhejiang), Qin Yongmin (Hubei), Xie Wangjun and Liu Lianjun (Shandong). Almost none were born after the 1970s. As we know, in any period of social change, young people in their 20s are the most politically active and idealistic. But there are almost no college students among these dissenters. This middle-aging of the Chinese dissenters sends an important message about the depoliticisation and secularisation among the student strata.

Third, livelihood. Many were imprisoned because of the June Fourth Incident and, after being released, have no steady job and home. Many are living at the same level as the lower class. They have long remained in the lower class and their personal experiences and feelings are remarkably different from the ones of the mainstream intellectuals. The two decades of economic reform have led to a considerably clear division of interest in the political mentality between the radical group and the college intellectuals. Their adoption of harsh criticism against the present system is largely because of their experiences in the lower class and their radical thoughts of liberalism formed in the June Fourth period. This indicates well enough the relationship between the economic situation and the standing mentality.

Fourth, mentality. Basically, in their application to found the party, the reason they gave clearly reflects the ideas of Western democracy in the June Fourth period. Their criticism of the current political regime is derived from the ideas of the radical-liberal group in the June Fourth period. This is evident from an article by a dissenter on the Internet "From the Beijing University Students to the Wretched Era." This author says:

> After coming to power, the Chinese Communist Party thoroughly controlled individuals where economy, mentality, education, occupation, household registration system, and organisations were concerned. This resulted has in there not being any individuality in this society, let alone freedom of speech and thought.

This judgment is not consistent with the changes and developments in reality. The article totally ignores the fact that in the last two decades China has transited from an autocratic totalitarian society to one with a relative amount of freedom. According to the author, there was not much change between the post-Deng political realities and the ones two decades ago when the Cultural Revolution came to an end. Thus, this indicates that their thoughts still remain in the time ten years ago. For this author, the choice they should make is to carry on with the traditional philosophy of struggle and through the struggle force the "autocratic regime" to compromise. The article also demonstrates the feeling of solitude and moral superiority associated with the radical-liberal group, which thinks "themselves are the ones awake while the rest are drunk. His view is that "human beings cannot be like pigs whose purpose of living is to eat." He looks down on the mainstream intellectuals who benefited from the current system. For instance, he point out, "some friends advised me not to be concerned about politics and instead try to earn money. Those who say this include ordinary people, but some are the holders of doctoral and master degrees."

THE FOUNDING OF THE CHINA DEMOCRATIC PARTY

Basically, we can divide the China Democratic Party Event into three major phases.

The first phase began in June 1998 and lasted until September of the same year. It is the initial stage where a democracy activist in Zhejiang, Wang Youcai, launched the effort to found the party.

In the second phase, the activists in Shandong, Xie Wangjun and Liu Lianjun, submitted an application to the Shandong Civil Administration Department for the founding of the party. Subsequently accepted by the officials, this triggered other individual activities in 11 provinces throughout the country where dissenters attempted to establish parties.

The third phase began in early 1998. A dissenter in Beijing, Xu Wenli launched a preparatory committee of the China Democratic Party at the national level. This further radicalised the movement and led to the government's firm suppressing and punishing the three major activists for 10 to 13 years

First Phase, the Zhejiang Event

It is worth noting that there was reason for the dissenters to choose mid-1998 as a time to initiate the party founding movement. As discussed previously, since the second half of 1997, politics in China began loosening. Furthermore, some factors that emerged in mid-1998 caused the democracy activists to think that the conditions had become more sound and promising than before. For instance, in a speech released overseas after the event, Yao Zhenxian, an activist in Shanghai, said that according to their judgment:

> The Chinese Communist Party has declared that it will sign in this year 'The International Conventional Concerning the Civilian Rights and Political Rights.' In addiction, the American President will visit China in June for the first time since the June Fourth Incident. For sure, the Chinese Communist Party will give a loosening gesture.

Hence, in their view, this was exactly the right time for them to found the party. Moreover, they thought, given the relative social stability in the country in 1998, the tolerance the Chinese Communist Party will have towards an opposition party should be higher. To use their words, "As long as (they) show that (they) are moderate and mild, do not give challenging comments that cater to the outside media and organisations, or do not have blatantly aggressive actions," they thought that they would not receive harsh suppression from the government.

On 25 June 1998, dissenters in Zhejiang, Wang Youcai, Wang Donghai, and Lin Hui, submitted to the Zhejiang Civil Adminstration Department "An Open Announcement of the Founding of the Zhejiang Preparatory Committee of China Democratic Party" an application for the founding of the party. In the application it was stated that the objective of the founding was to "realise the direct democratic election, construct constitutional democratic regime and shared power mechanism."

For the first time since the founding of the People's Republic of China, the dissenters made an open application to establish an opposition party and politically challenge the current regime. It was not until 10 July, after Clinton left China, that Wang Youcai was arrested. The democracy activists within and outside of China released an announcement and raised objections with the hope of getting international response. Fifty days after the arrest, on 30 August, Wang Youcai was released. This shows that the government's attitude towards this kind of incidents was much more self-controlled, compared to that of the Maoist era. In recent years, in handling the dissenters in the country, the government has adopted a method of "short term imprisonment." The dissenters in the country have been familiar enough with this method of "arrest and release, then arrest and release again." Clinton's visit to China only constituted an external factor to the controlled attitude of the Chinese government.

Second Phase, the Shandong Incident

On 5 September, before the Senior Official of Human Rights Affairs in the United Nations, Madam Robinson, visited China, three dissenters in Shandong, Xie Wangjun, Liu Lianjun, and Jiang Fuzhen, declared the founding of the Shandong Preparatory Committee of the China Democratic Party. They sent by post the declaration of the founding of the party and the application of the founding to the Shandong Civil Administration Department. In the application, they demonstrated a moderate strategy the same as that of Wang Youcai in Zhejiang. They stated,

> Considering the unique political and social realities in China, and also considering that China has to depend on laws and stability before she can smoothly realise the political and social reforms, we promise that, after the founding of Shandong Preparatory Committee of the China Democratic Party has been approved, we will support the Chairman Jiang Zemin as the leader of the country. We will also, in the period the political reform in China, recognise the Chinese Communist Party as the ruling party. The Shandong Preparatory Committee of the China Democratic Party will act as a party not in office and monitor as well as constrain the ruling party. We will also, within the scope allowed by the Constitution and laws, take part in political and social activities.

They thought that the wording they used would allow no excuse for the government, which had prepared to sign two international conventions concerning human rights, to outlaw them.

Surprisingly, the response from the Shandong Civil Administration Department was more moderate than the activists originally had expected. According to the recollection of the activists on the Internet, five days after Xie Wangjun sent out the letter, two officials of the Civil Administration formally received the activists. They explained that, according to the laws of social organisations, founding an organisation required four conditions–having $50,000 registration capital; declaring the office site; declaring the background of members of the level above the assistant secretary; and declaring that the organisation had more than 50 members. The activists in Shandong quickly disseminated through telex this news as "A Major Breakthrough! The Chinese Government Lifted the Party Ban!" and "A Better Turn for the Party Founding Attempt in Shandong!" After the news was spread, one after another the preparatory committees in different places submitted their applications. However, the Civil Administration Department in different places had different reactions and ways of handling of the cases. The activists in others places did not receive treatment as good as their counterparts in Shandong.

How to view the message from the Shandong Civil Administration Department? Actually, the Shandong Incident can be seen as an individual case. In my opinion, the officials in the Shandong Civil Administration Department, whether consciously or not, had linked the application to Jiang Zemin's promise to sign "International Convention Concerning Civil Rights and Political Rights." Though the department was criticised by the central government after the incident, this shows that the central government has no clear and fixed rules in this regard. As analysed previously, in the development of post-totalitarianism, there is a "gray area" where the central and local governments handle this kind of case. As a result of the loosened political control since 1997, coupled with the new development and the government's open attitude, some of the local government officials used their own interpretations to handle these cases. Not long afterwards, the local Public Security Department arrested Liu Lianjun and Xie Wangjun respectively with the accusation of "distorting social order." However, they were released some ten days later. By mid-October, all 13 activists in Shandong were released. This indicates that the Chinese government did not wish the incident to affect the open image it had established. Thus, the government did not want to change its self-controlled actions against and ambiguity towards the dissenters.

That the Shandong activists were received formally was a pleasant surprise to the domestic dissenters. They thus felt no more fear. In the short period afterwards, they received further encouragement by the radical groups from the overseas democracy activists. One after another activists in 11 provinces founded their own provincial level preparatory committees of the China Democratic Party. A number of the overseas activists also established "overseas offices of the China Democratic Party," with the hope of forging linkages with their counterparts in China. Wang Bingzhang, who was more radical than Wei Jingsheng, made an announcement overseas that openly applauded that the Chinese Democratic Party was "holding a red flag against a red flag," and "seized the right opportunity, environment, and people." This illustrated the interactions between the most radical groups overseas and the activists who attempted to found the China Democratic Party in China. These two forces were the most active in pushing the political trends in October 1998.

On the political stage, none of the moderate mainstream intellectuals took part in the event. Some came to know about it through information from the Internet and were not concerned about it. On the other hand, the majority of the overseas democracy activists still remained cautious and moderate. They gave their opinions, with much reservation, on the Internet. According to them, the conditions were not mature enough for the founding of the party in China. Giving the example of democratisation in Taiwan, they thought that only after the realisation of freedom of the press was the party founding possible. However, due to their stand as democratic groups, they had to give their moral support to the activities of party founding in China. Otherwise, the radical group would criticise them as "liking dragon the way Mr Ye does," and "giving up the stand of liberalism." In a month or two after October 1998, there seems have been some small fights between the Chinese government and the radical democracy activists both in and outside of China. The other political forces either kept a distance from or did not fully take part in the event.

Third Phase, Xu Wenli's Radical Activities

While Wang Youcai (Zhejiang), Xie Wangjun and Liu Lianjun (Shandong) maintained a moderate tone, Xu Wenli, an old activist in Beijing who perceived himself to be a leading figure in the democratic movement in China, marked a turning point that the China Democratic Party Event finally lost control and became radical.

Xu Wenli was the key figure in the event. He took part in the democratic movement in Beijing from 1978 to 1979. A professional democracy activist, he had conflicts with Ren Wanding and Wei Jingsheng. This is commonly known among the circle of the activists. As a matter of fact, Xu was not radical at all in the beginning. After the incidents of party founding took place in Zhejiang, Shandong and Northeast China, Wang Youcai and the rest telephoned him to invite him to found a party in Beijing. He once said that the time was not yet mature for the party formation and intended to take action slowly. However, when Ren Wanding, a "rival to his position as a leader in democratic movement," started preparing to found a "Beijing Preparatory Committee for Beijing Democratic Party," he changed his mind. On 6 November 1998, he suddenly declared the founding of "The Preparatory Work Team for National Congress of China Democracy Party." Besides, he also founded a "branch in the Beijing and Tianjin areas," trying to show that this was a "formal organisation" which, unlike other preparatory committees elsewhere, needed no approval from the government. He even successfully persuaded Qin Yongmin, an activist in Hubei, who subsequently established formally the "Hubei Branch of the China Democratic Party," dropping the name of the "Hubei Preparatory Committee."

More radically, in the proclamation of "The Preparatory Work Team for National Congress," Xu further announced that the party would gradually establish its own institutions of nation, religion, and Taiwan affairs, as well as research institutes on the national defense strategies. This demonstrated its wish to be the future ruling party. Also, shockingly, the proclamation openly welcomed the return of the democracy activists now exiled overseas, including Wang Bingzhang, Wang Dan, Wang Xizhe, Wei Jingsheng, Yan Jiaqi, Fang Lizhi, Liu Qing, as well as some wanted by the government, to become the leaders and advisors of the preparatory committee. This shows that he totally neglected the government which banned the exiles from coming back.

Few could understand the quick change of Xu Wenli. According to the public opinion in Hong Kong, this has to do with Xu's strong speculative mentality and expansive desire for power. On 27 November 1998, one of the Hong Kong newspaper headings was "Xu Wenli in Fight with Ren Wanding to be the Leader of the China Democratic Party." Besides, Ren also stated "Xu Wenli was overly pursuing power." For this, over the phone Xu fought back that Ren Wanding showed his "action as a weak" in saying that he would not found the party after being suppressed by the government. It appeared that, once the activities of party founding were initiated, internal conflicts quickly took place among the activists.

The active participation of overseas radical anticommunist activists, such as Wang Bingzhang, was the crucial factor that eventually led to the Chinese government's firm suppression. These overseas "hardcore activists" attempted, through various means, to influence the democratic movements in China and create mutually responding and supporting linkages between the people concerned in and outside of China. Though the moderate groups in the founding of the China Democratic Party did not wish the overseas activists to intervene, this was actually inevitable. This is because the overseas radical groups have always utilised all opportunities to influence the domestic democratic movements, in order to prove their existence and highlight their status as the "democracy fighter". There is nothing more important than this for them. According to them, the government suppression caused by their intervention precisely reflects their stand which has been correct all the time.

THE REASONS FOR THE GOVERNMENT HARD-LINE POLICIES AND ITS "LIMITED RESPONSE" MODEL

Apparently, Xu Wenli's took radical steps beyond the freedom scope originally formed between the government and the democracy activists. Without doubt, this upset the Chinese leaders who eventually changed the way they had been handling the transgressive democracy activists in recent years. Instead of "arrest and release, then arrest and release again," the government now made up its mind to resume a hard-line attitude.

There are other reasons behind the government's shift to tough measures. Politically, for the Chinese leaders, 1999 was a year fraught with "political hotspots and difficult points." These included the 80th Anniversary of the May Fourth Movement, the 10th Anniversary of the June Fourth Movement, the 50th Anniversary of the Founding of the People's Republic of China, and the return of Macau. All these activities could potentially provide opportunities for the democracy activists to initiate their movement and struggle that might trigger political upheaval. Moreover, taking advantage of the 10th Anniversary of the June Fourth Incident, the overseas democracy activists launched a signature campaign of a million people imposing pressure on the government to redress the June Fourth Incident. Undoubtedly this would further reinforce the democracy movements within China.

Where the Chinese society itself is concerned, the increased numbers of laid-off workers, the economic depression, employment disputes, and conflicts between the people and government still went on. From the viewpoint of the government, the activists of the China Democratic Party would make use of these factors and incite social unrest. What made the government worried most was whether the radical democracy activists would converge with the populace on the issue of bureaucratic corruption. According to the government, if suppression was done slowly, there would be a tendency for forces to combine within and outside of China.

On 21 December 1998, the same day Jiang Zemin returned from his visit to Russia, Xinhua New Agency published Li Peng's talk in an interview by foreign reporters. Li asserted, "An opposition party was totally not allowed." This became an indicator of the Chinese government's new shift to tightened political control. On 18 December, in the "20th Anniversary of the Third Plenary Session of the Eleventh Central Committee," Jiang officially announced a new policy that "the government has to be fully cautious about the intervention as well as the subversive and separatist activities of the rival forces within and outside the country, and have to resolutely annihilate them right from their embryonic stage." This was the hardest voice towards dissenters by the government heard in a year and a half.

By the end of 1998, the government smashed the activists who took part in the founding of the "China Democratic Party." It further tightened its control on news and publications and took up other restrictive measures. In the New Year Tea Meeting, Jiang Zemin specially announced that they "would pay particular attention to the destructive activities by the rival forces within and outside of China so as to secure the political and social stability." This set the tone of tightened political control for the coming year.

It is worth nothing that the way the Chinese government handled the Chinese Democratic Party Event still reflected what we can call a "limited response" model. The major features are as follows:

From the newspaper reports and the words used for the punishment upon Xu Wenli and the rest, it did not clearly use ideological language (such as socialism, the communist leadership, proletarian dictatorship, and Marxism) to state the political reasons for the suppression. More specifically, the government explained the event as destructing political stability and domestic security. This, compared to the explanation using revolutionary language, was much more moderate.

Meanwhile, the government did not carry out massive arrests of democracy activists. It should be pointed out specifically that such key figures as Xie Wanjun and Liu Lianjun (Shandong) and Ren Wanding (Beijing) were not prosecuted. With this, the government showed its differentiation among those participating in the event. Later on, the activists still carried out their activities underground, some even with the name of "The Preparatory Committee of the China Democratic Party".

By treating it as an individual case, the Chinese government tried to minimise the social implications of the event. The newspaper coverage of the event only occupied the less important column of the second page, with limited text. It emphasised that the tried were "those who re-breached the laws." There was no follow-up report afterwards, clearly showing the government's intention to handle the cases in as low-key a way as possible in order to avoid any chain response. Meanwhile, the government released Liu Nianchun, a democracy activist who was originally imprisoned, and allowed him to go with his family to the United States with the reason of "receiving medical treatment overseas." This was to reduce the negative implications on the communities in and outside of China about its authoritative handling of the case. Apparently, the government attempted to minimise as much as possible the psychological impact on the intellectuals and did not want it to be seen as a crucial turning point of the government policies.

We can reconfirm the "limited response model" from the recent talk by Jiang Zemin in the early 1999. Reported in all newspapers in China, "Jiang Zemin's talk in the National Meeting of Propaganda Ministers, 21 January" demonstrates the government's new policies after the "China Democratic Party." Generally speaking, the key message contained in the talk was to remind officials at all levels that "1999 will witness many great events and happy events, many difficult points and hotspots, thus requiring much heavier task to secure the stability in order to carry out the reform." It also asked "the compatriots in the propaganda lines to strengthen three major consciousnesses–of politics, of the whole situation, and of the responsibilities." It said:

> We must continue to sing the theme melody and bear in mind the whole situation. We must firmly control the correct direction of the public opinion. We must be clear about the things not right and with the calculation in our mind deal with them cool-headedly. We must not make hot the incorrect things and especially must not let them interrupt the whole situation of the country. On the issues pertaining to the principles, we must have a clear flag and idea about the correct and the wrong. We cannot let go the flows they way they are. We must pay particular attention to maintain the social and political stability." And,
>
> "We must comply with the political discipline and propaganda discipline. We must control those that need to be controlled. We must control rightly the field of propaganda and the means of propaganda. We cannot let the problem happen. We must maintain the unity, the whole situation, and stability. We must not pursue sensational effect.

How do we decipher the core meaning of these messages? For the things that need to be opposed, previously the government used such political ideas as "liberalisation of the bourgeoisie." This time, Jiang Zemin instead used less provocative and used such ambiguous ideas as "incorrect things." More specifically, everyone knew what Jiang was pointing to, but they were not clearly indicated so as to avoid "unnecessary polemics", which would disrupt the whole situation. It is worth noting that Jiang requested the propaganda departments at all levels not to "pursue sensational effect" and "make hot the incorrect things." This indicates a continuity of Deng Xiaoping's principle of "no polemic" and that Jiang follows the line attempting to avoid open ideological conflict with the political opposition. The ultimate objective was to prevent a chain reaction in society would affect political stability. This policy clearly indicates a shift from the principle based on revolutionary ideology and the model of "thorough attack" against political enemies. Now the government moved to the post-totalitarianism era with security as its utmost goal and adopted the model of "self-defense attack". This "limited response model" remarkably sets the post-totalitarianism era apart from the totalitarianism era.

In addition, the new policy showed that the government did not change much because of the China Democratic Party Event. There was still a limitation of the degree of the response, giving more space for the government to re-implement an open policy in the future when political stability was secure.

The model of handling the China Democratic Party Event was adopted at a time when there was no intervention from the revolutionary senior statesmen and no pressure from the old leftist officials. This basically reflects the essential features of the post-Deng political regime.

PREDICTIONS ABOUT POLITICAL INTERACTIONS UNDER THE "LIMITED RESPONSE MODEL"

Based on the foregoing discussion, in the foreseeable future, the political control and interactions in China's post-totalitarian society will demonstrate new models and features as follows.

The mainstream intellectuals have been basically a group benefiting from social differentiation. The secularisation, that is, not being fervent in ideology, to some extent has caused the intellectuals unconsciously to no longer take up responsibilities as value guardian and social critic. They will no longer mobilise the lower class to political activities against the current regime. Thus, in the mid- and long-term, it is unlikely to see any massive political opposition activity as in the June Fourth period, with widespread interaction, between the intellectuals and the populace.

The liberal group among the mainstream intellectuals is a moderate constitutionalist group, advocating the incremental realisation of democracy through reforming the institution of the People's Congress. (This kind of constitutionalism is in a way similar to the constitutionalist gentry group in the period of the implementation of liberal autocracy in the late Qing dynasty). This is because the constitutional reform under liberal autocracy will best protect their interests during the course of incrementally achieving democracy. As the aforementioned intellectuals have benefited from the market economy, they, as compared to those involved in the June Fourth period, have more in common with the government. Thus, the current political stability of the post-totalitarian era can be maintained.

Economically and politically disadvantaged, the liberal radical group among the marginal intellectuals will from time to time seize any opportunity to criticise the current political order and take over the mainstream intellectuals as leading and proactive critics. However, due to their limited numbers and influence, they are more easily controlled by the local public security departments. As they are conducting activities individually among themselves and not forming an authoritative leading and cohesive force, they will not achieve social influence as in the June Fourth period.

From the China Democratic Party Event, we can observe the radical propensity that can be generated among the marginal intellectuals. Influenced by various factors, a certain number of "professional revolutionaries" would lose their political self-control and easily lead the democracy movements in the populace to being radical. In order to expand their personal power, they would interpret their impractical political devices as an outgrowth of their "spirit of struggle" and "uncompromising attitude". Through this, they would highlight their voice as superior to that of their rivals. In this situation, the more radical one is, the more that one must exercise some "language hegemony" across the groups struggling for democracy. In contrast, in activities conducted among the general population, there have not been any such restrictions placed among themselves.

If there would be a spilt between the radical and moderate groups among the marginal intellectuals, then there would also be such a split among the groups overseas concerning the views on the situation in China. The overseas moderate group, which is more pragmatic, will voice cautious doubt and criticism concerning the potential repercussions of the actions taken by the domestic radical group. However, because each is acting individually, neither group will breed influence. On the other hand, the overseas radical group, because of controlling the high key "language superiority," will get hold of the initiative power. Their intervention will cause the government to adopt a harder stance. Thus, the combination of overseas intervention and being radical always leads to the government suppressing the political activities of the marginal intellectuals. The political tightening will defer incremental liberalisation and loosening of control that started to emerge some time ago. This kind of interaction will go on in the long-term.

However, the socioeconomic development and secularisation will still continue. With the moderate attitude of the populace and further political requests for liberalisation, and under the international macro environment, the aforementioned factors will function again to nurture political liberalisation. The new loosening will re-emerge. In the early 21st century, China will, in this recurrent process, gradually move into a new era that is politically more open and free.

THE ACTION BOUNDARIES OF THE CHINESE GOVERNMENT'S AUTHORITARIANISM FROM THE PERSPECTIVE OF POST-TOTALITARIANISM

While the departure of the former Soviet Union and East Europe countries from totalitarianism was realised through drastic and radical internal "explosions" and collapse, China demonstrates a totally new transition model. In the new model, China has, since the June Fourth Incident, realised limited non-political pluralism through the development of a market economy. We can call this transition model "post-totalitarianism," with which China and Vietnam are associated. The post-totalitarian regime as a result of the model is unprecedented in history.

The post-totalitarian regime has two features. First, it inherits the legacy of the totalitarian regime concerning social control, which is manifested in a strong public security system, the bureaucracy system, a mechanism assuring the implementation of political order from top to bottom, the control of media and propaganda, and so forth. Second, different from the totalitarian era, the post-totalitarian era witnesses the retreat of the leftist ideological force and revolutionary senior statesmen, constituting not much pressure on the technocratic political leaders. In the socio-economic sector emerged a pluralistic structure of a quasi-citizen society and a new mentality of citizen, which generally is not concerned much about political affairs. As discussed previously, Chinese intellectuals as a whole have become more politically moderate. Thus, the leaders face less pressure and challenges from the populace and intellectuals that were once strong in the June Fourth period.

As a result, the political science studies on the social structure of the Chinese post-totalitarian regime are a totally novel field. (The "post-totalitarian regime" discussed here is different from the concepts of post-totalitarianism held by Vaclav Havel. The latter refers to the East Europe countries after the death of Stalin where the societies were relatively close economically and open politically).

As discussed previously, without political challenge and a sense of crisis, the Chinese leaders of the post-totalitarian regime are likely to develop into openness. Meanwhile, the Chinese government will be more active in establishing a liberal image on the international political stage in order to lessen foreign political pressure and achieve international security. In order to secure China's position in international politics, the government will demonstrate flexibility with regard to human rights and domestic policies. The decision to sign two international conventions concerning human rights in mid-1998 precisely reflects the government's attitude towards moving into openness.

This, however, does not necessarily mean that, regardless of what situation it is, the Chinese leaders in the post-totalitarian era will always be open and lessen social control. The government is still fragile and unstable to bear all kinds of political challenges. Sensitive issues include requests from opposition forces for liberalisation and democracy, as well as the potential participation of the populace in making such requests. This is why the leaders are in a dilemma.

Given the dilemma, the behaviour of the Chinese leadership will demonstrate the following features. On the one hand, as discussed previously, when the situation becomes milder and the economy develops more smoothly, the leaders will display a certain degree of openness and tolerance. As analysed previously, on the issue of the China Democracy Party Event, the leadership revealed considerable tolerance and self-control unprecedented in the history of the Chinese Communist Party.

When the leadership subjectively thinks that there are more socially destabilising factors, the leaders will further tighten political control. Subsequently, they can easily make use of the legacy from the totalitarian regime and mobilise the whole security system, including measures controlling ideological propaganda.

On the other hand, the political tightening only constitutes an immediate "limited response," which does not have much scope nor time to implement. This is because the government has to take into consideration the international and domestic situations confronting the post-totalitarian regime. Besides, the leftist ideology is losing its hold and democracy is becoming a strong language in China as well as the international arena, setting an important standard by which the Chinese people evaluate the government in the 21st century. In fact, the limited scope and time of the response model reflects its lack of support of revolutionary ideological conviction and language. It also indicates that the era in which politics were controlled by ideology is now gone.

In the long term, Chinese leaders will adopt the "limited response model" to handle the complicated questions posed by political opposition forces. This shows that Chinese politics will not go backwards and return to the post-totalitarian era. Nor will the government sacrifice its political security and abandon its authoritative way of dealing with opposition groups. China in the early 21st century will witness the cycles of political loosening and tightening. It is only under the condition that civilian society achieves a certain degree of development that China will attain democracy through an incremental process. And this is going to be a long way.

ENDNOTE

1 Translated from the author's writing "Cong 'Zhongguo Minzudang' zudang shijian kan hou Deng shidai Zhongguo de zhengzhi zouxiang," *EAI Working Paper* (Chinese Series), No. 37, 21 January 2002. The author was a visiting research fellow at the East Asian Institute, National University of Singapore. He obtained his master's degree from Nanjing University in 1981 and is currently history professor in Shanghai Shifang University. Among the positions he holds are permanent committee member of the China Youth Studies Society, permanent committee member of China Society of State-Owned Enterprise Studies, and committee member of the Shanghai Federation of Social Sciences.

CHAPTER 14

Rule by Virtue: Jiang Zemin's Revival of the Party's Ideology

ZHENG YONGNIAN AND LAI HONGYI

JIANG'S IDEOLOGICAL PLATFORM

In February 2000, Jiang Zemin raised a new concept called the "three represents" (*sange daibiao*) when he visited Guangdong. According to this concept, the Chinese Communist Party (CCP) represents the most advanced mode of production, the most advanced culture, and the interests of the majority of the people[1] A year later, on 11 January 2001, at a meeting with officials in charge of propaganda, Jiang highlighted the concept of "rule by virtue" (*yide zhiguo*), which he had raised earlier. He apparently wanted the CCP to govern the country by combining the rule of law (*yifa zhiguo*) with the rule by virtue. While the CCP should make establishing the rule of law its priority, promoting the rule by virtue, he stated, could greatly enhance the rule of law.[2]

Even though Jiang Zemin had not fully explained his theory of the rule by virtue, it has attracted a great deal of attention. Many speculate that he was trying to revive old Confucian teachings in order to unify a populace that had become disillusioned with communism and was indulging in Western individualism. Soon after Jiang's talk, the CCP propaganda machines made strenuous efforts to spread the concept of rule by virtue among party cadres and government officials. On 1 February 2001, *People's Daily*, the party's mouthpiece, published an editorial pointing out that in order to build a market economy, it was necessary to promote the rule by virtue while developing the rule of law.[3]

Rule by virtue is inherent in the Chinese Confucian tradition. Confucians believed that a ruler has to be educated in Confucian virtues before he can be a legitimate ruler; the ruler should be, first of all, morally superior to his subjects and his primary role is to be a role model for the subjects to follow. The legalists, on the other hand, favoured the rule by law. Out of their conviction of the wickedness of human nature, they argued that a strong legal system should be established to deter people from doing evil. In reality, Chinese emperors governed by using a combination of the rule by law and the rule by virtue.

What is Jiang Zemin trying to achieve by reviving the concept of the rule by virtue? According to Liu Ji, a senior aide to Jiang and former deputy chairman of the Chinese Academy of Social Sciences, China should draw on its 5,000-year civilisation to guide its use of moral values to complement the legal system. A country that is solely governed by law can be unhealthy. Law must be complemented by moral values, human feelings and family concerns. Liu argued that if individualism, albeit permitted by law, went too far, it would become a cancer in society; and that China should not repeat the mistakes made by the West. Hence, communitarianism, not individualism, is more suitable for China.[4]

Rule by virtue has been controversial for centuries. Why did Jiang Zemin raise this concept now, especially during this period of power transition? Does he really believe in Confucianism? Does the CCP want to revive the Confucianism that it tried to destroy in the past several decades?[5] Will such an emphasis give rise to a distinctively Chinese version of socialism, i.e., Confucian socialism? Simply put, what is the political rationale for Jiang's new emphasis on virtue?

IDEOLOGICAL DECLINE AND MORAL CRISIS

In calling for rule by virtue, Jiang has tried to revive the declining ideology of the CCP in order to cope with a consequent moral crisis. Ideology and organisation have been the two pillars of the CCP. Ideology clarifies the party's mission, justifies the party's control and policies, and provides party cadres guidance in implementing policies and a sense of identity. This in turn aids party leaders in shaping the minds and behaviour of party members and political activists.[6]

In Mao's China, the official ideology consisted of Maoism and orthodox Marxist denunciations of capitalism. Maoism emphasised political correctness and public ownership. Orthodox Marxism upheld economic planning and public ownership and rejected capitalism and private ownership. What Mao Zedong achieved was tight political control, but a backward economy.

The decline of Maoist ideology was inevitable after Deng Xiaoping came back to power in the late 1970s. Guided by pragmatism, Deng downplayed the role of ideology, weakened the ideological controls of Maoism and orthodox Marxism, and encouraged officials and the people to experiment with reform initiatives. In 1978, he oversaw an ideological movement that refuted Maoism. This was the so-called first wave of mind-emancipation that undergirded China's economic reforms in the 1980s.

In the aftermath of the crackdown on the pro-democracy movement in 1989, China was caught in a heated debate about whether the country's development should be capitalistic or socialistic. Economic growth was again constrained by the revival of leftist ideology as well as economic sanctions imposed by the West. The leadership was ineffective in dealing with slower economic growth.

In response, 88-year-old Deng Xiaoping made a high-profile tour to southern China, i.e., his celebrated Nanxun, and initiated a second wave of mind-emancipation.[7] He put an end to the Mr. *Zi* vs. Mr. *She* (capitalism vs. socialism) debate. In order to achieve rapid economic development without being bogged down by ideology, Deng proposed the "no-debate" policy so that the party could focus on economic reforms. This was accepted by the top leadership.

Deng's de-ideologisation in the 1980s and 1990s fostered an atmosphere conducive to economic development. Despite several policy setbacks, including the Tiananmen Event, reformists eventually triumphed over conservatives in the party in the early 1990s. The party, cadres and the population were free to experiment with reform and embrace the market economy. And, without a public forum, orthodox and liberal ideologies lost their wide appeal, and the CCP was freed of any immediate ideological challenge.

However, the de-ideologisation did negatively affect the party and country. Many party members no longer accepted the ideological mission of the party as the vanguard of the working classes. Instead, they began to embrace a variety of alternative ideologies, including materialism, old and new leftism, Western liberalism, nationalism, religions, and cults.

For old leftists, the declining role of the state firms in the economy had weakened the CCP leadership. The new leftists, on the other hand, are concerned about the rise of bureaucratic capitalism and are calling for political democracy in the form of Mao's mass participation and redistribution of wealth to achieve social justice.[8] The liberals, on their part, support a multi-party system and inter-party competition.

Cults, such as Falun Gong, instill fear about doomsday and preach the need to faithfully follow superstitious beliefs in supernatural abilities and mystic self-cultivation. Despite the party's prohibiting party members from believing in religion, which it views as spiritual opium, 7 percent of regular members and 46 percent of the leading organisers of the Falun Gong movement in Shandong Province in the 1990s were party members.[9] After the movement was officially banned in July 1999, ideological cleansing of the party became especially urgent.

Without an ideological tool, the party's control over its members has been weakened, resulting in widespread abuse of power and corruption by party cadres which has severely undermined the party's legitimacy. The abuse of power has tyrannised the populace, and corruption has ranged from accepting monetary bribes or sexual favours to embezzlement and misappropriation of official funds.

In 1995, the year that Jiang started his ideological revival, the procuratorial organ in China investigated 2,153 officials at the county level and above for possible corruption crimes. This was up 27 percent from the previous year, and constituted the largest increase since the CCP came to power.[10] In that year, Chen Xitong and Wang Bosen, the Mayor and Vice Mayor of Beijing, were investigated for corruption. Wang committed suicide, and Chen was jailed.[11] By the late 1990s the situation had worsened. Corruption had infected officials from the top to the lowest levels, and the amount of money involved had soared from millions to billions of yuan. In addition, the variety of corruption broadened to bribes for promotion, sales of offices, promises of promotion in exchange for subordinates' support, exaggeration of performance, and deceiving the party's investigators of corruption.

Without an ideology, the party can no longer provide spiritual guidance for the population. Ideological decay and official moral laxity have taken their toll on professional and business ethics, resulting in shoddy, even deadly, products (such as poisonous wine) and deceitful financial schemes.

The party also has difficulty representing its traditional constituents as well as new classes. With the moral standing of the party cadres deteriorating, the party has lost its influence among its traditional constituents, namely, the workers and peasants. In recent years, new elites, including white-collar professionals at the non-state firms, private entrepreneurs, pop artists, etc, have emerged. However, according to its orthodox mission, the party is a vanguard of the workers and peasants, and the new elites are not allowed to join the party. Thus, the party has no influence or control over these new elites.

How should the party cope with the fallout arising from the ideological decline? There is no consensus among top leaders, though undoubtedly each has searched for a solution. Qiao Shi proposed the rule of law and political transparency. His proposal soon gained popularity within the party. In 1994, during the Second Session of the Eighth National People's Congress (NPC), 54 intellectual dissidents from Shanghai called on the NPC to speed up political reform. Qiao Shi, the head of the legislature, stressed on the role of democratic politics in his concluding speech at the session.[12] At the closing ceremony of the annual session of the NPC in March 1996, he formally proposed to "rule the country in accordance with law, and build a legally institutionalised socialist country." In an interview with a US columnist in December 1996, he stated that though the

NPC worked under the party's leadership, all party members needed to abide by the laws passed by the NPC.[13] He believed that many of the problems the party had encountered resulted from the fact that the party had stood above the law, and if it wanted to govern the country effectively, it itself had to first obey the law.

In 1995, Li Ruihuan, chairman of the conference of various satellite parties, stated plainly in his concluding speech at the Third Session of the Eighth Chinese People's Political Consultative Conference (CPPCC) that the CCP should confront popular discontent and remedy any defects in its work.[14] In 1996, he pushed the satellite parties to provide the CCP with practical help and consultation.[15]

Both Qiao and Li had served longer in the Political Bureau than Jiang, and were regarded as his potential challengers. Their calls for moderate political reform would not only strengthen the institutions they headed, but also diminish Jiang's power. To respond to a crippled ideology, and to thwart the challenges of his rivals, Jiang Zemin had to take new initiatives.

REVIVING MORAL ORDER BY RECONSTRUCTING IDEOLOGY

Jiang has made numerous attempts, on the one hand, to strengthen his leadership and weaken his political rivals, and, on the other, to combat the problems plaguing the party and to resurrect the ailing party. The call for a return to ideology and moral values has become the single most important means for Jiang to achieve his goals. Nevertheless, for Jiang, the ride has not always been smooth, and he has to proceed by trial and error.

From "Talking about Politics" to "Three Talks"

In 1995, Jiang initiated the "talking about politics" (*jiang zhengzhi*) notion in response to Qiao Shi's concept of the rule of law. At a meeting held in advance of the Fifth Plenum of the 14th Party Congress in September 1995, Jiang asked senior officials, including provincial party secretaries, governors, ministers, members of the CCP Central Committee, and members of the Political Bureau, to talk about politics. He called on them to be serious about political direction and to exercise political discipline, discretion, and sensitivity. He reminded them not to deviate from the party's aim of serving the people, and requested them not to attend night clubs or ballrooms. He declared that the party should concurrently carry out economic and ideological work.[16] In January 1996 his "talk-about-politics" speech was front page news in the government-run newspapers and party journals, attracting much attention.[17]

In March 1996, Jiang again urged the leading cadres to talk about (or stress) politics, virtue, and political studies, termed the "three talks" (*san jiang*). He criticised the then single-minded attention to economic construction, and tried to correct any misunderstanding about the "three talks" by declaring that they were designed to support, rather than replace, modernisation as the core of the party's politics. The "three talks" speech was published in the *Qiu Shi*, the party flagship organ, and set the tone for the party's ideological work until 1999.

By launching the "talk politics" and "three talks" campaigns, Jiang managed to consolidate his authority among the senior party cadres and the military. As the military newspapers took the lead in popularising the "three talks" campaign, Jiang's position within the military appeared to be established. Nevertheless, middle- and low-level party cadres viewed these campaigns as outdated Mao-style slogans, and were not enthusiastic about them. While senior officials acknowledged Jiang's leading role in formulating the party's ideology, few took up his ideas.

From "Three Represents" to "Rule of Law and by Virtue"

On his tour to Guangdong in February 2000, Jiang proposed the "three represents" (*sange daibiao*), meaning that the CCP represents the most advanced mode of production, the most advanced culture, and the interests of the majority of the people. He asked party members and leading cadres to use these "three represents" to guide their thought and behaviour. While conceding there were many problems plaguing the party members' outlook, organisation, and work attitude, Jiang called on the party committees at various levels to rebuild the party.

During the tour, Jiang also began to assert that the rule by virtue and the rule of law should be promoted hand-in-hand in reaffirming the Party's ethos and honest politics. By emphasising the rule by virtue, he wanted to indoctrinate the party members and cadres with a new set of proper work styles, such as working hard and in a down-to-earth manner, living plainly, maintaining a good reputation, sacrificing self-interest for the public good, and serving the people. Through virtues education, he believed that the quality and spirit of the cadres could be improved, and violation of laws and party discipline could be reduced. By the rule of law, he meant reducing legal loopholes, punishing criminals and violators of the party's rule, and thereby educating the party members and the populace of the "right" norms.[18]

Increasingly, Jiang has focused on rule by virtue. At a talk with the heads of the country's propaganda departments in January 2001, Jiang reaffirmed and explained in detail his notion of rule both by virtue and law. He stated that the party, in the course of building a socialist market economy, should strengthen the construction of both a socialist legal system and socialist morality. He argued that the rule of law and the rule by virtue should complement each other, receive equal attention, and be ultimately integrated.[19]

Nevertheless, Jiang himself did not explain clearly what rule by virtue means. A group of scholars in the Shanghai Academy of Social Sciences, who are Jiang's loyal theoretical thinkers, have advanced helpful definitions. They argued that rule by virtue referred to the role of morality, ideals (*lixiang*) and beliefs (*xinnian*) in governing the country.[20] More concretely, rule by virtue implies:

1) building socialist moral values compatible with the socialist legal system, and Marxism-Leninism, Mao Zedong Thought and Deng Xiaoping theory as its bases;

2) "to serve the people" as its core, collectivism as its principle, "to love the country, people, work, science and socialism" as its basic requirements;
3) constructing professional ethics, public morality and family virtue as a basic starting point;
4) placing an emphasis on moral standards when party cadres and government officials are selected and promoted;
5) leading party cadres have to serve as a role model for the people;
6) most importantly, that rule by virtue is based on the recognition of the importance of rule of law.[21]

Jiang has three objectives in his emphasis on the "three represents" and rule of virtue. First, as noted above, his "talk about politics" and "three talks" were given a cool reception by party members and local cadres. Simply taking up traditional ideological tools and concepts did not seem to work for Jiang. The "three represents" and rule of virtue can thus be seen as the fruit of Jiang's ongoing attempts to formulate a new party ideology.

Second, as power was passed from the third-generation leaders to the fourth in 2002, Jiang was apparently trying to inject his ideas into the party platform and instill them in the minds of the new leaders.

Finally, Jiang wants to establish a political legacy for himself by proposing his theory regarding the role of the CCP and party building under new conditions–a theory that is comparable to Deng's theory of building socialism with Chinese characteristics.

TOWARDS CONFUCIAN SOCIALISM?

The "rule of law", "three represents", and "rule by virtue"–all these concepts have guided Jiang's political actions since the passing of China's last political strongman, Deng Xiaoping. All these concepts provide a much-needed ideological, economic, and political platform for the party, and do help the CCP to reconcile the anti-corruption campaign and party building with economic reform.

Jiang is not the first Chinese leader since the end of the Qing Dynasty who introduced virtue and morals in their governance.

Modern China has seen its rulers frequently using moral values to govern the country. During the Republican period, Chiang Kai-shek implemented the New Life Movement to revive Confucian values. In a similar vein, Mao Zedong initiated the campaign of "learning from Comrade Lei Feng." After Deng Xiaoping began the reform and open-door policy, the leadership carried out waves of anti-bourgeois liberalisation campaigns while emphasising socialist virtue. Their use of morals echoes Confucian emphasis on official moral conduct in order to bring about a prosperous, orderly, and ideal society.

Although Jiang took up the Confucian emphasis on virtue, he needed to inject some new meanings to the concept, especially in redefining the role of the ruling regime, namely, the mandate for the Communist Party. So his loyal scholars argued that rule by virtue cannot only be understood only in the context of China's cultural development, but also in socio-economic progress. According to them, to emphasise the role of morality in directing China's political development is consistent with Jiang's ideal of three represents. Of these "three represents", one is that the party represents the most advanced culture, ranging from morals to healthy popular culture. The other two are that the party represents advanced productive forces and the interest of the majority of people.[22] In other words, by proposing the rule by virtue, Jiang does not mean to go back to such an ancient virtue. It is not meant to repeat China's traditional values but to modernise these values in modern socio-economic circumstances. What is the modern context of rule by virtue? According to Jiang's loyal interpreters mentioned above, its modernity lies in the context of China's modern practice of rule of law. The rule by virtue "is required not only by the need for spiritual development, but also by the need of rule of law per se".[23]

Jiang thus has once again raised a crucial issue, namely, the relationship among the rule of law, the rule by law, and the rule by virtue. The rule of law means that, first, the law must apply to every individual in a given society; second, the rulers as well as the ruled must follow the laws; and third, the rulers should govern in a predictable, transparent, and honest fashion. The rule by law, on the other hand, means that the rulers make use of the law to govern the country, and that the law only serves as an instrument.[24] While Westerners generally stress the rule of law, Asians have traditionally emphasised both the rule by law and the rule by virtue.

Thus, what is important is the relationship between rule of law and rule by virtue. For those who support the concept, rule of law and rule by virtue are not in conflict, but mutually complementary. First of all, both were aimed at developing good and discarding evil, purifying the social atmosphere, lifting the quality of citizens, and facilitating social progress. Second, when lawmakers make law and law implementers enforce the law, they must have a sense of morality. Without the support of rule by virtue, the system of rule of law itself will not work effectively. Some law enforcers feel no guilt in using their power to harass the innocent. They even see these acts as within their own legitimate scope of power. Third, even segments of the public lack a certain basic sense of morals and civility and disregard public interest. It is reported that 600,000 wads of chewing gum were spat on the Tiananmen Square during the National Day holiday in 2002. It cost the Beijing municipal authority a fortune to clean it all up. Since the reform and the opening of China, a large number of laws and regulations have been made, but they have not been enforced. An obstacle for law enforcement is a widespread lack of respect for morality, rules, and laws.

Assessment of Jiang's Promotion of Virtue

All the above historical campaigns, such as Chiang's New Life Movement, Mao's the campaign of "learning from Comrade Lei Feng," and Deng's socialist spiritual civilisation campaign, started with lofty intentions, yet ended with disappointing results.

How can rule by virtue become possible? Or how can such a system materialise? Jiang Zemin and his followers differ from the New Life Movement and the "Learning from Lei Feng" movement in this regard. Both Chiang Kai-shek and Mao Zedong were more ambitious and idealistic than Jiang. Chiang and Mao wanted to use the movement to educate not only party cadres and government officials, but also social members. Jiang is not able to launch a nationwide movement of this kind. He limits the movement to the party and government. According to Jiang's supporters, "rule by virtue means first to rule the party (government officials) rather than the people; furthermore, in order to rule the party, it is necessary to rule party cadres, especially high-rank cadres first."[25]

How can rule by virtue play an important role in educating party cadres and government officials? According to these proponents, in order to do so, the leadership has to: 1) emphasise the moral dimension of administration and social justice; 2) cultivate (*jiaohua*) party cadres and government officials–the most important function of rule by virtue; 3) demonstrate that they are moral rulers themselves; and 4) balance between law and morality during legislation and administration of justice.

There is also an institutional side of rule by virtue. Without certain institutions, virtue will not be able to play its proper role in government. As Jiang's supporters alleged, the realisation of virtue in government can be assured by building a set of institutions, including: 1) establishing a system of moral evaluation and moral supervision; 2) building ethics codes into different areas of administration, and political, economic and religious activities; and 3) developing individual professional ethics codes.[26]

Throughout history, China has suffered from a lack of institutional checks on corrupt officials and rulers, while Western society has been undermined by decay in individual morality and social unity. Jiang's synthesis of the rule of law and the rule by virtue is creative. The aim is to build a functioning market economy based on an effective yet comprehensive political-social control system.

Nevertheless, the challenge, or the reality rather, is that the Chinese are no longer interested moral indoctrination. They have undergone decades of devastating Maoist ideological campaigns, have been immersed in the ocean of market economic activities, and are confronting uncertainties in China's economic transition. They are more concerned with their daily livelihood and economic welfare than any ideological agenda. In addition, Jiang's reliance on the party-controlled mouthpiece and out-of-date ideological tools readily remind cadres, intellectuals, and populace of the resemblance to

Maoist political campaigns. Even though Jiang Zemin showed his genuine enthusiasm and even great passion over rule by virtue, and even though the party's propaganda made enormous efforts to spread the idea, the movement received a very cold reception. The movement only provided political conservatives with an opportunity to claim moral superiority of the party and justify its existing authoritarian rule. Naturally, the propaganda movement is very unpopular among Chinese liberal-minded intellectuals and serious criticism followed even with tight political control of media. It reminds them of the quasi-fascist nature of the New Life Movement, or the sterile slogans and Mao's personal cult during Maoist ideological campaign.[27]

Even among Jiang supporters, there is no consensus about rule by virtue. They seem to have reached an agreement that rule of law is China's basic strategy for political development, but they disagree with one another if rule by virtue can be assigned the same importance. While many would be willing to take rule by virtue as constituting another basic strategy for party building, and for moulding party cadres and government officials, they would object and doubt that rule by virtue should become a basic strategy for the country's political construction. Since rule by virtue must be implemented from above, without knowing what modern virtue is, it is dangerous to implement it.

Most importantly, what China needs the most is the building of organisations and the reforming of institutions in order to achieve rule of law. Jiang and his followers seem to exert much of their energy on touting virtue. They have, in contrast, done little to overhaul the existing political institutions to allow law to reign supreme. Such an evasive approach of placing sole emphasis on rule by virtue and merely paying lip service to rule of law will certainly undermine the progress of rule of law.[28]

ENDNOTES

1 "Jiang Zemin zai Guangdong kaocha gongzuo" ("Jiang Zemin Made An Inspection Tour to Guangdong'), *People's Daily*, 26 February 2000. Also see, The Xinhua News Agency, "Jiang Zemin tongzhi zai quanguo dangxiao gongzuo huiyi shang de jianghua" (9 June 2000) (Comrade Jiang Zemin's Talk at the National Party School Working Conference"), *People's Daily*, 17 July 2000.

2 *People's Daily*, 11 January 2001.

3 *People's Daily*, 1 February 2001.

4 Clara Li, "Culture as Vital as Law, says Jiang aide", *South China Morning Post*, 13 February 2001. On Confucian communitarianism, see David L. Hall and Roger T. Ames, *The Democracy of the Dead: Dewey, Confucius, and the Hope for Democracy in China* (Chicago: Open Court, 1999).

5 In 1971, following the downfall of Lin Biao, Mao launched a campaign to criticise "Confucianism". It has now come to light that the campaign was actually targeted at Zhou Enlai.

6 Franz Schurmann, *Ideology and Organisation in Communist China* (Berkeley, Los Angeles, and London: University of California Press, 1968), pp. 1-172.

7 For a discussion of Deng's southern tour on China's development, see John Wong and Zheng Yongnian (eds.), *The Nanxun Legacy and China's Development in the Post-Deng Era* (London & Singapore: Singapore University Press & World Scientific, 2001).

8 Zheng Yongnian, "The Politics of Power Succession", in Wang Gungwu & Zheng Yongnian (eds.), *Reform, Legitimacy and Dilemmas: China's Politics and Society* (London and Singapore: Singapore University Press & World Scientific, 2000), pp. 29-36.

9 This is based on the statistics compiled by the Organisation Department of the CCP's Shandong Provincial Committee. Zhonggong Shandong Shengwei Zuzhibu (Organisational Department of Shandong Provincial Committee of the CCP), "Cong Falun Gong wenti xiqu jiaoxun, qieshi jiaqiang he gaijin dang de zuzhi gongzuo" (Drawing a lesson from the Falun Gong Issue, Conscientiously Strengthen and Improve Organisational Work for the Party), *Dangjian Yanjiu Neican* (Internal References for Research on Party Construction), January-February, 2000, p. 2; cf. Wu Guoguang, "The Return of Ideology? Struggling to Organise Politics During Socio-economic Transitions", pp. 17, 27.

10 Mirror Post Editorial Department (ed.), *Jiang Zemin Yunchou Weiwo*, Hong Kong, 1999, p. 54.

11 Tang Yingwu, *Jueze: 1978 Nian yilai Zhongguo Gaige de Licheng* (Choice: A History of China's Reform Since 1978) (Beijing: Jingji Ribao Chubanshe, 1998), pp. 469-472.

12 Gao Xin, *Zhonggong Jutou Qiao Shi* (A Magnate of the CCP: Qiao Shi)(Taipei: Shijie Shujiu), p. 256.

13 Ren Huiwen, *Zhongnanhai Quanli Jiaoban Neimu* (Inside the Power Transfer at Zhongnanhai)(Hong Kong, 1997), pp. 145, 143.

14 Zi Ping, *Li Ruihuan Chuanshuo* (Legends of Li Ruihuan)(Hong Kong: Xiafeier Guoji Chuban Gongsi, 1999), pp. 340-41.

15 Ren Huiwen, *Zhongnanhai Quanli Jiaoban Neimu*, 1997.

16 Jiang Zemin, "Leading Cadres Must Talk Politics", *Lilun Tansuo* (Theoretical Exploration)(special edition, 1996), pp. 2-3.

17 Wu Guoguang, "The Return of Ideology", p. 10; Mirror Post Editorial Department (ed.), *Jiang Zemin Yunchou Weiwo* (Jiang Zemin Devises

Strategies within a Command Tent)(Hong Kong: The Mirror Post Cultural Enterprises Co., Ltd, 1999), p. 52.

18 "Jiang Zemin Stresses to Strengthen Party Building and Steadfastly Lead the People to Facilitate the Development of Productive Force in Light of New Historical Conditions", *People's Daily*, 18 May 2000.

19 "Jiang Zemin Stresses It Is Necessary to Rule the Country Both by Law and by Virtue," Zhongguo Xinwen She (China News Service), 10 January 2001.

20 Zhang Qian and Ji Haiqing, "Fade jianzhi, jianshe you Zhongguo tese shehuizhuyi fazhi guojia" ("Rule of Law cum Rule by Virtue: Building a Socialist State of Rule of Law with Chinese Characteristics"), *Shanghai shehui kexueyuan jikan* ("Quarterly Journal of the Shanghai Academy of Social Sciences"), No. 2 (2001), p. 189. This paper is a summary of a conference on Jiang's concept of rule by virtue, held in the Academy.

21 Zhang and Ji, "Fade jianzhi, jianshe you Zhongguo tese shehuizhuyi fazhi guojia"; and The Editorial and Writing Group, *Yifa zhiguo*, p. 16.

22 Zhang and Ji, "Fade jianzhi, jianshe you Zhongguo tese shehuizhuyi fazhi guojia", p. 189.

23 Ibid., pp. 189-90.

24 Zheng, 'The Rule by Law vs the Rule of Law", pp. 135-63.

25 Ibid., p. 189.

26 Ibid., p. 191.

27 For a serious criticism, see Wei Yi, "Zhongguo xin dezhi lunxi: gaige qian Zhongguo daode hua zhengzhi di lishi fanxi" ("An Analysis of New Theory of Rule by Virtue in China: A Historical Reflection of Chinese Moralised Politics in Pre-Reform China"), *Zhanlue yu guanli*, no. 2 (2001), pp. 25-38.

28 See *Zhang* and Ji, "Fade jianzhi, jianshe you Zhongguo tese shehuizhuyi fazhi guojia", pp. 189-92.

CHAPTER **15**

Embracing the Capitalists: The Chinese Communist Party to Brace Itself for Far-Reaching Changes

JOHN WONG AND ZHENG YONGNIAN

OPENING PANDORA'S BOX

In his controversial speech celebrating the 80th anniversary of the Chinese Communist Party (CCP) on 1 July 2001, Jiang Zemin called on the party to admit those "outstanding elements" of society such as private entrepreneurs, professionals, technical and managerial personnel from various non-state sectors, including those employed by MNCs.[1] According to Jiang, these are people who can also make a positive contribution to the rebuilding of China's socialism, and therefore they should not be excluded from the party. Whether they are politically progressive (*xianjin*) or backward (*luohou*) should not be judged purely by on whether they are property-owning classes.

"Private entrepreneurs"–actually an official euphemism for "capitalists" or "private businessmen"–were hitherto publicly barred from the party. The proposed membership relaxation has accordingly generated enthusiasm from many private businessmen wanting to join the party. Immediately after Jiang's speech, more than "100,000 private entrepreneurs" were reported to have submitted their applications to join the party. Its organisation department (headed by Zeng

Qinghong) was planning to recruit 200,000 private entrepreneurs before the 16th Congress in September 2002.[2]

Traditionally, the CCP was supposed to represent the interests of only five major groups, i.e., workers, peasants, intellectuals, members of the PLA (People's Liberation Army), and government officials and cadres. The majority of the original rank and file of the party was basically drawn from the "proletariat" background. In championing the causes of capitalists, Jiang's initiative was hailed by supporters as a theoretical breakthrough by throwing off the party's old dogmas, particularly the shackle of class. At the same time, for Jiang as General Secretary to openly embrace capitalists, the antithesis of the proletariat class, amounts to dropping an ideological bombshell on the conservative wing of the party. Naturally, the party's ideologues have raised a great hue and cry. But the strength of the opposition from these party diehards seems to have taken Jiang by surprise.

The opposition came into the open with the publication on the Chinese Internet of a widely-circulated *Wanyan-shu* or "a petition of ten-thousand words", attributed to a group of conservative party veterans led by the long-time leftist critic Deng Liqun (aged 86, and no relation to Deng Xiaoping). Before Jiang's "July 1" speech, several provincial party leaders such as Deputy Party Secretary of Jilin Province Lin Yanzhi had already spoken out against Jiang's scheme. In brief, apart from being accused of breaching the party's cardinal principle of courting members of the exploitative class, Jiang was blamed for his failure to address the burning issues of growing unemployment and widening income disparities, and failure to hold formal consultations within the party before making the announcement. Jiang was also criticised for promoting a personality cult for himself. This means that Jiang did not have strong party consensus on the issue, and that he has encountered not just ideological but also political opposition.

In response, Jiang quickly ordered the closure of the two theoretical magazines, *Zhenli De Zhuiqiu* (Seeking Truth) and *Zhongliu* (The Central-Pillar), which are the well-known mouthpieces of the leftists.[3] Subsequently, some leftist websites were also closed down.[4]

Party cadres throughout China, including officers of the PLA, have been instructed to hold study sessions of Jiang's "July 1" Speech. How much has Jiang's personal prestige been damaged?

Jiang, as the head of the ruling group, certainly has no shortages of opponents: the Falun Gong followers, losers from economic reform such as the *xiagang* (laid-off) workers of state enterprises, displaced rural migrants, disenchanted intellectuals and so on. But this motley group of opponents is unlikely to form a coalition of interests with the party's ideological diehards against Jiang. It is nonetheless clear that the event may well complicate or even weaken Jiang's role in the ongoing arrangements for the coming leadership transition. A big unknown to the outside is whether some factions at the party's top leadership (e.g., Li Peng's) might have exploited the issue to jockey their own proteges against Jiang's own in the leadership lineup at the next Party Congress. The question boils down to this: does Jiang really have sufficient political clout to openly restructure the party's ideological orthodoxy with himself remaining unscathed?

A careful examination of all the relevant background would suggest that the actual backlash against Jiang's bold initiative, as reported overseas, might well have been over-stated. In real terms, what Jiang is doing is merely an endorsement of what has already been happening to the party for years. China has been openly following capitalism after Deng Xiaoping officially sanctioned the concept of the "socialist market economy" in 1992. Following China's success in economic development and the rise in per-capita income, the party (also the government) is getting more "middle-class" in character. For the party to renew itself and to stay relevant, it needs to recruit younger and better-educated members regardless of their class origins. The party's organisation department has recently revealed that almost half of its current total membership are below 45 years old. More significantly, one in four of China's postgraduates are already party members and about one-third of China's university students have applied to join the party[5]–most university students in China today come from an urban middle class background.

The CCP has also been transformed in a "technocratic" way. During Mao Zedong's time, the CCP was a genuine revolutionary party with its members overwhelmingly from workers and peasants, who constituted 83 percent of the total membership in 1956 (this figure dropped to 48 percent in 1994). Furthermore, after his return to power, Deng started what may be called a "technocratic movement," replacing revolutionary cadres in party leadership positions with technocrats. This is crystal clear at the pinnacle of the party's power structure. All seven Standing Committee members of the current Political Bureau and 18 of the 24 Political Bureau members may be classified as "technocrats". In short, the CCP has long ceased to be an ideologically oriented party led by revolutionaries; it has become one that is under a "full-fledged technocratic leadership".[6]

Strangely, neither the proponents nor the opponents have bothered to define what is exactly meant by an "entrepreneur", who, in the Schumpeterian sense is a great innovator or risk-taking capitalist. In any society, there are precious few successful entrepreneurs. If an "entrepreneur" is defined broadly to mean just an ordinary capitalist or businessman, then one can find in China many "new capitalists" who have been created by economic reform. They would include, apart from conventional private businessmen, hundreds of thousands of party cadres who started the profit-maximising township and village enterprises (TVEs) as well as those who were assigned by the party to run the privatised state-owned enterprises, both in China and overseas. These cadres are practically "capitalists" or more correctly, "bureaucratic capitalists"–often dubbed "Red capitalists" overseas. Many of them are children of high-ranking officials.

In short, reform and development has bourgeoisified numerous existing party members and cadres. With rising affluence, there are fewer and fewer real "have-nots" among the party's rank and file. Viewed in this context, Jiang is actually not swimming against the tide when he came out to support capitalists publicly. He can see clearly that for the party to continue to grow and expand, it must embrace the better educated and the most enterprising in society, who, incidentally, include many children of the ruling elite. Many of the party ideologues opposing Jiang are themselves already marginalised. It seems clear that Jiang's scheme will eventually prevail unless the opposition is backed by a powerful group at the top with ulterior motives.

It may be argued that from the start Jiang has conceived the scheme of admitting capitalists and professionals to the party as a shrewd win-win move. Provided that he could ride out the initial resistance, he would be seen as doing what is necessary to arrest the decay of the party and he would eventually gain the credit of having revitalised the party. Nevertheless, in the longer run, the presence of many capitalists and professionals in a primarily socialistic party would inevitably sharpen its internal contradictions and hasten its structural and ideological metamorphosis.

Ultimately, the main body of the party might evolve into a kind of social democratic party, and for that Jiang would also be credited for opening the door to such a transformation. Mao has gained full credit for creating New China and Deng, for starting economic reform. Jiang will then leave as his legacy the successful transformation of the party, one way or the other.

THE RISE OF THE CAPITALIST CLASS

In the wake of the 1989 Tiananmen Event, China's top leadership was engaged in a hot debate as to which direction China's economic reform and development should take–more socialistic or less socialistic (i.e. more capitalistic)? Alarmed by the sudden collapse of the Soviet Union as a result of its dismal failure in economic reform, Deng Xiaoping was determined to lead China boldly to a faster reform route via the capitalistic means. Deng espoused the idea during his famous Nanxun or tour of South China in early 1992. He urged party leaders to liberate their thoughts and open up themselves so as to learn how China could best make use of the dynamic capitalist system to promote China's economic growth. In the event, Deng's Nanxun thus quickly put an end to the futile debate of "Mr. Socialism vs Mr. Capitalism" among the party's ideologues. In effect, this also paved the way for the party to accept capitalist mode of economic development as its new orthodoxy, which in turn sparked off a decade of spectacular economic growth for China.

In the pre-reform era, China under Mao Zedong was an ideologically organised society. As the noted China scholar Franz Schurmann correctly pointed out in the early 1960s, "Communist China is like a vast building made of different kinds of brick and stone. However it was put together, it stands. What holds it together is ideology and organisation".[7] Armed with his own brand of ideology, Mao could therefore use the party to mobilise peasants and workers for various political experiments, from the Great Leap Forward to the Cultural Revolution, in order to reshape China in accordance with his own utopian ideals. In actual effect, Mao used totalitarian state power to destroy all possible private space and politicised the Chinese society with scant regard for China's economic conditions.

After Mao, Deng Xiaoping had to pick up the pieces by reviving the economy and rebuilding the party. Deng followed a radically different path to organise society and manage the economy. He realised that too much ideological and political contention as manifested in Mao's numerous movements and campaigns simply would not be conducive to economic growth, which would require a certain pragmatism so as to exploit all sources of comparative advantage and productivity gains regardless of their ideological origins. Deng also realised that successful economic growth, in delivering more goods and material benefits to the people, would ultimately increase the party's legitimacy.

Consequently, Deng took a radical turn in 1992 by launching the concept of the "socialist market economy," which provided a fertile ground for society's most productive elements, the "private entrepreneurs", to emerge. Table 15.1 shows the rapid expansion of private enterprises employing more than eight workers, from 90,000 units in 1989 to 1.5 million in 1999. Individually-owned businesses also increased from 12.5 million units in 1989 to 28.5 million in 1997. In terms of output, the non-state sector has also grown rapidly along with the corresponding decline of the state sector, which in 1999 accounted for only 26 percent of total industrial output, down from 76 percent in 1980 (Table 15.2).

As can be expected, the rise of the entrepreneur class has brought about concomitant political and social changes, some of which may carry negative consequences for China in the transitional stage. First, as people soon saw private businesses were highly profitable and the quickest way to increase their incomes and wealth, many government officials and party cadres joined the private sector in a phenomenon known as *xiahai* (literally, "plunging into the sea"). Second, many party cadres and government officials who chose to stay on in the public sector soon learned how to market their official position and *guanxi* (connection) for their own personal gain. This led to a rapid growth of rent-seeking activities and open corruption, which have since developed into a serious endemic problem in China today.

TABLE 15.1 THE GROWTH OF THE PRIVATE SECTOR IN CHINA (1989-1999)

	Private Enterprises*				Individually-owned and -operated enterprises**			
	Number (thousand)	Change (%)	Employees (million)	Change (%)	Number (million)	Change (%)	Employees (10,000)	Change (%)
1989	90.6		1.6		12.5		19.4	
1990	98.1	8.3	1.7	3.7	13.3	6.5	20.9	7.8
1991	107.8	9.9	1.8	8.2	14.2	6.7	22.6	7.9
1992	139.6	29.5	2.3	26.1	15.3	8.3	24.7	9.3
1993	237.9	70.4	3.7	60.8	17.7	15.2	29.4	19.1
1994	432.2	81.7	6.5	73.3	21.9	23.8	37.8	28.5
1995	654.5	51.4	9.6	47.5	25.3	15.6	46.2	22.2
1996	819.3	25.2	11.7	22.2	27.1	7.0	50.2	8.7
1997	960.7	17.3	13.5	15.2	28.5	5.4	54.4	8.5
1998	1,201.0	25.0	1,709	26.7	n.a	n.a	n.a	n.a
1999	1,508.9	25.6	2,022	18.8				

* Refer to those with more than eight employees

** Refer to those with less than eight employees

Sources: Adapted from Zhang Houyi and Ming Zhili, eds., *Zhongguo siying qiye fazhan baogao 1978-1998* (A Report on the Development of Private Enterprises in China, 1978-1998), Beijing: Shehui kexue wenxuan chubanshe, 1999), pp. 60, 66; *Zhongguo siying jingji nianjian* (The Yearbook of Private Businesses in China, 2000), p. 402.

TABLE 15.2 GROSS INDUSTRIAL OUTPUT IN CHINA BY DIFFERENT SECTORS

Year	Total (%)	State-owned enterprises (%)	Collective-owned enterprises (%)	Individually-owned enterprises (%)	Other types of enterprises (%)
1980	100	76.0	23.5	0	0.5
1985	100	64.9	32.1	1.9	1.2
1990	100	54.6	35.6	5.4	4.4
1991	100	56.2	33.0	4.8	6.0
1992	100	51.5	35.1	5.8	7.6
1993	100	47.0	34.0	8.0	11.1
1994	100	37.3	37.7	10.1	14.8
1995	100	34.0	36.6	12.9	16.6
1996	100	33.7	36.5	14.4	15.4
1997	100	29.8	35.9	16.9	17.4
1998	100	26.5	36.0	16.0	21.5
1999	100	26.1	32.8	16.9	24.2

Source: calculated from *Zhongguo tongji nianjian 2000* (China Statistical Yearbook 2000), Beijing: Zhongguo tongji chubanshe, 2000, p. 409.

When political power is freely traded for economic benefits, corruption becomes inevitable. Widespread corruption not only produces deleterious social (i.e., reducing equity) and economic (i.e., misallocating resources) effects, but also saps the party apparatus at all levels. Previously, political loyalty was the main criterion for assessing party cadres and government officials; money or pecuniary benefits have now come to be used as an important yardstick. Accordingly, the effective functioning of the party as well as its image and legitimacy has suffered. The end result has been the social decline of the party.

In the meantime, the entrepreneur class has been rising high, socially and politically. Not surprisingly, the rise of this class has undermined the party's ideological orthodoxy, making it difficult for the party to employ its official ideology to regulate the daily life of party cadres and government officials. In fact, when the party comes to deal with the private sector, especially in regard to certain business decisions involving maximisation of profits, efficiency, or growth, the party's official ideology often has to take a back seat. As the party retreats, business interests advance.

At the local level, many private entrepreneurs have already directly or indirectly participated in local politics in order to influence policy. Many have joined the party. At the national level, however, political participation by private entrepreneurs remains small. For instance, only 46 out of more than 2,000 representatives of the Ninth Chinese People's Political Consultative Conference in 1998 were classified as "private entrepreneurs." It follows that Jiang's "July 1" speech was largely aimed at the political participation of private entrepreneurs at the national level.

THE CAPITALISTS IN JIANG'S NEW POLITICAL ORDER

It may be noted that the 15th Party Congress in 1997 had already legitimated the private sector, and a constitutional amendment in the following year further provided constitutional protection for private ownership. In February 2000, Jiang instructed party members to study his new theory based on the concept of *sange daibiao* (literally, the "three represents"). According to this theory, the party represents the "most advanced mode of productive force, the most advanced culture, and the interests of the majority of the population".[8] The three represents theory is undoubtedly the party's strongest affirmation yet of the importance of the non-state sector in the economy. It also implies that the party is flexible enough to accommodate the interests of the newly rising economic and social groups.

Many have argued that Jiang's three represents theory, put forth when he is about to pass on the party leadership baton to the fourth-generation leaders under Hu Jintao, is originally meant to be his own ideological legacy after his departure. Whatever his original intention, Jiang's theory has gone down quite well with the public. It provides clear indications that the party is finally giving up its past ideological rigidity by its willingness to embrace rising economic and social elites. In short, the party is seen to be getting politically and socially pluralistic. With such good public reaction, it now seems only logical for Jiang to make use of the occasion of the 80th Party anniversary to formally open the door to private capitalists and professionals.

Jiang's initiative is apparently motivated by other pragmatic political considerations as well. First, admitting private entrepreneurs is proof that the party is constantly adapting itself to China's changing political and social reality. As mentioned earlier, many private entrepreneurs are already party members. What the party leadership proposes to do today is to formally endorse their party membership while allowing others to join as new members. Second, by doing so, the leadership wants to expand the party's social base in order to revitalise itself. Over the years, capitalist mode of economic development has radically changed China's class structure. With the decline of the political and ideological importance of workers and peasants, the party has to embrace the rising new elites, from industrialists and international businessmen to property magnates and "dot.com" venture capitalists, in order to stay socially relevant.

Politically, the party's initiative to embrace these new social elites or new economic interest groups is clearly calculated to bolster its one-party domination. Mao could depend on class struggle and mass movements to govern China, and he could count on the support of millions of poor peasants and workers. China was then a backward agricultural economy, with peasants accounting for 80 percent of the total labour force. Today, China is a growing industrial economy, with peasants constituting less than 50 percent of the labour force–and many of them not even full-time farmers.

Specifically, Jiang (and much less for the younger leaders in future) simply cannot rule China today by mass political mobilization as Mao once did since the party's original power base has been fast eroded as a result of rapid economic development and social change. China is rapidly developing into a modern society, now with 130 million hand-phones and close to 30 million Internet users. The economy is increasingly integrated with international capitalism on account of China's growing foreign trade, foreign investment and foreign tourism. The populace is also getting increasingly literate, especially in urban areas.

On the other hand, state governance in China is not yet highly institutionalised, and the rule of law not firmly rooted. For the party to effectively rule such a vast and diverse country without sound democratic foundations, it is all the more crucial for the party leadership to build up a broad social consensus and a coalition of various interests. Clearly, the party just cannot exclude the "outstanding elements" of society from the private sector. For China's emerging political order to remain viable, the party must be socially more broadly based.

TOWARDS A SOCIAL DEMOCRATIC PARTY?

However, the party will have to bear some long-term costs for admitting capitalists and professionals. Leftist critics have warned that the recruitment of the bourgeoisie into the party will inevitably create more corruption in the party, making it easier for the "money for power" phenomenon to take place. Some critics have even suggested that capitalists may eventually take over the party's leadership.[9]

This is actually already happening in many party branches in the rural areas where businessmen are reported to use their financial power to manipulate local elections or simply take over local party branches. Suffice it to say that with capitalists inside the party, they will certainly act as potential catalysts to quicken the transformation of the party. Judging by the way Chinese society is evolving, there is a real possibility that the party, in admitting capitalists, has also let in the Trojan horse.

Jiang Zemin may genuinely believe that he is doing what it takes to strengthen the party-state by broadening its social base. In future, as the party steps up its process of metamorphosis and evolves into a kind of social democratic party, he will still be favourably judged by history for leading the way for such a transformation. In short, he will have left a legacy in both strengthening the party and facilitating its transformation – a win-win situation for him. The loser, however, is clearly the Chinese Communist Party itself.

ENDNOTES

1 Jiang Zemin, "Jiang Zemin's Speech at the Conference Celebrating the Eightieth Anniversary of the Chinese Communist Party, July 1, 2001, *Renmin Ribao* (People's Daily), Beijing, 2 July 2001. Also, "Entrepreneurs From non-Public Sector Hail Jiang's Speech", *Beijing Review* (9 August 2001).

2 *Ming Pao*, 23 July 2001.

3 "Showdown of ideologies", *South China Morning Post* (August 15, 2001); and "Party closes leftist journal that opposed Jiang", *op cit* (August 14, 2001).

4 "Dissenting leftist Websites taken off (from) Internet", *South China Morning Post* (September 3, 2001).

5 "Party more attractive to Chinese youth", *China Daily* (June 6, 2001).

6 Li Cheng and Lynn White, "The Fifteenth Central Committee of the Chinese Communist Party: Full-Fledged Technocratic Leadership with Partial Control by Jiang Zemin", *Asian Survey*, Vol. xxxviii, No. 3 (March 1998), pp. 231-264; David Shambaugh, "The CCP's Fifteenth Congress: Technocrats in Command", *Issues and Studies*, Vol. 34, No. 1 (January 1998), pp. 1-37.

7 Franz Schurmann, *Ideology and Organization in Communist China* (Berkeley, CA.: University of California Press, 1968), p. 1.

8 The Xinhua News Agency, "Jiang Zemin tongzhi zai quanguo dangxiao gongzuo huiyi shang de jianghua" (9 June 2000) ("Comrade Jiang Zemin's Talk in National Party Schools Working Conference"), *People's Daily*, 17 July 2000.

9 Lin Yanzhi, Deputy Secretary of Jilin province stated: "The key to controlling the socialist market economy is to control the bourgeoisie and its capitalistic component; the key to control the bourgeoisie is ensure that they are not in the party, and the party has to see clearly their true colour", "The CCP Must Lead and Control the New Bourgeoisie", *Zhengli de zhuiqiu* (Seeking Truth), No. 5 (2001), p. 7.

Index